Dwellings, Identities and Homes

Dwellings, Identities and Homes

European Housing Culture from the
Viking Age to the Renaissance

Edited by Mette Svart Kristiansen & Kate Giles

JUTLAND ARCHAEOLOGICAL SOCIETY

Dwellings, Identities and Homes

European Housing Culture from the Viking Age to the Renaissance

Layout & prepress: Louise Hilmar
Cover: Louise Hilmar
English revision: Jens Damm
Type: Palatino Linotype
Printed by Narayana Press, Gylling
Front cover: A bourgeois family at home, print by Benedict Buchpinder, Augsburg 1488
Printed in Denmark

ISBN: 978-87-88415-89-6
ISSN: 0107-2854

Jutland Archaeological Society Publications Vol. 84

Published by:
Jutland Archaeological Society
Moesgaard Museum
DK-8270 Højbjerg

Distributed by:
Aarhus University Press
Langelandsgade 177
DK-8200 Aarhus N
www.unipress.dk

Published with financial support of:
The Aarhus University Research Foundation
Queen Margrethe II's Archaeological Foundation

FSC
www.fsc.org

MIX
Papir fra
ansvarlige kilder
FSC® C010651

Contents

Part 3. Houses, Homes and Social Strategies

Introduction

Kate Giles & Mette Svart Kristiansen

The study of houses, dwellings, homes and identities is a rapidly-expanding field within medieval archaeology. In order to establish a shared forum for theoretical, methodological and empirical ideas about housing across research teams, national borders and disciplines, the section for Medieval and Renaissance Archaeology at Aarhus University organised an international and interdisciplinary conference in December 2010. The aim of the conference was to address changing forms of living and their social background and symbolic content in Europe over 800 years, primarily during the period 800-1600 AD but also beyond this. It brought together a group of young as well as internationally established university- and museum-based scholars from across Europe, speaking on a wide range of subjects, including current theoretical perspectives on homes and houses, the reappraisal of traditional approaches and syntheses, and recent fieldwork on individual buildings. The conference was generously supported by the Globalisation research programme, the Department of Anthropology, Archaeology and Linguistics and the Section for Medieval and Renaissance Archaeology and this publication has been facilitated by generous donations from The Aarhus University Research Foundation and Queen Margrethe II's Archaeological Foundation.

The conference engendered lively and engaging debate, which is reflected in the structure of the volume into three different sections. The papers in each section address similar themes, but often do so from very different theoretical and methodological perspectives, using different kinds of evidence and interpretive approaches. What emerges from the juxtaposition of papers is a wealth of detailed evidence and nuanced interpretation, demonstrating the ongoing potential of research in the field. The volume highlights the need for further comparative and cross-national research in order to better understand the chronological and geographical spread of ideas, not just within the Northwest European countries, which dominates the volume, but also between East and West, South and North. It also highlights the need for more detailed intra-regional studies, comparing and contrasting houses in different forms of settlement, landscape and social setting, in order to understand the diversity in use of building materials, technologies, plan forms, fixtures and fittings. Many of the papers in the volume also demonstrate the potential of studying buildings within their wider cultural and ideological frameworks, and the methodological challenges that this presents.

The first section of the volume 'Exploring domestic and social space', engages with some of the dominant theoretical paradigms and models which have informed the study of domestic architecture. Kate Giles's paper uses recent theoretical debates in anthropology and archaeology to reconsider traditional typological approaches to the form, function and meaning of medieval vernacular houses in the UK. Her analysis stresses the historical specificity and diversity of medieval 'ways of living', whereas Ole Grøn's paper draws on experimental social psychology and ethnoarchaeological data to outline a basic non-verbal, cross-cultural syntax of human spatial behaviour in dwellings from the Mesolithic period to the present day. Thomas Kühtreiber's paper explores theoretical and methodological models which help to illuminate the construction of cultural identities and ideological frameworks in the analysis of the appearance, access routes and furnishing of middling to high-status Austrian tower houses and castles and surviving documentary sources. Christina Schmid also explores the methodological challenges and possibilities of analysing the process of dwelling, but through the excavation and stratigraphic interpretation of the fixtures, fittings and artefacts recovered from French and German urban townhouses, Swiss castles and Swedish rural dwellings.

The second section of the volume, 'Regions and regionality', examines the regionality of house types and constructions as well as dwelling practices. Eva Svensson identifies elements of a common architectural heritage between the houses of the European elite and those lower down the social scale. She also suggests that some phenomena, such as the transformation of multi-functional buildings into purpose-designed communal structures may be more fruitfully explored at a global, rather than a regional, or even European level. In Peter Dragsbo's paper, the political and cultural basis for regional typologies are explored – and challenged – by a reconsideration of 'The Schleswig Farmstead' in the light of nationalistic research agendas framed by the Danish-German border. The last two papers in this section also consider particular types of houses in relation to aspects of regionality. Charlotte Boje Hilligsø Andersen and Anne-Louise Haack Olsen suggest that the reappearance of turf houses in Jutland after several hundred years of post-built houses must be understood as a response both to contemporary environmental conditions and external influences from coastal areas farther south. Mogens Skanning Ravnsbjerg Høesgsberg's paper revaluates the established house typology of Norse Greenland and argues that regionality is the key to understanding greater similarities between the building customs and house typologies of the Greenland Norse and Iceland, than have been acknowledged by previous studies.

The third and final section of the volume, 'Houses, homes and social strategies', presents a series of case studies exploring the relationship between the form and function of houses and the relationship between dwelling and identity. The vibrancy of scholarship on Viking houses is reflected in a set of papers, including Sarah Croix's synthetic analysis of the excavated evidence for daily rural life and household relations

in the houses of Southern Scandinavia, in Norway and Iceland. In Anna Beck's article, the potential of focusing on one architectural element, such as the location and form of doorways in the Viking Age longhouse, is demonstrated in the study of the emergence of a cultural ideal of hospitality in Viking Age society. A 15th century, consciously antiquarian evocation of 11th century Norwegian and Icelandic 'housing culture' is then explored by Teva Vidal, using the literary source of 'Grettis saga'.

An interdisciplinary approach is used by Mette Svart Kristiansen, whose paper explores how a range of source material, including houses, inventories, and murals in churches can be approached in an interdisciplinary way to shed light on 'proper living' in affluent rural and urban households in medieval Denmark. The series of papers which follow Svart Kristiansen's article explore the ways in which houses shed light on both functional and cultural 'ways of living'. In her study, Danae Tankard explores the cultural and ideological meanings of medieval English peasant houses. She, too, advocates an inter-disciplinary approach, analysing middling-status rural plans in the light of contemporary written discourses of household and husbandry to assess their possible use and meaning for the medieval peasantry. Issues of meaning are also raised by Jill Campbell's re-evaluation of the design and appearance of medieval English gentry houses. Both these papers explore how houses were used to reflect and structure the distinctive ways of living of those in the middle of medieval society. Adam Bolander explores how the construction and use of smoke houses in the settlements of Örja and Skegrie may tell us something meaningful not only about the entrepreneurial activities and international trading links of medieval Scanian peasants, but also elements of ritual practice within the household.

The final papers of the volume explore house form and function in the context of structural and technological innovation and distinctive 'ways of living'. Rainer Atzbach's paper traces the relationship between different forms of heating systems, particularly the tile stove and the emergence of 'smoke-free living' in the reorganisation of domestic spaces in houses in the circum-Alpine zone and its diffusion into Southern Scandinavia by the 16th century. The relationship between heating, domestic space and the orientation of houses within the wider townscape, is also explored by Christian Klinge's analysis of the detailed excavation evidence of houses from Aalborg, Denmark. The potential of the fine-grained analysis of the remains of burned-down townhouses to shed light on domestic activity is also discussed in Anne Katrine Thaastrup-Leth's analysis of the remains of four medieval houses from Odense, Denmark. The two final papers in the volume provide a detailed overview of the use and meaning of houses within a larger region. Paola Galetti's explores the complex evolution of both urban and rural houses in Italy between the 5th and 12th centuries, and Bouwmeester the evolution of Dutch townhouses between 700-1300. Bouwmeester shows how early townhouses appropriated and transformed existing ways of building to cope with the challenges of building on unstable substraits, and he suggests that house building was an important strategy by which emerging groups of traders and craftsmen constructed a distinctive sense of bourgeois identity in the late medieval town.

Ways of understanding; ways of living

Although, as noted above, 'Houses, shaping dwellings, identities and homes' marked the beginning, rather than the conclusion of debates in the field of medieval housing culture, particular issues and themes emerged clearly from the discussions during the conference and published papers. The conference highlighted the diversity of approaches within and between archaeologists, architectural historians, ethnologists and historians not only across Europe but also within the historiographical traditions of each country. It is clear that our understanding of houses is a product of a recursive relationship between the conditions of excavation, and quality and nature of excavated data or of standing buildings, the survival or absence of contemporary documentary and literary or other cultural evidence, as well as the different theoretical models applied to the study of houses.

The conference revealed interesting and profound differences in the chronological frameworks and theoretical underpinning of studies of housing culture. For some scholars, such as Grøn, houses can be understood within cross-cultural, pan-chronological frameworks stretching from the Mesolithic to the modern era. For others, such as Giles, greater chronological specificity and context is required. However, whereas most Scandinavian scholars were comfortable discussing the relationship of medieval houses with the Iron Age and Viking precursors, this was much rarer in the UK, where the divisions between prehistoric and historical archaeology are much more profound. For scholars such as Svensson, the origins and diffusion of ideas across social groups about how to organise space, was of interest; for others, such as Dragsbo and Høesgsberg the spread of such ideas regionally or across a cultural diaspora, formed the focus of debate.

For many scholars, the desire to find evidence of continuity and similarity in house forms was balanced by the desire to acknowledge the difference and distinctiveness of the use and meaning of houses by their inhabitants. Several authors, including Svensson, Kühtreiber, Høegsberg and Tankard, sought to challenge established typologies and raised important questions about the diffusion of ideas or the existence of shared cultural norms within and between status groups and across regions. As Giles, Grøn, Kühtreiber, and Schmid argue, a greater understanding of the ideological, political and theoretical assumptions underpinning typologies and models of diffusion, emulation and distinctiveness as well as historiographical traditions discussed by Svart Kristiansen inform debate, even if they often challenge the search for consensus.

Several scholars highlighted clear differences in the nature of the surviving evidence, and the extent of rural and urban excavations between different European countries. In some regions, such as Denmark, discussed by Svart Kristiansen, there are very few surviving buildings, limiting the potential to understand surviving structures and placing greater emphasis on excavated material. Elsewhere, as Bouwmeester and Giles demonstrate, systematic programmes of survey and tree-ring dating hold great potential for refining understanding of the chronological pattern of house development in both urban and rural contexts. Bolander's paper notes that the extent of excavation across a settlement also has implications for understanding the full range of domestic and industrial buildings on a site. Klinge and Thaastrup-Leth similarly argue that the limited scope of commercially-driven urban excavations can prevent archaeologists from fully understanding the relationship between houses, plots and streetscapes. These papers reveal a clear need for future excavations and studies to explore houses in their wider settlement context, and to understanding the changing relationship between houses of different status, and between houses and other industrial, agricultural and communal buildings, as Svensson suggests.

Several of the papers highlight the potential but also the challenges of archaeological methodologies. Schmid, Boje Hilligsø Andersen and Haack Olsen, Croix, Klinge, Thaastrup-Leth, and Bolander explore the potential of detailed stratigraphic examination of the context of deposition and use within the household. Bolander highlights the opportunity to explore elements of ritual and votive practices in this way. Beck, meanwhile, shows how the stratigraphic analysis of a particular architectural feature forces us to re-examine the evidence for distinctive cultural practices, such as hospitality, within the home. The detailed archaeological recording of houses also has the potential to reveal the relationship of construction methods to the surrounding landscape, as Boje Hilligsø Andersen and Haack Olsen, and Høesgsberg's papers demonstrate, and to different social contexts, as discussed in Bouwmeester's and Galetti's papers.

Finally, the papers present early attempts by many scholars to move beyond an understanding of the form of medieval houses in order to understand the 'ways of living' proposed by Svart Kristiansen as one of the major themes of the conference and the volume.

For many contributors, the re-examination of house forms through formal spatial analysis techniques such as planning analysis, access analysis and social psychological and ethnoarchaeological theory, certainly offer one avenue of potential. The relationship between access routes, including the position of doorways, creation of sightlines, placement of fixtures and fittings, including portable artefacts and decoration, is one of the most exciting and challenging areas for further research. In some areas, such evidence will be purely archaeological. However, in others, contemporary literary and documentary sources may shed light on the more ephemeral uses and meanings of space, for domestic, working and ritual practices. Many of the papers in the volume draw on a combination of these approaches. However, such interdisciplinary study also requires careful theorisation. It is too easy for archaeologists to mine the source material of historians or literary scholars in search of a mimetic relationship between forms of cultural production in the past. Developing greater sensitivity to the potential, as well as the limitations, of interdisciplinary study is likely to be one of the greatest challenges for household archaeologists in the future.

The study of buildings, houses and homes is a fundamental research field in archaeology, but it is an area of research shared by many other disciplines, including architects and historians, ethnologists, anthropologists and sociologists. Although most participants in the conference and contributors to this volume were medieval archaeologists, the conference succeeded in bringing together researchers from several disciplines and prompted lively debate about the very different traditions, perspectives, data and research objectives within this continuously growing field. We hope that this volume heralds the start of discussions about what medieval archaeology can bring to the study of houses and ways of living in pre-modern Europe.

PART 1

Exploring Domestic and Social Space

Ways of Living in Medieval England

Kate Giles

Abstract

Archaeologists in England are fortunate to be able to study medieval houses from a wealth of data, including excavated and standing buildings, as well as surviving documentary sources and artefacts. Traditionally, the study of medieval English houses has focused largely on the post-Norman Conquest period, seeking to establish the development of particular construction methods and the diffusion of the open hall and tripartite plan from high status houses to those lower down the social scale. However, over the past two decades, such studies have been informed by new data and by overtly theoretical approaches to the use and meaning of domestic space and 'ways of living'. This paper highlights the potential of recent theoretical developments to shed new light on the existing historiography of English medieval houses. It focuses in particular on the rural houses of those in the middling levels of medieval society, exploring evidence for their investment in housing and for a distinctively 'flexible' way of living in the home.

Introduction

Medieval archaeology in the UK has been relatively slow to embrace the theoretical shifts which swept through the social sciences and humanities in the latter years of the 20th century (see Gilchrist 2009; McClain 2012). In part, this reflects the relatively late development of 'medieval archaeology' as a discipline distinct from prehistoric and Roman archaeology (Gerrard 2003; Gilchrist 1997; Gilchrist & Reynolds 2009). Within the discipline too, there are profound period divisions between 'early' medieval archaeology, which studies the post-Roman period to the Norman Conquest, late medieval archaeology, which focuses on the Norman Conquest to the 16th century, and post-medieval archaeology, which encompasses the early modern and modern periods. These divisions have had profound consequences for the study of material culture, such as houses, which tend to be studied more as the origin or context for an explanation of the post-medieval house, than as a continuation of prehistoric domestic building traditions (although see Gardiner 2000; 2008; Walker 2007 for important recent contributions to this debate).

The study of surviving, as well as excavated, medieval houses has also encouraged archaeologists in the UK to engage closely with vernacular architecture studies. During the latter part of the 20th century, this led to the explicit debates about the value and potential of theory, especially with regard to the study of medieval houses (Dyer 1997; Johnson 1997; Mercer 1997; and see also Currie 2004).

Theorising architectural space: building and dwelling

The theoretical approaches underpinning the study of buildings in British archaeology must be understood within the broader paradigmatic shift from functionalist ('processualist') to structuralist to postmodernist ('post-processualist') theory (Johnson 2010a). They also draw on wider theoretical debates about how meaning is attached to the built environment. Ingold (2000) provides a useful sketch of two very different theoretical traditions or 'perspectives'

13

in the field. The 'building perspective' is influenced by structuralist theory and maintains that people must construct the world cognitively in their heads, before they are capable of acting in it. The organisation of space is therefore believed to cognitively precede its material expression; in other words, buildings are 'thought' before they are built (Ingold 2000: 182). Ingold contrasts the 'building perspective' with the 'dwelling perspective', which draws on the phenomenological theory of Heidegger (1979) and Merleau-Ponty (1962). Phenomenology emphasises that the human experience of existence is one of 'being-in-the-world', where the body, not the mind, is the subject of perception. In this perspective building and dwelling are thought of not as separate processes:

> "Building then, cannot be understood as a simple process of transcription, of a pre-existing design of the final product onto a raw material substrate… The forms people build (in imagination or on the ground) arise within the current of their involved activity, in the specific relational contexts of their practical engagement with their surroundings" (Ingold 2000: 186).

Archaeologists have been attracted to the 'building perspective' because it appears to offer cross-cultural and cross-temporal generalising frameworks, within which the cultural and social frameworks of any society can be decoded from the built form of its architecture, regardless of the presence or absence of extensive contextual information about that society (see, for example, Kent 1990; Rapoport 1969: 1990). Because culture is thought to consist of imposing a framework of symbolic meaning upon the environment, 'building theory' approaches tend to be concerned with 'decoding' the social and cultural principles, 'rules' or 'grammar', which underlie the design of past buildings and environments.

One of the most popular forms of spatial analysis to have emerged from this theoretical tradition is 'space syntax', or 'access analysis', pioneered by Hiller and Hanson (1984; Hanson 1998; Hiller 1996). The technique analyses the degree of integration of architectural space to shed light on the relative importance of inhabitant-inhabitant and inhabitant-visitor interfaces which are perceived to be the 'fundamental social generators of buildings' (Hanson 1998). In England this technique has been used to explore how the configuration of space in spatially-complex elite buildings, such as castles, palaces and monasteries, both reflected and structured contemporary attitudes to elite and gender identities and social relations (Fairclough 1992; Fradley 2006; Gilchrist 1997; 1999; Mathieu 1999; Phillips 2005; Richardson 2003). Johnson (1993a, after Glassie 1979) has also used the structuralist idea of a 'grammar' as a means of understanding the mental templates which underpinned the organisation and use of space in medieval and early modern housing.

Medieval archaeologists have been more wary of adopting theories associated explicitly with the 'dwelling perspective' and phenomenology (Giles 2007; McClain 2012). They have tended instead to seek to qualify techniques such as access analysis by drawing on the work of post-structuralists such as Giddens' idea of the 'locale' – a physically bounded space which provides the settings for 'institutionally embedded social encounters and practices' and whose meanings can be transformed by the presence or absence of people and the social practices in which they are engaged (Giddens 1984: 118f). Kleinschmidt's (2000: 60) assertion that medieval place should be thought of as the "aggregate sum of qualitatively different places occupied by persons, groups or objects and not as the space in between persons, groups and objects", has considerable resonance with this approach. Bourdieu's (1977: 87, 93f) concept of 'habitus', the embodied practical skills which enable people to negotiate social life has also greatly informed archaeologists' engagement with the historicity and sensory experience of medieval space (Casey 1997; Giles 2007; Graves 1989; 2000; 2007; and see Woolgar 2006). Such approaches have been tempered by a more rigorous understanding of concepts such as 'public' and 'private' space, as reflected in medieval etymology and contemporary legal codes (Arnade, Howell & Simons 2002; Austin 1998; Hanawalt & Kobialka 2000).

What is perhaps most useful about these recent theoretical debates is the call for a more subtle, historically nuanced and less generalised understanding of the relationship between architectural structures, plan forms and distinctive 'ways of living' in the past. Ingold's 'dwelling perspective' offers a particularly useful way of thinking these issues through. It is not that people do not have ideas about space, or that these do not influence architectural form, but rather that mental representations or spatial templates are not simply *imposed* on the environment. The forms of buildings must be understood as the result of intimate, local negotiations and interpreted in the context, not of global, national, cultural models or 'types', but rather the lived lives of men and women inhabiting particular buildings, at particular times in the past.

Excavating the foundations: studies of English medieval housing

England is fortunate to preserve extensive standing remains of medieval houses, from the palaces and castles of the elite, to the much humbler dwellings of merchants, artisans and peasants. During the late 19th and early 20th centuries, scholars focused primarily on the castles, palaces and manor houses of the elite (Turner and Parker 1851; 1853; 1859). However, during the course of the 20th century research extended to the houses of those lower down the social scale (Addy 1898; Innocent 1916). Fox and Raglan's (1951) volume on Monmouthshire houses (Wales) also provided a powerful model for regional studies of vernacular buildings.

The mid-20th century marked a turning point for the study of vernacular houses, with the foundation of the Vernacular Architecture Group in 1952 and the Society for Medieval Archaeology in 1956/7 (Gilchrist & Reynolds 2009). Peasant houses began to form an important part of archaeologists' study of 'deserted' medieval settlements such as Wharram Percy by Beresford (1954), inspired by the work of Danish archaeologists such as Axel Steensberg (Grenville 1997: 123f). The bombing and post-war redevelopment of towns also afforded greater opportunity for the excavation and survey of medieval urban houses by scholars such as Pantin (1962-3; Gerrard 2003: 95-99). More systematic and in-depth regional, rural

and urban 'inventories' of buildings were also provided by the Royal Commission on Historic Monuments (see for example, RCHM(E) Cambridgeshire 1968; 1972). A series of important regional studies have subsequently been produced by RCHME and others, including those for North Avon and South Gloucestershire (Hall 1983), North Yorkshire (Harrison and Hutton 1984), Lancashire (RCHM(E) 1985), West Yorkshire (RCHM(E) 1986), Hertfordshire (Smith 1992), Suffolk (Johnson 1993a), Kent (Pearson 1994), Hampshire (Roberts 2003), Shropshire (Moran 2003) and most recently, the West Midlands (Alcock & Miles 2013). The journal *Vernacular Architecture* has also published numerous individual case studies of medieval houses, as have local and regional archaeological journals (see Pattison 1992, 1999 for a useful published bibliography and Moir et al 2012 for a new online database initiative (BARD)).

Ways of building: the investment of the middling sort

In England, there are very few surviving examples of houses dating to before c 1380 which can be linked with certainty to those in the middle or lower levels of medieval society. However, at some point during the late 14th century, these groups appear to have embarked on a process of building, and rebuilding, their houses, on a significant scale. This process has been described in the literature as a 'late medieval upsurge in building activity' (Smith 1970: 126) and even a 'housing explosion' (Mercer 1997: 10). The process is particularly apparent in the south-east of England, where it was argued that this period constituted the 'first great rebuilding', during which previous houses were swept away and large numbers of houses began to be built to a standard which ensured their survival. Although it was acknowledged that the data reflected evidence of survival, rather than construction, most scholars agreed that meaningful patterns could be drawn from the surviving evidence, particularly when similar patterns seemed to emerge from statistically-sampled regional data, as in West Yorkshire (RCHM(E) 1985: 26-37), or the Midlands (Dyer 1986; 1997: 3f).

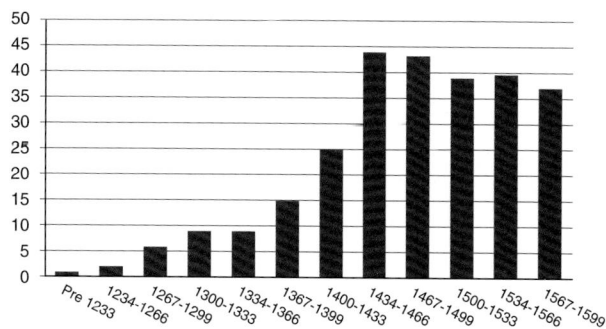

Tree ring dating of rural medieval vernacular houses
(270 examples, sampled 1980-2001)

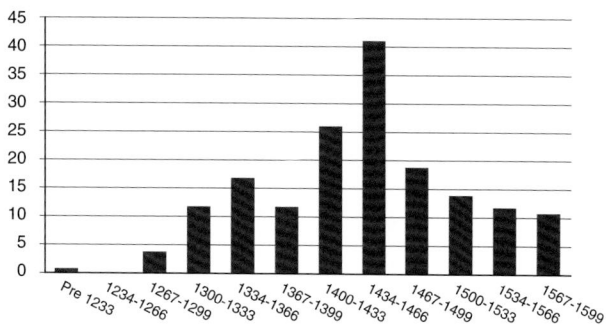

Tree ring dating of urban medieval houses (status not differentiated)
(169 examples, sampled 1980-2001)

Figure 1. Ways of building: a summary of trends in house construction derived from dendrochronological data. After Pearson 2001: Figures 2 and 3.

A more recent 'scientific' analysis of the national picture has been provided by Pearson (1997; 2001 and see also Meeson 2012). Pearson analysed patterns in published dendrochronological dates for episodes of construction and major rebuilding of 270 examples of rural vernacular houses (defined as those beneath aristocratic and gentry level) and 169 urban buildings (of undifferentiated status). The results, plotted in 33-year blocks, are consistent across the four years separating the two studies (Figure 1). They demonstrate a clear rise in the numbers of houses constructed or rebuilt from 1400 onwards and particularly, throughout the 15th century. In towns, a slightly different pattern emerges, with higher numbers being built during the later 14th century and again in the first part of the 15th century, followed by a drop in the later part of the century. These figures appear to be supported by dendrochronological dating associated with regional studies, such as that of Hampshire (Roberts 2003). Here, rural buildings showed a

slight delay in comparison with the national picture, with a particular surge from 1440-1550. Urban buildings showed an upsurge just prior to 1348, but also a continuation of building through the later part of the 14th century. Hampshire did not experience an upsurge in buildings in the early 15th century, but numbers did rise from 1425 onwards and continued to remain steady until 1500.

The chronological pattern which emerges from the data is significant because it suggests that building activity does not correlate exactly with current models of economic prosperity in medieval England. Traditionally, the post-Black Death period was described as a golden age of the European peasantry. However, there does not appear to be evidence for large-scale building in rural areas in the immediate post-Black Death period. This may reveal the disproportionate impact of the plague on rural communities (Pearson 2001: 69). However, it may also be an important reminder of the 'ways of living' of medieval peasants. Investment in houses was probably not their first priority, but rather followed the engrossment of land and investment in animals, crops and agricultural equipment. This may also partly explain the pattern observed in Goldberg's (2008; 2011) recent analysis of rural household inventories, which suggests that investment in domestic possessions did not appear to be a prosperous peasant priority.

The dendrochronological data also raise interesting questions about the decision of urban inhabitants to invest in houses throughout the middle years of the fifteenth century; a period identified by urban historians as one of apparent economic decline. Once again, this may tell us something meaningful about urban 'ways of living'. Did town dwellers seek to build themselves out of recession, a pattern observed in levels of investment in public buildings during the same period? Or was investment in the domestic comforts and the workshops which tended to be accommodated under the same roof in the urban home always more of a priority for artisans and merchants, as the evidence of their inventories might suggest (Goldberg 2011)?

What is also apparent from such analysis, and from the wealth of data emerging from regional studies, is that it is dangerous to try and generalise about 'rural' or 'urban' patterns of investment. The decision to build and the design of a building reflected the particular interplay of social structure, inheritance customs and market opportunities at particular moments in time (Smith 1970: 146). Chatwin's (2003) detailed analysis of a series of Sussex parishes suggests that in some areas at least, greater levels of social differentiation between inhabitants tended to result in the preservation of relatively-unaltered houses, whilst greater levels of competition between status groups resulted in far higher rates of adaptation and rebuilding. Buildings, like their inhabitants, experienced life cycles of prosperity and investment, and decline and neglect. Developing a greater understanding of these cycles is certainly an important area for future research.

Ways of building: semi-permanence and flexibility?

Between the tenth and thirteenth centuries, important changes occurred in the construction methods used in lower-status medieval houses. Early medieval houses tended to be of earthfast post construction, with simple lap and halved joints and stave-built, or wattle walls. By the 13th century, this was gradually replaced by techniques that set principal posts above ground level, such as the use of uninterrupted sills and padstones, or stylobates (see Grenville 1997: 30-37 for a useful summary of this debate). Such changes were facilitated by the development of more complex joint types, such as mortice and tenon joints. A great deal of information about these buildings emerged from the excavation of 'deserted medieval villages' such as Wharram Percy (North Yorkshire), Hangleton (Sussex), Upton (Gloucesstershire), Gomeldon (Wiltshire), Dartmoor (Devon), Grenstein (Norfolk) during the 1950s-1980s (Astill 1988; Austin 1990). The consensus which emerged initially from this work was that peasant houses were rather flimsy and impermanent structures, which had to be rebuilt every 20-30 years. It led Mercer (1975: 8) for example, to conclude that 'rural vernacular houses prior to the late middle ages appear from the evidence of

excavation, to have been of uniformly poor quality throughout the whole of England'.

However, during the 1980s, several important challenges to this hypothesis emerged (see Grenville 1997: 123-128). Initial challenges came from historians such as Dyer (1986), highlighting a range of documentary evidence to suggest a reasonably high standard of living amongst the peasantry in the post-Black Death period. Evidence from the study of surviving buildings in North Yorkshire (Harrison and Hutton 1984) and sites deserted only in the 18th century, such as West Whelpington (Northumberland) encouraged the re-examination of the excavated evidence to suggest that such buildings were originally cruck-framed – a much more permanent form of construction than previously thought (Wrathmell 1989). From this work a new consensus has emerged of a distinctively 'semi-permanent' approach to construction methods in late medieval houses.

The mapping of regional construction traditions has long been a focus of vernacular studies in the UK. In some areas, stone was part of the English medieval vernacular tradition (Clifton-Taylor & Ireson 1994; Parsons 1990), and the significance of earth as a building material at all status levels is also beginning to be recognised (Dyer 2008). However, the most common form of medieval house construction in England was that of timber-framing, and scholarship has therefore centred around the analysis of two, or three distinctive 'schools of carpentry' as reflected in the wall frames and roof structures of timber-framed buildings of the lowland zone of the east and south-east (characterised by close studs but also crown posts and clasped purlins); the highland zone of the midlands, south and south-west (characterised by square and ornamental panelling and cruck-framing); and the north (characterised by the use of crucks and king posts) (Smith 1965; Harris 1989; 1993; Walker 2011). Recent settlement studies and place-name evidence have also shed important new light on the availability of timber as a medieval building resource (Roberts & Wrathmell 2000: 18-23). Although these models have been very useful in highlighting the close relationship between regional resources, landscapes and building materials, they have been less successful in explaining the distribution of particular construction techniques, such as cruck construction, about which there continues to be debate (see Alcock 1981; 1997; 2006; Alcock & Blair 1986; Hill & Alcock 2007; Mercer 1996; 1998; Smith 1975 and see Le Patourel 1991).

What is perhaps most interesting for the purpose of this paper is increasing evidence of the ways in which apparently distinctive construction traditions, such as crucks and box-framing, could be found not only within the same region, town or parish (James 2011), but also the same house. Such evidence comes from both urban and rural areas, including Leicestershire (Cherry & Messanger 1988) and Shropshire (Moran 2003: 43). In Hampshire Roberts (2003: 23) too, has identified three examples where 'hybrid crucks' were used to create spacious halls in otherwise contemporary box-framed medieval houses, at Manor Farm, Weston Patrick, Uncle Dick's Cottage, North Hayling and Boarhunt (now at the Weald & Downland Open Air Museum, Singleton, Sussex). Many of these examples occur in 'border regions' between construction traditions and suggest that both patrons and craftsmen were willing to combine different forms of construction within the same building, selecting particular structures according to their suitability for the spaces they were intended to create within the house (Cherry & Messenger 1988: 9).

The significance of previous studies of construction techniques and the evidence for intra-, as well as inter-regional variation in timber-framing is that it appears to reveal evidence of a deliberately-flexible approach to both construction methods and structural form in the houses of those at the middling levels of society. The houses of the wealthy rural peasantry and urban bourgeoisie may have been far more flexible than those of the elite. The choice of these particular structural forms also had profound implications for the ability of a building to be adapted and altered over time (Currie 1988; 1990).

The active role played by patrons and craftsmen in designing medieval houses is reflected in the survival of formal contracts between those of middling status and professional carpenters (Dyer 1986; Dymond 1998). These indicate a concern with standards and a willingness to litigate when work fell short of the mark (Dyer 1986: 27-9)! But they also indicate clear

evidence of competitive emulation *between* middling-status home-owners. The details of surviving rural and rural 15th-century building contracts indicate the deliberate copying of features from the fashionable houses, referred to by the names of their owners, and a concern with placing the most elaborate jettied and framed façade of the building, towards the street (Dymond 1998: 281). Apparent evidence of emulation can also be found in surviving buildings, as at East Meon (Hampshire), where a pair of single-aisled late medieval halls of slightly different dates and construction traditions but similar appearance, face each other across an abandoned medieval street (Roberts 2003: 14). These examples are a reminder of the need to re-think and explore medieval attitudes to displaying status in the appearance, as well as the structure and plan form, of vernacular buildings (Cooper 2002).

Ways of living: plan form and rural life

The typological analysis of plan form has also been fundamental to understanding 'ways of living' in the English medieval home. In England, this has been dominated by the model of the 'open hall'. Longcroft (2002) has outlined the origin of this typology in the RCHM(E) West Cambridgeshire (1968, *xlvi-xlvii*) and North-East Cambridgeshire (1972, *xliii-xlv*) volumes. This featured idealised amalgams of individual examples from which all later additions had been stripped away to reveal their original, 'intended' plan (Figure 2). The typology establishes an important distinction between houses that are 'mediaeval, or in the mediaeval tradition, and are characterised by the existence of a hall open to the roof' (RCHME 1968, *xlvi*) and those which incorporated upper floors, which were dated to the post-medieval period. This typological framework became an important dating mechanism and underpinned all subsequent studies and syntheses (Mercer 1975).

In high-status buildings, the open hall was at the centre of a 'tripartite' arrangement (Grenville 1997: 89; see also Quiney 1990; Wood 1965). At the 'high' end of the hall was a raised dais, beyond which lay a

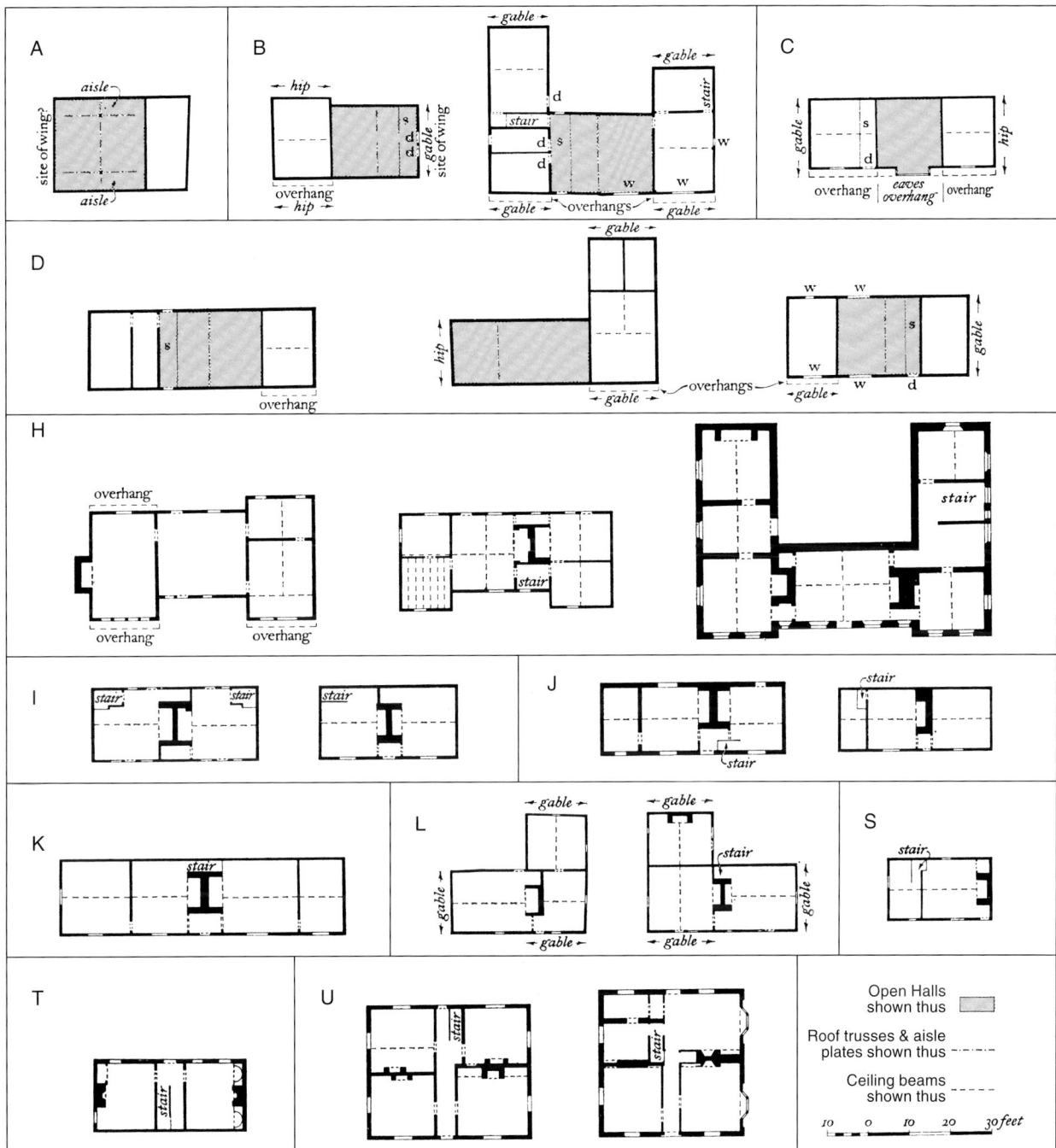

Figure 2. Types of medieval houses. Types A, B, C, D all contain open halls with aisles, cross wings, and end bays roofed in line ('Wealdens'), or as an extension of the hall in association with a cross wing. Types H onwards, with an upper floor, was noted as first appearing in the 16th century, and types I, J, K and L in the 17th century. Two new types, F and G, where the hall only was ceiled, were added in the RCHME's 1972 volume on north-east Cambridgeshire. Once again these types were associated with changes of the mid-16th century. © Crown Copyright RCHME 1968, p.xlvii. Reproduced by kind permission of English Heritage Archives.

range, often storeyed, containing private accommodation such as the solar, chamber or parlour. At the 'low' end was often a passage, separated by screen and providing access via a set of two or three doors to the services of buttery, pantry and further accommodation. The tripartite arrangement was traditionally thought to have emerged at some point between the tenth and thirteenth centuries from where it was diffused gradually down the social scale "for that was the convention" (Mercer 1975: 20; see also Thompson 1995: 132-143). However, Gardiner (2000: 175) has recently argued that the 'medieval plan' can be identified as early as the 13th century, in *excavated* 'vernacular' buildings. Further, he suggests that other elements of supposedly 'high-status' planning, such as detached 'chamber blocks', may also have existed at lower status sites (Gardiner 2000: 170). Parallels have also been drawn between the axial plans of early surviving peasant houses and higher status halls with 'ends-in-line' (Grenville 1997: 130).

An apparently distinctive form of peasant house was the 'longhouse' – a single-storey, dual-function building, designed to house both people and animals under the same roof (Mercer 1975: 34). Longhouses are common in upland zones, such as south-west, north-west and north-east of England, but are much rarer in the Midlands, East Anglia and south-east of England (Astill 1988; Gardiner 2000: 167f). Much of the debate about this building has centred on the need to identify unequivocal evidence for this dual function, in the form of a byre or shippon (Alcock & Smith 1972: 145f; Austin 1985: 75). However, the fact that distinctions between longhouses and other single-storeyed tripartite plans are notoriously difficult to recognise archaeologically, is significant. At Hill Top Farm, Langdon (Staffordshire), for example, close attention to archaeological recording revealed evidence of a byre in what was thought to be a standard medieval hall-house (Meeson 2001). This is an important reminder of the strategic priorities of rural ways of medieval living. Byres were always multiple-functioning spaces, being used for a host of other agricultural activities, such as dairying activities and the storage and processing of goods and tools, when animals were not present (Barley 1986: 160 and see Harrison & Hutton 1991). Gardiner (2000: 168) has therefore concluded that the longhouse should therefore be understood as a regional variation or adaptation of the tripartite plan, rather than a distinctive type of medieval house (Figure 3).

Some of the most impressive examples of rural 'middle-class' houses are the hall-houses of the south-eastern counties of Essex, Kent, Suffolk, Sussex and Surrey (Mercer 1975; Quiney 1990: 89-92).

However, open halls are also found in most other regions of the country. These houses accommodated the late medieval plan within a variety of structural forms, from halls with a single, or two cross wings, to Wealdens, in which the hall and jettied-cross wings were accommodated under a single roof, and end-jetties, where the end bays of the house were jettied only at the ends. Open halls in middling status rural houses could be visually and structurally impressive, incorporating formal dais ends, emphasised by painted partitions and coving, screens passages and formal service ends. Shieling Hall, Langley (Kent) is a typical example. Built between 1480-1520, it is a Wealden house, with a formerly open, 2-bay hall, an 'overshot' passage (in which the screens passage lay beneath part of the chamber above the services); an upper end providing access to a parlour. The dais end of the hall was emphasised by a plank and muntin partition and the parlour was also decorated with surviving panelling (RCHME 1994a: 91; 1994b: 78).

Gardiner (2000: 169f, 179) has suggested that one explanation for similarities between the house forms of the lower levels of the gentry and upper levels of the peasantry may be that it facilitated easy comparison between the two. Nevertheless, he has also called for the need to debate further this 'remarkable consensus' in the organisation of medieval domestic space. Johnson (1993a: 57; 1997: 14f; 2010b) continues to provide the most theoretically-informed interpretation of the medieval hall as a *leitmotif* of feudal society, providing a powerful sense of community within which there was an asymmetrical, hierarchical framework of upper and lower ends which could be used to differentiate gender and status within and between members of the household community. The open hall features prominently in his 'grammar' of medieval houses, where it is juxtaposed against the gradual abandonment of the form in the 16th and 17th centuries, through a process he terms 'closure'.

The decision to invest in an open hall certainly tells us something meaningful about the 'ways of living' of prosperous medieval peasants. However, we need to look beyond the apparent similarities of form between high and low-status buildings, to the detail of their structure, in order to understand the complexity of their past use and meanings. Such an

a

b

Figure 3. The rural open-hall house and the longhouse. Pearson 2005: Figure 3.5. © reproduced by kind permission of Maney Publishing, Leeds.

analysis then begins to reveal considerable variation in the realisation of the 'tripartite plan', which often involved encroachment of other spaces onto, or into, the hall.

The services might occupy an extra long bay. Indeed, in some cases, the service end was longer and more impressive than the 'parlour' end, reversing the apparent hierarchy of the hall and creating a high-status chamber at first floor level (Alcock & Currie 1989; Smith 1970: 123-5). Services did not always follow the tripartite model of division between buttery and pantry. In Hampshire (Roberts 2003: 130) and Kent (RCHM(E) 1994: 102) there are examples of service bays which appear to have been open to the roof. The function of these spaces is unclear, but may have been both domestic and/or storage-related, facilitat-

ing the insertion of temporary joists and floors when required. In Somerset, this may well have served an agricultural function (Austin & de Zouche Hall 1972: 90). In West Yorkshire, it has been argued that the large, lower rooms of aisled halls may have been used for workshop or storage associated with the cloth industry (RCHM(E) 1986: 31). Overall, the evidence suggests that service functions in rural houses may have been provided in a variety of ways and buildings (Pearson 2012).

The use of internal jetties which projected into upper end of the domestic plan creating large chambers at first floor level, was also common. In Hampshire, there are a number of such 'overshot halls', dating to the mid-15th century and later, such as Batchelors, North Waltham (Roberts 2003: 134),

Garden Cottage, West Meon (Hampshire) (Lewis et al 1988: 18). In Devon, a series of late medieval houses with internal jetties have also been identified. The example of Glebe House, Whitestone preserved a particularly impressive chamber with a surviving four-light, trefoil-headed window (Alcock & Laithwaite 1973). These impressive first floor chambers may have been used for a variety of functions, including private and domestic activities, but also were sufficiently well-lit to accommodate household working activities, such as spinning. The changing preferences of prosperous rural peasants for locating their principal chamber at the low or high ends of their halls, and at ground- or first-floor level has been charted by Barley (1991) and Alcock & Currie (1989).

Traditionally, these aspects of medieval rural planning have tended to be interpreted as variations of the tripartite arrangement, which did not impinge on the integrity or meaning open hall. I would suggest that such variations constitute evidence of greater 'flexibility' in the late medieval domestic plan than has previously been recognised. They are a reminder that the relatively limited spaces in these houses had to be used in multiple ways, to accommodate a diverse range of activities. Moreover, the use of terms such as 'encroachment' and 'intrusion' by previous scholars are meaningful. For whilst at one level, internal jetties might reinforce the symbolism of the hall, by creating a canopy over the dais end, they also made a powerful statement about the status of the room encroaching upon it. What emerges from this analysis is an apparent flexibility of the structure and spaces within the medieval home.

This flexibility is particularly apparent in a recent scholarly exchange in *Vernacular Architecture* which focused on the issue of whether a series of storeyed buildings in Kent were *either* 'detached kitchens' *or* domestic buildings accommodating members of an extended household (Martin 2000; Martin & Martin 1997; Meeson 2000; Smith 2001). Documentary evidence of agreements to accommodate young married couples and elderly relatives in converted service and agricultural buildings is well attested and has been used to explain several plan form arrangements across England (Austin 1990: 61; Dyer 1986; Fox & Raglan 1951: 75; Mason 1964: 29; Smith 1970: 186-18).

However, for the purposes of this paper the crucial issue is that these buildings were sufficiently flexible to be used for multiple purposes in the past, and interpreted in different ways, in the present. As the Martins (2001: 31) conclude:

"The tendency to classify everything we study.... risks forming artificial barriers which our ancestors would not have recognised. They lived and worked from home. Inevitably some farming operations would have spilled over into the domestic areas and vice versa. Furthermore the extent to which this occurred would have varied from household to household and from generation to generation."

Ways of living: in transition?

The gradual alteration and adaptation of medieval houses in the early modern period has been bound up with the narrative of the 16th-century Great Rebuilding (Hoskins 1953; see subsequent debate in Alcock 1983; Machin 1977a; 1977b; Johnson 1993b). Gradually, the open hall was abandoned and continuous first floors were created. New forms of heating and access arrangements were introduced and the tripartite plan was ultimately abandoned. Discussion of the timing and meaning of this process has proved one of the most interesting areas of debate in vernacular architecture in recent years, not least because of Johnson's contributions to the debate (Johnson 1993a; 2010b). The evidence emerging from dendrochronologically-informed studies in Kent and Hampshire reveals evidence of an incredibly complex and long period of 'transition'. Open halls persisted in both areas well into the 16th century, but some halls had begun to be partially-floored over as early as the 1470s, and new fully-floored, storeyed buildings were also being built in the late 15th and early 16th century (RCHM(E) 1994: 134; Roberts 2003: 148-149). At Overton Court in Hampshire, the late medieval demesne lessees chose to convert the former open hall into services, whilst building themselves fully-floored houses with internal chimney stacks and elaborate chambers designed for 'semi-public' functions such as entertaining the household of the Bishop of Winchester (Roberts 1995).

It is clear that one of the most interesting areas for future research in rural houses is the explanation of the relationship between the variation and flexibility of medieval house structure and layout discussed above, and the widespread process of partial or 'piecemeal' rebuilding which case studies suggest may have affected up to 40% of houses in regions such as Sussex from the late 15th century onwards (Martin and Martin 1987; 1999; Martin 2000). Theoretical analyses of the structure and use of space might well offer one means of doing this. Martin's (2003) application of 'planning analysis' (a slightly simpler version of 'access analysis') to the transitional houses of Sussex (Figure 4), for example, revealed the creation of new access routes and 'suites' of rooms which raise important questions about changing 'ways of living' in the late medieval and early modern home.

Urban ways of living

Thus far, this paper has focused predominantly on the analysis of medieval rural houses. However, it is worth briefly reviewing the historiography of urban houses because it resonates with some of the ideas presented above. Until recently, late medieval urban houses had been presumed to be an urban variant of the tripartite plan, diffused from elite and rural houses, into the urban context. Their analysis had been informed by Pantin's (1962-3) 'parallel' and 'right angle' types which seemed to reinforce the idea of the universality of the tripartite plan across medieval building types (see Grenville 1997: 157-193; Quiney 2003; Schofield 1995; also see Grenville 2008 for a theoretically informed discussion of the ways in which this facilitated ontological security between town and country).

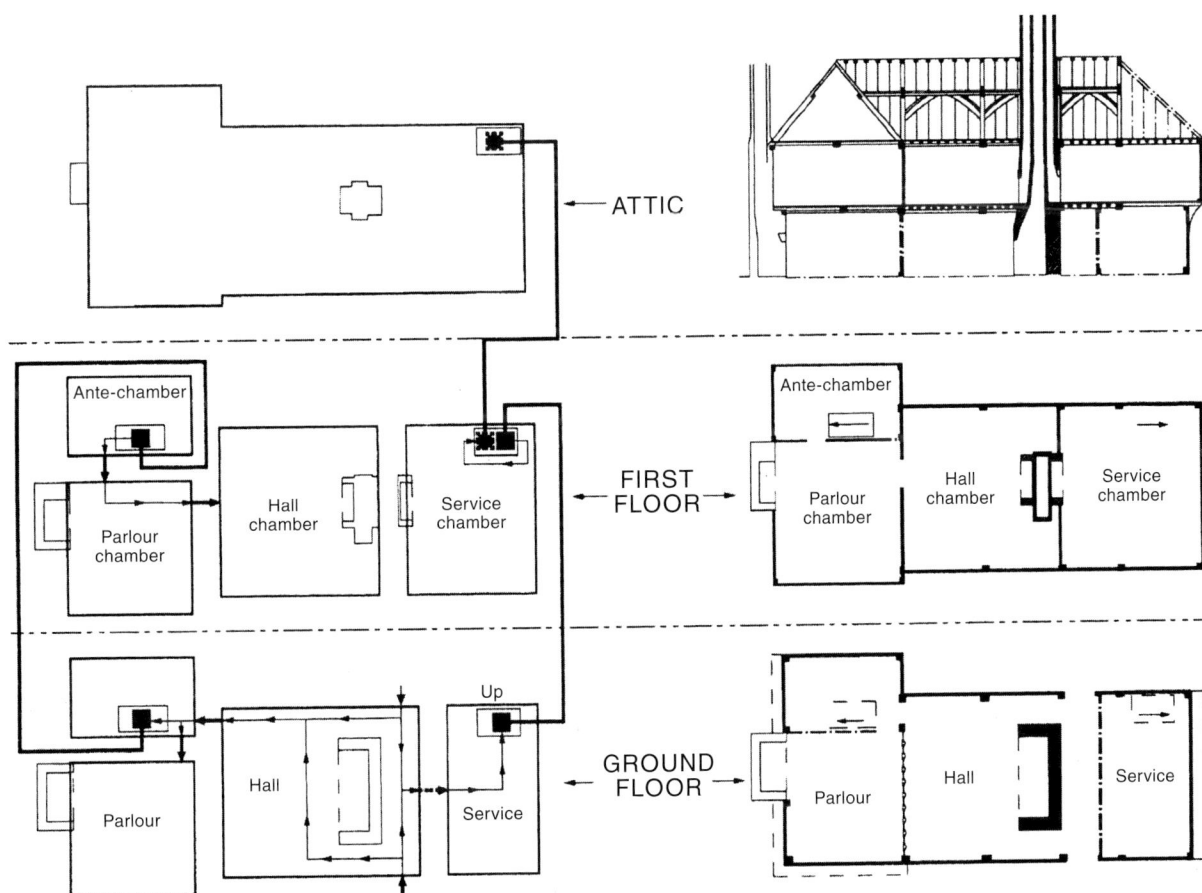

Figure 4. Planning analysis of Brooks, Northiam (Sussex). Martin 2003: Figure 2. © Reproduced by kind permission of Maney publishing, Leeds.

However, recently this consensus has been challenged by Pearson (2005; 2009) who has argued that urban life and thus urban ways of living, were distinct, and that towns may have encouraged innovation, rather than emulation in the structure and plan forms of medieval houses. Such innovations included the use of storeyed accommodation and jetties to maximise the use of space (Pearson 2005: 47-50). Indeed, she suggests that the 'Wealden type' of house, in which a recessed hall is flanked by two jettied, storeyed ends under a single roof, may be an important example of such innovation. The dating of the earliest Wealden in England at 35 High Street Winchester (Hampshire) to 1339/40 appears to support her hypothesis, since it suggests that the earliest Wealdens may be found in towns, rather than the Weald of Kent, where they have traditionally been thought to originate. It may also explain the popularity of terraces of half Wealdens at Upper Spon Street in Coventry and Battle, Sussex (Quiney 2003: 266) and terraces of cruck-built houses in Much Wenlock, Shropshire (Moran 1992; 2010).

Although archaeologists have long acknowledged the existence of a distinctive way of treating the façade of medieval urban buildings, especially shops (Stenning 1985; Clark 2000; Quiney 2003: 247), it has taken them much longer to recognise the implications of a diversity of plan form. Pearson (2005: 53) however, raises important questions about the 'universality' of the tripartite plan and the open hall in late medieval urban houses, cautioning that piecemeal rebuilding may result in plan forms that look deceptively similar. There were, of course, elaborate, tripartite halls in most towns. York and Salisbury, for example, have about 15 surviving examples in each city (RCHM(E) 1980; 1981), whilst the Chester Rows project has revealed a very distinctive solution to accommodating undercrofts, halls and rows of shops to the topography and morphology of the city (Brown 1999). However, the constraints of space meant that the location of services and screens passages associated with halls varied greatly. Urban houses often incorporated several rooms at the lower or upper end of the hall which may have accommodated a variety of shop or workshop functions (see Alston 2004 for an excellent case study of medi-

eval workshops in Suffolk). These could encroach upon the open hall, reducing it to one or one and a half bays. Indeed some cases, the urban first-floor chamber or 'solar' seems to have taken precedence over the hall as the most high-status room of the house (Roberts 2003: 144). The analysis of surviving decoration and the evidence of late medieval probate inventories, sheds important light on the multiple, as well as the distinctive uses of these spaces and their intended audiences (Goldberg 2011; Leech 2000).

Pearson's seminal work encourages us to re-examine the precise evidence of urban houses and to acknowledge the ways in which subtle variations reflect the differing priorities of the diverse community of merchants and artisans who made up the late medieval middling urban sort. It highlights the importance of engaging with the historical and literary evidence for urban bourgeois culture (Goldberg 2008; Rees Jones 2003), and for ritual as well as social practices in the home (Gilchrist 2012; Grenville 2008; Riddy 2008). It also, however, encourages us to re-examine the ways in structural innovations in towns, such as the creation of continuous jetties, partial flooring and internal galleries related to the process of 'transition' (Roberts 2003: 44-46).

Conclusion

This paper started by reviewing some of the ways in which recent theories about the use and meaning of the built environment may be relevant to the analysis of medieval 'ways of living'. In particular, it highlighted the potential of the 'dwelling perspective' (after Ingold 2000) as a means of understanding buildings, not as a materialisation of an abstract idea into material form, but rather as a product of the practical engagement of people with their surroundings. This theoretical approach was then used to question and re-examine existing evidence of the late medieval houses of the rural 'middling sort'. Evidence of a large-scale rebuilding of houses during the late medieval period in distinctively 'semi-permanent' and flexible ways was emphasised. So too was the flexibility of the tripartite plan within these houses. Rather than representing a homogenous and static appropriation of a 'consensus' about building, the article sought evidence for variation and adaptation of houses, to accommodate particular forms of service and chambered accommodation, which often encroached upon, the open hall. This re-interpretation of trends long-established within the literature raises questions about debates within and between scholars of rural and urban houses. It may well be that rural middle-class houses are more innovative and diverse than has recently been acknowledged. But it also highlights the need for a more subtle and nuanced understanding of the medieval house, as a building used to structure, accommodate and symbolise the working identity of the late medieval household in a distinctively flexible way. Future work in this field may therefore allow medieval archaeologists to contribute more meaningfully to explanations of how – and why – houses were subsequently transformed in the post-medieval period.

References

Addy, S.O. (1898) *The Evolution of the English House*. London: Swan Sonnenschein.

Alcock, N.W. (1981) *Cruck Construction*. CBA Research Report 42. London: CBA.

Alcock, N. (1997) A reponse to: cruck distribution: a social explanation, *Vernacular Architecture* 28, 92-93.

Alcock, N.W. (1983) The Great Rebuilding and its later stages, *Vernacular Architecture* 14, 45-9.

Alcock, N.W. (2006) The origin of crucks: innocence or naiveté? A response, *Vernacular Architecture* 37, 50-53.

Alcock, N.W. & J. Blair (1986) Crucks: new documentary evidence, *Vernacular Architecture* 17, 36-38.

Alcock, N.W. & C.R.J. Currie (1989) Upstairs or Downstairs? *Vernacular Architecture* 20, 21-3.

Alcock, N.W. & M. Laithwaite (1973) Medieval houses in Devon and their modernisation, *Medieval Archaeology* 17, 100-125.

Alcock, N. & D. Miles (2012) *The Medieval Peasant House in Midland England*. Oxford: Oxbow.

Alcock, N.W. & P. Smith (1972) The long house: a plea for clarity, *Medieval Archaeology* 16, 145-6.

Alston, L. (2004) Late medieval workshops in East Anglia. In: *The vernacular workshop from craft to industry 1400-1900*, eds. P.S. Barnwell, M. Palmer & M. Airs, 38-60. York: Council for British Archaeology.

Arnade, P., M. Howell & W. Simons (2002) Fertile spaces: the productivity of urban space in Northern Europe, *Journal of Interdisciplinary History* 32(4), 515-548.

Astill, G.G. (1988) Rural settlement: the toft and croft. In: *The Countryside of Medieval England*, eds. G.G. Astill & A. Grant, 36-61. Oxford: Basil Blackwell.

Austin, C. & R. de Zouche Hall (1972) The medieval houses of Stocklinch, Somerset, *Proceedings of the Somserset Archaeological and Natural History Society* 116, 86-99.

Austin, D. (1985) Dartmoor and the upland villages of the southwest of England. In: *Medieval villages. A Review of Current Work*, ed. D. Hooke, 71-79. Oxford: Oxford University Committee for Archaeology.

Austin, D. (1990) The 'proper' study of medieval archaeology: a case study. In: *From the Baltic to the Black Sea: Studies in Medieval Archaeology*, eds. D. Austin & L. Alcock, 43-78. London: Unwin Hyman.

Austin, D. (1998) Private and public: an archaeological consideration of things. In: *Die Vielfalt der Dinge: Neue Wege zur Analyse mittelalterlicher Sachkultur*, eds. H. Hundsbichler, G. Jaritz & T. Kuhtreiber, 163-206. Wien: Verlag der Österreichischen Akademie der Wissenschaften.

Barley, M.W. (1986) *Houses and History*. London: Faber & Faber.

Barley, M.W. (1991) The use of upper floors in rural houses, *Vernacular Architecture* 22, 2-23.

Beresford, M.W. (1954) *The Lost Villages of England*. London: Lutterworth Press.

Bourdieu, P. (1977) *Outline of a Theory of Practice*. Cambridge: Cambridge University Press. Transl. R. Nice.

Brown, A. (1999) *The Chester Rows Research Project*. London: English Heritage.

Casey, E. (1997) *The Fate of Place: A Philosophical History*. Berkeley: University of California Press.

Chatwin, D. (2003) Variation in the survival rate of timber framed buildings in two Sussex parishes, *Vernacular Architecture* 34, 32-36.

Cherry, M. & P. Messanger (1988) A medieval hall and cross-wing house in Queniborough, *Transactions of the Leicestershire Archaeological and Historical Society* 62, 9-15.

Clark, D. (2000) The shop within: an analysis of architectural evidence for medieval shops, *Architectural History* 43, 58-87.

Clifton-Taylor, A. & A.S. Ireson (1994) *English Stone Building*. London: Victor Gollancz.

Cooper, N. (2002) Display, status and the vernacular tradition, *Vernacular Architecture* 33, 28-33.

Currie, C.R.J (1988) Time and chance: modelling the attrition of old houses, *Vernacular Architecture* 19, 1-9.

Currie, C.R.J. (1990) Time and chance: a reply to comments, *Vernacular Architecture* 21, 5-9.

Currie, C.R.J. (2004) The unfulfilled potential of the documentary sources, *Vernacular Architecture* 35, 1-11.

Dyer, C. (1986) English peasant buildings in the later Middle Ages (1200-1500), *Medieval Archaeology* 30, 19-45.

Dyer, C. (1997) History and vernacular architecture, *Vernacular Architecture* 28, 1-8.

Dyer, C. (2008) Building in earth in late-medieval England, *Vernacular Architecture* 39, 63-70.

Dymond, D. (1998) Five building contracts from fifteenth-century Suffolk, *Antiquaries Journal* 78, 269-87.

Fairclough, G. (1992) Meaningful constructions: spatial and functional analysis of medieval buildings, *Antiquity* 66, 348-66.

Fox, C. & F.R.S. Raglan (1951) *Monmouthshire Houses; a Study of Building Techniques and Smaller House-plans in the Fifteenth to Seventeenth Centuries Volume 1.* Cardiff: National Museum of Wales.

Fradley, M. (2006) Space and structure at Caernarfon Castle, *Medieval Archaeology* 50, 165-178.

Gardiner, M. (2000) Vernacular buildings and the development of the late medieval domestic plan in England, *Medieval Archaeology* 44, 159-179.

Gardiner, M. (2008) Buttery and pantry and their antecedents: idea and architecture in the English medieval house. In: *Medieval Domesticity. Home, Housing and Household in Medieval England*, eds. M. Kowaleski & P.J.P. Goldberg, 37-65. Cambridge: Cambridge University Press.

Gerrard, C. (2003) *Medieval Archaeology. Understanding Traditions and Contemporary Approaches.* London & New York: Routledge.

Giddens, A. (1984) *The Constitution of Society: Outline of a Theory of Structuration.* Cambridge: Polity Press.

Gilchrist, R. (1997) *Gender and Material Culture: The Archaeology of Religious Women.* London: Routledge.

Gilchrist, R. (1999) *Gender and Archaeology: Contesting the Past.* London: Routledge.

Gilchrist, R. (2009) Medieval archaeology and theory: a disciplinary leap of faith. In: *Reflections: 50 Years of Medieval Archaeology, 1957-2007*, eds. R. Gilchrist & A. Reynolds, 385-408. London: Maney Publishing.

Gilchrist, R. & A. Reynolds (eds.)(2009) *Reflections: 50 Years of Medieval Archaeology, 1957-2007.* London: Maney Publishing.

Gilchrist, R. (2012) *Medieval Life: Archaeology and the Life Course.* Woodbridge: Boydell Press.

Giles, K. (2005) Public space in town and village. In: *Town and Country 1100-1500*, eds. K. Giles & C. Dyer, 293-312. Leeds: Maney Publishing.

Giles, K. (2007) Seeing and believing: visuality and space in pre-modern England, *World Archaeology* 39(1): 105-121.

Glassie, H. (1979) *Folk Housing in Middle Virginia.* Knoxville: University of Tennessee Press.

Goldberg, P.J.P. (2008) The fashioning of urban domesticity in later medieval England: a material culture perspective. In: *Medieval Domesticity. Home, Housing and Household in Medieval England*, eds. M. Kowaleski & P.J.P. Goldberg, 124-144. Cambridge: Cambridge University Press.

Goldberg, P.J.P. (2011) Space and Gender in the later medieval English House, *Viator* 42(2), 1-28.

Graves, P. (1989) Social space in the English medieval parish church, *Economy and Society* 18(3), 297-322.

Graves, P. (2000) *The Form and Fabric of Belief: An Archaeology of the Lay Experience of Religion in Medieval Norfolk and Devon.* British Archaeological Reports 311. Oxford: Archaeopress.

Graves, P. (2007) Sensing and believing: exploring worlds of difference in pre-modern England: a contribution to the debate opened by Kate Giles, *World Archaeology* 39(4), 515-531.

Grenville, J. (1997) *Medieval Housing.* Leicester: Leicester University Press.

Grenville, J. (2008) Urban and rural houses and households in the late Middle Ages: a case study from Yorkshire. In: *Medieval Domesticity. Home, Housing and Household in Medieval England*, eds. M. Kowaleski & P.J.P. Goldberg, 92-123. Cambridge: Cambridge University Press.

Hall, L. (1983) *The Rural Houses of North Avon and South Gloucestershire 1400-1720.* Bristol: City of Bristol Museum and Art Gallery Monograph 6.

Hanawalt, B. & M. Kobialka (2000) *Medieval Practices of Space.* Minneapolis: University of Minnesota Press.

Hanson, J. (1998) *Decoding Homes and Houses.* Cambridge: Cambridge University Press.

Heidegger, M. (1979) *Basic Writings: from Being and Time(1927) to the Task of Thinking.* New York: Harper & Row.

Harris, R. (1989) The grammar of carpentry, *Vernacular Architecture* 20, 1-8.

Harris, R. (1993) *Discovering Timber-framed Buildings.* Princes Risborough: Shire Publications.

Harrison, B. & B. Hutton (1984) *Vernacular Houses of North Yorkshire and Cleveland.* Edinburgh: John Donald.

Harrison, B. (1991) Longhouses in the Vale of York, *Vernacular Architecture* 22, 31-9.

Hill, N. & N.W. Alcock. (2007) The origin of crucks and a rejoinder, *Vernacular Architecture* 38, 8-14.

Hillier, B. (1996) *Space is the Machine: A Configurational Theory of Architecture.* Cambridge: Cambridge University Press.

Hillier, B. & J. Hanson (1988) *The Social Logic of Space.* Cambridge: Cambridge University Press.

Hoskins, W.G. (1953) The rebuilding of rural England, 1570-1640, *Past and Present* 4, 44-59.

Ingold, T. (2000) *The Perception of the Environment: essays on livelihood, dwelling and skill.* London: Routledge.

Innocent, C.F. (1916) *The Development of English Building Construction.* Cambridge: Cambridge University Press.

James, D. (2011) On the need to acknowledge the parochial nature of timber-framing: some thoughts on the unrealised potential in the detailed recording of buildings, *Vernacular Architecture* 42, 1-13.

Johnson, M.H. (1993a) *Housing Culture.* London: UCL Press.

Johnson, M.H. (1993b) Rethinking the great rebuilding, *Oxford Journal of Archaeology* 12, 117-125.

Johnson, M. (1997) Vernacular Architecture: the loss of innocence, *Vernacular Architecture* 28, 13-19.

Johnson, M. (2010a) *Archaeological Theory: An Introduction.* Malden, MA: Wiley Blackwell.

Johnson, M. (2010b) *English Houses 1300-1800: Vernacular*

Architecture; Social Life. Harlow: Pearson Education Limited.

Kent, S. (1990) *Domestic Architecture and the Use of Space: An Interdisciplinary, Cross-Cultural Study.* Cambridge: Cambridge University Press.

Kleinschmidt, H. (2000) *Understanding the middle ages: The Transformation of Ideas and Attitudes in the Medieval World.* Woodbridge: Boydell Press.

Le Patourel, H.E.J. (1991) Rural building in England. In: *The Agrarian History of England and Wales,* vol. 3: 1348-1500, ed. E Miller, 869-881. Cambridge: Cambridge University Press.

Leech, R. (2000) The Symbolic Hall: historical context and merchant culture in the early modern city, *Vernacular Architecture* 31, 1-10.

Lewis, E., E. Roberts, & K. Roberts (1988) *Medieval Hall Houses of the Winchester Area.* Winchester: Winchester Museum.

Longcroft, A. (2002) Plan forms in smaller post-medieval houses: a case study from Norfolk, *Vernacular Architecture* 33, 34-56.

Machin, R. (1977a) The Great Rebuilding: A Reassessment, *Past and Present* 77, 33-56.

Machin, R. (1977b) The Mechanism of the Pre-Industrial Building Cycle, *Vernacular Architecture* 8, 819-824.

Martin, D. (2000) End reversal during the conversion of medieval houses in Sussex, *Vernacular Architecture* 31, 26-31.

Martin, D. (2003) The configuration of inner rooms and chambers in the transitional houses of Eastern Sussex, *Vernacular Architecture* 34, 35-71.

Martin, D. & B. Martin (1997) Detached kitchens in Eastern Sussex, *Vernacular Architecture* 31, 85-91.

Martin, D. & Martin, B. (1999) Adapting houses to changing needs. Multi-phased medieval and transitional houses in Eastern Sussex, *Sussex Archaeological Collections* 137, 121-32.

Martin, D. & B. Martin (2001) Detached kitchens or adjoining houses? – a reponse, *Vernacular Architecture* 32, 2-33.

Mason, R.T. (1964) *Framed Buildings of the Weald.* Handcross: Author.

Mathieu, J. (1999) New methods on old castles: generating new ways of seeing, *Medieval Archaeology* 43, 115-42.

McClain, A. (2012) Theory, disciplinary perspectives and the archaeology of later medieval England, *Medieval Archaeology* 56, 131-169.

Meeson, B. (2000) Detached kitchens or service blocks? *Vernacular Architecture* 31, 73-75.

Meeson, B. (2001) Archaeological Evidence and Analysis: A Case Study from Staffordshire, *Vernacular Architecture* 32, 1-15.

Meeson, B. (2012) Structural insights in English medieval buildings: new insights from dendrochronology, *Vernacular Architecture* 43, 58-75.

Mercer, E. (1975) *English Vernacular Houses.* London: HMSO.

Mercer, E. (1996) Cruck distribution: a social explanation, *Vernacular Architecture* 27, 1-2.

Mercer, E. (1997) The unfulfilled implications of vernacular architecture studies, *Vernacular Architecture* 28, 9-12.

Mercer, E. (1998) Cruck distribution: a brief note, *Vernacular Architecture* 29, 57.

Merleau-Ponty, M. (1962) *The Phenomenology of Perception.* London: Routledge. Transl.C. Smith.

Moir, A., R. Wild, & R. Haddlesey (2012) An Internet-accessible building archaeology research database (BARD), *Vernacular Architecture* 43, 1-6.

Moran, M. (1992) A terrace of crucks at Much Wenlock, Shropshire, *Vernacular Architecture* 23, 10-14.

Moran, M. (2010) A second terrace of crucks in Much Wenlock, Shropshire, *Vernacular Architecture* 41, 45-50.

Moran, M. (2003) *Vernacular Buildings of Shropshire.* Almeley: Logaston Press.

Pantin, W.A. (1962-3) Medieval English town-house plans, *Medieval Archaeology* 6-7, 202-39.

Parsons, D. (1990) *Stone Quarrying and Building in England, AD43-1525.* Chichester, Sussex: Phillimore.

Pattison, I.R., D.S. Pattison & N.W. Alcock (1992) *A Bibliography of Vernacular Architecture, Volume 3: 1977-1989.* Aberystwyth: Vernacular Architecture Group.

Pattison, I.R., D.S. Pattison & N.W. Alcock (1999) *A Bibliography of Vernacular Architecture, Volume 4: 1990-94.* Aberystwyth: Vernacular Architecture Group.

Pearson, S. (1997) Tree-ring dating: a review, *Vernacular Architecture* 28, 25-39.

Pearson, S. (2001) The chronological distribution of tree-ring dates 1980-2001: an update, *Vernacular Architecture* 32, 68-69.

Pearson, S. (2005) Rural and urban houses 1100-1500. In: *Town and Country 1100-1500,* eds C. Dyer & K. Giles, 43-63. The society for medieval archaeology monograph 22. Leeds: Maney Publishing Publishing.

Pearson, S. (2009) Medieval Houses in English Towns: Form and Location, *Vernacular Architecture* 40, 1-22.

Pearson, S. (2012) The provision of services in medieval houses in Kent, *Vernacular Architecture* 43, 28-46.

Phillips, K. (2005) The invisible man: body and ritual in a fifteenth-century noble household, *Journal of Medieval History* 31(2), 143-162.

Quiney, A. (1990) *The Traditional Buildings of England.* London: Thames & Hudson.

Quiney, A. (2003) *Town Houses of Medieval Britain.* New York & London: Yale.

Rapoport, A. (1969) *House Form and Culture.* Englewood Cliffs: Prentice Hall.

Rapoport, A. (1990) *The Meaning of the Built Environment: a Nonverbal Communication Approach.* Tucson: University of Arizona Press.

Rees Jones, S. (2003) Womens' influence on the design of urban homes. In: *Gendering the Master Narrative: Women and Power in the Middle Ages,* eds. M.C. Erler & M. Kowaleski, 190-211. Ithaca, New York: Cornell University Press.

Richardson, A. (2003) Gender and space in English Royal Palaces c1160-c1547: a study in access analysis and imagery, *Medieval Archaeology* 47, 131-165.

Riddy, F. (2008) "Burgeis" domesticity in in late medieval England. In: *Medieval Domesticity: Home, Housing and Household*, eds. M. Kowaleski & P.J.P. Goldberg, 14-36. Cambridge: Cambridge University Press.

Roberts, B.K. & S. Wrathmell (2000) *An Atlas of Rural Settlement in England*. London: English Heritage.

Roberts, E. (1995) Overton Court Farm and the late-medieval farmhouses of demesne lessees in Hampshire, *Proceedings of the Hampshire Field Club Archaeology Society* 51, 89-106.

Roberts, E. (2003) *Hampshire Houses 1250-1700*. Southampton: Hampshire County Council.

RCHM(E) (1968) *An Inventory of the Historical Monuments in the county of Cambridge, Vol 1: West Cambridgeshire*. London: HMSO.

RCHM(E) (1972) *An Inventory of the Historical Monuments in the county of Cambridge, Vol 1: West Cambridgeshire*. London: HMSO.

RCHM(E) (1981) *An inventory of the historical monuments in the city of York. Volume 5: York: The Central Area*. London: HMSO.

RCHM(E) (1985) *Rural Houses of the Lancashire Pennines 1560-1760*. London: HMSO

Turner, T.H. & Parker, J.H. (1851, 1853, 1859) *Some Account of Domestic Architecture in England, 3 vols*. Oxford: J.H. Parker.

RCHM(E) (1986) *Rural Houses of West Yorkshire 1400-1830*. London: HMSO.

RCHM(E) (1994) *The Medieval Houses of Kent. An Historical Analysis*. London: HMSO.

Schofield, J. (1995) *Medieval London Houses*. New Haven, Conn.: Yale University Press

Smith, J.T. (1965) Timber-framed building in England: its development and regional differences, *Archaeological Journal* 122, 133-58.

Smith, J.T. (1970) The evolution of the English peasant house to the late Seventeenth Century: the evidence of buildings, *Journal of the British Archaeological Association* 3rd Series 33, 27-44.

Smith, J.T. (1975) Cruck distributions: an interpretation of some recent maps, *Vernacular Architecture* 6, 3-17.

Smith, J.T. (1992) *English Houses 1200-1800: The Hertfordshire Evidence*. London: HMSO

Smith, J.T. (2001) Detached kitchens or adjoining houses? *Vernacular Architecture* 32, 16-19.

Stenning, D. (1985) Timber-framed shops 1300-1600: comparative plans, *Vernacular Architecture* 16, 35-9.

Thompson, M. (1995) *The Medieval Hall. The Basis of Secular Domestic Life 600-1600AD*. Aldershot: Scolar Press.

Walker, J. (2007) *The Ideology of the Early Medieval Hall in the North Sea Region*. PhD thesis, University of York. T488.

Walker, J. (2011) *The English Medieval Roof: Crownpost to Kingpost*. Chelmsford: Essex Historic Buildings Group.

Wood, M. (1965) *The English Medieval House*. Ferndale: London.

Woolgar, C. (2006) *The Senses in Late Medieval England*. New Haven, London: Yale University Press.

Wrathmell, S. (1989) *Domestic Settlement 2: Medieval Peasant Farmsteads*. York University Archaeological Publications VIII. London: The Soc. for Medieval Archaeology.

Human Spatial Behaviour in Dwellings and Social Psychology

Ole Grøn

Abstract

The focus of the present paper is the spatial organisation of daily life in dwellings related by their occupying households, or to sub-groups of these. Experimental social psychology and ethnoarchaeological data provide a basic syntax for human spatial behaviour in dwellings. The present paper makes use of this in outlining and discussing a framework for the interpretation of the spatial organisation of archaeological dwellings, on the basis of repeated organisational patterns observed in excavated dwellings, drawing further on the analysis of recent ethnographic contexts and existing experimental social-psychological data about humans' non-verbal interaction in space. This paper deliberately engages with a very broad chronological and cultural range of domestic buildings, in order to make the best use of the detailed recording of prehistoric, as well as historic material.

Introduction – the extremes of ordinary human dwellings

Human inhabitations show great structural and ornamental variety, elements of which challenge our ideas about the function of a dwelling. In some cases, rudimentary windbreaks are used under quite harsh climatic conditions, demonstrating that a dwelling does not necessarily provide effective protection from the elements (Figure 1). This point of view is taken to its extreme by Lord Raglan who, in his book 'The Temple and the House', argues that the original purpose of dwelling structures was ritual and religious, equivalent to that of a temple, rather than providing shelter (Raglan 1964: 2): "House-building is still by no means universal. Many tribes of South-East Asia, Australia and South America have no regular dwellings, and the Ona [= Selk'nam], who live in the almost Arctic climate of Tierra del Fuego, though they know how to make conical huts, and make quite elaborate ones for their religious ceremonies, usually content themselves with a windbreak of skins. And this though they have no proper clothing, but only skin cloaks. If people who can build houses can be content to live in such conditions without them, it can hardly be maintained that people who had never heard of houses, and who lived in more equable climates, would necessarily build them".

In reference to a group of Bushmen, Elisabeth Marshall Thomas writes (Marshall Thomas 1959: 196): "Looking around, we saw that only the two families lived here, for there were only two sleeping-places, set, for the sake of privacy, on the opposite sides of one of the scrawny trees. The women had not built huts, but had scooped little hollows for themselves and their husbands which they had lined with soft grass bedding, and had put up two arching sticks at each of these hollows to mark the place where the door would be if a 'scherm' [a hut or shelter] had been there, for the Kung as well as the Gikwe need a sense of place."

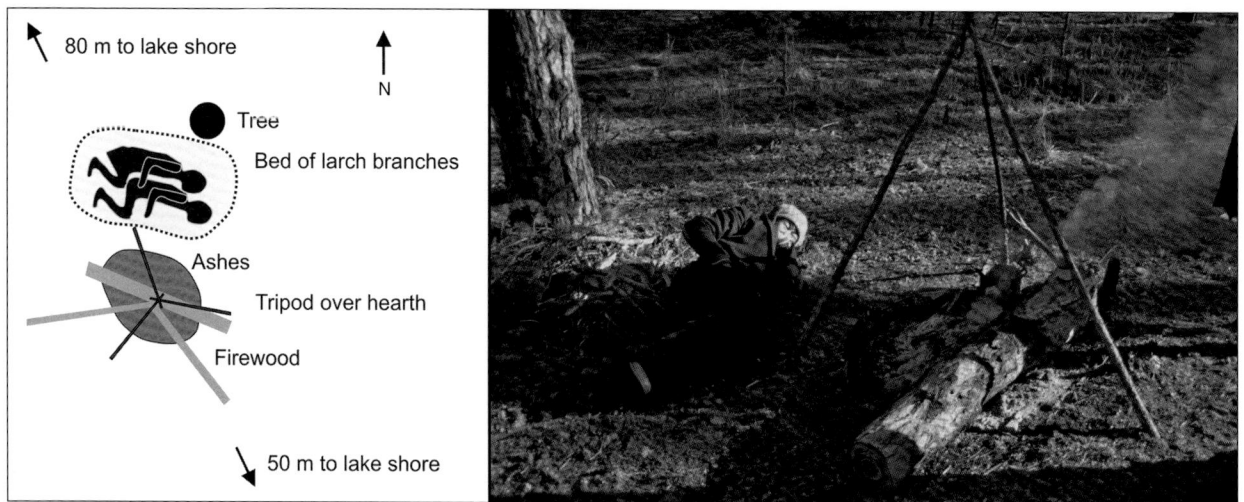

Figure 1. Ludmilla and Valeria Malchikitov's sleeping place for a night at Chikalowski Lake, Chitinskaya Oblast = Chita County, Siberia, 1997. Valeria lay nearest to the hearth, as is the custom of Evenk men, with Ludmilla behind him. In the photo, Valeria demonstrates how he lay sleeping. Ludmilla's part of the bed has already been taken up by a heap of freshly caught fish for our breakfast. Photo Ole Grøn 1997.

Apparently factors other than passive physical screening, *ie* dwelling structures and clothing, can protect humans against the climate. In his Alaskan experimental comparison of Inuit people and American base personnel, Kåre Rodahl demonstrated that an important factor in the Inuit's ability to withstand cold conditions is a 15% increase in their basal metabolism due to their high protein diet (Rodahl 1954).

At the other end of the scale some structures, even those of hunter-gatherer societies, deviate from our general ideas about the dwellings of such societies by being extremely large (both as structures and in terms of the built space per person in the household) and elaborate; for instance the houses of the NW Coast Indians (*eg* Thornton Emmons & de Laguna 1991: 58-72) (Figure 2).

It seems obvious that the role and function of the dwelling is highly variable in human societies and that the more important aspects of socio-cultural activity are not necessarily associated with its physical features. Rapoport, in his extensive investigation of dwellings, makes a couple of important observations about dwellings that appear to have a general validity: ".... that shelter is only one function of architecture and that other, and more important, functions are the symbolic, place-defining and socio-cultural – to any environment in which people live,

whether built or not built" (Rapoport 1975). In a discussion of cross-cultural comparison of dwellings he states that "... many activities which take place within what we call a dwelling may occur in a widely dispersed system of settings in another culture which also, apparently, has dwellings. The units to be compared, therefore, are not the (...) dwellings but the system of settings within which a particular system of activities takes place." (Rapoport 1997).

Human dwellings as socio-cultural spatial units

A general aspect of prehistoric dwellings of interest from an archaeological point of view is that they seem to be organised spatially in accordance with a culturally-specific code that reflects the social organisation of the household (Deetz 1968; Grøn 1991; 1995; 2003).

Gustav Ränk was probably the first social anthropologist to deal with the symbolic and social organisation of human dwelling spaces on a general basis. In his study of the spatial organisation of the dwellings of the North Eurasian peoples he reaches the general conclusion that: "In an emblematic sense the organization of space thus in small scale depicts the structure of the total society of the people concerned. It reflects a concentrate of all observable relations between the different generations, age groups, classes of the community, kin, and the division of labour between these. Since this system of order so to say has grown in an organic way from an economic-social basis as well as from numerous religious conceptions, this means that it must be perceived as a function of economic-social and spiritual life." (Ränk 1951: 141, author's translation).

Gordon Childe was arguably the first archaeologist to use ethnological/ethnographical information in order to understand the organisation of dwelling space in the interpretation of prehistoric dwelling spaces. In his book on the Neolithic Skara Brae settlement, he makes a detailed comparison between the repeated interior organisation of the Skara Brae dwellings and the general lay-out of the traditional Scottish black houses of historic and early modern times: "The vitality of the adaptation to the inclement climate of North Scotland that we have described is demonstrated by survivals of elements of the Skara Brae culture, especially architectural, in the Highlands and Islands till last century. The so-called black houses in which peasantry normally dwelt less than a hundred years ago were in many ways extraordinarily like our Skara Brae huts." (Childe 1931: 182).

Mellaart's excavation of the Neolithic 'town' of Catal Hüyük in Anatolia also revealed a very strict and uniform organisation of the dwellings, and of the activities within the rooms (Mellaart 1967: 54-63). Since excavations of well-preserved dwellings dating from subsequent periods have revealed similarities in organisational patterns in all cultures all over the globe and from the Old Stone Age to the medieval period (eg Agorsah 1984; Bawden 1993; Grøn 2003; Haarnagel 1979; Hill 1968; Hurst 1972; Jameson 1993; Kapches 1990; Myhre 1975), there seems to be strong

Figure 2. A traditional Haida house, the 'monster' house of Chief Wi:ha:, Haida Gwai. Photo Edward Dossetter, 1881. This house is actually an enormous sunken-floored building (pit-house) (Blackman 1972).

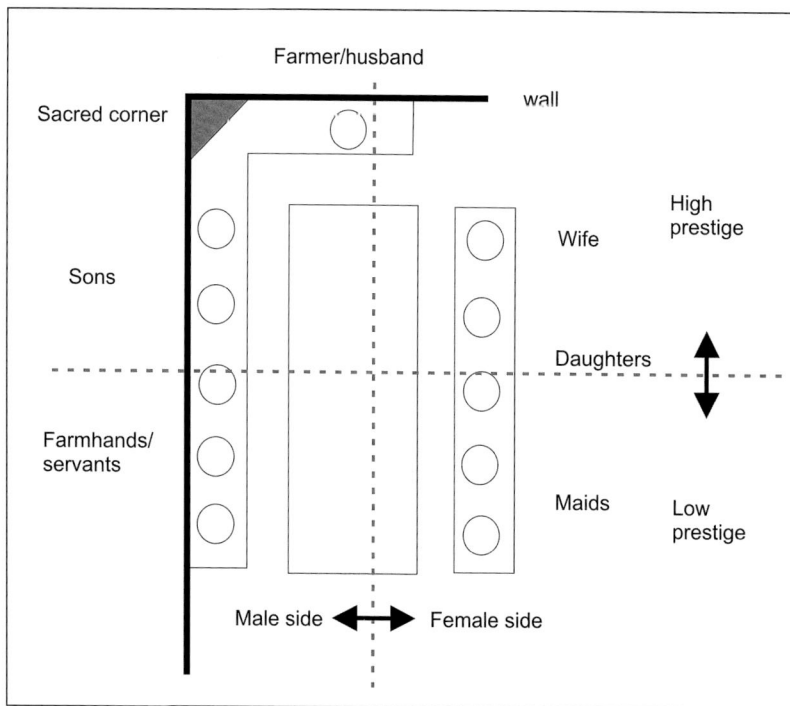

Figure 3. Typical organisation of the sacred corner in a farmhouse.

archaeological evidence for the social organisation of human cultures being reflected in their micro-scale use of dwelling space.

According to the information we can obtain from recent cultures, the strictest organisation of the dwelling space seems to be in the zone where the household eats (Figure 3). In larger dwellings, the organisation of the space outside the 'eating zone' can be quite variable. In Eurasian and European farmhouses people ate within a narrow zone running up to the 'sacred corner'. Within this zone, the household would be arranged in strict order around the table: the farmer/husband at the 'upper' end, the sons and farmhands/servants in order along the side of the table by the wall and likewise the wife, daughters and maids arranged along a bench on the outer side of the table. Consequently, there was a male and a female side and an 'upper' and 'lower' end in this spatial pattern. Sacred objects, or the vodka/snaps bottle, were kept in the sacred corner within reach of the farmer/husband (Rapoport 1969: 54; Ränk 1949).

In smaller dwellings, in which the eating zone more or less conjoins with the dwelling area, all of this is usually strictly spatially organised (Figure 4).

An interesting problem, in relation to repeated organisational patterns in prehistoric dwellings, is how we should understand the relationship between archaeological cultural units defined on the basis of variation in artefact types and style, on the one hand, and on the basis of cultural-behavioural patterns as reflected in the spatial organisation of the dwelling, on the other.

In the case of the Mesolithic, it looks as if the territories outlined by similarity in the spatial organisation of the dwellings can be significantly larger than the Mesolithic 'cultures' established on the basis of typological and stylistic differences (Grøn 2003). Similarly, in the Scandinavian Iron Age, the established typological/stylistic zones tend to be significantly smaller than those reflected by similarity in dwelling design (Neumann 1982: 49-51, 85; Jensen 2003: 115-142; 2004: 29-49).

When studying such aspects in recent cultures we are faced with the problem that the 'ethnic groups', as defined in social anthropology, do not in many cases solely reflect ethnic aspects but also practical categorisations as defined by modern administrators, etc. As the formation and dissolution of 'ethnic'

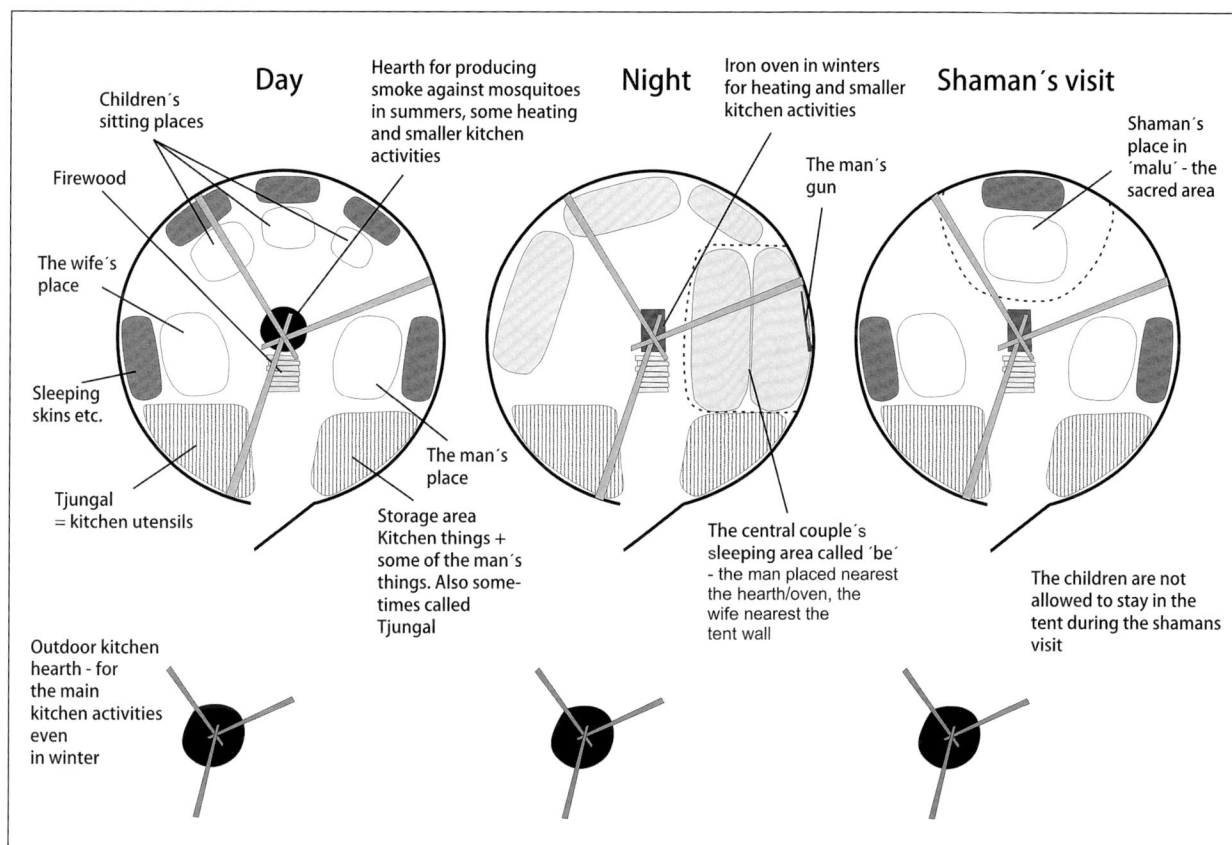

Figure 4. The Evenk spatial code for the use of tent space.

groupings must, furthermore, be seen as a dynamic historical process (Barth 1978; 1987; Shirokogoroff 1935: 12-39), and as our information concerning the impact of different 'ethnic groupings' on each other's spatial dwelling organisation is unfortunately rudimentary (Grøn 2006; Levin & Potapov 1961: 198-223), it is presently difficult to achieve a precise and detailed understanding of the relationship between ethnic borders and borders between different patterns of dwelling organisation in both recent and prehistoric societies.

However, material, linguistic, spiritual and ritual cultures normally show significant small-scale variation at clan level, within what is considered as a single cultural/ethnic grouping (Barth 1978; 1987; Best 2003: 158-171; Donner 1915: 75; Grøn et al 2009; Shirokogoroff 1935: 12-39; Wiessner 1983; 1984). According to my own observations, the spatial organisation of the dwelling – especially the

tents – of the Siberian Evenk displays surprising uniformity over an enormous area. According to the Evenk, this strict and uniform spatial code is necessary to avoid situations in which 'one makes a fool of one-self when visiting other Evenk'. The fact that they speak a dialect which other Evenk may not be able to understand, and that their culture varies in other aspects, is not important. But if a person takes up a position in the dwelling which is incorrect in relation to his or her status, sex etc., this is extremely embarrassing. The spatial behaviour within and organisation of the dwelling space seems, therefore, to be of crucial importance in the Evenk culture. Seen from this perspective, the stylistic variation apparent in the diagnostic artefacts of the European Mesolithic might well identify sub-groups of more extensive cultural groupings with a single spatial dwelling code, rather than a larger number of individual 'cultures'.

Spatial behaviour, non-verbal communication and experimental social psychology

It is interesting that spatial codes can play such an important role in social and cultural life. Is this likely to be a general tendency in human culture? There are some indications that the latter may be the case. Non-verbal communication, including spatial behaviour, has been demonstrated by social psychology to be a much more uniform and universal 'language' than verbal communication, which can display significant small-scale variation (*eg* Argyle 2007: 1-10; Grøn et al 2009; Hall 1966: 1-6; Mehrabian 2010: 1-15).

According to experimental social psychology, human spatial behaviour is regulated by a series of syntax elements. These constitute the relative distance between individuals, their orientation and attitude relative to each other, their orientation in relation to and their relative distance from elements in the dwelling space, for instance entrances and central focal points such as hearths.

In the 1950s, Hall – as a basic element in his 'proxemics' – discovered that the preferred distance between two people when interacting is proportional to their 'social' distance and that a number of 'distance-zones' mark different levels of intimacy: intimate distance (1.5-4feet), social-consultative distance (4-10feet) and public distance (more than 10feet) (Hall 1966: 112-122).

In the 1960s, Sommer demonstrated that the orientation of two people relative to each other also reflects their relation to one another (Figure 5). It was shown experimentally that two people seated at a round table preferred to sit beside each other when conversing and collaborating, whereas in co-acting (studying for different exams) and competition they chose to sit opposite each other. Similar tendencies were found at rectangular tables (Gifford 1982; Kaplan et al 1983; Sommer 1965).

Sight is central to spatial communication and the degree of eye contact between individuals is an important element in their social communication, for instance in the communication of status relations, degree of sympathy etc. (Argyle & Dean 1965; Chance & Jolly 1970: 171-175; Dovido & Ellyson 1982;

PERCENTAGE OF Ss CHOOSING THIS ARRANGEMENT

Seating arrangement	Condition 1 (conversing)	Condition 2 (cooperating)	Condition 3 (co-acting)	Condition 4 (competing)
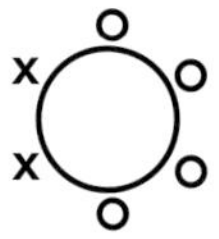	63	83	13	12
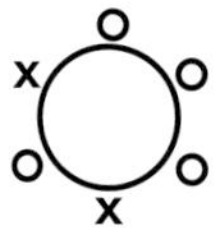	17	7	36	25
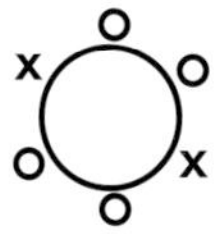	20	10	51	63
Total	100	100	100	100

Figure 5. Robert Sommer's analysis of round-table situations involving two people. The preferred positions vary with task type. After Sommer 1965: 345, Figure 2.

Exline 1971; Goldberg et al 1969; Mehrabian 1969; Nachshon & Wapner 1967; Strongman & Champness 1968). As a result, the members of smaller groups involved in internal communication will normally arrange themselves in something approaching a regular circle or oval (in a rectangle when seated around a rectangular table) facing a common centre, thereby facilitating visual communication within the group (Alexander et al 1977: 858f; Patterson et al 1979; Steinzor 1950).

The degree of visual dominance is found to be proportional to the ratio between looking while speaking (maintaining direct eye contact) and looking while listening. Consequently, extreme dominance will be practised by looking while speaking and not looking while listening (Dovido & Ellyson 1982).

In the early 1960s, Sommer observed that leaders tend to choose positions at the ends of long rectangular tables (Sommer 1961). However, in circular groups, dominant people tended to mark their position by maintaining a greater distance to their neighbours than that seen between 'ordinary' members of the group. An important factor is probably that dominant individuals seek to make themselves more visible and thereby place themselves in a more visually-dominant position (Giesen & McLaren 1976;

Silverstein & Stang 1976; Steinzor 1950). Hare and Bales also observed in their experiments that the most dominant individuals preferred to sit at the end of the oblong rectangular table from where they could face the door (Hare & Bales 1963). Just as leader types seek out 'leader positions' to dominate visually, individuals who are placed in a dominant position will, by virtue of its visual dominance, assume a more dominant role (Howells & Becker 1962).

The study of task-oriented discussion in small circular groups shows that these produce communication lines between individuals situated more or less directly facing each other. Individuals sitting beside each other in the circle (a more difficult position for maintaining direct eye-contact) will communicate less during task-oriented discussion. In contrast, communication of a social nature mainly produces communication lines between neighbours or, in other words, between positions not ideal for visual communication (Hare & Bales 1963; Steinzor 1950). This corresponds to Sommer's results concerning the placing of two people around, for example, rectangular tables where 'side by side', 'around a corner', 'front to front at opposite sides', and 'more distant' situations reflect decreasing intimacy (Brewer 1968; Hall 1966: 112-122; King 1966; Little 1965; Sommer 1968). Furthermore, where sympathy and close social relations are signalled physically through closeness between individuals, closeness is found to produce and support sympathy between people – especially between individuals of the opposite sex (Kahn & McGaughey 1977).

In conclusion, it can be said that individuals in small groups tend to organise themselves spatially in circular arrangements so that they face a common centre, and so that the various individuals are located near to those with whom they share 'close' relations, but at a greater distance from those with whom they have more 'distant' relations. In task-oriented discussions an individual will often find him or herself 'confronted' with individuals with whom they share more distant relations, whereas social communication will mainly take place between neighbours, involving people with relatively close relations (Cook 1970: 70-72; Lott & Sommer 1967; Rosenfeld 1965). These spatial structures relating to

placing and communication must be seen as 'conservative' factors maintaining and strengthening the existing structure of a group.

Different distance intervals for the various interpersonal distances exist within different cultures. This means that the boundaries between the different degrees of intimacy or closeness are found at different distances, but in the same relative order as observed by Hall (Brewer 1968; Hall 1966: 112-122; Sommer 1968). This suggests that this principle is universal for human beings, a point of view supported by the fact that the ethnographic literature – as already mentioned – provides numerous examples of spatial behaviour within dwellings conforming to the principles experimentally observed in social psychology.

Where several couples occupy the same dwelling comprising a single room, in a circular arrangement it is nearly always seen such that the succession around the circle is wife 1, man 1, man 2, wife 2, wife 3, ... and so on – where these numbers identify the different couples (eg Jenness 1970: 65-76; Ränk 1951: 32-34, 87-90; Tanner 1979: 84-86). In terms of social psychology this apparently prevents individuals of the opposite sex from different couples developing too much intimacy due to their spatial proximity (Kahn & McGaughey 1977).

Besides maintaining the lines of communication between the members of households, and their mutual social relations, the fixed spatial organisation of the dwelling space seems to serve another purpose. Each individual – according to his or her role – has a restricted and sharply defined 'personal area'. This apparently makes it possible for them to 'identify' mentally with this area and thus to segregate themselves from what is going on outside it. One important element in this isolation behaviour is to avoid eye contact with the other occupants (Argyle & Dean 1965; Binford 1983: 163f; Briggs 1970: 77f; Hall 1966: 39-47; Sommer 1965: 347). The fact that purely symbolic divisions of the space within the dwellings of 'primitive' cultures are, in numerous cases, used in place of a physical screen (e .g. Ränk 1949: 24-68; 1951: 31-57) must be seen in the light of this ability to restrict attention to a limited part of the immediately available space (Cook 1970: 69).

In households, members of subgroups who, in certain situations, might wish to 'isolate' themselves from the others (*eg* families, women etc) should be expected to hold positions close to each other so that they could isolate themselves without interruption by individuals taking up positions in their lines of communication. The groups studied in experimental social psychology did not, in most cases, have sufficient time to stabilise their social and spatial relations. Therefore, the tendencies that can be identified from these experiments can be expected to display themselves more clearly in the spatial structure of the households examined in ethnographic studies, since the latter have had a much longer time to develop a stabile spatial relation between individuals with different social/cultural roles in their actual societies.

Discussion

The focus of the present paper is the spatial organisation of daily life in dwellings related to their occupying households or to sub-groups of these. The purpose is to establish that human spatial behaviour within such a framework is controlled by a restricted number of social psychological factors which, together with other important cultural factors, are integrated as central elements into the basic cultural syntax. It seems likely that an improved understanding of this spatial-cultural 'grammar' can facilitate an improved understanding of the cultural and individual identity relations reflected in the archaeological material of the larger and more complex habitations from the Viking Age to the Renaissance.

It is important to be aware that experimental social psychology and social anthropology, in conjunction, provide a solid platform for the understanding of the organisation and function of archaeological dwelling spaces. Even though Lord Raglan seems to overstress the importance of ritual and religion as the original reason for the development of human dwellings, factors other than the immediately practical and functional ones obviously seem to control the spatial syntax of the human behaviour in dwellings. The location of the household's members within the eating zone seems to be an expression of central cultural values of the utmost importance for archaeological interpretation of the social organisation at household level.

A central question arising from the discussion of the spatial behaviour in the dwellings of prehistoric cultures is whether their spatial syntax forms a better basis for cultural categorisation and classification than that provided by object shapes and ornament patterns which has so far formed the spine of archaeological classification. On the face of it, one should think that the former, as a more direct reflection of the basic cultural values in play, should be preferred, even though reliable information about the spatial behaviour in archaeological dwellings is more difficult to obtain.

The maintenance and visibility of cultural spatial patterns in the material evidence depends on the degree of non-distinguishable overlap between different settlement phases, re-deposition during and after the occupation, animal activity, etc (Grøn & Kuznetsov 2003). However, the increasing awareness of spatial patterning, underpinned by improved excavation techniques and tools for recording and analysis, today supports archaeology's ability to deal with complex dwelling space issues (*eg* Bamforth et al 2005; Keeler 2007; Sergeant et al 2006).

References

Agorsah, K. (1984) Patterns of Spatial Behavior among the Nchumuru, *NYAME AKUMA* No. 23, 6-10.

Alexander, C., S. Ishikawa & M. Silverstein (1977) *A Pattern Language. Towns, Buildings, Constructions*. Oxford: Oxford University Press.

Argyle, M. (2007) *Bodily Communication*. London: Routledge.

Argyle, M. & J. Dean (1965) Eye-contact, distance and affiliation, *Sociometry* 28(1), 289-304.

Bamforth, D.B., M. Becker & J. Hudson (2005) Intrasite Spatial Analysis, Ethnoarchaeology, and Paleoindian Land-Use on the Great Plains: The Allen Site, *American Antiquity* 70(3), 561-580.

Barth, F. (1978) Conclusions. In: *Scale and Social Organization*, ed. F. Barth, 253-285. Oslo: Universitetsforlaget.

Barth, F. (1987) *Cosmologies in the making. A generative approach to cultural variation in inner New Guinea*. Cambridge: Cambridge University Press.

Bawden, G. (1993) Domestic space and social structure in pre-Colombian northern Peru. In: *Domestic Architecture and the Use of Space. An interdisciplinary cross-cultural study*, ed. S. Kent, 92-113.Cambridge: Cambridge University Press.

Best, A. (2003) *Regional Variation in the Material Culture of Hunter-Gatherers. Social and Ecological Approaches to Ethnograpnic Objects from Queensland, Australia*. BAR International Series S1149. Oxford: Archaeopress.

Binford, L.R. (1983) *In pursuit of the past: Decoding the archaeological record*. London: Thames and Hudson.

Blackman, M.B. (1972) Nei:wɔns, the 'monster' house of Chief Wi:ha: an exercise in ethnohistorical, archaeological, and ethnological reasoning, *SYESIS* 5, 212-225.

Brewer, M.B. (1968) Determinants of social distance among East African tribal groups, *Journal of Personality and Social Psychology* 10(3), 279-289.

Briggs, J.L. (1970) *Never in anger. Portrait of an Eskimo Family*. Cambridge Mass: Aldine Publishing Company.

Chance, M.R.A. & C.J. Jolly (1970) *Social Groups of Monkeys, Apes and Men*. London: Jonathan Cape.

Childe, V.G. (1931) *Skara Brae. A Pictish Village in Orkney*. London: Kegan Paul, Trench, Trubner & Co., ltd.

Cook, M. (1970) Experiments on orientation and proxemics, *Human Relations* 23(1), 61-76.

Deetz, J. (1968) Cultural Patterning of Behavior as Reflected by Archaeological Materials. In: *Settlement Archaeology*, ed. K.C. Chang, 31-42. Palo Alto, California: National Press Books.

Donner. K. (1915) *Bland Samojeder i Sibirien åren 1911-1913, 1914*. Helsingfors: Söderstrom and Co.

Dovido, J. F.& S.L. Ellyson (1982) Decoding visual dominance: attributes of power based on relative percentages of looking while speaking and looking while listening, *Social Psychology Quarterly* 45(2), 106-113.

Exline, R.V. (1971) Visual interaction: The glances of power and preference. In: *Nebraska Symposium on Motivation*, ed. J.K. Cole, 163-206. Lincoln: University of Nebraska Press.

Giesen, M. & H.A. McLaren (1976) Discussion, distance and sex: changes in impressions and attraction during small group interaction, *Sociometry* 39(1), 60-70.

Gifford, R. (1982) Projected interpersonal distance and orientation choices: Personality, sex, and social situation, *Social psychology Quarterly* 45(3), 145-152.

Goldberg, G. N., C.A. Kiesler & B.E. Collins (1969) Visual behaviour and face-to-face distance during interaction, *Sociometry* 32(1), 43-53.

Grøn, O. (1991) A method for reconstruction of social organization in prehistoric societies and examples of practical application. In: *Social Space. Proceedings of an Interdisciplinary conference on human spatial behaviour in dwellings and settlements*, eds. O. Grøn, E. Engelstad & I. Lindblom, 100-117. Odense: Odense University Press.

Grøn, O. (1995) *The Maglemose Culture. The reconstruction of the social organization of a Mesolithic culture in Northern Europe*. BAR International Series 616. Oxford: Archaeopress.

Grøn, O. (2003) Mesolithic dwelling places in south Scandinavia: their definitions and social interpretation, *Antiquity* 77, 298, Dec 2003, 685-708.

Grøn, O. (2006) Comments on David G. Anderson: Dwellings, Storage and Summer Site Structure among Siberian Orochen Evenkis: Hunter-Gatherer Vernacular Architecture under Post-Socialist Conditions. Norwegian Archaeological Review 39, 1-26, *Norwegian Archaeological Review* 39(2), 165-168.

Grøn, O., T. Klokkernes & M.G. Turov (2009) Cultural small-scale variations in a hunter-gatherer society: or 'everybody wants to be a little bit different!' An ethnoarchaeological study from Siberia. In: *Mesolithic Horizons. Papers presented at the Seventh International Conference on the Mesolithic in Europe, Belfast 2005*, eds. S. McCartan, R. Schulting, G. Warre & P. Woodman, 203-209. Oxford: Oxbow Books.

Grøn, O. & O. Kuznetsov (2003) Ethno-archaeology among Evenkian forest hunters. Preliminary results and a different approach to reality! *Mesolithic on the Move. Papers presented at the Sixth International Conference on the Mesolithic in Europe, Stockholm 2000*, eds. L. Larsson, H. Kindgren, K. Knutson, D. Loeffler & A. Åkerlund, 216-221. Oxford: Oxbow Books.

Haarnagel, W. (1979) *Die Grabung Feddersen Wierde. Methode, Hausbau, Siedlungs- und Wirtschaftsformen sowie Sozialstruktur*. Wiesbaden: Franz Steiner Verlag.

Hall, E.T. (1966) *The Hidden Dimension*. New York: Doubleday & Company, Inc.

Hare, A.P. & R.E. Bales (1963). Seating position and small group interaction, *Sociometry* 26(1), 480-486.

Hill, J.H. (1968) Broken K Pueblo: Paterns of Form and Function. In: *New Perspectives in Archaeology*, eds. S.R. & L.R. Binford, 103-142. New York: Aldine Publishing Company

Howells, L.T. & S.W. Becker (1962). Seating arrangement and leadership emergence, *Journal of Abnormal and Social Psychology* 64(2), 148-150.

Hurst, J.G. (1972) The changing medieval village in England. In: *Man, Settlement and urbanism*, eds. P. Ucko, R. Tringham & G.W. Dimbleby, 531-540. London: Duckworth,

Jameson, M.H. (1993) Domestic space in the Greek city-state. In: *Domestic Architecture and the Use of Space. An interdisciplinary cross-cultural study*, ed. S. Kent, 92-113. Cambridge: Cambridge University Press.

Jenness, D. (1970) *The Life of the Copper Eskimos*. Part A of vol. XII. New York: Johnson Reprint Corp.

Jensen, J. (2003) *Danmarks Oldtid. Ældre Jernalder 500 f.Kr.-400 e.Kr.* Copenhagen: Gyldendal.

Jensen, J. (2004) *Danmarks Oldtid. Yngre Jernalder og Vikingetid 400 e.Kr.-1050 e.Kr.* Copenhagen: Gyldendal.

Kahn, A. & T.A. McGaughey (1977) Distance and liking: When moving close produces increased liking, *Sociometry* 40(2), 138-144.

Kapches, M. (1990) The Spatial Dynamics of Ontario Iroquoian Longhouses, *American Antiquity* 55(1), 49-67.

Kaplan, K.J., I.J. Firestone, K.W. Klein & C. Sodikoff (1983) Distance in dyads: A comparison of four models, *Social psychology Quarterly* 46(2), 108-115.

Keeler, D. (2007) Intrasite Spatial Analysis of a Late Upper Paleolithic French Site Using Geographic Information Systems, *Journal of World Anthropology*, Occasional Papers, volume III, number 1, 1-40. http://wings.buffalo.edu/research/anthrogis/JWA/V3N1/

King, M.G. (1966) Interpersonal relations in preschool children and average approach distance, *The Journal of Genetic Psychology* 109, 109-116

Levin, M.G. & L.P. Potapov (1961) *Istoriko-Etnografitcheskii Altas Sibiri*, Historical-Ethnographical Atlas of Siberia. Moscow: Isdatelstvo Akademii Nauk SSSR.

Little, K.B. (1965) Personal space, *Journal of Experimental Social Psychology* 1, 237-247.

Lott, D.E. & R. Sommer (1967) Seating arrangement and status, *Journal of Personality and Social Psychology* 7(1), 90-95.

Mehrabian, A. (1969) Significance of posture and position in the communication of attitude and status relationships, *Psychological Bulletin* 71(5), 26-30.

Mehrabian, A. (2010) *Nonverbal Communication*. London: Aldine Transactions.

Mellaart, J. (1967) *Catal Hüyük. A Neolithic Town in Anatolia*. London: Thames and Hudson.

Myhre, B. (1975) Gårdshusenes konstruksjon og funksjon, *Arkeologiske skrifter fra Historisk Museum, Universitetet i Bergen* 2, 73-105.

Nachshon, I. & S. Wapner (1967) Effect of eye contact and physiognomy on perceived location of other person, *Journal of Personality and Social Psychology* 7(1), 82-89.

Neumann, H. (1982) *Olgerdiget – et bidrag til Danmarks tidligste historie*. Haderslev: Haderslev Museum.

Patterson, M. L., C.E. Kelley, B.A. Kondracki & L.J. Wulf (1979) Effects of seating arrangement on small-group behaviour, *Social Psychology Quarterly* 42, 180-185.

Raglan, Lord (1964) *The Temple and the House*. London: Routledge and Kegan Paul.

Rapoport, A. (1969) *House Form and Culture*. Englewood Cliffs, N.J.: Prentice-Hall inc.

Rapoport, A. (1975) Australian aborigines and the definition of place. In: *Shelter, Sign & Symbol*, ed. P. Oliver, 38-51. London: Barrie & Jenkins.

Rapoport, A. (1997) Systems of activities and systems of settings. In: *Domestic architecture and the use of space. An interdisciplinary cross-cultural study*, ed. S. Kent, 9-20. Cambridge: Cambridge University Press.

Rodahl, K. (1954) *Eskimo Metabolism. A Study of Racial Factors in Basal Metabolism*. Oslo: Brøggers Boktrykkeris Forlag.

Ränk, G. (1949-51) (vol. I. 1949, vol. II: 1951) *Das System der Raumeinteilung in den Behausungen der Nordeuroasischen Völker*. Tierp: Hugo Löjdquist Bocktryckeri.

Rosenfeld, H.M. (1965) Effect of an approval-seeking induction on interpersonal proximity, *Psychological Reports* 17, 120-122.

Sergant, J., P. Crombe & Y. Perdaen (2006) The 'invisible' hearths: a contribution to the discernment of Mesolithic non-structured surface hearths, *Journal of Archaeological Science* 33, 999-1007.

Shirokogoroff, S.M. (1935) *Psychomental Complex of the Tungus*. London: Kegan Paul, Trench, Trubner & Co., ltd.

Silverstein, C.H. & D.J. Stang (1976) Seating position and interaction in triads: A field study, *Sociometry* 39(2), 166-171.

Sommer, R. (1961) Leadership and Group Geography, *Sociometry* 24(1), 99-110.

Sommer, R. (1965) Further studies of small group ecology, *Sociometry* 28(1), 337-348.

Sommer, R. (1968) Intimacy ratings in five countries, *International Journal of Psychology* 3(2), 109-114.

Steinzor, B. (1950) The spatial factor in face to face discussion groups, *Journal of Abnormal and Social Psychology* 45, 552-555.

Strongman, K.T. & B.G. Champness (1968) Dominance hierachies and conflict in eye contact, *Acta Psychologica* XXVIII, 376-386.

Tanner, A. (1979) *Bringing home animals. Religious ideology and mode of production of the Mistassini Cree hunters*. London: C. Hurst & Company.

Thomas, E. (1959) *The Harmless People*. London: Secker & Warburg.

Thornton Emmons, G. & F. de Laguna, (1991) *The Tlingit Indians*. New York: American Museum of Natural History.

Wiessner, P. (1983) Style and social information in Kalahari San projectile points, *American Antiquity* 48(2), 253-76.

Wiessner, P. (1984) Reconsidering the Behavioral Basis for Style: A Case Study among the Kalahari San, *Journal of Anthropological Archaeology* 3, 190-234.

The Investigation of Domesticated Space in Archaeology – Architecture and Human Beings

Thomas Kühtreiber

Abstract

Houses do not only reflect social structures, in many cultural context the idea of 'house' and 'households' is used as a metaphor in philosophical and religious discourse. Thus we may assume that the material relicts of houses offer traces through which it is possible to decode and interpret features as materialisations of social space. The paper delineates recent theoretical and methodological approaches which seek to explore the integration of human actors into debates about houses as crucial elements through which cultural identities were constructed in the past.

Introduction

What does it mean "to make oneself at home in the world" from the human perspective (Ingold 2000: 172)? As Tim Ingold points out, there are strong similarities between human or animal inhabitations, because both act based on their biological and social needs and the environmental resources available to them (Ingold 2000: 173f). Antique and post-antique texts emphasize another approach, however, associated with structuring of the environment through design and the idea of 'order'. Quoting Xenophon "There is nothing, which is so useful and beautiful to mankind like order". Only when all things are on their proper place, a household can be kept in divine sense (Xenophon 1828: 1090). Therefore it can be suggested that the arrangement of things reflects social systems. A concept familiar in both antiquity and the Middle Ages is the term 'household'. The household as a model of 'god-given' social order may refer to the family unit (in culturally differing structures) as well as to the whole community (see further Lemmer 1991; Meyer 1998; Richarz 1991). In this context one has to keep in mind that the concept of household is not always identical with that of the house. Whereas in many societies the household is the smallest social unit of a community, houses are physical units, which may be congruent with household but may also be part of more complex household systems. Nevertheless, the metaphorical use of the term 'house' is deeply related to concepts of dynasty and descent. Thus conceptions of houses reflect models of communities and beyond this, 'world views' reflecting transcendence (see Derks 1996; critical: Opitz 1994; Weiß 2001). Houses can therefore be analyzed both as social categories and as physical structures.

From a sociological point of view, space can be seen as a system of social goods or of people, which/who concurrently define a social order (Löw 2001: 234). Space becomes constituted by iterative interaction between social activities and social structures; it is result and pre-condition of individual and social behavior (Löw, Steets & Stoetzer 2008: 63, see also for this and the following C. Schmid in this volume). Therefore, space is not only the setting for activities, but also the product of them. People arrange objects as well as themselves, and thereby influence spatial organization; thus human actors are the crucial factors in the social constitution of space. However, artifacts are not merely as passive objects. They affect the qualities of space by means of the senses and perception (*ie* smells, sounds). Space can therefore only be fully analyzed by looking at the relationships between all of these constitutive elements (Löw, Steets & Stoetzer 2008: 65).

This approach can be applied particularly to architecture in the sense of the 'built environment' (for the term see Rapoport 1990: 13): Buildings constitute and represent social realities through their spatial organization (see also Hillier & Hanson 1987: 198). Therefore they bear social and cultural information in their design and structure. Both elements of spatial organization are used as social media to exercise control over activities inside of the building (Allison 2002: 1).

Bearing these points in mind the paper will focus on three methodological aspects: place and space in built environments, detecting individuals and collective as actors within housing culture and networks and boundaries as metaphors for social as well as for architectural studies.

Place and space in built environments

The theoretical framing of building history and building archaeology within cultural studies coincides with recent theoretical developments in the field of landscape archaeology. In both cases mankind is studied as a knowledgeable being acting within a particular historical perspective. The main question which has arisen in both these contexts in the last two decades is how identity is constructed spatially. I would suggest that the answer to this is embedded within the idea of 'colonization'. Colonization is the concept of the transforming process from natural to cultural environment (see for example the pioneering work of the Center for Environmental History, University of Klagenfurt in cooperation with Rolf-Peter Sieferle 1997). Of course, humans are not only biological and social organisms but as Tim Ingold (2000: 172) notes, they are 'divided' between the biological and cultural sphere, and are therefore active mediators between these two milieus.

By acting intentionally in the natural environment, human beings transform ecofacts into artifacts, and these artifacts integrate 'ecological' qualities or information, such as material, and cultural information, such as design. Moreover, humans build the 'bridge' between these two spheres not only by transforming the shapes and substance of the physical world, but also by giving all these phenomena specific cultural meanings. It can be argued that it is less important to understand whether a concept of things precedes the production of the material objects or vice versa. What is important is that the mental act of giving meaning to specific objects within the perceived world is a means of acculturation. Following Ingold (2002: 173), inhabiting the world can be understood as the main human practice of acculturation. In terms of spatial analysis these inhabited spheres can be correlated with physical space on the one hand and the cognitive space on the other, filtered by human perception and imagination (Hartmann 1980, see also: Doneus & Kühtreiber 2013). From this perspective, landscape is understood as both physical and cognitive space. Physical space is the basic framework, transformed by intentional and by unconscious acts of individuals and collectives.

Places play a central role in this model of humans as spatial actors; they are the nodal points, around which a network of human communicative interaction with the environment occurs. Individual as well as collective experiences are memorized spatially and therefore play a crucial role in the development and stability of both individual and collective identities, as *lieux de memoire* (Csaky 2004; Löw 2001). It is interesting that places are often only perceived when they appear on the 'radar screen' of subjective attitudes or needs. They become spatially-bound resources, loaded with meaning by individual or social expectations. Such places do not simply exist on the large scale, they also become freighted with meaning in small-scale settlements and buildings. Once again, memory plays an important role in this process. Story-telling and shared 'acting out' of collective memories is one way in which we know this occurs ethnologically. The problem for archaeologists is that we do not always know these tales and stories. We are cultural outsiders and have to try and decode or decipher these multiple meanings from the traces they leave behind. It is therefore often easier to understand the collective, rather than the individual meanings of culture, drawing on Klaus P. Hansen's (2009: 17-19) understanding of culture as a process and product of the standardization of individual attitudes and acting habits. Since culture requires a communicative agreement of the collective society or community, then individual attitudes and habits can be understood as part of a larger cultural canon. We therefore need to explore whether we can detect the relationship between the cultural life of the individual and the collective in the archaeological record.

The Individual and the Collective

In this paper there is not enough space to reconsider the last 20 years' discussion of the implementation of sociological approaches in theoretical archaeology. However, one of the main areas of discussion within this field has been the issue of how to represent the individual actor's perspective and agency in the interpretation of archaeological evidence. Of course, as Schmid discusses in this volume, not all human activities produced archaeological records and there are multiple filters in the transformation of past social activity into archaeological contexts. One way of approaching this is to acknowledge that physical traces of human behaviour are relicts of former meaningful action or agency, because every human being acts in a culturally- and temporally-specific environment and social position, and operates with a certain level of technological knowledge and competences. These create possibilities as well as limitations for intentional and unconscious forms of behavior, but nevertheless, make each social action meaningful and, because they are influenced by the individual's enculturation, also rational and logical. This approach, known as the 'structural-individualistic approach', and pioneered by Siegwart Lindenberg (1985), sees humans as Resourceful, Restricted, Expecting, Evaluating, Maximizing Man (RREEMM-Model). The relationship between individuals and collectives can be theorized using the macro-micro-macro-Model of

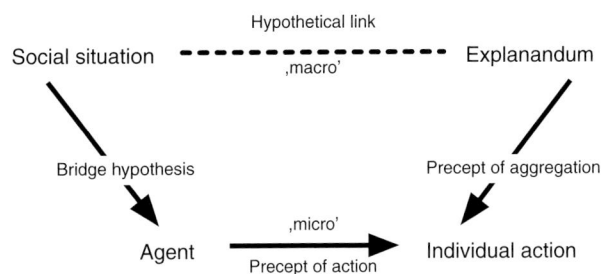

Figure 1. Macro-micro-macro-Model after Coleman ('Coleman's bathtub').

James Samuel Coleman (2010; Figure 1). Here, culture is seen as an aggregate which stands in an unknown relationship to individual phenomena. This requires the development of a 'bridge hypothesis' to explain the relationships between individual behavior and wider social and cultural contexts. Volker Kunz (2004: 107ff) proposes four different ways of bridging this issue:
- the testing of different assumptions through simulations ('analytic constructions')
- the postulation of 'obvious', common sense ideas
- the theory of social production functions (see also Lindenberg 1996)
- direct empirical construction through questioning and written documents

In the following example two of these methodological approaches will be applied to one specific phenomenon in rural architecture. Looking on houses as 'social goods' (point 3) the paper explores the possible functions but also symbolic meanings of particular architectural features within a specific cultural context. This is achieved first, by the comparative analysis of the building type in space and time, and second, through the evaluation of the hypothesis in the context of contemporary written sources (point 4).

The tower and the castle: bridging cultural norms

It is possible to explore the relationship between collective cultural norms and individual perceptions and actions in the context of high-status domestic buildings in medieval Europe through the motif of the tower. From the 9th/10th centuries onwards, towers, together with surrounding walls and great halls, became one of the key elements of castle buildings. Indeed, towers sometimes stand in documentary, literary sources for the idea of the castle itself, since they comprise the iconographic features of a high building with massive walls, crowned with battlements, prominent entrances and windows (Kühtreiber 2009: 65-67; Wheatley 2004: 29). From the 13th century onwards, it is possible to identify attempts across Europe to legislate or regulate the construction of castles, in contradistinction to 'normal' buildings. A building needed permission if it was higher than two storeys, had a surrounding fence or wall higher than a horseman was able to reach with his hands, sitting on his horse, and had an entrance set higher than knee-level (Kühtreiber 2009: 64). These criteria of height are also reflected in the German word used for a castle, 'Burg', which is related to 'Berg' (mountain) and means 'guarding by being founded in a high position' (Gebuhr & Gebuhr 2001: 421f).

If we take a look at the architectural spread of tower-like buildings in Middle Europe we find a group of architectural complexes which seem to oscillate between castles and farmsteads (Figure 2). On the one hand, they do not feature fortifications such as moats, ramparts or massive surrounding walls; on the other these farmstead complexes contain tower houses, which are sometimes integrated in the main building, and sometimes standing isolated in the farmstead area. The impression of a high-status building was consolidated by the provision of a decorative façade which highlighted the details of doors, windows and angles (Figure 3). In the scholarly debate many of these building complexes are regarded as 'castles at low level', sometimes identified with medieval terms like *curia* or *curtis* (Kühtreiber & Reichhalter 2009; Kühtreiber & Reichhalter forthcoming). These buildings parallel tower houses in the border regions of England as well as more secular 'fortified manor houses', which often acquired licences to crenellate in England during the same period (Johnson 2002: 23f).

The example of the castle and the tower can be used as a means of illustrating the potential of bridge hypotheses discussed above. The castle was perceived within society as a high status building, built by those at the upper levels of society. Over time, one defining element of the castle, namely the tower, was appropriated by those lower down the social scale. The explanation of this process can be developed in relation to what has been described as the etic/outsider or emic/insider-position (Doneus & Kühtreiber 2013). In order to explore these ideas further it is necessary to think about the original

Figure 2. 'Kälberhof' farmstead, Lower Austria, with tower-house. Photo author 2008.

Figure 3. Storage building in Lungau, Salzburg (Austria). Photo Gerhard Reichhalter.

motivations of the builders of castles, which, following Rössler (1999: 76f) can be conceptualized as both meeting well-being or biological needs and creating social esteem. Medieval castles clearly fulfilled both of these functions. Castles might indeed provide effective military protection but their design also represented and symbolized the capacity to enact military authority without this actually needing to be enacted (Kühtreiber 2009; see also Creighton 2002: 65ff; Liddiard 2005: 46ff). Over time, towers appropriated this symbolic meaning and thus it is possible to find towers integrated into castles which served little or no military function but rather reflected the power of lords over surrounding landscapes, settlements and households.

Reviewing the evidence of more than 60 surviving 'tower-like' buildings as parts of farmsteads of the 13th to the 18th centuries in the Eastern parts of

Austria, reveals important evidence of their function (Kühtreiber & Reichhalter 2009). Most of the 'towers' have at least two entrances, one at ground level or leading into a basement, the other set at a slightly higher level. The windows of these towers are often very small and secured with grills, but only very few of them have formal features of fortification, such as battlements or arrow or gun loops. Moreover, in contrast to 'normal castles' there is no evidence either for the provision of residential functions such as heating, water provision, toilets etc. So if these were neither military or residential, what was their original function? Here, it is useful to look more closely at their relationship to other buildings within the farmstead. Sometimes, tower buildings are integrated in another building; normally a 3-5-room structure which features a central entrance at the longside of the building with residential and cooking rooms toward the principle façade and the tower building to the rear (Figure 4). An alternative variation on this layout features a two-storey structure which has a larger mass and form than the rest of the building, but which is not a tower *per se*. Archaeological investigations in high-medieval deserted villages in Moravia suggests that this morphological structure has its origin in the dual function of single-room dwelling houses with storage pits. From the 13th century onwards, the storage pit was replaced by massive buildings, which became gradually integrated in the dwelling house by the construction of a corridor (Frolec 1982; Nekuda 2003). It can therefore be suggested that the towers of late medieval and early modern farmsteads in Austria functioned as storage buildings and that their 'fortified' features were protective, rather than militaristic in function and in meaning. These massive buildings, which included vaults at first-floor level preventing the spread of fire, whilst their small windows and high-level entrances protected the goods within from daylight, humidity and rodents. From this perspective, such storage towers have clear precedents in the wooden buildings known as 'Rutenberge' or 'Bergfried' in German, a term which itself seems to be borrowed from medieval castle terminology, as Hermann Hinz (1971; see also Zimmermann 1991; 1995) suggests.

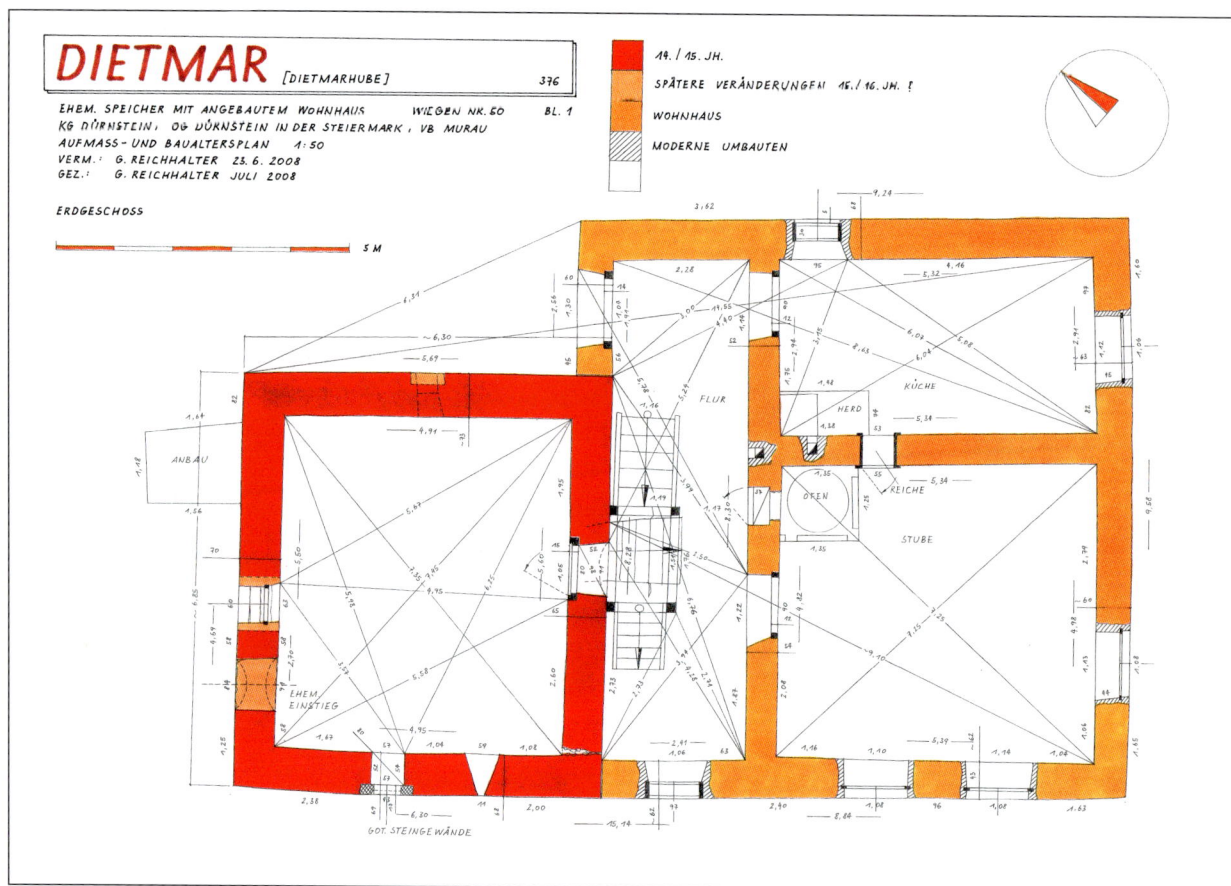

Figure 4. 'Dietmar' farmstead, Dürnstein, Styria (Austria). Groundplan and interpretation: Gerhard Reichhalter.

This interpretation provides a means of returning to the idea of the 'bridge hypothesis' outlined above. The lives of the builders of these farmstead 'towers' and storage builders were rooted in the 'rural sphere', where the precious goods stored within such buildings were the basis of livelihood, economic welfare and thus the status of the household. At one level, these meanings might seem very different to the symbolic meanings of high-status castle towers discussed above. Yet such towers were also often used for storage functions. Further light can be shed on the meanings of these structures by returning to the insider-emic perspective mentioned above, and to the legislative requirements of castle building.

Importantly, two of the three criteria outlined above, namely the number of floors and the high-leveled position, characterize such storage towers. Indeed, a closer inspection of multiple storey towers reveals that all of them are built against a slope, presenting '3 floors' to visitors (Figure 5). The entrances, too, fit the criteria of the castle. All storage towers have high-level entrances into the first or second floors; however, many also feature a second entrance, into basement level. Using these criteria it is possible to draw a fine distinction between storage buildings and aristocratic towers, which is also reflected in another aspect of the latter, which is not regulated in contemporary land laws. Whilst the wall thickness of storage buildings is usually between 0.9 m-1.2 m (3-4 feet), most of the castle towers have wall thicknesses over 1.5 m and more. The fact that wall thickness was also part of the cultural norms of tower construction is indicated by a tantalizing reference in a charter dated to 1262 between Abbot Hermann of Niederaltaich and his vassal Tyrolf of Purchstal. In it the abbot forbid Tyrolf from completing the construction of a tower, permitting him rather to store his possessions in a *cellarium* which was to have walls no thicker than 3 feet (Chmel 1848: Nr. 36).

In summary, it is possible to suggest that 'towers' in late medieval or early modern farmsteads fulfilled two functions. They protected agricultural goods and were thus of crucial importance for the socio-economic well-being and status of the owner, his family and his household. Ethnographic sources reveal the enduring importance of both crops and household tools and objects for family members at this level of society (Hinz 1981: 99ff). However, this valuable socio-economic function was communicated to the outside world through the appropriation of the symbolic militaristic meaning of the tower from contemporary aristocratic architecture.

Networks and Boundaries: Architecture as social mirror?

This paper started by exploring useful sociological models for explaining intercultural phenomena, particularly the relationship between past social structures and forms of architectural and spatial organization. Archaeologists must also, however, model the ways in which these cultural and spatial relationships change over time. Two models propose themselves here. The first is the classic metaphor for biological and social evolution, namely the 'life tree' (Ingold 2000: 134ff). This is a model for how initial ideas grow and develop over time and space. For Ingold this metaphor informs genealogical concepts of cultural development, where descent plays a crucial role in identity, either defining your place in a community based on your ancestors or by integrating ancestor cults in everyday life. In contrast, Deleuze and Guattari (1988: 15) propose what they term the 'Rhizome model', where the idea of a network is used to explain how the individual actor defines his/her position in the world in a dynamic and communicative relation to all other participants, whether living or non-living objects. Although the latter seems more appropriate for our understanding of the modern world, the genealogical model has considerable resonance with antique and medieval emphases on divine and patriarchial order, in society and at household level (Handzel 2011: 26ff; Schmidt 2008: 302). It is possible, for example, to see this reflected in concepts of the household having an inner sphere, which has its center at the hearth fire and is connoted to the housewife, whereas the outer sphere including the economic and social interaction with the 'world outside' is the male side of the

Figure 5. 'Moar' farmstead, Adendorf, Styria (Austria): View from the Southeast. Photo Gerhard Reichhalter.

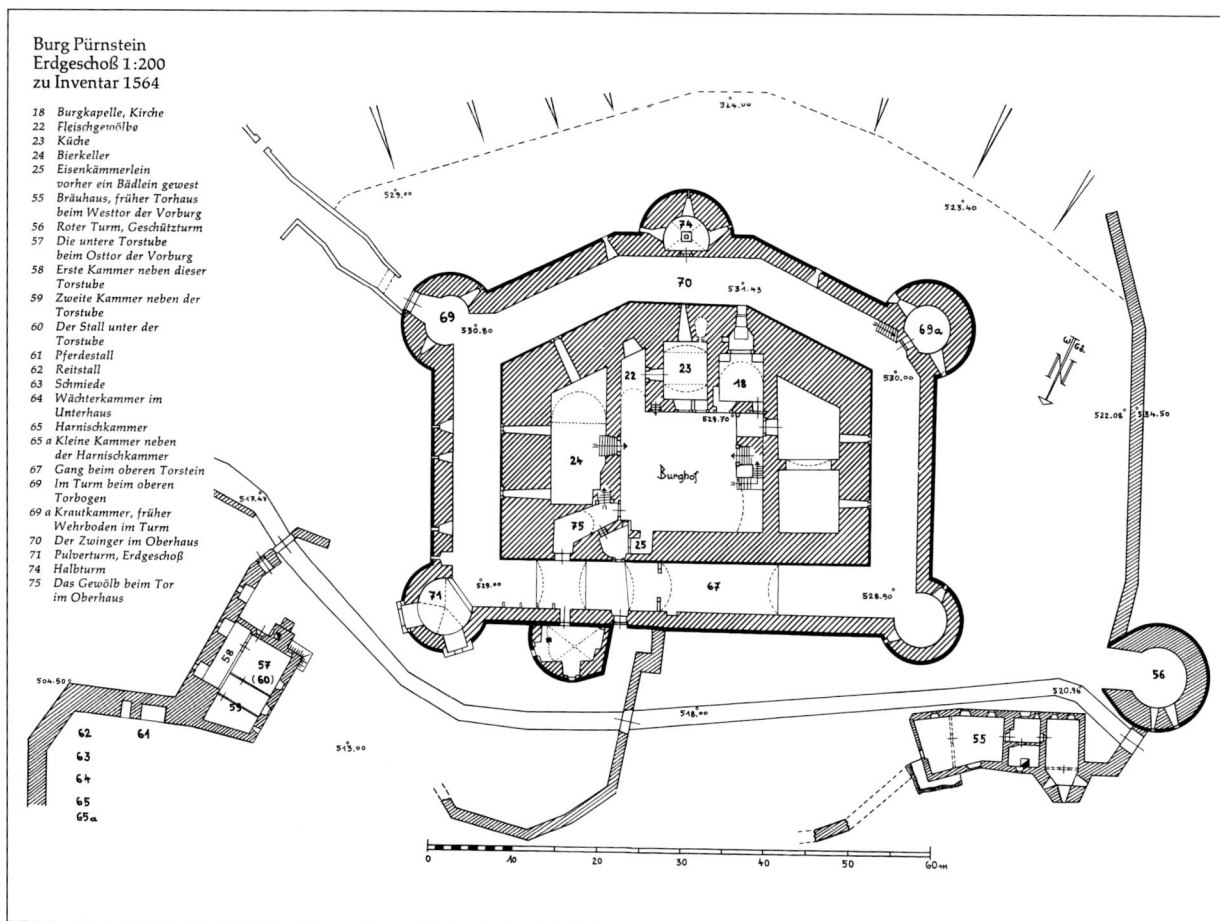

Figure 6. Pürnstein Castle, Upper Austria: Groundplan. After Götting 1976.

household (Wigley 1992). Although there are no contemporary documentary or literary sources which shed specific light on the structuring frameworks behind the organization of domestic space within farmhouses in medieval Central Europe, it might be possible to map this binary opposition of inside/female: outside/male spheres onto the layout of the typical Central European late medieval farmhouse of the 'Middle-Corridor-Type' plan, which is divided into residential/domestic: storage/service functions.

Such a division can also be argued to exist in high-status architecture, and here, it is possible to compare architecture and written sources in some specific examples. In the middle of the 15th century members of the landlords of Starhemberg built a new castle in Pürnstein, Upper Austria (Figure 6). This noble residence was modern in its design; a symmetrical three-wing-building enclosed by two concentric rings of massive, turetted walls (Götting & Grüll 1967: 171-190). The northern wing, situated next to the main entrance, containing the Great Hall and the main staircase, is set opposite the south wing, which contains residential rooms linked to the courtyard by means of an external stair. A central wing integrates the residential rooms with a chapel and with the kitchen adjacent to the Great Hall. In the upper floor there are also corridors which link the residential rooms with the Great Hall. An inventory dating to 1564, around 100 years after the building of Pürnstein Castle, provides a detailed description of the wings, their rooms and their fittings and fixtures. Here, it is interesting to note that the term used for the northern wing was named 'Herrenhalb' or 'Herrenzimmer', which means 'the male half' or 'Lord's apartment', whereas the southern wing is named 'Frauenzimmer', *ie* 'Lady's apartment'. These terms are also supported by the apparent functions and fittings and fixtures of the rooms within them (Grüll 1976; Handzel 2011: 128).

In this high status building it is possible to identify the architectural and functional division of the castle into different sections for living, storage and access routes and to explore how this mapped onto near-contemporary peceptions of gendered elite space. An access analysis diagram, based on the architectural structures of approximately 1450 (Figure 7) and the room functions around 1564 (Figure 8; Handzel & Kühtreiber forthcomming), reveals the careful control of access to the castle, its interior spaces and its inhabitants which fits medieval concepts of a gradual retreat from public to private space (see Meckseper 2002). It can also be argued that such analysis reinforces the association of the 'public' with the male sphere, while the 'private sphere' is associated with the 'female part' of the household. However, there are changes between 1450 and 1560, which are indicated by the division of the lordly apartment in two separate apartments. During this period the lord moved to the northern wing, and residential rooms were installed above the Great Hall. This evidence may find its expression in theoretical architectural literature of the Renaissance, which recommends the strict division of male and female spheres in the (noble) household to ensure the effective control of 'weak wives' (Handzel 2011: 32; Wigley 1992: 332f). These changes are associated with an apparent rise in the ability of the Lord to control and survey other parts of the castle complex during this period. The new Lord's apartment facilitated visual control over a cluster of guest rooms, servant's rooms and the Great Hall and rooms such as the spinning room which was occupied by young female members of the household, but also over access routes into the castle and even the inner courtyard. It could therefore be argued that the agency, especially of female members of the Pürnstein castle household, became increasingly restricted during this period. Such architectural conceptions of gendered separation has been identified until now only in new built royal and high aristocratic castles up from the 1550s (Hoppe

2000). Pürnstein castle is not only the first example of this phenomenon in a landlord's context, but also for the adaption of an older building for such concepts.

However, the 1564 inventory also reminds us of the need to explore the 'gaps' or slippages between architectural design and social practice. The inventory reveals the ways in which the strict separation of gendered spheres was undermined in reality by the presence of personal belonging of the Lord in the Lady's chamber. Similar evidence for such practices in a princely context can be found for instance at the Augustusburg near Chemnitz, built in the years around/after 1568 (Hoppe 2000: Abb. 9).

When we take a last look at the shape of access diagrams of late medieval castles, it is possible to argue that their design shows similarities with the 'lifetree'-model of genealogically-based societies. Is this a mere coincidence, given that access diagrams analysis of medieval castles normally highlight patriarchal conceptions of social control? The analysis of Pürnstein suggests that (following Wunder 1992: 58f) the heated 'Stube' was the centre of the medieval household. However, between the 15th and 16th centuries, the relationship of the Lord's apartments to other spaces had become more complex, the potential of gaining access to the Lord more restricted. At the same time, the Lord had gained increasing visual control over the surrounding buildings. Whilst this seems to reinforce the idea of the patriarchal household, the analysis of gendered objects in the Pürnstein castle inventory of 1564 demonstrates that such spatial hierarchies constructed in stone, could also be negotiated and contested by everyday life and practice.

Conclusion

To come to an end, it is time to reconsider. Like other social goods, buildings are not only designed by societies but also affect social behavior. Architectural space must therefore be seen both as a setting for – and as a product of – human activities. In consequence it is necessary to analyze buildings by applying a combination of structural and behavioral perspectives drawn from sociology and other cognate disciplines. Using houses to understand the construc-

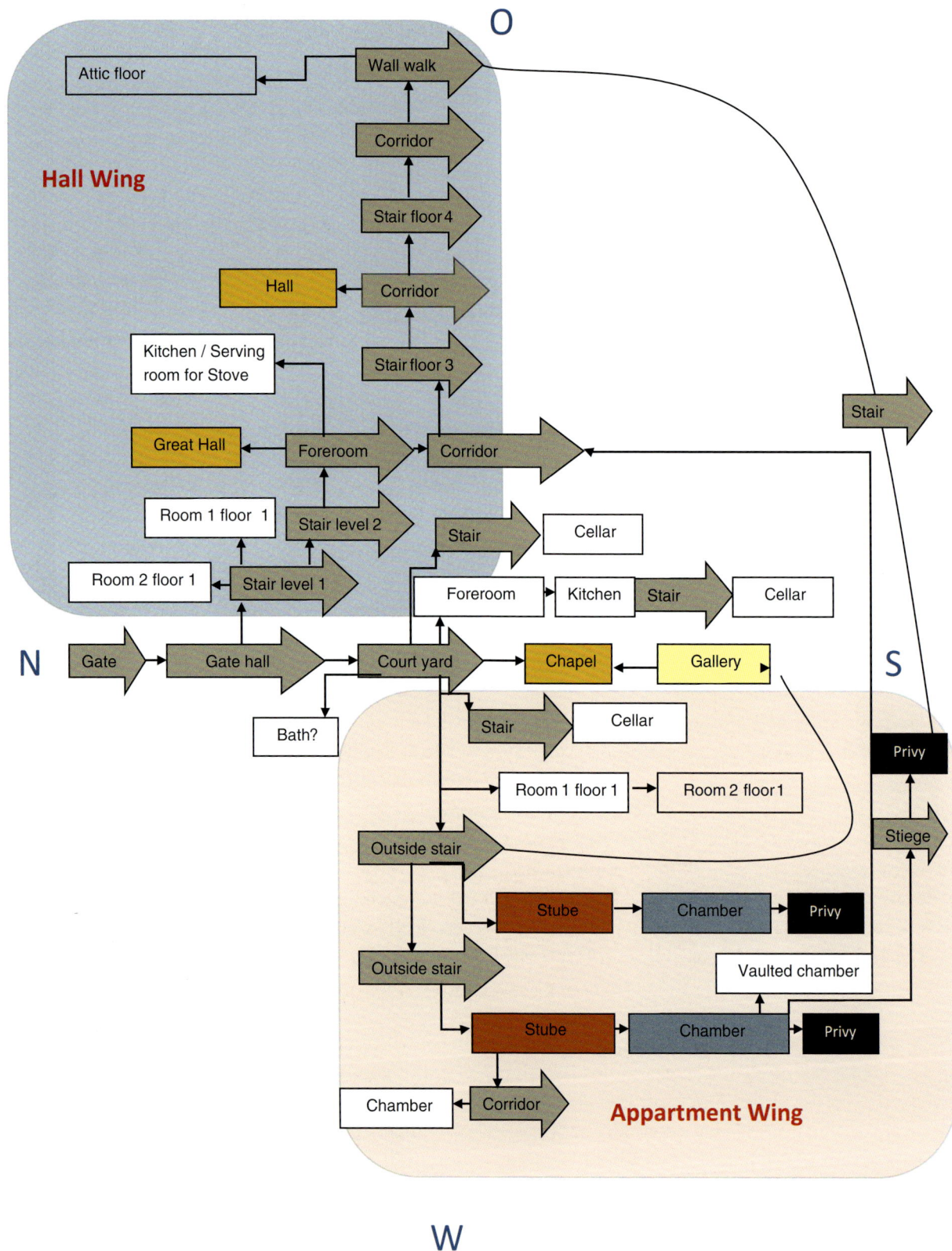

Hall Wing

Attic floor

O

Wall walk

Corridor

Stair floor 4

Hall

Corridor

Kitchen / Serving room for Stove

Stair floor 3

Great Hall

Foreroom

Corridor

Stair

Room 1 floor 1

Stair level 2

Stair

Cellar

Room 2 floor 1

Stair level 1

Foreroom

Kitchen

Stair

Cellar

N

Gate

Gate hall

Court yard

Chapel

Gallery

S

Bath?

Stair

Cellar

Stair

Privy

Room 1 floor 1

Room 2 floor 1

Stiege

Outside stair

Stube

Chamber

Privy

Outside stair

Vaulted chamber

Stube

Chamber

Privy

Chamber

Corridor

Appartment Wing

W

Figure 7. Pürnstein Castle. Access Diagram a. 1450.

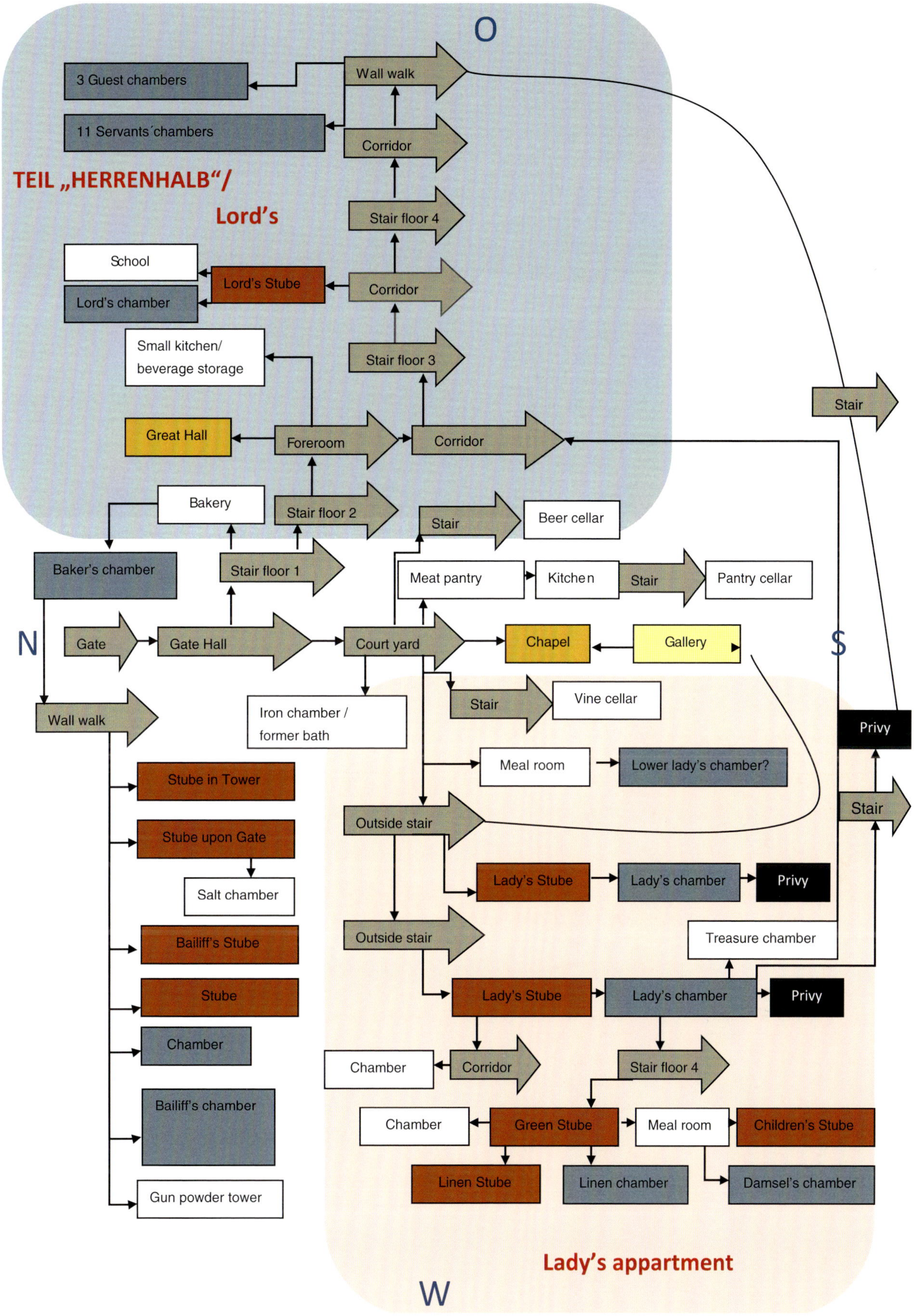

Figure 8. Pürnstein Castle, Access Diagram a. 1560.

Diagram labels:

O

3 Guest chambers
11 Servants´chambers

TEIL „HERRENHALB"/
Lord's

School
Lord's Stube
Lord's chamber
Small kitchen/
beverage storage
Great Hall
Bakery
Baker's chamber

Wall walk
Corridor
Stair floor 4
Corridor
Stair floor 3
Foreroom
Corridor
Stair floor 2
Stair floor 1
Stair
Beer cellar
Meat pantry
Kitchen
Stair
Pantry cellar

N

Gate
Gate Hall
Court yard
Chapel
Gallery

Wall walk
Iron chamber /
former bath
Stair
Vine cellar

Stube in Tower
Stube upon Gate
Salt chamber
Bailiff's Stube
Stube
Chamber
Bailiff's chamber
Gun powder tower

Meal room
Lower lady's chamber?

Outside stair
Lady's Stube
Lady's chamber
Privy

Outside stair
Lady's Stube
Lady's chamber
Privy
Treasure chamber

Chamber
Corridor
Stair floor 4

Chamber
Green Stube
Meal room
Children's Stube
Linen Stube
Linen chamber
Damsel's chamber

Stair
Privy
Stair
S

Lady's appartment

W

tion of individual and collective social identities and cultural norms is challenging. However, combining archaeological analysis with that of contemporary historical sources and these theories sheds important new light on deeply-embedded cultural concepts in the past. As Winston Churchill noted, "There is no doubt whatever about the influence of architecture and structure upon human character and action. We make our building and afterward they make us." (Lockton 2011, quoting Churchill 1924).

References

Allison, P.M. (2002) Introduction. In: *The Archaeology of Household Activities*, ed. P.M. Allison, 1-18. London: Routledge.

Chmel, J. (1848) Auszüge aus einer Pergamenthandschrift des 13. Jahrhunderts, von dem Abbte Hermann von Nieder-Altaich begonnen, und mehreren seiner Nachfolger fortgesetzt, *Archiv für Österreichische Geschichte* 1/1, 1-72.

Coleman, J.S. (2010) *Grundlagen der Sozialtheorie. Band 1: Handlungen und Handlungssysteme*. Scientia nova 1. München: Oldenbourg.

Creighton, O. (2002) *Castles and Landscapes*. London: Continuum.

Csaky, M. (2004) Die Mehrdeutigkeit von Gedächtnis und Erinnerung. Ein kritischer Beitrag zur historischen Gedächtnisforschung. In: *Digitales Handbuch zur Geschichte und Kultur Russlands und Osteuropas*. Virtuelle Fachbibliothek Osteuropa (http://epub.ub.uni-muenchen.de/603/1/csaky-gedaechtnis.pdf, last access 2011-11-18).

Deleuze, G. & F. Guattari (1988) *A thousand plateaus: capitalism and schizophrenia* (trans. B. Massumi). London: Athlone Press.

Derks, H. (1996) Über die Faszination des „Ganzen Hauses", *Geschichte und Gesellschaft* 22, 221-242.

Doneus, M. & T. Kühtreiber (2013) Landscape, the Individual and Society: Subjective Expected Utilities in a Monastic Landscape near Mannersdorf am Leithagebirge, Lower Austria. In: *Historical Archaeology in Central Europe*, ed. N. Mehler, 339-364. Society of Historical Archaeology Special Publications no. 10. Germantown: Society of Historical Archaeology.

Frolec, J. (1982) Interpretaci geneze trojdílého komorvého domu (Ve světle archeologických výzkumů na jihozápadní Moravě), *Archaeologia historica* 7, 67-78.

Gebuhr, K. & R. Gebuhr (2001) Bemerkungen zum Begriff „Burg". In: *Sein & Sinn / Burg & Mensch*, eds. F. Daim & T. Kühtreiber, 418-426. Katalog des Niederösterreichischen Landesmuseums N.F. Part 434. St. Pölten: Amt der NÖ Landesregierung – Abteilung Kultur und Wissenschaft.

Götting, W. & G. Grüll (1967) *Burgen in Oberösterreich*. Schriftenreihe der oberösterreichischen Landesbaudirektion 21. Wels: OÖ Landesbaudirektion.

Götting, W. (1976) *Burg Pürnstein. Inventar vom Jahr 1564 (Maps)*. Linz: Oberösterreichischer Landesverlag.

Grüll, G. (1976) *Burg Pürnstein. Inventar vom Jahr 1564 (Text)*. Linz: Oberösterreichischer Landesverlag.

Handzel, J. (2011) „Von erst in der grossen Stuben"– Adelige Sach- und Wohnkultur im ausgehenden Mittelalter und der frühen Neuzeit im Gebiet des heutigen Österreich. Phil. Diss. Univ. of Vienna (http://othes.univie.ac.at/15348/, 2012-12-13).

Handzel, J. & T. Kühtreiber (forthcoming) Herrenstube und Frauenzimmer. Sozial konnotierte Lebensräume auf Burg Pürnstein in textlicher und materieller Repräsentation. In: *Raumstrukturen und Raumausstattung auf Burgen in Mittelalter und früher Neuzeit*, eds. K. Holzner-Tobisch, G. Klug, T. Kühtreiber & C. Schmid. Salzburg: Institut für Realienkunde des Mittelalters und der frühen Neuzeit.

Hansen, K.-P. (2009) Kultur und Kollektiv: Eine essayistische Heuristik für Archäologen. In: *Kulturraum und Territorialität*, eds. D. Krausse & O. Nakoinz, 17-26. Rahden/Westf.: Leidorf.

Hartmann, N. (1980) *Philosophie der Natur. Abriß der speziellen Kategorienlehre*. Berlin: de Gruyter.

Hillier, B. & J. Hanson (1987) Introduction: A Second Paradigm, *Architecture et Comportement/Architecture and Behaviour* 3/3, 197-199.

Hinz, H. (1971) Bergfried – Burgturm und bäuerlicher Speicher. In: *Burgen- und Siedlungsarchäologie des Mittelalters*, 45-50. Veröffentlichungen der Österreichischen Arbeitsgemeinschaft für Ur- und Frühgeschichte 5. Wien: Österreichische Arbeitsgemeinschaft für Ur- und Frühgeschichte.

Hinz, H. (1981). *Motte und Donjon. Zur Frühgeschichte der mittelalterlichen Adelsburg*, Zeitschrift für Archäologie des Mittelalters, Beiheft 1. Köln : Rheinland-Verlag.

Hoppe, S. (2000) Bauliche Gestalt und Lage von Frauenwohnräumen in deutschen Residenzschlössern des späten 15. und 16. Jahrhunderts. In: *Das Frauenzimmer. Die Frau bei Hofe in Spätmittelalter und früher Neuzeit*, eds. J. Hirschbiegel & W. Paravicini, 151-174. Residenzenforschung 11. Stuttgart: Jan Thorbecke.

Ingold, T. (2000) *The Perception of the Environment. Essays in livelihood, dwelling and skill*. London and New York: Routledge.

Johnson, M. (2002) *Behind the Castle Gate: Medieval to Renaissance*. London & New York: Routledge.

Kühtreiber, T. (2009): Die Ikonologie der Burg. In: *Die imaginäre Burg*, eds. O. Wagener, H. Laß, T. Kühtreiber & P. Dinzelbacher, 53-92. Beihefte zur Mediävistik 11. Frankfurt am Main: Peter Lang.

Kühtreiber, T. & G. Reichhalter (2009) Ländliche Speicherbauten. Turmartige Gebäude zwischen Funktion und Repräsentation unter besonderer Berücksichtigung Ostösterreichs. In: *Lebenswelten im ländlichen Raum. Siedlung, Infrastruktur und Wirtschaft*, eds. S. Felgenhauer-Schmiedt, P. Csendes & A. Eibner. Beiträge zur Mittelalterarchäologie in Österreich 25, 285-288. Wien: Österreichische Gesellschaft für Mittelalterarchäologie.

Kühtreiber, T. & G. Reichhalter (forthcoming) *Turmartige Speicherbauten in Ostösterreich. Charakteristika, Entwicklung und Deutungsansätze eines wenig beachteten Bautyps*. Beiträge zur Mittelalterarchäologie in Österreich. Vienna: Österreichische Gesellschaft für Mittelalterarchäologie

Kunz, V. (2004) *Rational choice*. Campus-Einführungen. Frankfurt am Main: Campus-Verlag.

Lemmer, M. (1991) Haushalt und Familie aus der Sicht der Hausväterliteratur. In: *Haushalt und Familie in Mittelalter und früher Neuzeit*, ed. T. Ehlert, 181-191. Sigmaringen: Jan Thorbecke.

Liddiard, R. (2005) *Castles in Context: Power, Symbolism and Landscape, 1066 to 1500*. Macclesfield: Windgather Press.

Lindenberg, S. (1985) An Assessment of the New Political Economy: Its Potential for the Social Sciences and for Sociology in Particular, *Sociological Theory* 3, 99-114.

Lindenberg, S. (1996) Die Relevanz theoriereicher Brückenannahmen, *Kölner Zeitschrift für Soziologie und Sozialpsychologie* 48, 126-140.

Lockton, D. (2011) Architecture, urbanism, design and behaviour: a brief review. In: *Design with Intent Blog* (http://architectures.danlockton.co.uk/2011/09/12/architecture-urbanism-design-and-behaviour-a-brief-review/, 2012-12-13).

Löw, M. (2001) *Raumsoziologie*. Frankfurt a. M.: Suhrkamp Verlag.

Löw, M., S. Steets & S. Stoetzer (2008): *Einführung in die Stadt- und Raumsoziologie*. Opladen: Barbara Budrich.

Meckseper, C. (2002) Raumdifferenzierungen im hochmittelalterlichen Burgenbau Mitteleuropas, *Chateau Gaillard. Etudes de Castellologie medievale* 20, 163-171.

Meyer, U. (1998) *Soziales Handeln im Zeichen des ‚Hauses'. Zur Ökonomik in der Spätantike und im frühen Mittelalter*. Göttingen: Vandenhoeck und Ruprecht.

Nekuda, R. (2003) Construction development of granaries in Mstenice, *Ve Službach Archeologie* 4, 2003, 147-149.

Nekuda, V. (1975) *Pfaffenschlag. Zaniklá středověká ves u Slavonic*. Brno: Moravské muzeum v Brně.

Opitz, C. (1994) Neue Wege der Sozialgeschichte? Ein kritischer Blick auf Otto Brunners Konzept des ‚ganzen Hauses', *Geschichte und Gesellschaft* 20, 88-98.

Rössler, M. (1999) *Wirtschaftsethnologie. Eine Einführung. Zweite, überarbeitete und erweiterte Auflage*. Berlin: Dietrich Reimer Verlag.

Sandkühler, H.-J. (2009) *Kritik der Repräsentation: Einführung in die Theorie der Überzeugungen, der Wissenskulturen und des Wissens*. Frankfurt: Suhrkamp.

Schmidt, H.R. (2008) „Nothurfft vnd Hußbruch". Haus, Gemeinde und Sittenzucht im Reformiertentum. In: *Ehe – Familie –Verwandtschaft. Vergesellschaftung in Religion und sozialer Lebenswelt*, eds. A. Holzelm & I. Weber, 301-328. Paderborn, Wien, München, Zürich: Ferdinand Schöning.

Sieferle, R.-P. (1997) Kulturelle Evolution des Gesellschaft-Natur-Verhältnisses. In: *Gesellschaftlicher Stoffwechsel und Kolonisierung der Natur. Ein Versuch in Sozialer Ökologie*, eds. M. Fischer-Kowalski, H. Haberl, W. Hüttler, H. Payer, H. Schandl, V. Winiwarter & H. Zangerl-Weisz, 37-56. Amsterdam: G+B Verlag Fakultas.

Richarz, I. (1991) *Oikos, Haus und Haushalt. Ursprung und Geschichte der Haushaltsökonomik*. Göttingen: Vandenhoeck und Ruprecht.

Rapoport, A. (1990) *The meaning of the built environment: a nonverbal communication approach*. Tucson: University of Arizona Press.

Weiß, S. (2001) Otto Brunner und das Ganze Haus. Oder: Zwei Arten der Wirtschaftsgeschichte, *Historische Zeitschrift* 273, 335-369.

Wheatley, A. (2004) *The Idea of the Castle in Medieval England*. York: York Medieval Press.

Wigley, M. (1992) Untitled: The housing of Gender. In: *Sexuality and Space*, ed. B. Colomina, 327-389. Princeton: Princeton Architectural Press (http://www.colorado.edu/envd/courses/envd4114-001/Spring %2006/Theory/Wigley.pdf, 2012-12-13).

Wunder, H. (1992) *'Er ist die Sonn, sie ist der Mond'. Frauen in der Frühen Neuzeit*. München: C.H. Beck.

Xenophon (1828) Von der Haushaltungskunst und Hiero oder Herrscherleben. In: *Xenophon's von Athens Werke*. Dritte Abteilung, Neuntes Bändchen, ed. A.H. Christian. Stuttgart: Verlag der J.B. Metzler'schen Buchhandlung.

Zimmermann, W.H. (1991) Erntebergung in Rutenberg und Diemen aus ethnographischer und archäologischer Sicht, *Néprajzi Értesitö a Néprajzi Muzeum Evkönyve* 71-104.

Zimmermann, W.H. (1995) Der Rutenberg – Ein landwirtschaftliches Nebengebäude zum Bergen von Feldfrüchten und Heu. In: *Der sassen speyghel. Sachsenspiegel – Recht – Alltag*, ed. M. Fansa, 207-216. Archäologische Mitteilungen aus Nordwestdeutschland 10. Oldenburg: Stadtmuseum Oldenburg.

The Investigation of Domesticated Space in Archaeology – Beyond Architecture

Christina Schmid

Abstract

When studying historical settings, the behaviour of human beings – who played an important role as actors in specific historical contexts – cannot be included in the research as it is impossible to investigate their personal circumstances and ways of living by interview or observance. Thus, 'dwelling' as action and attitude is not directly empirically comprehensible. It can only be made accessible in an indirect way, by analysing housing space and objects related to housing. The physical structure of houses makes up the material framework for social actions, yet architectural settings can accommodate many different kinds of activities. As there is no direct interrelation between architecture and activities, human activity cannot be understood by merely analysing the static elements of a setting. Rather, evidence for behavioural patterns can be found in its mobile elements. In comparison with more constant parameters such as floor plans and construction methods, fittings and furniture can more easily be changed, and therefore become a good indicator for changing social, economic and cultural relationships over time.

Within the last decade, there have been rising demands for collaboration between archaeologists and building historians in terms of developing an 'archaeology of the house'. Increasingly often, traces of usage in buildings are documented. These can provide information on the use of a room. House contents, which are often found in large number among archaeological remains and are not part of the architecture, but rather part of the household, play an important role in structuring the behaviour of households and the relationship between social actions and material objects. In this article, the opportunities and drawbacks of using spatial analysis in the archaeology of the middle ages will be investigated, with particular consideration of houses and their fixtures and fittings. This paper will focus on the specific strengths, but also the limitations of archaeology for researching dwellings and the activities carried out within and around them.

Introduction

Unlike prehistoric archaeology, the archaeology of the Middle Ages and early modern period only rarely explores the potential of detecting human activities in the archaeological record by means of spatial analysis. But why are these methods so far only being used sporadically? Is there a difference in the scientific paradigms of prehistoric archaeology and historical archaeology, or are there differences in the nature of the features which do not allow for or encourage the application of these methods? What could be the possible differences between prehistoric and historic features?

Firstly, spatial analyses are often carried out at prehistoric (and especially Stone Age) sites which were used for only a rather short period of time. This means that – in the best of cases – they feature traces of activities which originate from one single form of activity carried out at a particular place for a certain time. In addition, the shorter the period during which a site was in use, the lower the number of cleaning processes which wipe out such traces of activity. Secondly, houses in the Middle Ages often comprised two or more floors. These upper floor levels are mostly not found in situ, but rather as debris, and are therefore hard to investigate archaeologically. Actions performed on now-collapsed floors cannot be investigated by examining occupation layers, as they no longer exist in their original spatial location. Due to these limitations, we can see a predominance of studies which emphasize the importance of analysing surviving medieval buildings, rather than excavated structures (Allison 2002: 4).

Yet the special strengths of historic features lie in the possibility of linking information gained from archaeological features to information derived from structural remains. Additionally, where there are no structural remains and no other sources (such as written or pictorial source material) at hand to investigate, archaeological information often remains the only way of gaining information on activities carried out at a site. These are some of the reasons that can be considered responsible for the rare application of spatial analysis to research on historic dwellings. In the following paper, the opportunities of its application to features from the Middle Ages are investigated. First, some general remarks are made on architecture on which the argument advanced below is based.

Buildings constitute and represent aspects of social reality. Dwellings – as well as cities – own a constitutional quality: they organise space (Hillier & Hanson 1987: 198). The room layout of houses exerts influence on the localisation of activities and they are the material framework for actions (Kaspar 1998: 211; Sommer 1991: 134). Not only objects, but also rooms, experience a life cycle. This life cycle can consist of many steps, from the primary use to the abandonment due to complete redundancy (Sommer 1991: 104). During this life cycle, rooms are subject to constant processes of conversion and adaptation. The longer a dwelling exists, the less it may correspond to the changing needs of its users. The costs and effort of modifications are decisive factors in the conversion of buildings. Changes in dwellings built of stone are difficult and labour-intensive, whereas architecture made of clay or wood can be adapted more quickly in response to changes in social circumstances (Dafinger 2010: 129; Sommer 1991: 104). If the structural environment inhibits conversion, the spatial organisation may no longer directly serve or

reflect the needs of its inhabitants (Altwasser 2000: 45; Sommer 1991: 104). Households might occupy spaces over whose design they had little or no influence because they were built by unrelated ancestors or distant individuals or simply other members of a contemporary extended family or community (Allison 2002: 4; see also Blanton 1994: 6). The ways these inhabitants lived might vary greatly from the original intention of its builders. Therefore, the research of structural remains does not automatically lead to an understanding of the perceptions of those who inhabited them (Allison 2002: 4). Contrarily, the most recent layers of occupation at a site are very likely to reflect the activities that were carried out only during its last phase of occupation – and certainly do not tell the entire history of usage of a site (Bernbeck 1997: 189).

In order to identify the use of a room, parameters such as accessibility, location and view, size and shape, building material and technologies used, the relation of a room to other rooms or central areas, opening directions of doors, defensive features or entrances can be useful (for these aspects see Meckseper 2002: 169; Virágos 2006: 88f). Architectural remains can, for example, be investigated applying methods such as *Space Syntax* and *'access analysis'*. These methods were developed in order to gain information on the ways buildings were used; they are regularly being applied to Middle Age or early modern sites today.

Space Syntax tries to find social relationships expressed in architecture.[1] This method was, to name one example, applied to investigate medieval structures in the town 's-Hertogenbosch in the Netherlands. In her study, Marlous Craane tried to find correlations between areas with high 'to-movement potential' (which means a high 'integration level') and urban economic areas. On the basis of a comparison between reconstructed city maps and the so called 'topological choice maps', Craane demonstrated that the choice of the location of a certain professional sector correlates with the expected movements of the potential customers (Craane 2009: 5, 12).[2] But there are also limitations to the application of the *Space Syntax*-model. Ethnological studies carried out by Andreas Dafinger showed that without an integration of the semantic level, that is without knowledge about the users and inhabitants of the rooms and their relationships, no meaningful assertions on descriptive and normative aspects of spatial systems could be made. Only the combination of information gained from permeability maps with information on the movement through a room and the knowledge of concrete relationships of the members of a social group would allow for broad conclusions (Dafinger 2010: 135, 138. He does, however, consider permeability maps to be a useful form of *emic* modelling).

When studying historical settings, the behaviour of human beings cannot directly be included in the research as it is impossible to investigate their personal circumstances and ways of living by interview or observance. Thus, 'dwelling' as action and attitude has to be made accessible in an indirect way, by analysing housing space and objects related to housing (Bedal 1993: 86; 2004: 32).

Access Analysis analyses the spatial (and therefore social) patterning and the relationships expressed in the structures of architectonical demarcations and entrances (Steadman 1996: 67). This method was in many cases applied to the research of castles in England, as they frequently show extraordinary preservation conditions of the building structures. Analysing the succession of rooms, their position within the building and their accessibility should allow for comprehending the spatial impression intended when the building was erected (see, for example Dixon 1998). This approach to the investigation of social space, however, reduces to seeing architecture as floor plans and buildings as two-dimensional concepts. Archaeological remains (including structural remains) are usually preserved three-dimensionally, and these aspects should also be included in the research (Allison 2002: 4. For critique of access analysis, see also Grenville 1997: 17-20).

Amos Rapoport, the Polish architect and psychologist, assumed that there was a connection between human behaviour and built environment.[3] He defined built environment as consisting of fixed-feature elements (including buildings, floors, walls etc.), semi fixed-feature elements (consisting of furnishing, inside and outside), and non fixed-feature elements (these include the human beings, their

activities and their behaviour) (Rapoport 1990a: 13; 1990b: 88). If the house contents are defined as semi-fixed-feature respectively as non-fixed-feature elements, all three of these types of elements can be found in the archaeological record (Rapoport 1990b: especially 89, 97; see also Allison 2002: 6; Steadman 1996: 70).

An architectural setting can accommodate different activities. Settings guide behaviour not only through the fixed-feature elements of architecture. Rather, the specific fixtures or the indications of them allow reconstructing the function or one of the functions of a room (Bedal 2004: 32). These semi-fixed-feature elements are decisive and meaningful for the activities carried out in a room and can therefore be indicators for behavioural patterns. They can change more easily and vary with the activities – in guiding them, but also in reacting to them (Rapoport 1990a: 13; see also Bedal 2004: 34). Through changes in the mobile elements and changing activities of its users, the same room can become a different setting. This shows that there is no direct interrelation between architecture and activities. Therefore, it is not sufficient to analyse only the static elements of a setting; the functions of a room cannot be reconstructed only through an analysis of a room's design and position. Not least, besides semi-fixed-feature elements, human action also constitutes space. The presence or absence of humans and evidence of the activities in which they were engaged are also valuable signals (Rapoport 1990a: 13, 18).

More recent sociological research on space therefore tends to highlight the close connection of human beings, material objects and space: Space is seen as "relational arrangement of social goods and human beings at places".[4] Space comes into existence by linking social goods through their material qualities, and on the basis of space the material goods unfold their symbolic properties. Human beings are included in this constitution of space in two ways: on the one hand as components of the elements which are linked as space, on the other hand, because this linking itself is bound to human activity (Löw 2001: 234). However, as noted above, these cannot always be directly included in the research of historical space. For an analysis of humans' experience of dwellings, we often have to draw on sources other than the archaeological data (*eg* Alexandre 1990; Locock 1994).

Considering the above, it becomes clear that a comprehensive analysis of houses can only be made through multi- or inter-disciplinary analysis of different sources and disciplines (*cf* Kaspar 1998: 211). For historical settings, it is possible to draw upon many sources which shed light on how houses were experienced. An integration of contextual information, documentary and material culture evidence is therefore essential (Johnson 2000: 227).

The archaeology of the house

In the remainder of this paper, the potential of the archaeological contribution to the research of houses and dwelling functions shall be explored. Here, I will always have to come back to other kinds of sources, as it is impossible and illegitimate to strictly separate them. It is, for example, impossible to draw a sharp line between features relevant to archaeology and those relevant to building history. Within the last decade, there have been rising demands for a collaboration of archaeologists and building historians in terms of an "archaeology of the house" (Baeriswyl 2000: 21). Increasingly often, traces of usage in buildings are documented.[5] These traces can be divided into those connected to the house and those not connected to the house (Klein 2007: 107).

Traces connected to the house can be layers of paint, slots related to the location of light sources (often small pieces of wood or candles), or traces of fixings such as hooks for hanging foodstuffs on the wall, traces of windows, or drainage features in a kitchen. A blocked notch or a sooty wall can be signs of a subsequently- removed oven.[6] Furniture can leave marks on the floor and thus also allow for a reconstruction of a room's fittings and fixtures (*cf* Bedal 2004: 32; Klein 2007: 108f; Uhl 2004).[7]

Traces that are not connected to the house are, for instance, objects which were deposited in the house, lost objects, fillings or sedimentary material (Klein 2007: 110-112). Objects are also regularly found in redundant floor surfaces. The dry storage conditions underneath these floors can often preserve even wooden objects. Microstratigraphical research

in buildings opens up new opportunities of gaining information. Sediments in upper floor levels can also be documented archaeologically and used to construct fine stratigraphies (*cf* Altwasser 2000: 56; Altwasser & Klein 2007: 54; Klein 2007: 112).

The so-called 'house contents', which are among the most important sources for the archaeologist, are also traces that are not connected to the house. These non-fixed-feature elements are often found in great number in archaeological excavations. They are not part of the architecture, but part of the household (on this see Allison 2002: 5f). In comparison to more constant parameters such as floor plan and construction, fittings and furniture can more easily be changed, and therefore become a good indicator for activities, social and economic basis, cultural relationships and their particular changes (Bedal 2004: 38; Rapoport 1990a: 13). Yet furnishings, particularly wooden furniture is short-lived, highly moveable and perishable. This can present difficulties in its interpretation (Bedal 2004: 34; Virágos 2006: 114). Additionally, the social interpretation of material culture remains problematic. The Hungarian archaeologist Gábor Virágos, for instance, showed by the example of several Hungarian castles, that loss of social status as seen in written sources and current building stock does not necessarily correlate with a decline in the material culture (Virágos 2006: 126).

It has been pointed out that the functional analysis of the objects found in a room or a certain area can be useful when investigating the character of a room. The following analysis explores how activities are reflected in the archaeological material and how these archaeologically-relevant traces of human activity can be interpreted by archaeologists.

The spatial analysis of archaeological remains

Starting with a functional approach in archaeology, spatial analyses have been carried out since the middle of the 20th century. In the course of this, the inter-relation between the spatial patterning of artefacts and architecture within sites, as well as the way in which past societies worked as systems, were explained (Seibert 2006: xiii). In prehistoric archaeology, so called intrasite and intrastructure analyses focussing on domestic architecture were carried out, questioning social and economic structures (Steadman 1996: 52). These analyses were then expanded to the study of settlements or landscapes, trying to find intercultural and inter-temporal regularities by analysing the spatial distribution of architecture and artefacts (Seibert 2006: xiv). The first movers in this respect were the exponents of 'New' (Processual) Archaeology (Sommer 1991: 55-57). Their objective was to find regularities which were presumed to underlie human behaviour (Eggert 2006: 194). By interpreting ethno-archaeological observations, the formation of features and sites could be explained (*cf* Gramsch 2000: 6). In the 1960s, models to make the formation of find assemblages comprehensible were designed by Robert Ascher, Michael Schiffer or Lewis Binford, to name only a few (*cf* Binford 1981; 1983; Schiffer 1976; 1996: 21f; see on this Frommer 2007: 223f and Sommer 1991: 55, 62-64).

Those models were strongly debated (*cf* Frommer 2007: 162-170). It was argued that space was seen as a relationship between objects, and social space was reduced to its physical description. Patterns of spatial distribution were seen as passive and random reflections of social practice (Saunders 1990: 182). Culture cannot be seen as mere adaptation to environmental conditions. Distributional analysis cannot be used to explain economic systems and social relationships (on this see among others Bernbeck 1997: 38; Gramsch 2000: 7; Grenville 2000: 310; Schmidt 2005: 242f). The wide gap between human action and what is left of it in the form of archaeological remains has been one of the most frequently-voiced objections to these models (*cf* Hakelberg 1996: 105). Even if the models and claims of Processual Archaeology are no longer up-to-date, the request for replacing subjective assertions by traceable and comprehensible approaches is of great importance (Kienlin 1998: 103).

The approaches of New Archaeology did not elicit much response in Medieval Archaeology (Scholkmann 1997/98: 15). Within historical archaeology, Stanley South was first to systematically integrate elements of Processual archaeology, such as pattern recognition to his 1970s analysis of patterns in the

material residues of excavated abandoned settlements of North America (South 2002). In the following decades, based upon the works of Processual Archaeology and the activity area studies of functionalist archaeology, so called Household Archaeology was developed mainly in the Anglo-Saxon countries. It also deals with the spatial components of a system, but within a much smaller research area (Seibert 2006: xv). The paradigm of Processual Archaeology was followed by Post-processual (or 'interpretive') Archaeologies (on these see Shanks & Hodder 2006). These schools of thought questioned the normative assumptions of the processualists, which led to an investigation of human behaviour from a less deterministic perspective. Social, cognitive and cultural aspects of spatial analyses came to the fore (Seibert 2006: xv-xvi. For the influence of Post-processual schools on medieval archaeology, see Scholkmann 1997/98: 16/footnote 40).

Spatial structures have to be seen as means of structuring, as well as a product, of human activity. Physical space is a social product, formed by historically-specific social practices. From this perspective, space is understood as the materialization of social practices and therefore plays an important role in social action (Saunders 1990: 183). Space comes into being in the constant mutual configuration of social action and social structures which are both the result and the condition for proceedings (Löw, Steets & Stoetzer 2008: 64). Agency and structure are intertwined, as each is the product of the other (Johnson 2000: 226). Yet, this behaviour of human beings, who take on important roles as actors and non-fixed-feature elements, as pointed out before, cannot often be directly included in the research (Rapoport 1990a: 13).

Visibility of activities in archaeological data

The underlying assumption of this argument is that human activities can – under certain circumstances – be reflected in the archaeological record and be made visible to and be interpreted by the archaeologist. An activity can be defined as consisting of four components: the activity itself; how it is being carried out; how it is associated with other activities and combined in systems of activities; as well as the meaning of the activity (Rapoport 1990a: 11; 1990b: 15). An activity area can be seen as a spatially-definable place, at which one certain activity was carried out by one or more persons. Activity area analysis is the investigation of spatial relations of objects, the aim of these analyses is to identify recurrent patterns of activities (Bernbeck 1997: 186; Sommer 1991: 130; Steadman 1996: 63).

Before trying to identify activities in archaeological data, we have to clarify what the conditions for the archaeological visibility of actions or artefacts are. In 1978, Diane Gifford specified the following three conditions (Gifford 1978: 98; cf Sommer 1991: 59f): Firstly, human action must have material consequences. Secondly, these material consequences need to have the opportunity of being preserved. Thirdly, natural processes have to have such impact on the material consequences of an action that they are being preserved. The German archaeologist Ulrike Sommer added a fourth criterion. The traces have to be identifiable to the archaeologist. So, there are processes and criteria referring to the pre-depositional archaeological visibility, whereas factors like modern use of land or research intensity can have an effect on post-depositional visibility (Sommer 1991: 60).

Yet, the main question when trying to interpret spatial distributions remains: which objects become parts of archaeological sediments, and why? As shown before, the question of how to interpret the formation of find assemblages and their results visible to the archaeologist have been subject to heated debates between scholars from the most different paradigms. The German archaeologist Sören Frommer discussed the formation processes of archaeological assemblages in his book published in 2007 (Frommer 2007). In it, he sums up the discussion in a very pragmatic way. Relevant aspects of the primary formation of finds can be divided into positive selection (I want something to be that way), negative selection (I do no longer want something to be that way) and de-facto-selection without intentional character (these are all processes concerning the taking of the definite stratigraphic position that are not inten-

tional). For the relevant aspects of the primary formation of features, Frommer differentiates between positive selection (I want this structure to be that way) and the de-facto-selection without intentional character. Yet, he points out that this concept cannot be used as a methodically backed-up step in the interpretation (Frommer 2007: 224f).

Frommer differentiated between four formation processes that could have an effect on the form of appearance of archaeological contexts:

Primary formation: This includes all sedimentation processes in historic reality which led to the formation of an archaeological context (Frommer 2007: 138, 385-388).

Secondary formation: This includes the external influences which affect sedimentation; naturally- and culturally-determined transformations of the archaeological context during the bedding phase in the ground. These influences could be natural, like moisture, changes in temperature, natural earth pressure and so on, or manipulation by human beings (like grave openings or densification of the soil in the course of the use of heavy agricultural machinery). What remains after the processes of secondary formation have occurred (the so called "archaeological context"), can be regarded as the source of archaeology.

Tertiary formation: In tertiary formation, the transformation effects of the archaeological excavation and the subsequent storage have an impact on the archaeological context. What remains after this is the archaeological feature, which forms the basis of our scientific work.

Quaternary formation: Before these archaeological documentations can be evaluated and interpreted, reductive formation processes become effective.

Activity analyses on the basis of spatial distribution patterns

The conditions under which the deposition of archaeological finds took place are crucial regarding the analysis of the composition of finds assemblages at a site. Archaeological features, which have undergone all of the above-named formation processes, are able to reflect historical spatial relationships. These can be understood as the record of material interactions in primary formation (Frommer 2007: 224). These finds assemblages can therefore, under certain favourable circumstances, serve as indicators for activity areas. However, localising activity areas on the basis of the archaeological record holds high potential for error. Some of these preconditions shall be explained in the following.

The sedimentation processes in primary formation are strongly influenced by the performance of human beings. Activities can only be localised when they are connected with material requirements as well as with loss of material. Activities for which no material is needed or in the course of which only little waste is produced can hardly be seen in the archaeological record and will be under-represented in such analyses (cf Kühtreiber 2006: 161; Virágos 2006: 87). Cleaning processes also have a wide influence on the composition of the find material. The common and important activity of 'cooking' can be named as an example. The material produced in this activity will be either consumed, discarded or will simply decompose (Ciolek-Torrello 1984: 133). Repetitive activities are also easier to understand and detect in the archaeological material than activities which occurred only once (Sommer 1991: 61 and 138; see also Rapoport 1990a: 11). Activities bound to a fixed element, to an installation, are more likely to be archaeologically visible than those which can be carried out at different places (Sommer 1991: 139).

Even though a site may not show traces of intense subsequent (human) disturbance, many processes in secondary and tertiary formation can and are likely to have taken place – and many of these will not be identifiable to the archaeologists. When defining activity areas on the basis of mobile objects, one first has to make sure these objects were found in the place at which they were used, lost or thrown away (Bernbeck 1997: 182; Sommer 1991: 130). Before the naturally- and culturally-determined transformations in the ground (see above and cf Frommer 2007: 388) take effect, objects are at the place and in the state they were produced, used, dumped or lost by human beings. The position of an object within an archaeological feature usually allows an assertion on its last historical movement, which does certainly not give any information on the degree of closeness to its primary historical context of use (Frommer 2007: 224; Frommer & Kottmann 2003: 118).

Sites that were systematically abandoned usually show finds patterns which are different to sites that were left abruptly and unexpectedly. A house which was left in the course of or after a damaging event and was subsequently not searched for objects, reused or rebuilt, will provide an entirely different archaeological picture than a house which was systematically given up. For a successful analysis of patterns of spatial distribution, excellent conditions of conservation have to occur: ideally, the complete destruction of a house, a whole settlement or a castle by fire or other damaging events (cf Bernbeck 1997: 189). Such features are often referred to as 'in situ'-situations. Their last part of primary formation was a damaging event like fire, earth quake or flooding. Due to these damaging events, the human beings at the site had no or only a little time to exert influence on the position of the artefacts and the composition of the artefact assemblages (Hakelberg 1996: 106). One can therefore assume that by the position of the objects or their association with other finds it is possible to infer how and what they were used for. Objects found in these features can be assigned to the topographic context they were found in. They were deposited at this place in the course of their last historical movement (Frommer 2007: 224). In the best examples, the feature shows a topographic link between repetitive, waste-producing processes, a good state of preservation of the characteristic objects and a lack of subsequent disturbances (Frommer & Kottmann 2003: 143). Because of their extraordinary depositional circumstances, features like these are often used in research on household activities (cf Allison 2002).

These archaeological features usually show the last state of usage of different objects, installations and buildings (Bernbeck 1997: 66f, 189). We have to consider the fact that the finds in these contexts were not discarded unselected and at the same time. Normally, material is discarded in a piecemeal fashion. Most of what we find archaeologically had contemporarily been considered and treated as waste (Bernbeck 1997: 66f; LaMotta & Schiffer 2002; on the

'Pompei-premise' see Frommer 2007: 223f and Sommer 1991). When an artefact is taken out of use, this usually goes along with spatial or formal changes (Neustupný 2009: 50). Even in houses that were still in use, you could find objects in archaeological contexts (*eg* objects in the dirt on the floors of houses at castle Romrod, Hessen/Germany; see Friedrich 2006: 166 and below). Furthermore, finds and features documented archaeologically do not necessarily have to reflect 'everyday life'. The destruction of a building might have been preceded by a longer period of exceptional living conditions, such as war or siege, for instance. Former inhabitants or others might also have returned to recover precious or useful objects (Sommer 1991: 105, 107).[8]

Some examples for domesticated space as seen in archaeological features

In the following, I would like to explore how distributional analyses can be used in medieval archaeology (with particular attention to houses) and what can be the specific strengths of the application of the different methods (for more examples regarding castles *cf* Schmid 2011).

Room functions

Distributional analysis within a site can be significant regarding the activities carried out within buildings. One of the methodological problems of the archaeological investigation of houses is the fact that mostly, upper floors are no longer extant. In situ-remains of occupation layers are often found in cellars or ground floors, whereas the surfaces of upper floors are often found as debris in these cellars or on ground level and can therefore not be documented in their original position. However, occasionally it is possible to detect floors which have collapsed in the course of a catastrophic event.

Intrasite analysis on a small scale was used to understand the functions of rooms and areas within a house at a site in Bourgogne in France. The results of this excavation were published in 1975 by Françoise

Piponnier and Jean-Marie Pesez. In an abandoned medieval settlement, the remains of house no. 2 were outstandingly well-preserved. It was destroyed by fire; its destruction was archaeologically dated to the 14th century. The layers of debris that covered the ruins could be separated and interpreted. The two front rooms showed trampled clay floors which seem to have been thoroughly cleared during the time the house was in use, as there were no traces of waste to be documented. These two front rooms had heating opportunities, one a hearth, and the other one a chimney. The inner rooms, which could not be entered from the outside but only through the front rooms, had rougher surfaces which appeared to have resulted in a greater preservation of surface deposits (Pesez 1975: 148; Piponnier 1975: 161/figure 16, 17). In the debris that covered the surfaces of the inner rooms, a layer of trampled clay was interpreted as the remains of an upper floor which had collapsed during the course of the fire. This assumption was also backed up by the position of broken and complete pots in these rooms (Pesez 1975: 147). One reason for the more thorough cleaning of the front rooms could have been the direct connection to the outside; the more uneven surfaces in the back rooms could also have added to this. However, the fixed-feature elements (hearth and chimney) as well as the differences in the regularity and intensity of their cleaning could also indicate diverging uses of the front and the back rooms, for example for living or storage.

In the outer bailey of the Swiss castle Mörsburg (Canton Zurich/Switzerland), the cellar of a house destroyed in a devastating fire around the year 1300 was also documented. The fire seems to have escalated so quickly, that no or only a few objects were retrieved. The cellar floors were covered with debris from the ground floor. Besides the skeleton of a cat that obviously got killed in the fire, the charred remains of plants and cereals were discovered, as well as – among other things – sickles, a knife and iron mounting and locks, most likely belonging to the doors of the cellar. The assemblage of the finds as well as the absence of objects directly related to dwelling supported the interpretation that the house was used as storage building (Kühn, Szostek & Windler 2002: 277-297).

The features discussed above are rare examples derived from outstanding preservation conditions. However, these provide a valuable insight into the use of a room or an outdoor area. One such small-scale feature shows an extraordinary linking of a fixed-feature element and a non-fixed-feature element at Castle Scheidegg (Canton Basel-Land/Switzerland), which was destroyed in a fire around the year 1320 and was excavated in 1975. In the inner castle, the remains of a tiled stove which was destroyed in the fire were documented. On top of the pile of stove tiles lay the remains of an aquamanile, a vessel used for washing hands before a meal was taken. This vessel which was made out of bronze is likely to have been put on top of the oven in order to warm the water before its use (Ewald & Tauber 1975: 38/Abb. 28, 84; Meyer 1975: 12).

In the town of Einbeck (Lower Saxony/Germany), a house destroyed in a devastating fire in 1540 was documented. The building was not rebuilt, and therefore the occupation layers were in a good state of preservation. The archaeologists were able to reconstruct the arrangement of the rooms. In one of these, the destruction layers showed no traces of subsequent disruption. In the debris at ground floor level, there were several tools (hammer, pliers, drill), and other useful objects (stud, knife, key, fire steel, dice, scale etc.). As all these finds were documented on an area of less than half a square meter, in a layer of burnt clay, it was assumed that these things had fallen down from an upper floor level from where they had perhaps been stored in a chest or drawer (Heege 2005: 20-24/figure 32; Heege & Frey-Kupper 2000).

Use of settlement areas

Distributional analysis can be used to understand the distribution of finds at a site and in this way find out about the use of different areas in a settlement. As Rapoport pointed out, it is not sufficient to only investigate single activities or buildings, but rather the systems of activities which take place in systems of settings should be investigated (Rapoport 1990a: 15).

An analysis of the spatial distribution of objects can facilitate the location of different activities in

sites, as well as the reconstruction of the activity areas of distinctive social groups: In 2008, Eva Svensson published her research on two Swedish villages (Skinnerud/Skramle) and two castles (Saxholmen/Edsholm). As part of this investigation, she carried out analyses of the distribution patterns of the finds at these sites. She divided the finds into 13 categories of activities such as handicraft, trade or home furnishings and building activity. On the basis of these data, she mapped the different activity areas with regard to spatial structures. Svensson evaluated the distribution maps regarding the different categories with special attention to their relationship with excavated constructions and, amongst others, chronological aspects (Svensson 2008: 154f, 260-266). In a final step, she connected the 13 find categories to categories such as gender or social position.[9] At castle Romrod (Hessen/Germany), due to extraordinary preservation conditions, the provisional wooden dwellings from the first building phase (dendrochronologically dated to 1193) could be documented. No social gradations could be inferred from their size and design (Friedrich 2006: 166). However, spatial analysis of the small finds which were found in great number in these buildings showed clear concentrations of objects which could be ascribed to certain areas of life or work or certain social groups (Friedrich 2006: 171/figure 8, 9).

The distribution of archaeological objects (including animal bones) can provide valuable information about 'everyday' processes. At castle Lanzenkirchen (Lower Austria/Austria), the ratio of fish scales to fishbone in different layers was analysed. In occupation layers, a lot of fish scales, but few fishbones were found. In refuse pits more fishbone and fewer fish scales were identified. Accordingly, it was possible to suggest that the activity of scaling fish seems to have taken place in the working areas of the castle, whereas most of the fishbones seem to have been discarded in refuse pits immediately after cooking and consumption (Galik 1999: 201/figure 4).

Distributional analysis can also allow for inferences about the changing use of buildings within a settlement or a castle over time. At Castle Scheidegg (Canton Basel-Land/Switzerland), distribution maps of the metal objects at the site show an area with a high number of metal objects and another with almost no metal objects. The area that was rich in finds seems to have been buried by the debris of a dwelling which was still in use – whereas the main tower, the older part of the castle, seems to have become redundant before the fire and had been thoroughly cleared of all valuable or useful objects (Ewald & Tauber 1975: 83, 113, 87/figure 53-55).

Conclusion

What kinds of information can be derived from spatial analysis? When looking for traces of activities in archaeologically-relevant features in houses, we must conclude that at the moment we are working with a very restricted data base. This makes it very hard to identify patterns or processes. Yet, it can be seen from the few examples I have chosen, that comprehensive spatial analysis can – as in the example of the comparison of hamlets and castles in Sweden by Eva Svensson – make visible differences and changes in ways of living in different surroundings. Intrasite analyses in buildings with dwelling functions but also in workshops or storage buildings can widen our understanding of how space was domesticated and used.

Trying to find a way of overcoming the polarities of historical-individualistic and sociological-natural scientific positions (on this see Gramsch 2000: 8, 10), we should dare to explore the full potential of the methods of spatial analysis. This implies, however, that we have to turn our attention in excavations to the distribution of small finds, in connection with a thorough documentation of the stratigraphy at a site. Regarding the search for agency, Matthew Johnson has called for the use of small-scale-studies as representatives of wider changes in both a temporal and spatial sense (Johnson 2000: 227). I am confident that the realization of a larger number of such small-scale-studies is an attainable goal for medieval archaeology and will provide a solid data set from which to start this study.

Notes

1. Assuming that it is possible to find social relationships by describing and analysing spatial relations (Hillier/ Hanson 1987: 198).

2. These maps were developed on the basis of assumptions regarding the decision processes according to which humans are moving within a system.
3. For an overview of Rapoport's work see Steadman 1996: 68-70.
4. In this context, by 'social goods' („soziale Güter") M. Löw primarily means 'material goods' („materielle Güter"), as only those can be placed („da nur diese platzierbar sind") (Löw 2001: 234).
5. For the different methods and on the interdisciplinary demands of this type of sources see Grenville 1997: 1-22; Altwasser/Klein 2000 and Baeriswyl 2000.
6. As an example, fixed feature-elements such as the platform of a tiled stove in a room with wall paintings at castle Rehberg in Krems/Austria can be named (Kreitner 1993: 110f/Abb. 17, 18).
7. On the second floor of the town house "Zum Schwert" in Zurich/Switzerland, the organisation of a hotel kitchen built in 1762 could be 'read' from the traces of wear on the sand stone floor (Schneider, Wyss & Hanser 1996: 17 and 20/figures 36, 37). As further examples for traces of usage which are connected to the house, the negative imprints of wooden chambers which have been found at several castles and town houses in Austria and Germany can be named. These smoke-free rooms are likely to have been used as parlours (Reichhalter 2006).
8. An example can be named from the town of Einbeck (Lower Saxony, Germany), which was destroyed in a devastating fire in 1540. In the burnt layers markedly little material was found, apart from nails, stove tiles or roof tiles. These layers seem to have been searched for usable items after the fire or in the course of the rebuilding (Heege 2005: 19).
9. For the hypotheses on gender and social status used by Svensson see Svensson 2008: 157/footnote 5.

References

Alexandre, D. (1990) Home, sweet home: confort et bien-être domestique aux XIVe et XVe siècles à travers les miniatures. In: *L'idée de bonheur au moyen âge*, ed. D. Buschinger, 31-48. Göppinger Arbeiten zur Germanistik 414. Göppingen: Kümmerle.

Allison, P.M. (2002 (1999)) Introduction. In: *The Archaeology of Household Activities*, ed. P.M. Allison, 1-18. London: Routledge.

Altwasser, E. (2000) Archäologie im Obergeschoss. In: *Bauforschung und Archäologie. Stadt- und Siedlungsentwicklung im Spiegel der Baustrukturen*, ed. D. Schumann, 44-60. Berlin: Lukas.

Altwasser, E. & U. Klein (2000) Heutiger Stand und zukünftige Entwicklungsmöglichkeiten einer Archäologie des Hauses. In: *Freilichtmuseum und Sachkultur*, eds. J. Carstensen & J. Kleinmanns, 41-59. Münster/New York/München/Berlin: Waxmann.

Baeriswyl, A. (2000) Wo ist die Höhe Null? Über die angebliche Grenze zwischen Bauforschung und Bodenarchäologie. In: *Bauforschung und Archäologie. Stadt- und Siedlungsentwicklung im Spiegel der Baustrukturen*, ed. D. Schumann, 21-31. Berlin: Lukas.

Bedal, K. (1993) *Historische Hausforschung. Eine Einführung in Arbeitsweise, Begriffe und Literatur.* Quellen und Materialien zur Hausforschung in Bayern 6 = Schriften und Kataloge des Fränkischen Freilandmuseums Bad Windsheim 18. Bad Windsheim: Fränkisches Freilandmuseum.

Bedal, K. (2004) Über die Bedeutung der Ausstattung für die Hausforschung. In: *Historische Ausstattung, Jahrbuch für Hausforschung 50*, eds. U. Großmann et al, 31-39. Marburg: Jonas.

Bernbeck, R. (1997) *Theorien in der Archäologie.* Tübingen: A. Francke.

Binford, L. (1981) Behavioral Archaeology and the Pompeji Premise, *Journal of Anthropological Research 37*, 195-208.

Binford, L. (1983) *In Pursuit of the Past: Decoding the Archaeological Record.* London: Thames and Hudson.

Blanton, R.E. (1994) *Houses and Households. A Comparative Study.* Interdisciplinary Contributions to Archaeology. New York: Plenum Press.

Ciolek-Torrello, R. (1984) An alternative model of room function from Grasshopper Pueblo, Arizona. In: *Intrasite Spatial Analysis in Archaeology*, ed. H. Hietala, 127-153. Cambridge: CUP Archive.

Craane, M. (2009) The Medieval Urban 'Movement Economy'. Using Space Syntax in the Study of Medieval Towns as Exemplified by the Town of 's-Hertogenbosch, the Netherlands. In: *Proceedings of the 7th International Space Syntax Symposium*, eds. D. Koch, L. Marcus Lars & J. Jesper, 019:1-14. Stockholm: Royal Institute of Technology. Online: http://www.sss7.org/Proceedings_list.html (19.01.2012).

Dafinger, A. (2010) Die Durchlässigkeit des Raums: Potenzial und Grenzen des *Space-Syntax*-Modells aus sozialanthropologischer Sicht. In: *Der gebaute Raum. Bausteine einer Architektursoziologie vormoderner Gesellschaften*, eds. P. Trebsche & N. Müller-Scheeßel & S. Reinhold, 123-142. Tübinger Archäologische Taschenbücher 7. Münster/New York/München/Berlin: Waxmann.

Dixon, P. (1998) Design in castle-building: the controlling of access to the Lord, *Château Gaillard. Etudes de Castellologie medievale 18*, 47-57.

Eggert, M.K.H. (2006) *Archäologie: Grundzüge einer Historischen Kulturwissenschaft.* Tübingen: Francke.

Ewald, J. & J. Tauber (1975) *Die Burgruine Scheidegg bei Gelterkinden.* Schweizer Beiträge zur Kulturgeschichte und Archäologie des Mittelalters 2. Olten/Freiburg i. Br.: Walter.

Friedrich, W. (2006) Die sozialen Strukturen in der Burg Romrod anhand des archäologischen Fundmaterials, *Château Gaillard. Etudes de Castellologie medievale 22*, 163-174.

Frommer, S. (2007) *Historische Archäologie. Versuch einer methodologischen Grundlegung der Archäologie als Geschichtswissenschaft.* Tübinger Forschungen zur historischen Archäologie 2. Büchenbach: Dr. Faustus.

Frommer, S. & A. Kottmann (2003) Zur archäologischen Rekonstruktion von Produktionssequenzen. Das Beispiel der Flachglasproduktion Glaswasen, *Zeitschrift für Archäologie des Mittelalters 31*, 115-144.

Galik, A. (1999) Fischreste aus mittelalterlichen bis neuzeitlichen Fundstellen: Bedeutung und Aussagekraft dieser kleinen archäozoologischen Funde, *Beiträge zur Mittelalterarchäologie in Österreich 15*, 197-206.

Gifford, D.P. (1978) Ethnoarchaeological observations of natural processes affecting cultural materials. In: *Explorations in Ethnoarchaeology*, ed. R. Gould Richard, 77-101. Albuquerque, New Mexico: University of Mexico Press.

Gramsch, A. (2000) Vom Vergleichen in der Archäologie – Zur Einführung. In: *Vergleichen als archäologische Methode: Analogien in den Archäologien*, ed. A. Gramsch, 3-17. British Archaeological Reports, International Series 825. Oxford: Archaeopress.

Grenville, J. (1997) *Medieval Housing.* The Archaeology of Medieval Britain. London: Leicester University Press.

Grenville, J. (2000) Houses and Households in Late Medieval England: An Archaeological Perspective. In: *Medieval women: Texts and Contexts in late medieval Britain 3*, ed. J. Wogan-Browne et al., 309-328. Turnhout: Brepols.

Hakelberg, D. (1996) Materielle Kultur: Zu Überlieferung und Interpretation. Realienforschung und historische Quellen, *Archäologische Mitteilungen aus Nordwestdeutschland* Beiheft 15, 101-114.

Heege, A. (2005) Einbeck 1540: Brandstiftung! Der Einbecker Stadtbrand vom 26. Juli 1540 – Archäologischer Befund und politische Hintergründe. Einbeck: Einbecker Geschichtsverein.

Heege, A. & S. Frey-Kupper (2000) Großvaters Truhe?, *Archäologie in Niedersachsen 3*, 114-115.

Hillier, B. & J. Hanson (1987) Introduction: A Second Paradigm, *Architecture et Comportement/Architecture and Behaviour 3/3*, 197-199.

Johnson, M.H. (2000) Conceptions of Agency in Archaeological Interpretation. In: *Interpretive Archaeology: a Reader*, ed. J. Thomas, 211-227. London: Leicester University Press.

Kaspar, F. (1998) Das mittelalterliche Haus als öffentlicher und privater Raum. In: *Die Vielfalt der Dinge. Neue Wege zur Analyse mittelalterlicher Sachkultur*, eds. H. Hundsbichler, G. Jaritz & T. Kühtreiber, 207-235. Forschungen des Instituts für Realienkunde des Mittelalters und der frühen Neuzeit. Diskussionen und Materialien 3. Wien: Verlag der Österreichischen Akademie der Wissenschaften.

Kienlin, T.L. (1998) Die britische Processual Archaeology und die Rolle David L. Clarkes und Colin Renfrews: Herausbildung, Struktur, Einfluß. In: *Theorie in der Archäologie. Zur englischsprachigen Diskussion*, eds.

M.K.H. Eggert & U. Veit, 67-114. Tübinger Archäologische Taschenbücher 1. Münster: Waxmann.

Klein, U. (2007) Spuren von Nutzungen – Nutzungsspuren. In: *Spuren der Nutzung in historischen Bauten,* eds. M. Goer et al, 105-114. Jahrbuch für Hausforschung 54. Marburg: Jonas.

Kreitner, T. (1993) Ausgrabungsarbeiten auf der Burgruine Rehberg, *Fundberichte aus Österreich* 31/1992, 107-119. Horn: Bundesdenkmalamt.

Kühn, M., R. Szostek & R. Windler (2002) Äpfel, Birnen und Nüsse – Funde und Befunde eines Speicherbaus des 13. Jahrhunderts bei der Mörsburg, *Archäologie im Kanton Zürich* 1999-2000, 271-308.

Kühtreiber, K. (2006) Archäologisch erschließbare Nutzungsräume und -areale in der Burg Dunkelstein, Niederösterreich – Ein Vorbericht. In: *Castrum Bene 8 – Burg und Funktion,* eds. M. Krenn & A. Krenn-Leeb, 145-164. Wien: Österreichische Gesellschaft für Ur- und Frühgeschichte.

LaMotta, V.M. & M.B. Schiffer (1999) Introduction. In: *The Archaeology of Household Activities,* ed. P.M. Allison, 19-26. London: Routledge.

Locock, M. (ed.) (1994) *Meaningful Architecture: Social Interpretations of Buildings.* Worldwide Archaeology Series 9. Avebury: Aldershot.

Löw, M. (2001) *Raumsoziologie.* Frankfurt a. M.: Suhrkamp Verlag.

Löw, M., S. Steets & S. Stoetzer (2008) *Einführung in die Stadt- und Raumsoziologie.* Opladen: Barbara Budrich.

Meckseper, C. (2002) Raumdifferenzierungen im hochmittelalterlichen Burgenbau Mitteleuropas, *Château Gaillard. Etudes de Castellologie medievale* 20, 163-171.

Meyer, W. (1975) Der historische Rahmen. In: *Die Burgruine Scheidegg bei Gelterkinden,* eds. J. Ewald & J. Tauber, 120-128. Schweizer Beiträge zur Kulturgeschichte und Archäologie des Mittelalters 2. Olten/Freiburg i. Br.: Walter.

Neustupný, E. (2009) *Archaeological Method.* Cambridge: Cambridge University Press.

Pesez, J.M. (1975) Une maison villageoise au XIVe siècle: les structures, *Rotterdam Papers* II, 139-149.

Piponnier, F. (1975) Une maison villageoise au XIVe siècle: le mobilier, *Rotterdam Papers* II, 151-170.

Rapoport, A. (1990a) Systems of activities and systems of settings. In: *Domestic architecture and the use of space: an interdisciplinary cross-cultural study,* ed. S. Kent, 9-20. New Directions in Archaeology. Cambridge: Cambridge University Press.

Rapoport, A. (1990b) *The Meaning of the Built Environment: a Nonverbal Communication Approach.* Tucson: University of Arizona Press.

Reichhalter, G. (2006) „Blockwerkkammern" des 13. bis 15. Jahrhunderts aus österreichischen Burgen. In: *Castrum Bene 8 – Burg und Funktion,* eds. M. Krenn & A. Krenn-Leeb, 179-192. Wien: Österreichische Gesellschaft für Ur- und Frühgeschichte.

Saunders, T. (1990) The Feudal Construction of Space: Power and Domination in the Nucleated Village. In: *The Social Archaeology of Houses,* ed. R. Samson, 181-195. Edinburgh: Edinburgh University Press.

Schiffer, M. B. (1976) *Behavioral Archaeology.* New York: Academic Press.

Schiffer, M. B. (1996) *Formation Processes of the Archaeological Record.* Salt Lake City: University of Utah Press.

Schmid, C. (2011) Raumfunktionen und Ausstattungsmuster auf Burgen – die Möglichkeiten der Archäologie, *Mittelalter – Moyen Age – Medioevo – Temp medieval* 4/2011, 155-180.

Schmidt, D. (2005) Die Lesbarkeit des Abfalls: Zur Entdeckung materieller Unkultur als Objekt archäologischen Wissens. In: *Die Dinge als Zeichen: Kulturelles Wissen und materielle Kultur,* ed. T. Kienlin, 239-254. Universitätsforschungen zur Prähistorischen Archäologie 127. Bonn: Habelt.

Schneider, J.E.,F. Wysss & J. Hanser (1996) Das Haus „Zum Schwert" in Zürich – vom Wohnturm zur Standes- und Nobelherberge am Limmatbrückenkopf, *Mittelalter – Moyen Age – Medioevo – Temp medieval* 1/1, 3-28.

Scholkmann, B. (1997/98) Archäologie des Mittelalters und der Neuzeit heute. Eine Standortbestimmung im interdisziplinären Kontext, *Zeitschrift für Archäologie des Mittelalters* 25/26, 7-18.

Shanks, M. & I. Hodder (2006) Processual, postprocessual and interpretive archaeologies. In: *Interpreting Archaeology. Finding meanings in the past,* eds. I. Hodder, M. Shanks & A. Alexandrini et al, 3-29. Oxon: Routledge.

Seibert, J. (2006) Introduction. In: *Space and Spatial Analysis in Archaeology* (Papers originally presented at the Conference: Space and Spatial Analysis in Archaeology held at the University of Calgary, Nov. 18th, 2002), eds. E.C. Robertson et al, xiii-xxiv. Calgary: University of Calgary Press.

Sommer, U. (1991) Zur Entstehung archäologischer Fundvergesellschaftungen. Versuch einer archäologischen Taphonomie, *Universitätsforschungen zur Prähistorischen Archäologie* 6, 53-193.

South, S. (2002) *Method and Theory in Historical Archaeology.* New York: Percheron Press.

Steadman, S.R. (1996) Recent Research in the Archaeology of Architecture: Beyond the Foundations, *Journal of Archaeological Research* 4/1, 51-90.

Svensson, E. (2008) *The Medieval Household. Daily Life in Castles and Farmsteads. Scandinavian Examples in their European Context.* The Medieval Countryside 2. Turnhout: Brepols.

Uhl, S. (2004) Das Hauptgebäude der Burgruine Albeck bei Sulz a. N. Dübel- und Klobenlöcher als Hinweise auf Grundrissgliederung und Wohnausstattung, *Burgen und Schlösser. Zeitschrift der Deutschen Burgenvereinigung e.V. für Burgenkunde und Denkmalpflege* 45/4, 225-232.

Virágos, G. (2006) *The Social Archaeology of Residential Sites.* British Archaeological Reports International Series 1583, Central European Series 3. Oxford: Archaeolingua.

PART 2

Regions and Regionality

The Rural Home. Local or 'European' Style?

Eva Svensson

Abstract

Nobles and castles are often referred to as a European heritage, whereas peasants and rural settlements are considered part of regional or local contexts. In this article the participation of peasants in cross-regional or international trading networks are also explored. Also, a few rural settlements from different part of Europe are compared to common themes occurring on medieval castles. From this examination two possible observations emerge. First, that a more closed spatial structuring of buildings on rural settlements could have been inspired by the shape of castles. Second, that the, on older rural sites, common multifunctional longhouses were transformed and inserted as space for community both at castles and at rural settlements in medieval times. However, the longhouse being rather a global than a European phenomenon, suggests a global perspective to be more fruitful than a European.

Introduction

When investigating rural settlements and peasants' homes, we often refer our findings to local or regional historical traditions. In contrast, castles, lords and knights are associated with more European cultural, elitist expressions, even if the castle and the village were close neighbours in space and time, and might, upon closer examination, share several traits. In fact they are seldom compared, because they were seldom excavated or investigated by the same scholar, at the same time, in the same context or in the same research framework.

In this article I will look more closely at some high- and late-middle age rural settlements from a comparative perspective, using the concepts of spatial and social identities. Although rural settlements from different parts of Europe are drawn into the discussion, the core of the investigation will be the Swedish context.[1] I will start by discussing the concepts of local and regional identity, 'Europeanization' and social collectives, then move on to castles and rural settlements and end by discussing the style of daily life at home in rural contexts.

Local and regional identity (?)

There are long-standing traditions of studying rural population and settlements from regional or local perspectives (Rösener 1995: 7). When industrialization and urbanization in the 19th century radically changed both demographic and social landscapes, history, tradition and nature stood out as stabilizing factors in a troubled world (Skoglund & Svensson 2010; Ödmann et al 1982). Nature reserves and open-air museums displaying rural homes from different regions with specific regional properties were created as means of educating the growing working class and creating common national values. The Swedish open air-museum *Skansen* in Stockholm hosted farmsteads from various parts of Sweden. In this way, urban workers, many of whom had moved into Stockholm from the countryside, were still able to find places resembling traditional concepts of 'home' on a Sunday visit with their families.

The assumption that peasants were strongly influenced by traditions and by awareness of local and regional identity was also emphasized by the ethnologists who studied ancient peasant society mainly in the early 20th century. Different ways of designing tools, fences and houses were considered parts of the regional and local peasant identity (eg Erixon & Campbell 1957). Also, local, traditional costumes were part of the 'localisation' of peasants in the academic world and history writing, and are still regularly worn as part of costumed interpretation at folk life museums and heritage attractions and on festive occasions.

This approach to heritage derived from ethnologists had a powerful impact on the comparatively late move by Swedish medieval archaeologists to study the countryside (Bentz 2008). The regionalized types of houses, fences, modes of agriculture and shapes of tools organized by the ethnologists often served as models for interpretation of archaeological remains. As the archaeological remains appeared to meet preconceived expectations, the information from the ethnologists seemed very useful. But these ethnological types also risked to serve as a blue-print for archaeological interpretation thus, uncritically, enforcing the idea of a regionalized countryside and preventing archaeologists from developing new analyses of the data.

Of course, regionality and locality were an important part of Swedish and European rural life, and exerted a profound effect on material culture. An example is the 'high loft cottage' (Swedish: 'högloftsstuga'). This type has been of significance in generating a distinctive sense of identity to the former border areas between medieval Denmark and Sweden. The same areas were also known for the peasants from both sides of the borders taking political initiatives and making their own peace treaties in times of national, or royal, war enterprises (Andrén 2000, see also Anglert 2008).

Perhaps a more useful question for archaeologists to ask is therefore whether peasant life was limited to the local and regional arena? Furthermore, it might be useful to question the apparent homogeneity of peasant material culture and question what the evidence might be for social, economic and political differences within and between different peasant communities.

'Europeanization' (?)

For some time there has been an opinion that a collective modern EU identity, with flairs of cultural superiority, can be forged from ethno-cultural attributes such as origin, cultural heritage, religion and so forth (Hansen 2000, see also Duroselle 1990). However, there is a danger that this modern emphasis on the homogeneity of the European community is a Eurocentric trap, especially when the emergence of the European Union is presented as the inevitable end of an historical process. Influential studies of 'the making of' medieval Europe depart from Western Europe as the norm, based on the heritage from the Roman empire, channeled through the Carolingian empire, together with the Catholic church and intellectual traditions from the classic literature and science (Bartlett 1994; Dawson 2003; Le Goff 2005).

In contrast to studies on 'the making of Europe' which search deliberately for common roots, it has been suggested that a process of 'Europeanization' took place in the period 1100-1400. This is a variation on Immanuel Wallerstein's world systems theory, at the centre of which was the network, ideology and organization of the Catholic Church (Blomkvist 2004; Wallerstein 1974-89). Trade has been argued to have been an alternative driver for another world system with a more global scope, emerging from the European subsystem in the 13th and 14th centuries (Abu-Lughod 1999).

Whether discussing the roots of Europe, or the process of 'Europeanization', the concept of European identity is often an elite identity centered around the Catholic Church, and the system of knights and castles, not peasants and farmsteads, and in fundamental opposition to the Muslim world. Ideology, the technology of warfare, architecture and fashion were features which supposedly united representatives of a European elite. However, it is worth noting that although exceptions were made for individual rulers, in fact Continental observers often struggled to include the Nordic region as a whole within the chivalric sphere. The Nordic variation of chivalry had limitations that were probably linked to economic restrictions and a very different domestic mentality. For instance, representations of courtesy and chivalric love appear to have been difficult to digest in Scandinavia (Bengtsson 1999). Indeed, there are more tournaments taking place in Sweden today, than there were during the medieval period!

Because peasants were not considered part of the pan European elite identity, there have been few attempts to explore the existence of a common 'peasant culture' within medieval Europe. However, if the idea of a common elite identity throughout medieval Europe is abandoned and the idea of 'Europeanization' and the two world systems models described above are reconsidered, other possibilities present themselves. The importance of trade should be emphasized. We know that objects and raw-materials travelled far from the place of production or extraction, as 'alien' objects and materials are often found in excavations not just of high-status medieval sites such as towns, castles and ecclesiastical institutions but also rural settlements. Moreover, objects did not travel alone but were usually accompanied by people. In contrast to the picture of the immovable peasant painted by earlier research, several recent studies have shown that peasants, not least from so-called marginal mountainous and forested areas, were active parts of trading networks (see examples *eg* in Andersson et al 1998, Holm et al 2005). Thus, it seems likely that medieval peasants not only encountered material culture from other parts of the world, but also people and ideas.

Social collectives

In the past, a nobleman was recognizable simply by being taller than others, but there were also other means of distinguishing between people such as fashion and a manner of speaking (Reuter 2000). Thus there were observable differences and similarities communicated among and between people and groups. The term 'social collective' emphasises the presence of a binding set of ideas about what was or should be shared by a group (Hermansson 2004). This social identity was then communicated inside and outside the group, not least through material culture. Here, nobles and peasants are considered to be two social collectives that were institutionalised during the medieval period into different estates. Unlike many other European countries, Swedish peasants were a separate estate as opposed to being in the so-called third estate together with the bourgeoisie.

The consolidation of different social collectives as estates was part of a major process of change experienced by Swedish society during the medieval period. This process also included the emergence of the state, the enhanced power of the king and the institutionalization of the Catholic Church. The emergence of estates had consequences not only for the privileges and obligations of medieval society, but also required the construction and reproduction of different social, and collective, identities as markers of distinction. The overt demonstration of aristocratic identity and ideology through the adoption of court culture was vital to the nobility. In reality, however, the boundaries between peasants and nobles were not absolute, and there was mobility between these two social groups (Småberg 2004).

Nobles emerged mainly from the peasant collective, and there were many points of contact between the groups throughout the medieval period, not least because both groups were ultimately living off the land. Unlike the nobility, there is little evidence that the peasantry sought to express a demonstratively idealized self-portrait of themselves. That does not mean that the peasantry did not have ideals concerning behavior and appearance, but the written source materials permit few meetings with medieval peasants, few opportunities to gain an insight into individual fates. Peasants are therefore often presumed having monotonous lives governed by the seasons and harvests.

Peasantry did not express identity that corresponded to the court culture. Or, if they did, it was not channeled through the written source material. Instead, our understanding of medieval peasants has much to do with opinions about the peasantry expressed by other social groups, and of our own views of lower orders in the modern period. One thing that makes it harder to understand the nature of a medieval peasant, is the confusion between our modern, urban, description of a profession and a medieval social identity or position. In Swedish, the term for peasant (Swedish: 'bonde') originally indicated a propertied person who lived on the land, and had access to possibilities in society (Dovring 1953: 92). The relegation of the peasantry to a lower social position was intimately connected with the estab-

Figure 1. 'Heraldic' mount found at the medieval hamlet of Skramle, Sweden. The mount should be interpreted as a means of communicating that peasants should be seen as a strong social station in society. Photo Bengt Holter, Projekt Skramle. After Svensson 2008: fig. 45.

lishment of nobles as a separate social status group in the late 13th century.

Compared with the rest of Europe, Swedish peasants held a relatively strong social position and this, to some extent, must have been due to the large numbers of property-owning peasants within Swedish society (Figure 1). According to the first records of land ownership dating from the early 16th century, around 50% of estates were taxed and owned by the peasants, with the remainder rented out and inhabited by tenants. Of the total amount of leased land, around 5% was owned by the crown, 21% by the nobility and the church respectively. It is estimated that the proportion of types of land (tax classification) remained relatively constant after the latter part of the 14th century and that the proportion of taxed land was previously larger (Lindkvist & Ågren 1985: 30ff). It is also probable that the kind of social and political culture which emerges from sources for early modern Sweden, with clear evidence of negotiation and compromise between power elites and subalterns, was also in place in the medieval period. Written sources from the early modern period present the peasantry as active and self-aware in dialogue with the authorities (Österberg 1989, see also Aronsson 1992).

Of course, neither nobles nor peasants formed homogenous social collectives. Economic status and potential varied both within and between the collectives. There were also other kinds of networks which impacted on daily life, not least those related to trade. These networks are clearly visible in Swedish homes, regardless of whether they were castles or farmsteads.

Castles

When assigning a common set of ideals and perceptions to the European nobility it seems likely that such ideals should form part of the 'package'. However, in Sweden and Scandinavia few noble families owned castles, as castle building during most of the Middle Ages was a royal prerogative. Castles were therefore more likely to be built by the Crown and inhabited by royal bailiffs collecting taxes, rather than the homes of the nobility.

Many medieval Swedish castles appear relatively small and simple in comparison with their European counterparts (Figure 2). The timber construction of these buildings may also have added a sense of ephemerality to the impression they made on visitors. This was underlined by the fact that most Swedish castles were burned down in the Engelbrekt rebellion of 1434 and not rebuilt (Lovén 1996). In Sweden castles never came to characterize rural or urban landscapes, although there were regional exceptions such as Småland, with a relatively large number of nobles, where large and important castles were more common and influential in the landscape (Hansson 2001). When comparing Swedish castles and their 'cousins' in other marginal corners of Europe, with the grander castles in more central Continental areas, differences seem readily apparent. However, when examined more closely a number of similarities are also evident. A good way of describing the phenomenon is by using the concept of grammar. There seems to have been an overarching castle grammar shared by small and grand castles, masonry and wooden castles, and those owned by the aristocracy and royal

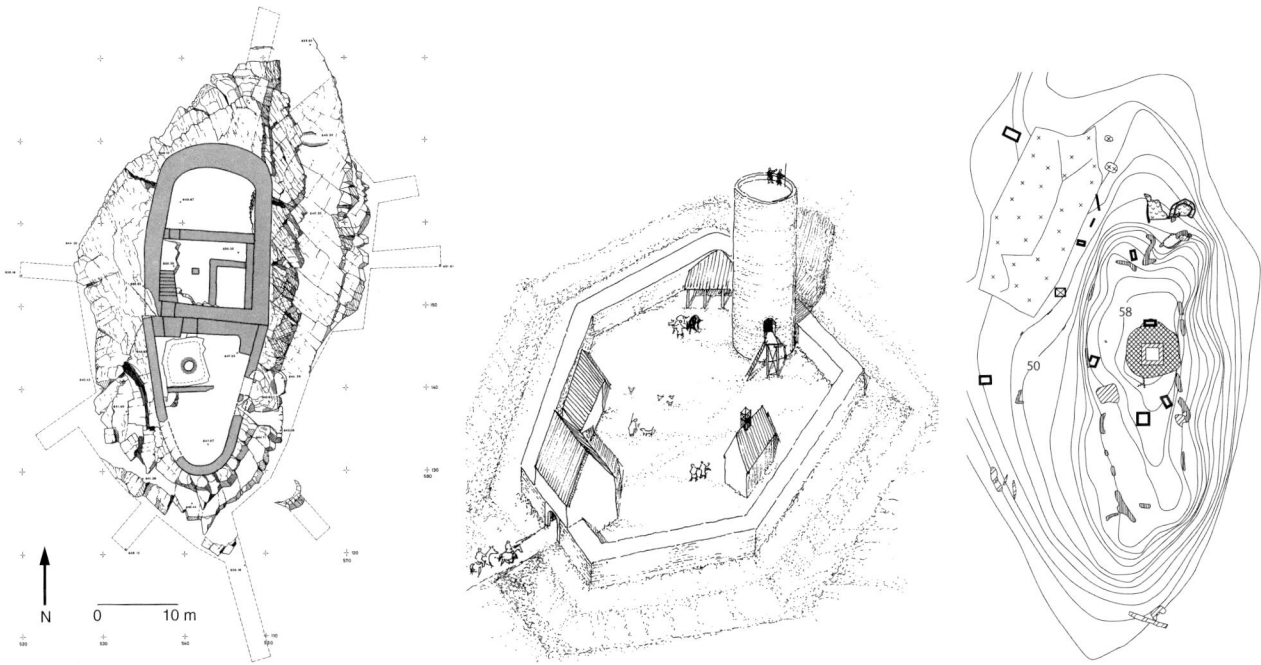

Figure 2. The castles of Alt-Warburg, Switzerland (left); Schnellerts, Germany (middle); Saxholmen, Sweden (right). Alt-Warburg after Meyer 1974: fig. 4; Schnellerts after Krauskopf 1995: fig. 20. Figure compiled by author.

castles (see *eg* Dixon 1998; Hansson 2006; Johnson 2002; Svensson 2008).

First, castles seek to dominate or control the landscape in which they are located. The physical or visual dominance or 'control' of roads, towns or a geographical area is a common feature of this relationship, often achieved through the setting or construction of the castle in an elevated position. Second, and closely related to this, castles tend to have a distinctive relationship with water, often surrounded by an artificial moat, or set on an island and thus surrounded by a lake. Third, castles tend to have a rounded shape, at least before the arrival of cannons had made an impact on castle architecture. Fourth, the interior of castles is characterized by the social segregation of space. Over time the basic division between main castle and bailey, which can be shaped in various ways, is supplemented with more refined means of segregation such as different table practices. Also, there is spatial gender division highlighted by the ladies' quarter where femininity was displayed and practiced in various ways such as sewing. Fifth, paradoxically, there were special assembly buildings or rooms, halls, in the castle uniting the otherwise segregated garrison at least on festive occasions.

Lastly, even if the surroundings were played in different ways, and both proximity and distance to 'lay' settlement were used as means of enforcing control or power, there were still common elements acted out in the landscape such as fish ponds and deer parks. Not all castles possessed all of the elements of this grammar, but enough to communicate a sense of 'castle-ness' to their audiences. This raises the question of whether aspects of this grammar influenced the structuring of adjacent rural settlements as well?

Rural settlements – a trip across Europe

Rural settlements are even more erratic than castles. Economy, topography, demography, climate, community, local and regional traditions, ownership or not, were, to name some, factors at play in shaping rural settlements; villages, hamlets or dispersed settlements. The following section explores four examples, from the British Isles in the west to the Czech Republic in the east (Figure 3).

In Derbyshire, England, a site called *Hill Top Farm* was excavated in 1992-95 (Makepeace 2001). The site was dated to *c* the 13th and 14th centuries. The settlement, a single farmstead, was part of a general upland expansion associated with sheep, and the increased trade in wool and fleece. The farmstead consisted of two houses (buildings B and C) adjacent to a courtyard and a long barn off the courtyard. House B was a dwelling house, whereas the function of house C is unknown. The houses were built in limestone with shell walls (double walls) with rubble filling. Older building traditions, based on wooden constructions had been ignored in favour of the local limestone. The largest building, the long barn, measured 20 x 5 m. It was one-aisled, with remaining limestone walls over half a meter high.

The finds material included pottery, nails, knives, spindle whorls, a few items relating to clothing and personal adornment and animal bones. Among the finds were some items of copper, *eg* a buckle, a fragment of jet and an oyster shell.

The inhabitants of Hill Top Farm were involved in a commercial enterprise, raising sheep and producing wool, centered on a market. They appear to have been fairly well off, eating oysters, and also bold enough to break old traditions like using the traditional building material, wood. Maybe the limestone buildings were modeled after desirable originals encountered in new places?

Across the channel, in Holland on the arm of river Daver, the rural settlement of *Huis Malburg* was excavated in 1997-98 (Oudhof et al. 2000). The settlement was an agrarian unit, focused on cattle breeding. Most of the remains were dated to *c* AD 1050-1225 (period 4), but there were also indications of earlier settlements at the site. From period 4 there were traces of seven buildings with different subphases, four wells and seven round stack barns.

According to the excavation results a standard farmstead at Huis Malburg comprised living quarters, farm buildings, a number of stack barns and a well. The convex, or ship-like, buildings with daubed, plaited walls match the super-regional building traditions (Gasselte type buildings), but there were also special local characteristics, for

instance roof tiles. The finds material was relatively rich, for instance several buckles including an exclusive clasp from Limoges, several spurs, arrowheads and coins. Thus, the settlement appears to have been fairly well off, and it is not known why it was deserted.

Northwest of Huis Malburg, in northern Germany, large parts of the rural settlement of *Dalem* were excavated in 1977-86 (Zimmerman 1991). The settlement could be dated to AD 600-1340, when the inhabitants moved to the grounds of a monastery.

From the outset, the settlement structure was characterized by special-purpose buildings housing different activities instead of multi-functional long houses. Until the 10th century a 'standard' farmstead in Dalem consisted of a one-aisled main building, used for household activities and related handicrafts, a stable / cattle byre, and sunken floor buildings often used for weaving. In the 9th/10th centuries the rectangular houses were replaced by ship-formed buildings. In turn these were sometimes later replaced by rectangular buildings. With the change in building style the farms in Dalem consisted of these dwelling houses, storage houses, stackbarns and stables /cattle byres until the desertion.

In Dalem there was also, during the period AD 800-1300, a special building. It was an unusually large, *c* 36 m long and 9-10 m wide, rectangular wooden building. The building was rebuilt a couple of times, but remained a constant feature in Dalem until the time of desertion. Due to the finds material not having been processed, the status of the village is hard to assess.

From Germany we move to the Czech Republic in the east. The archaeological investigations at the village of *Bystřec*, north-east of the city of Brno were carried out between 1975 and 1998. Bystřec has been almost completely examined, and parts of the material have been published over the years (*eg* Belcredi 2000). The village was established in the 13th century and deserted in the early 15th century, probably due to military unrest. It was quite a large village situated on both banks of a river along a trading route. During the excavations nineteen farmsteads on sixteen tofts were identified, but there are probably a few more farmsteads left to discover.

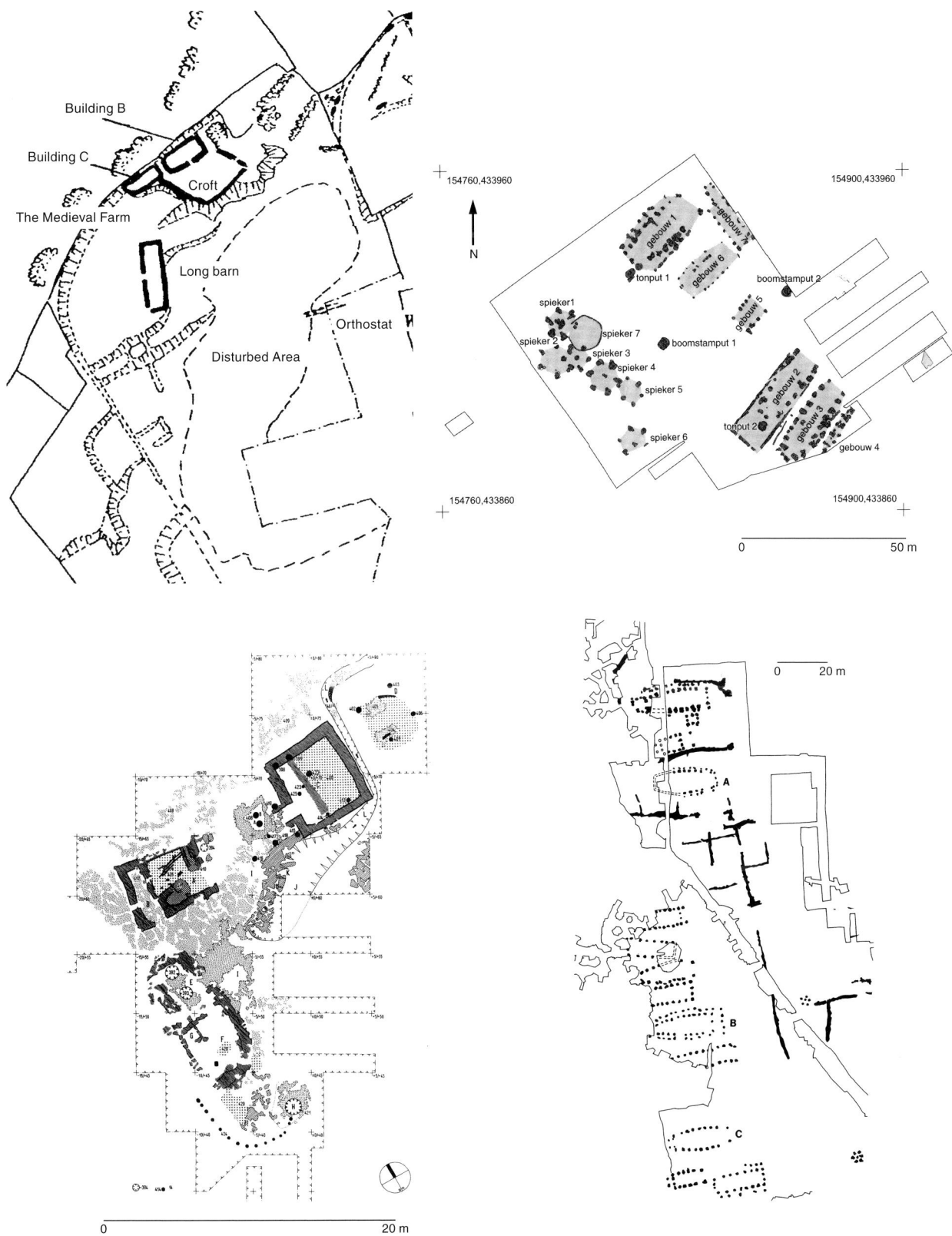

*Figure 3. The rural settlements Hill Top Farm (above, left); Huis Malburg (above right), Byst*ř*ec, farmstead X (below, left); Dalem (below, right). Hill Top Farm after Makepeace 2001, detail of fig. 2; Huis Malburg after Oudhof et al. 2000: fig. 3:6; Byst*ř*ec after Belcredi 2000: fig. 4; Dalem after Zimmerman 1991: fig. 7. Figure compiled by author.*

The individual farmsteads were very similar, L-shaped with stone-paved courtyards. Initially, the houses were built in daubed wattle, later replaced by timber buildings with stone cellars or buildings entirely of stone. There were also other features discovered in the village such as threshing floor, grain store and other stores, wells and dunghills. In the finds material there were coins, arrowheads, knives and some weapons.

Bystřec stands out as a large and fairly well off village, connected with a larger world through the trading route passing by the village. Still, the village was not strong enough to survive uneasy times.

The four rural settlements have, and rightly so, been placed in their local and regional contexts. When it comes to Hill Top Farm, the importance of market forces have also been emphasized. The settlements have been built in local or regional traditions, apart from Hill Top Farm, using local material. But if shifting perspective to a broader view (see Figure 3), there are two observations worth noting. First, in the two older settlements Huis Malburg and Dalem, the buildings and structures are placed in rows as if along a path or a green. In the younger settlements Hill Top

Farm and Bystřec, the buildings are rather organized in relation to a yard in an encircling, almost closing, way. In Bystřec these two spatial principles meet, as the tofts in the village were placed in rows on the river banks, but the buildings in the individual tofts related to yard in an L-shaped manner. Second, long buildings, be it dwelling houses, assembly houses or barns/outhouses, stand out as significant markers in the settlements even if the practice of the multifunctional longhouse was abandoned.

Moving north...

The sparsely populated mountainous or forested areas of Scandinavia are often suggested to be fundamentally different from the rest of Europe (*eg* Sandnes 1991: 213). Two excavated examples of rural settlements, *Skinnerud* and *Skramle*, located in the sparsely populated, forested areas of western Sweden are here used to explore similarities in the 'grammar' of space with the Swedish castles discussed above (Andersson & Svensson 2002; Emanuelsson et al. 2003) (Figure 4).

To Skinnerud and Skramle the surrounding forested landscapes were of great importance for both

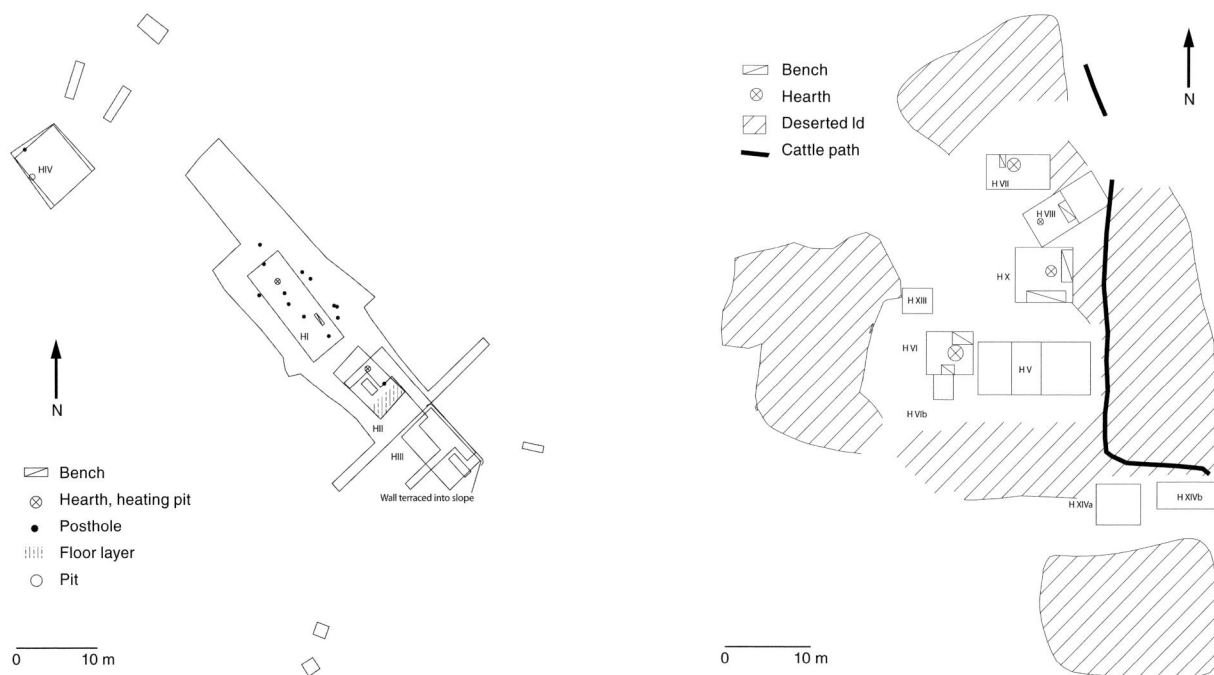

Figure 4. Skinnerud (left) and Skramle (right). After Svensson 2008: figs. 16 and 24.

subsistence and identity. Bloomery iron production, fur hunting, elk catching in pitfalls, soapstone production, forest grazing including use of shielings, haymaking on mires and cereal cultivation in the outland were some of the activities carried out (Svensson 1998). These activities generated income for the peasantry, and produced ways of life that required men to be absent from home for periods of time, and afforded opportunities for women to hold more power within the household and become more actively involved in co-operative production in farming, the development of domestic industries and travel for the purpose of trade.

Skinnerud was excavated in 1996, 1998 and 1999 (Emanuelsson et al 2003). The excavations yielded the remains of a single farmstead that had been established outside the main village on prime agricultural land. There was only one settlement phase dating from the 10th to the 13th centuries. Skinnerud was probably deserted *c* AD 1250, or at the latest by AD 1300. The excavations revealed the remains of four buildings: a hall, a dwelling house/cooking house, a probable cattle byre and an outhouse. Older field layers and slags from blacksmithing were unearthed. The houses were probably built of wood, most likely in the regional tradition of log timbering, apart from the hall that is thought to have been timber-framed. The finds were characterized by everyday, functional items, but there were also some more exclusive artefacts such as beads and bronze items related to dress.

The peasants at Skinnerud therefore appear to have been fairly affluent, perhaps as a result of the exploitation of the surrounding resources of the forested outland including bloomery iron, antler and skins and furs that were processed into goods for sale to the market. However, in the early 13th century the market for these products declined radically, causing a crisis in these communities. Skinnerud was most likely deserted due to this phenomenon.

The hamlet of Skramle was excavated between 1990 and 1992-98 (Andersson & Svensson 2002). Settlement remains from the 6th to the 16th centuries were discovered, but most of the cultural layers and artefacts dated to *c* AD 1250-1350 (Period III). Five dwelling houses, one of which had an adjacent smithy, a long outhouse, a smaller outhouse, a combined barn and cattle byre, with a cattle path, and fossilized field systems were also discovered. During the 13th century the hamlet consisted of three households (dwelling houses), and during the early 14th century of two households. One dwelling house was used during the whole period. The long outhouse was the best built, and most ostentatiously located, building in the hamlet, and had an old Nordic runestone re-set in its sill. It was divided in parts for the individual households in the hamlet and could be interpreted to symbolize the hamlet, and one part was abandoned *c* AD 1300. The houses were log-timbered, which was the regional building tradition. But inside two dwelling houses there were also 'imported' smoke ovens with bricks, an otherwise urban phenomenon. The finds were dominated by functional everyday items, but also a few more exclusive items related to dress such as a brass buckle, ring brooch and a heraldic mount (Figure 1).

Skramle stands out as a fairly wealthy hamlet, due to its production of furs destined for a more distant market and soapstone products aimed at the local market. The hamlet was probably deserted due to the Black Death, or at least very suddenly as the cultural layers indicate that the houses were left standing with everything intact. However, the desertion appears to have been preceded by a downturn when the number of households was reduced from three to two.

Skinnerud and Skramle belong to their local and regional contexts, but they were also connected to wider networks due to their market activities. When compared with the four settlements discussed above, they do not stand out as particularly odd. The older Skinnerud follows the spatial principle with the buildings organized in a row, whereas the buildings in the younger Skramle tend to encircle a yard. And, in both settlements, there was a long building of significance or importance, a hall in Skinnerud and a special outhouse in Skramle.

The rural home – some reflections

Rural settlements are often, rightly, discussed and interpreted in local and regional contexts. There are usually good arguments for such interpretations

Figure 5. Reconstruction of houses and fields in Skramle, around AD 1250-1300. Note the tendency of encircling the yard. Also, note the imposing long house. Photo Bengt Holter, Bengt Andersson. After Svensson 2008: fig. 2.

such as similarities with nearby sites. However, the interpretation of rural settlements can also be extended beyond the local and the regional. If we try and free ourselves from some of the older research traditions and images of medieval peasants, there are other perspectives which can be adopted.

First, I would like to recall the two world system-theories presented above; both the one based on the Catholic Church and the one based on trade. The Catholic Church was a unifying ideology, and the churches, even if different at scale, physical representations understood by everybody connected to the church. Also, going on pilgrimage meant encountering new environments. Like pilgrimage, trade could mean travel. As the self-sufficient peasant was an historical impossibility, we can safely say that information on trade and production for sale is under-reported in rural archaeology. Peasants were using the landscape for production of various goods for sale, and thus connected to markets of different range.

Second, I would like to put forward the interaction between the 'European' nobles and the 'region-al' peasants. To peasants of means the aristocratic lifestyle must have been tempting to imitate. There may also have been social competition between the estates (see Figure 1 with caption). One observation made above concerning the rural settlements is relevant here, and could well be a result of inspiration from castles, namely the tendency that the slightly later rural settlements organized buildings in relation to a yard in an encircling, almost enclosing, manner (Figure 5).

When it comes to the long house, it could well be the other way around. The older multi-functional longhouse, the important meeting place, was transformed both at rural settlements and castles. At the rural settlements investigated here, there was a long house of both functional and symbolic importance. In the castles the hall had inherited the function of the longhouse, and remained a feature uniting people also when social segregation also became an increasingly important structuring factor of castle life.

Could the longhouse be considered a European heritage? Considering the fact that there are and have been long houses all over the world, that would too narrow a perspective. I would therefore like to put forward 'global' approach as an alternative and perhaps more productive way of viewing medieval rural domestic life.

Note

1. This paper is based on the book *The medieval household. Daily life in castles and farmsteads. Scandinavian examples in their European context* (Svensson 2008). In this book two castles, Saxholmen and Edsholm, and two rural settlements, Skinnerud and Skramle, were studied in detail.

References

Abu-Lughod, J. (1999) *Before European hegemony. The world system A.D. 1250-1350.* New York & Oxford: Oxford University Press.

Andersson, H., L. Ersgård & E. Svensson (eds.) (1998) *Outland use in preindustrial Europe.* Stockholm: Almqvist & Wiksell International.

Andersson, S. & E. Svensson (eds.) (2002) *Skramle – the true story of a deserted medieval farmstead.* Stockholm: Almkvist & Wiksell International.

Andrén, A. (2000) Against War! Regional Identity across a national border in late medieval and early modern Scandinavia, *International Journal of Historical Archaeology* vol. 4 no. 4, 315-334.

Anglert, M. (ed.) (2008) *Landskap bortom traditionen. Historisk arkeologi i nordvästra Skåne.* Stockholm: Riksantikvarieämbetet.

Aronsson, P. (1992) *Bönder gör politik. Det lokala självstyret som social arena i tre smålandssocknar, 1680-1850.* Lund: Lund University Press.

Bartlett, R. (1994 (1993)) *The making of Europe. Conquest, Civilization and Cultural Change 950-1350.* London: Penguin.

Belcredi, L. (2000) Colonization, development and desertion of the medieval village of Bystrec. In: *Ruralia III,* ed. J. Klápště, 187-201. Prague: Institute of Archaeology.

Bengtsson, H. (1999) *Den höviska kulturen i Norden. En konsthistorisk undersökning.* Stockholm: Almqvist & Wiksell International.

Bentz, E. (2008) *I stadens skugga: den medeltida landsbygden som arkeologiskt forskningsfält.* Lund Studies in Historical Archaeology. Dissertation. Lund: Lund University.

Blomkvist, N. (2004) The medieval catholic world-system and the making of Europe. In: *The European Frontier. Clashes and Compromises in the Middle Ages,* ed. J. Staecker, 15-33. Stockholm: Almkvist & Wiksell International.

Dawson, C. (2003 (1932)) *The making of Europe. An introduction to the history of European unity.* Washington: The Catholic University of America Press.

Dixon, P. (1998) Design in castle-building: the controlling of access to the Lord. In: *Château Gaillard. Etudes de Castellologie medievale XVIII,* 47-57. Köln: Centre de recerces archéologiques médievales, Université de Caen.

Dovring, F. (1953) *Agrarhistorien. En översikt av dess uppgifter, forskningsmetoder och resultat.* Stockholm: Geber.

Duroselle, J.-B. (1990) *Europe. A History of its Peoples.* London: Viking.

Emanuelsson, M., A. Johansson, S. Nilsson, S. Pettersson & E. Svensson (2003) *Settlement, Shieling & Landscape. The Local History of a Forest Hamlet.* Lund Studies in Medieval Archaeology 32. Stockholm: Almkvist & Wiksell International.

Erixon, S. & Å. Campbell (1957) *Atlas över svensk folkkultur. 1. Materiell och social kultur.* Uppsala: Lundequistska bokhandeln.

Hansen, P. (2000) *Europeans only? Essays on identity politics and the European Union.* Dissertation. Umeå: Umeå University.

Hansson, M. (2001) *Huvudgårdar och herravälden: en studie av småländsk medeltid.* Stockholm: Almqvist & Wiksell International.

Hansson, M. (2006) *Aristocratic Landscape: Spatial Ideology of the Medieval Aristocracy.* Lund Studies in Historical Archaeology Stockholm: Almqvist & Wiksell International.

Hermansson, L. (2004) *Släkt, vänner och makt. En studie av elitens politiska kultur i 1100-talets Danmark.* Dissertation. Göteborg: Göteborgs University.

Holm, I., S.M. Innselset & I. Øye (eds.) (2005) *"Utmark": the outfield as industry and ideology in the Iron Age and the Middle Ages.* Bergen: Department of Archaeology, University of Bergen.

Johnson, M. (2002) *Behind the Castle Gate: Medieval to Renaissance.* London & New York: Routledge.

Krauskopf, C. (1995) *"..davon nur noch wenige Rutera zu sehen seyn sollen…" Archäologische Ausgrabungen in der Burgruine Schnellerts. Kultur- und Lebensformen in Mittelalter und Neuzeit.* Band 1. Bamberg: Scrîpvaz.

Le Goff, J. (2005) *The Birth of Europe.* Malden: MA Blackwell.

Lindkvist, T. & K. Ågren (1985) *Sveriges medeltid.* Solna: Esselte Studium.

Lovén, C. (1996) *Borgar och befästningar i det medeltida Sverige.* Stockholm: Almqvist & Wiksell International.

Makepeace, G.A. (2001) Report on the excavations of a medieval farm at Hill Top Farm, Aldwark, Near Brassington, Derbyshire 1992-95, *Derbyshire Archaeological Journal* Vol. 121, 162-89.

Meyer, W. (1974) *Die Burgruine Alt-Wartburg im Kanton Aargau: Bericht über die Forschungen 1966/67.* Olten & Freiburg: Walter-Verlag.

Oudhof, J.W.M., J. Dijkstra & A.A.A. Verhoeven (eds.) (2000) *'Huis Malburg' van spoor tot spoor; een middeleeuwse nederzetting in Kerk-Avezaath.* Amersfoort: Rikjsdienst voor het Oudheidkundig Bodemonderzoek.

Reuter, T. (2000) Nobles and others. The social and cultural expression of power relations in the middle ages. In: *Nobles and Nobility in Medieval Europe. Concepts, Origins, Transformations,* ed. A.J. Duggan, 85-98. Woodbridge: The Boydell Press.

Rösener, W. (1995 (1994)) *The Peasantry of Europe. The making of Europe.* Oxford & Cambridge: Blackwell.

Sandnes, J. (1991) Utmarksdrift og resursutnyttelse i Norge i eldre tid. In: *Plov og pen. Festskrift til Svend Gissel 4. januar 1991,* eds. H. Ilsøe & B. Jørgensen, 213-221. København: Det kongelige Bibliotek.

Skoglund, P. & E. Svensson (2010). Discourses of nature conservation and heritage management in the past, present and future: discussing heritage and sustainable development from Swedish experiences, *European Journal of Archaeology* Vol. 13 No. 3, 368–385.

Småberg, T. (2004) *Det stängda frälset. Makt och eliter i det medeltida lokalsamhället: Marks och Kinds härader i Västergöt-*

land ca 1390-1520. Dissertation. Göteborg: Göteborgs University

Svensson, E. (1998) *Människor i utmark.* Stockholm: Almkvist and Wiksell International.

Svensson, E. (2008) *The Medieval Household. Daily Life in Castles and Farmsteads. Scandinavian Examples in their European Context.* The Medieval Countryside 2. Turnhout: Brepols

Wallerstein, I. (1974, 1980, 1989) *The Modern World-System* I-III. New York: Academic Press.

Zimmermann, W.H. (1991) Die früh- bis hochmittelalterliche Wüstung Dalem, Gem. Langen-Neuenwalde, Kr. Cuxhaven. Archäologische Untersuchungen in einem Dorf des 7. – 14. Jahrhunderts. In: *Die Salier. Siedlungen und Landesausbau zur Salierzeit,* Band 1, ed. H-W. Böhme, 37-46. Mainz: Jan Thorbecke Verlag Sigmaringen.

Ödmann, E., E. Bucht & M. Nordström (1982) *Vildmarken och välfärden. Om naturskyddslagstiftningens tillkomst.* Stockholm: LiberFörlag.

Österberg, E. (1989) Bönder och centralmakt i det tidigmoderna Sverige. Konflikt – kompromiss – politisk kultur, *Scandia. Tidskrift för historisk forskning* 55:1, 73-95.

'The Schleswig Farmstead'
– A Key to the Dynamics of Culture in the Danish-German Borderland from Medieval to Recent Times

Peter Dragsbo

Abstract

This paper deals with the traditional farmhouses of the former duchy of Schleswig, which, since 1920, has been divided between Denmark and Germany. From not later than the 16th century until the 19th century, the middle and southern parts of Schleswig were dominated by a farm-type with a 'Wohnstallhaus', that is a main wing with dwelling and byre together, which is very different from the Danish quadrangle farmhouse type as well as the North German hall house (German: 'Hallenhaus'). During more than 200 years, the farm-types of Schleswig were drawn into nationalistic arguments about of Danish or German culture. Now, however, we can consider the existence of the 'Schleswig framhaus' without the burden of nationalism, and in this paper I will try to outline some possible explanations of the puzzling existence of the Wohnstallhaus farms of Schleswig.

Introduction

The main aim of cultural history in the 19th century was to support the formation of nation states by demonstrating the ancient, noble heritage and lineage of 'the people', using folk culture to identify the proper boundaries of the nation. Throughout Europe there was a focus on vernacular architecture as a symbol of this folk culture; living proof of the dream that 'the farmer's dwelling' could be linked to the peoples and tribes of our forefathers back in the dim mists of time (Figure 1).

In the first half of the 20th century, new interest was aroused in the spatial dimension of material culture by such cultural historical theories as diffusionism and the 'Kulturkreis' theories; and the work done in the preparation of the Atlas projects of European culture documented the spread of a great number of elements, from table manners to flails

(Dragsbo & Ravn 2003; Stoklund 2003b: 61ff). Later, the Atlas work fell into disrepute, and the main figure in the Danish work being done on the Atlas, Ole Højrup, commented a few years before his death that if the spread of all the charted elements were to be marked on one map, the result would be a Christmas cake with very runny icing!

This paper argues that it is useful to revisit the work of those associated with the Atlas projects. Although such work was a product of functionalist paradigms of thought, these scholars also acknowledged that important elements of material culture did not only stem from functional needs, but also to a large extent from their role as cultural symbols – for example as symbols of similarity, signalling membership of a 'reference group', or as symbols of dissimilarity, signalling distinction. Some objects,

Figure 1. An excellent example of the so-called 'one-wing' Schleswig farmhouses: The Duus farm of Fjelby, Alsen, dating from ca. 1780. Photo Halvor Zangenberg, National Museum of Copenhagen.

Figure 2. Not all innovations came from the South: The Danish four-wing farmhouse, which since late medieval times had dominated the northeastern part of Schleswig, spread in the 18th century southwards along the east and west coasts of the duchy and was even, in large parts of the midlands, combined with the traditional Wohnstallhaus main wing. Late 18th century farmhouse, Skast. Photo Peter Dragsbo 1994.

such as flails, reflected no doubt the choice of crops and local natural resources, whereas others, such as houses and dwellings, have always been important markers of identity in time and space.

This paper draws on a classic ethnological theme of the distribution of types of farm buildings in a classical ethnological area – Schleswig, but in an unusual and chronologically-difficult period. It focuses on the period from the 13th to the 16th centuries, in which archaeology and ethnology attempt to meet each other, but a period about which we know less about vital and central cultural elements, than we do, for example, about some aspects of Palaeolithic culture.

The 'Schleswig Farmhouse' and its role in nationalist debate

In the southern parts of the Schleswig region, now divided by the German-Danish border of 1920, the traditional farmsteads consisting of a main long-house – a Wohnstallhaus – comprised of a dwelling and byre under one roof, have been supplemented by other buildings, resulting in a variety of forms, such as traditional Danish quadrangle farms (Figure 2), three-wing farms, the 'hook' farms of Als and single-wing longhouses with barns and stacks (Ravn & Dragsbo 2002). These farms can be clearly distin-

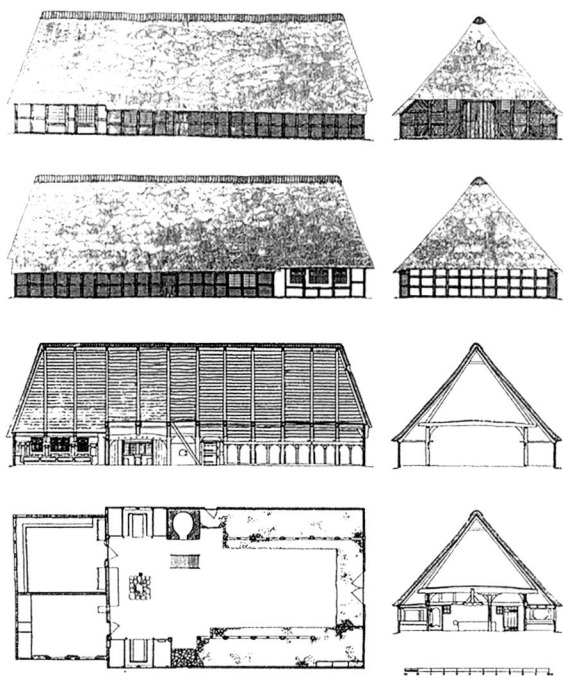

Figure 3. The North German Hallenhaus did not spread further northward in Schleswig than the region of the Iron Age-Viking Age defence wall of Danevirke. But elements of the Hallenhaus spread northwards in the second half of the 18th century – and may even have inspired the development of the Schleswig farmstead in general. After Michelsen 1976: 33.

guished from the type of the quadrangle farm found in the northernmost parts of Schleswig and most parts of 'old' Denmark and southern Sweden. These farms consist of one wing used solely for dwelling purposes, and to the south, the type of the three-aisled hall, the north German Hallenhaus (Figure 3). Although the 'Schleswig' dwelling-byre main wing has its parallels in the Wohnstallhäuser of other parts of Europe and can be traced through the Friesian landscapes along the North Sea Coast as well as in minor farmsteads in Northern Jutland, it has been argued, up to the present day, to be one of the cultural characteristics of the southern parts of Schleswig. In landscapes such as Als and the Schleswig midlands, the farmsteads have until recently continued to preserve the physical proximity of cattle and people, agriculture and dwelling, in clear contrast to the Danish quadrangle farmsteads, in which a clear distancing between dwelling and 'outhouses' can be identified from the 19th century onwards.

Formerly, the Schleswig farmhouse was drawn into nationalist debates between Danish and German scholars, in which each party sought to prove the 'Danishness' or 'Germanness' of the multilingual and multiethnic region of Schleswig. Today, research on vernacular buildings of the region has, finally, been freed from the harness of national aspirations and is now able to cast a new light on this old evidence. In brief, Danish researchers from the 1840s to the 1930s tried to prove that the Danish or Nordic building customs reached down to the Danevirke. German researchers in turn tried to isolate the Schleswig building customs from the Danish by using such terms as 'Cimbrian house' or 'Jutland farm' to describe these buildings. As early as 1892, the Danish scholar of vernacular architecture, Reinhold Mejborg, had to admit that there were several other types of farms in Schleswig besides the 'national' quadrangle farm. However in 1895, the amateur historian Peter Lauridsen produced what Bjarne Stoklund has called 'the Columbian egg': that the so-called 'one-winged' farm which was, as clearly demonstrated by the variety of forms in the Schleswig area, not so 'one-winged' after all– was in reality the original type of Danish house, the prehistoric long-house. This argument tended to settle the battle of the 'Danishness' of the Schleswig farmhouses for almost 100 years (Stoklund 1999; 2003a).

New archaeological evidence, new explanations?

Archaeological excavations of Iron-Age farms in the 1930s, along with the discovery of the presumed 'relics' of 'one-winged' farms in North Jutland, seemed to confirm the theory. The results of the forty years of excavations of farms from the Viking Age appeared to prove beyond doubt that the period of the three-aisled Wohnstallhäuser ended with the Viking Age, giving way to farm complexes with a central hall on the pattern of the Trelleborg house, combined with several barns, byres etc. It has therefore been argued that the Wohnstallhaus type survived only in the Friesian marshland areas along the North Sea coast.

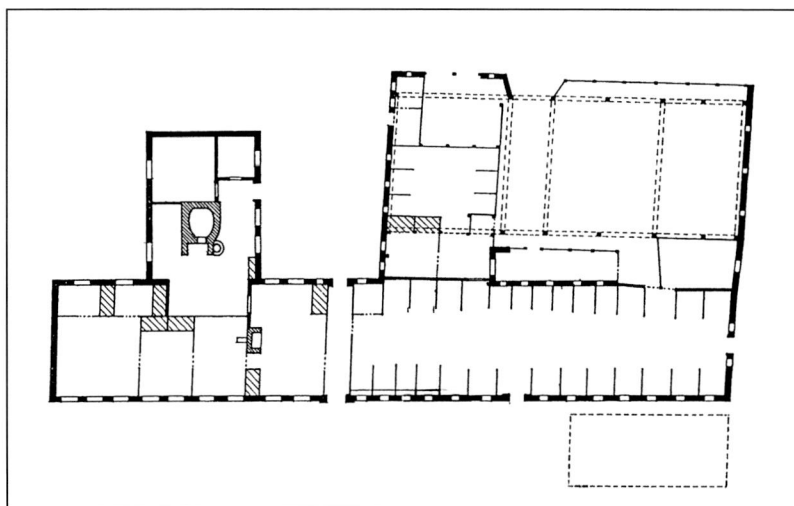

Figure 4. The farmstead from Sønder Sejerslev near Tønder/Tondern in the Open Air Museum of Copenhagen dates from the 18th and 19th centuries and shows a gradual development from an original Wohnstallhaus to a large complex with barns and byres. After Køster 1973: 41.

This argument is problematized by the spread of the Schleswig farmstead since the 16th and 17th centuries across an area stretching from North Friesland and Dithmarschen in the West to Lyø and Ærø in the East, and from the Danevirke wall in the South to a line running roughly from Ribe to Aabenraa in the North, with scattered incidences further north, such as the 17th-century Vinkel farmhouse in Northern Jutland and the main wing of the so-called 'parallel farms' of the northernmost Jutland. This distribution suggests that the Wohnstallhaus has either continued to exist in spite of the testimony of the archaeological evidence – or has, at some time in the medieval period, reappeared and spread as a result of an innovation process.

This phenomenon cannot be explained as a consequence of economic recession. The most characteristic Schleswig farmhouses are found in what have always been the most prosperous areas of West and East Schleswig. Bjarne Stoklund has advanced the theory that the European Wohnstallhäuser are especially linked to cattle-farming areas, symbolically placing the livestock nearest to the living-rooms. But this does not explain the distribution in Schleswig, where the form is found both in areas where cattle farming was dominant, and in areas where arable farming was dominant. This paper suggests that the Schleswig farmhouse must therefore be seen as a radically new cultural element appearing after the end of the Viking Age, not the 'reappearance' of a

particular type of farm lay-out. Parallel to this is the appearance of the three-aisled house in the 13th and 14th centuries (Sørensen 2011; Svart Kristiansen 2008). Here we can see a new development, in which former small extensions, in Danish 'udskud', in German 'Kübbungen', developed into whole-length side-aisles in the one building. In this context it is also worth mentioning the large European three-aisled monastery barns and tithe barns from the 12th and 13th centuries, which probably influenced the development of the Danish three-aisled manor house barns of the Renaissance, and possibly even to the North German Hallenhaus and the Dutch Gulf-house (Figure 4).

A series of possible explanations

Several explanations of the emergence of the Schleswig farmhouse can be tentatively advanced here. The first explanation might be that the Wohnstallhaus continued to be the typical farmhouse of the Friesian marshlands throughout the Middle Ages. This type of farmhouse may then have spread north-eastwards, either because it became associated with the booming economy of the marshlands, or more generally with the prestige of the Friesian culture itself, which continued to have an influence on dwellings right up to the 19th century. However, the spread of this type of building especially in Schleswig, as far as the South Funen islands, might first of all reflect the fact that in some ways Schleswig became a separate cultural unit after its seclusion as a separate duchy from the 13th and 14th centuries onwards, from 1460 linked with Holstein as the 'Duchies' inside the Danish monarchy, consisting of the Danish Kingdom, Norway (till 1814), the Duchies (till 1864), Iceland (till 1943) and the Faroe Islands.

An alternative explanation might be that Schleswig was an ancient national border area, and consequently had a tradition for cultural diversity and the mixing of cultures. On this basis, the Schleswig farmhouse could be regarded as a 'compromise' between the two types of farmhouse that arose in areas bordering on Schleswig in the late Medieval period: the North German Hallenhaus and the Danish quadrangle farmstead; combining the multi-functional, northern European Einhaus and the Danish building custom using wings, divided into rooms, perhaps under the influence of the new fashion of having several living rooms that spread northwards in the 16th and 17th centuries. This theory of 'mixture' might explain the mere fact that there are, especially in the Schleswig midlands, several examples of buildings where a main Wohnstallhaus wing is combined with Danish quadrangle farm lay-out (a series of farmsteads of this type, dating from the decades around 1800 were documented by the Danish National Museum in the 1950s and -60s) (Figure 5).

However, it could also be suggested that the main wing of the Schleswig farmsteads with dwelling and byre under one roof, separated by a cross-section, and often divided into a passage (Danish: 'framgulv') and a threshing floor (Danish: 'lo') is a regional version of the North German Hallenhaus. Here, it is worth recalling that the oldest Hallenhäuser in Northwest Germany seem to have had three sections: the 'Diele' (byre and barn), the 'Flett' (multi-functional room with a hearth) and the 'Kammerfach' (living rooms). This parallels the oldest-known farm-houses of the Schleswig type in Southern Schleswig (Stoklund 2008: 33). In this interpretation, the Schleswig farmstead could be seen as being developed in conjunction with influences from Holstein, reflecting the prestige of Holstein farming. If so, the contrast between the Holstein hall house and the Schleswig farmstead, hailed by Danish nationalist scholars, might simply be the meeting point between two variations of the same principle.

Another possibility is that the Wohnstallhaus was connected with the general distribution of longhouses in Scandinavia, in recent times documented in various regions, such as Northern Jutland, South-Western Norway and the islands of the North Atlantic (Jespersen 1961; Myhre et al 1982; Zangenberg 1925). Thus, it might reflect two different waves of innovation during the period following the Viking Age: the first was a wave of longhouses reaching most of Denmark and even further to southern Norway; the second was the development of the quadrangle farm in the 15th and 16th century, overlying

Figure 5. The Schleswig farmstead still dominates large parts of the old duchy, where the close connection between dwelling and byre remained as a preferred feature until the beginnings of the 20th century. Midland farm of the 1850s. Photo Peter Dragsbo 2010.

Figure 6. This old farm of the Angel landscape south of Flensborg Fjord is a real showpiece of cultural encounter: The overall lay-out is typical of the Schleswig farmstead, but the byre and barn-part of the house has been extended with a three-aisled construction, very similar of the Hallenhäuser. Nevertheless, the Angel farmers in the 19th century changed their farms into three-winged manor-like farms together with a change of language and accept of a more urban life-style. After Mejborg 1892: 146.

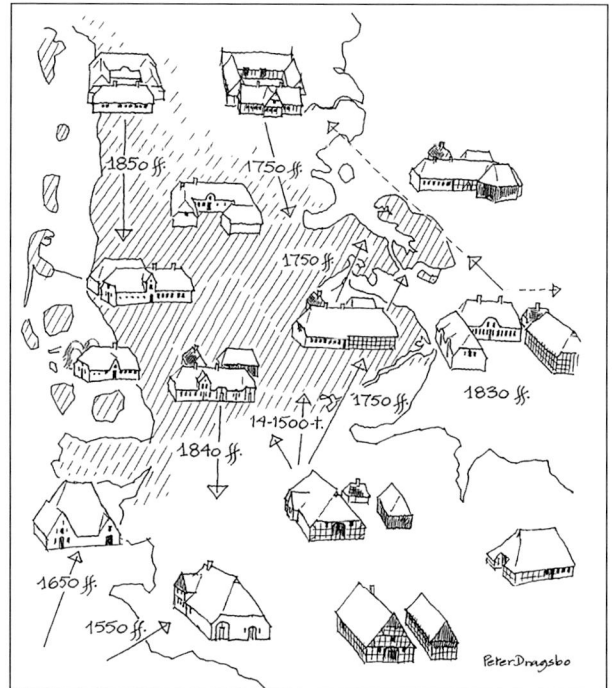

Figure 7. In this drawing, I have tried to show the cultural dynamics of the vernacular architecture of Schleswig, showing innovations from the South and North as well as interior developments. Peter Dragsbo 2008.

the former longhouse area. This kind of explanation takes us back to such diffusionist explanations of 'relict areas', suggesting that the middle and southern area of Schleswig as well as northern Jutland, preserve the relic form of the longhouse from the period prior to the development of the quadrangle farm. This theory requires us to accept the impact of two different waves of innovation concerning building customs between 1200 and 1500, but may well be worth considering in an era where archaeologists freed from political and nationalistic concerns are prepared to accept evidence of cultural change as well as continuity, in the past (Figure 6).

Conclusion

At present, these hypotheses must remain speculation, as we have not had many excavations of farmsteads in the Schleswig area dating from the 14th to the 16th centuries – and in the absence of a systematic understanding of those already recovered. Nor have we analysed the written sources in museums and archives, example given in the rich registers from the ducal lands of Gottorp, dating from the first decades of the 18th century that might also illuminate these issues. We therefore need to try to cast some light on 'the dark gap' between our archaeological knowledge of 12th- to 13th-century vernacular buildings

and our ethnological knowledge of the oldest extant houses from the 16th and 17th centuries (Figure 7).

Nevertheless, as a starting point for future common research projects we should, in my opinion, first of all drop any prejudices concerning continuity between prehistoric and more recent times, unless this can be proved with certainty. All the farm types of Southern Scandinavia and North Germany – the quadrangle farmstead, the Schleswig farm and the Hallenhaus – seem to be the results of waves of innovation in high-medieval times or even later.

Secondly, the Schleswig farm must be studied as one of several cultural elements of a cultural borderland, characterised since medieval times by a higher degree of cultural variation and flux than its neighbouring regions of North Jutland or Holstein. So, in the discussion of the Schleswig farmhouse type, we must also take account of other cultural features, such as language, clothing and furniture.

Finally, the introduction of the *Wohnstallhaus* in Schleswig – and maybe further north – should, in my opinion, make us reconsider the prejudice, often vaunted by architects and even sometimes by archaeologists, that 'form follows function'. Taking a critical view of the 'functionalist' point of view in the study of houses could maybe enable us to see medieval and renaissance vernacular architecture as defined just as much by cultural and political influences as the simultaneous upper-class culture – or modern material culture.

References

Dragsbo, P. (ed.) (2008) *Haus und Hof in Schleswig und Nordeuropa*. Heide: Boyens Verlag.

Dragsbo, P. (2003) Folkegrænse og byggeskik. Myter og realiteter i Claus Eskildsens påstande om dansk og tysk byggeskik i Sønderjylland, *Sønderjyske Museer*, 11-20.

Dragsbo, P. & H. Ravn (2003) Levende egnsforskelle i det 20. århundrede. In: *Forskellige mennesker? Regionale forskelle og kulturelle særtræk*, eds. I. Adriansen & P.O. Christiansen, 55-72. Ebeltoft: Skippershoved.

Eskildsen, C. (1936) *Dansk Grænselære*. København: C.A. Reitzel.

Køster, J. (1973) *Gården fra Sønder Sejerslev*. København: Frilandsmuseet.

Lauridsen, P. (1895) Om dansk og tysk Byggeskik i Sønderjylland, *Historisk Tidsskrift* 6. Rk. VI., 43-113.

Mejborg, R. (1892) *Nordiske Bøndergaarde i det XVIde, XVIIde og XVIIIde Aarhundrede: Slesvig*. København: Lehmann & Stage.

Michelsen, P. (1976) *Ostenfeldgården på Frilandsmuseet*. København: Frilandsmuseet.

Myhre, J. et al (eds.) (1982) *Vestnordisk byggeskikk gjenom to tusen år: Tradisjon og forandring fra romertid til det 19. Århundre/ West Nordic Building Customs from the Roman Period to the 19*[th] *Century (with English summary)*. AmS-Skrifter 7. Stavanger: Arkeologisk museum i Stavanger.

Rasmussen, C.P. (2013) Bondens gård. In: *Det Sønderjyske landbrugs historie 1544-1830*, ed. C.P. Rasmussen, 368-390. Aabenraa: Historisk Samfund fra Sønderjylland.

Ravn, H. & P. Dragsbo (2002) *Taks og trempel – Havekultur og byggeskik på Als gennem 200 år*. Sønderborg: Historisk Samfund for Als og Sundeved & Museet på Sønderborg Slot.

Stoklund, B. (1999) Bondebygninger og folkekarakter. Striden om "den etnografiske grænse" mellem dansk og tysk 1840-1940. In: *Kulturens nationalisering. Et etnologisk perspektiv på det nationale*, ed. Bjarne Stoklund, 48-65. København: Museum Tusculanums Forlag & University of Copenhagen.

Stoklund, B. (2003a) Gårdformer og boligformer. Om at tolke landlig byggeskik. In: *Tingenes kulturhistorie. Etnologiske studier i den materielle kultur*, ed. B. Stoklund, 79-110. København: Museum Tusculanums Forlag & University of Copenhagen.

Stoklund, B. (2003b) Høriven som studieobjekt. Et stykke kritisk faghistorie. In: *Tingenes kulturhistorie. Etnologiske studier i den materielle kultur*, ed. B. Stoklund. 61-78. København: Museum Tusculanums Forlag & University of Copenhagen.

Stoklund, B. (2008) Der schleswigsche Hof und die dänische Bauernhausforschung. In: *Haus und Hof in Schleswig und Nordeuropa*, ed. Dragsbo, 24-43. Heide: Boyens Verlag.

Sørensen, A.B. (2011) Østergård. Vikingetid og *middelalder*. Skrifter fra Museum Sønderjylland, vol. 5. Haderslev: Museum Sønderjyllands Forlag.

Svart Kristiansen, M. (2008) Der dänische Bauernhof im Mittelalter. Daten und Deutung. In: *Haus und Hof in Schleswig und Nordeuropa*, ed. Dragsbo, 108-126. Heide: Boyens Verlag.

Zangenberg, H. (1925) *Danske Bøndergaarde. Grundplaner og Konstruktioner*. København: Det Schønbergske Forlag.

Medieval Turf Houses in Jutland, Denmark – A Regional Building Practice?

Charlotte Boje Hilligsø Andersen & Anne-Louise Haack Olsen

Abstract

In recent years, more and more turf-built houses from the medieval period have been found in the North Western part of Jutland, Denmark. Due to good preservation conditions these houses contain a great deal of information on household conditions and daily life of the period. This paper describes houses from the site of Sjørring, Thy, with a special focus on the turf walls and their construction. The reappearance of this type of house after several hundred years of post-built houses is interpreted as a response both to contemporary environmental conditions and external influences from coastal areas farther south. The paper also questions whether the present geographical distribution of Danish medieval turf houses reflects their regional distribution during the period, or rather particular preservation conditions in the intervening centuries. This raises important questions for further research.

Background

The first medieval turf houses in Denmark were excavated in 1946 at Nødskov Hede in North Western Jutland by the ethnologist Axel Steensberg (1952: 257ff) (Figure 1.1). For many years they stood completely alone in the Danish material, and they were not considered as being in any way representative of Danish medieval building practice (Liebgott 1989: 28). During the last two decades, however, increasing numbers of medieval houses with turf-built walls have appeared at several sites in Western and especially North Western Jutland (Figure 1). This article focuses on the numerous finds in the area of Thy, although a number of locations are also known from the neighbouring island of Mors, including the site of Tæbring (Figure 1.3) (Mikkelsen et al 2008). Medieval turf houses moreover occur scattered along the West Coast of Jutland, including the well-documented site of Fjand just south of Nissum Fjord (Figure 1.2) (Henningsen 2000). The only occurrence so far in

the eastern part of Denmark has been found in the medieval village of Tårnby, near Copenhagen (Svart Kristiansen 2005: 254). In addition, turf walls have been found in a few medieval castles (Engberg & Frandsen 2011: 36; Hyldgård 1988).

The site of Sjørring

Among the sites with turf houses in the region of Thy, the settlement of Sjørring (Figure 1.4) is key, as it has an unusually large number of turf houses for a single locality (Olsen 2005). Sjørring is situated in a strategic location where an old road passes over a narrow piece of land between two former lakes, which have now both been drained. It boasts a runic stone from around AD 1000, an impressive medieval fortress, and a Romanesque granite church from around 1150-1200 with exceptionally rich decoration. The site is mentioned in 'Kong Valdemars Jordebog', an inven-

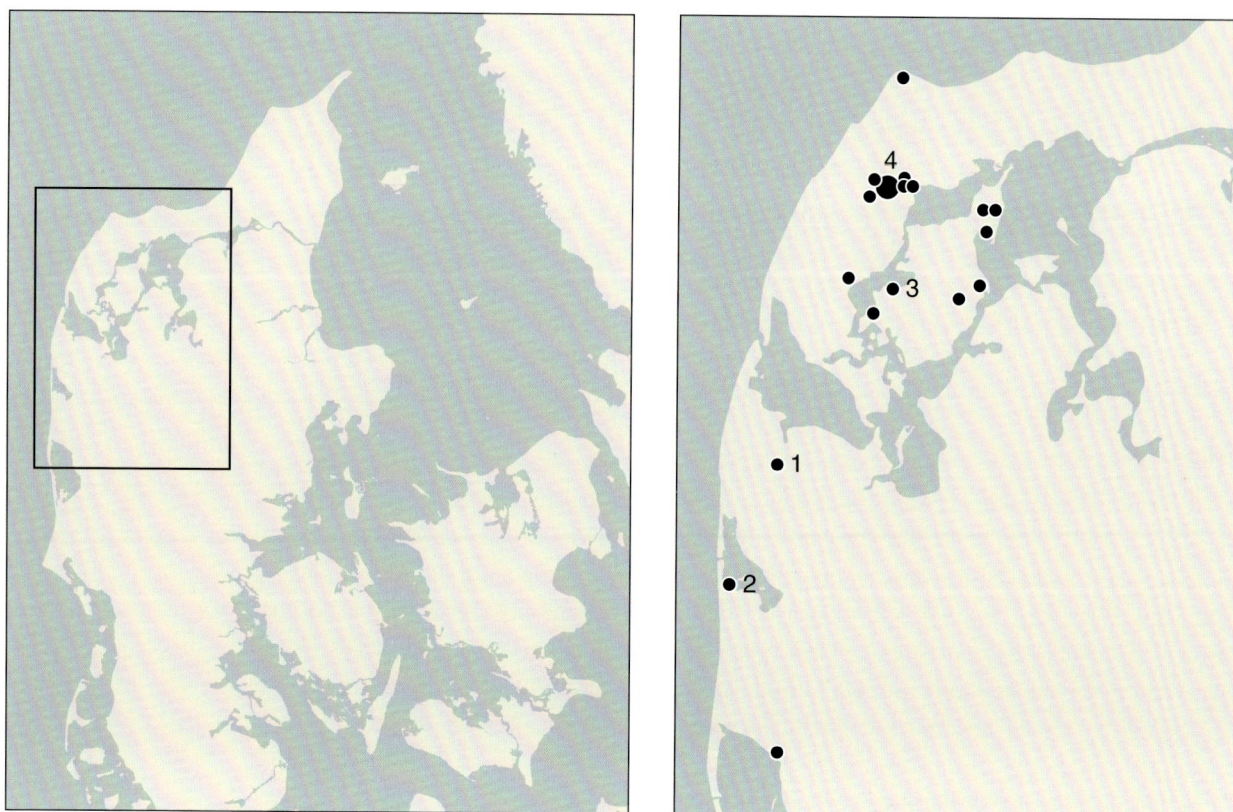

Figure 1. Map of Denmark with detail showing sites of medieval turf houses in North Western Jutland. The sites mentioned in the text are: 1. Nødskov Hede; 2. Fjand; 3. Tæbring on the island of Mors; 4. Sjørring in Thy (enlarged signature). A small number of sites are also found along the West Coast of Jutland south of the enlarged area. Copyright the National Survey and Cadastre.

tory of the property of the Danish crown around 1230 (la Cour & Stiesdal 1957: 117). Below the present town are traces of a settlement dating to the Viking Age and medieval period, but only small fragments of this had been uncovered until the excavation of a large area on the outskirts of the present town began in 1995. This was excavated in three consecutive campaigns driven by building development.[1]

The settlement

Within an area of approximately 40.000 m² settlement traces were excavated dating from the late Viking Age to the 11th-12th centuries, comprising ten medieval 12th century turf-built houses scattered over the area in small groups. Other features from the culture layer comprise turf-built dykes, and paths and roads paved with gravel and small stones. A number of

ditches were seen both in the culture layer and in the subsoil. Some of these were interpreted as marking boundaries between plots. The reason why the culture layer was preserved is the presence of a deep overburden of soil, which has protected the medieval layers from destruction by modern agriculture. This consisted of layers of soil which had accumulated as a result of distinctive farming techniques practised at least until the 19th century, where discarded turves from dykes and ditches were mixed with manure and spread in the fields, thereby contributing to a growing layer of topsoil. This agricultural practice is well documented in written sources from Thy and Mors (Aaby & Vegger 1996: 33).

Beside the turf-built medieval houses, a number of post-built houses were found at the site, dating from the Late Neolithic, the Early Bronze Age, the late Viking Age and the Middle Ages. In some cases, the medieval post-built houses antedate the turf houses, while others appear to be contemporary. This means that the site contained post-built houses which appear to be in use at the same time as turf houses. This paper focuses on the turf houses, since only a few examples have been published to date, and they contain a large amount of information relevant to the questions of daily life in the Early Middle Ages, regionality, cultural contacts with the outside world and the influence of the physical environment on house construction.

The turf houses

The excavated medieval turf houses had many features in common. The walls of these houses were about 80-100 m thick and were turf-built, while the roof was carried by a central row of posts. Some of the posts seem to have rested on padstones, and therefore they could not always be identified in excavation. The houses were fairly narrow, only 3-4 m wide on the interior, and around 10-17 m long. In many cases the length was impossible to determine with accuracy, as the gables were missing. Three

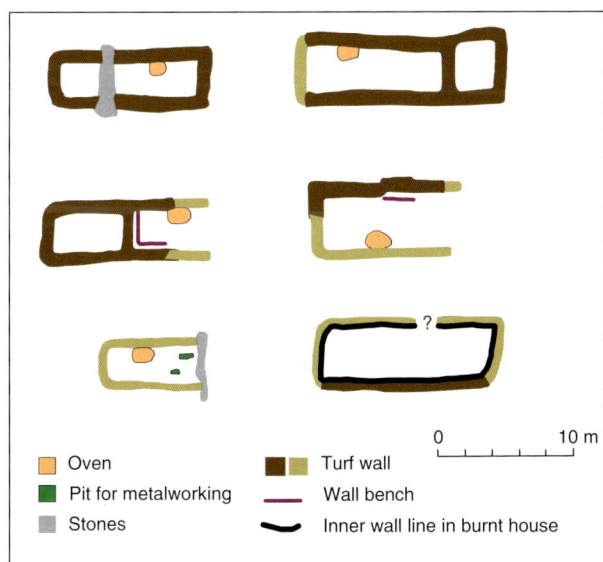

Figure 2. Examples of turf houses from Sjørring, Thy, showing selected elements of construction. The different shading of the turf walls shows varying degrees of certainty. Entrances could not be seen in all cases. For a more detailed house-plan with postholes see Figure 3.

houses were divided by a turf-built wall into a larger room with an oven, and a smaller room without permanent heating (Figures 2 and 3). A number of houses had two opposed entrances in the long walls, connected by a stone-paved passage. All the turf-houses, except one, had remains of an oven with a clay-dome and an underlying stone pavement. The identification of the houses in the first place was often based on the presence of a clay floor and an oven.

The only example of a structure without an oven had been burnt down, and the turf wall was only present along one side. This house has been interpreted as a non-domestic building (Figure 2, lower right). It seems likely that there were other more ephemeral turf-built non-domestic buildings which do not survive in the archaeological record. This means that it is not possible to reconstruct the entirety of the farm complex from the surviving archaeological evidence.

Living in turf houses

The floors in the turf houses consisted partly of clay, especially in the area around the oven. Between the two corresponding entrances there was often an irregular area of stone paving which appeared to reflect the extra wear from the traffic in this area (Figure 3). Normally, every house had an oven with a clay-dome and an underlying stone pavement, which served to absorb the heat from the fire and ensure a more stable temperature. The oven was heated by peat and heather turves, and firing took place from the front. In addition to the ovens, open hearths in the floor were also documented. The oven occupied a central place in the household as it was used for heating as well as baking and probably cooking. Normally it was placed along the wall, no doubt on account of the limited floor-space of the house. The smoke probably left the room through a hole or louvre in the roof. In a few examples, evidence for wall-benches, built of earth and clay, was discovered.

The turf houses measured typically 30-40 m² internally, exclusive of the occasional extra room. Once the oven and wall benches were constructed, this did not leave a lot of space for the inhabitants. Nevertheless, the archaeological evidence indicates that multiple activities took place within these build-

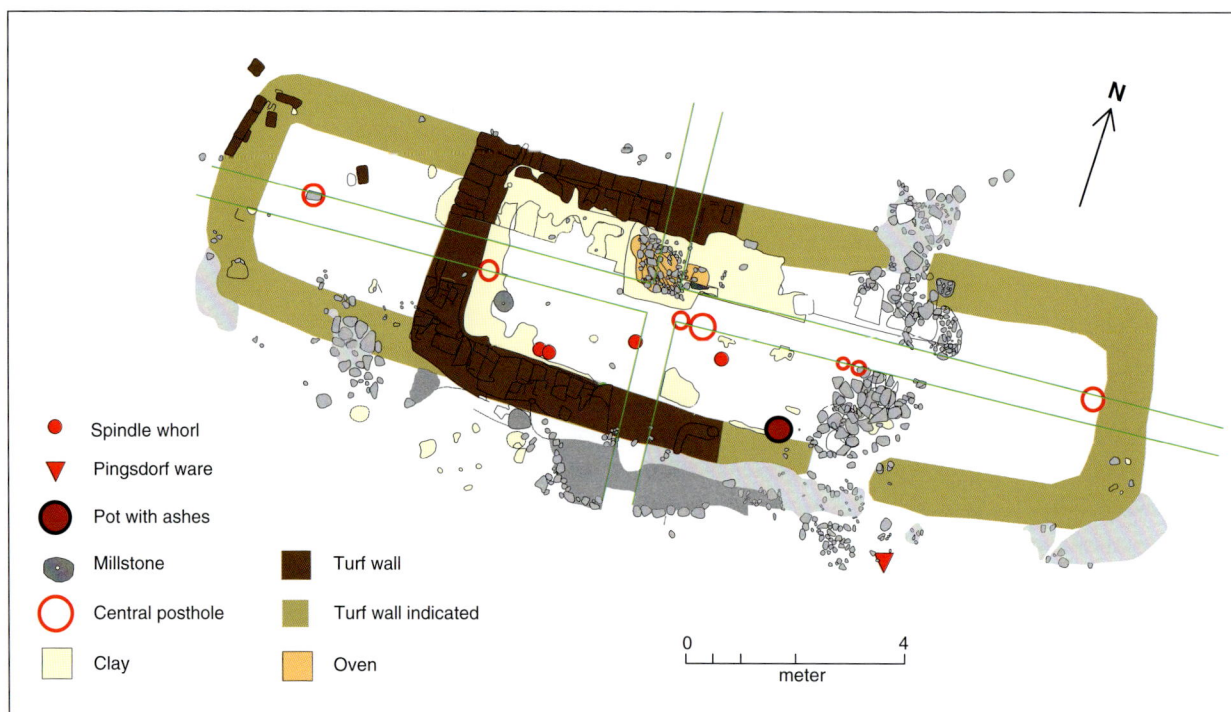

Figure 3. Plan of a typical turf-built longhouse, House 22, from Sjørring. It is interpreted as having an extra western room, which may, however, have been a later addition. The turf wall was extremely well preserved in some places, and invisible in other parts. Along the south wall were areas with stones and gravel (darker and lighter grey). The house is 14C dated to AD 1037-1160.

ings. There was clear evidence of cooking and textile work. Floor layers contained charcoal, turf ashes and burnt cereals from household activities. Oat and barley appear to have been the preferred cereals, but rye and some evidence of wheat were also found. Millstones of mica-schist were often found in secondary positions as foundations under ovens or in pavements. Based on the sheer number of examples discovered, it can be assumed that each household had its own grinder. The millstones were imported from Hyllestad in the South Western part of Norway[2] (*cf* Carelli & Kresten 1997). Several finds of spindle whorls made of burnt clay are clear indications that textile work went on inside the houses (Figure 3). Scissors also indicate the handling of wool.

In one of the houses a clay pot was placed just inside the door (see Figure 3 above). It was filled with red ashes containing traces of burnt cereal, seeds and heather turves. A circular hole in the bottom of the pot was filled with clay, so it was probably not a drain. It may have been used as a container for ashes,

or for gathering a liquid material. Residue analysis might reveal the nature of this substance. It is possible that it was urine, and that the ashes absorbed bad odours to enable the mixture to be used as a kind of soap or lye. A ritual function is another possibility, but there are no parallels from other turf houses.

Metal working also took place inside the turf houses. In one example two pits used for different metal-working activities were found (see Figure 2 above). The pits contained traces of both forging and casting, and indicated evidence of handling iron as well as bronze[3]. Later, this building was converted into a more conventional dwelling house, as its industrial pits were filled up and sealed by a floor layer with clay patches, containing finds of spindle whorls, whetstones and ceramics indicating normal domestic activities.

Although metal and prestige objects are not frequent finds from the turf houses, they do occur, indicating trading contacts and a certain amount of information about the social structure of the community. Keys, knifes, different tools, riding gear, weights and coins are found in clear association with the house or immediately outside it. The ceramics are mostly locally-produced pots, but sherds of imported yellow Pingsdorf ware have also been found and are interpreted as clear indications of trading beyond local markets (see Figure 3 above). The finds of these turf-built houses therefore indicate their occupation by households of a similar social and economic status to the contemporary post-built houses at Sjørring.

The medieval sites with turf houses in Thy, as well as in the rest of North West Jutland, generally have a rural character. However, as mentioned above, the settlement of Sjørring also includes the remains of the medieval castle Sjørring Volde (la Cour & Stiesdal 1957: 97-118). The precise date of the castle is unknown. It has traditionally been argued to date to the 12th century but could date from the 14th century, like most Danish castles (Liebgott 1989: 86-103). The question therefore remains as to whether the turf houses of Sjørring should be seen as a normal form of proto-urban settlement, or as being in some way connected to or influenced by the castle.

Dating

House 22 (Figure 3) is 14C dated to AD 1037-1160 with a 95.4% probability (AAR-14985 and AAR-14986 combined). Another turf house, House 1, from Sjør-ring, excavated in 1996, is 14C-dated to AD 1155-1220 with 68.2% probability, and between AD 1040-1250 with 95.4% probability (AAR-9206 and AAR-9207 combined). The floor layer of the latter also contained a coin struck by King Valdemar I who reigned from 1157 to 1182.[4] The house is therefore most likely to date to the second half of the 12th century, which means that it may be contemporary with the building of the Romanesque church and possibly with the castle as well. The dating of the castle in Sjør-ring is therefore a research priority which may shed important light on the relationship between castle and turf houses.

Turf walls

The preservation conditions of the turf walls varied greatly, even within the same house, and in almost every house there were parts of the outer wall that could not be identified in excavation. In some instances, however, the turf walls could be documented in detail, and in a few cases two or three layers of turves could be seen, making it possible to unravel the inner structure of the wall. The turves were normally rectangular, 25-30 cm wide and up to 60 cm long. In one section the turves could be seen to have been placed upside down, with the thin dark vegetation-layer of one turf placed directly on top of the subsoil layer from the turf below (Figure 4).

Figure 4. Section of turf wall. To the right three levels of turves placed upside down are visible, with the vegetation layer from the fourth level on top.

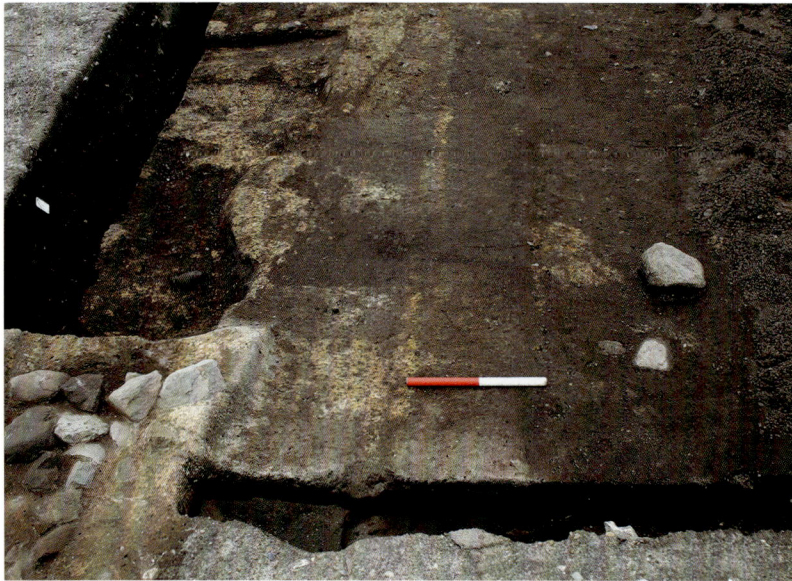

Figure 5. Part of the north wall in house 22, with the visible turf construction seen from the east. The same part of the wall, viewed from the south, is seen in Figure 6. Part of the clay and stone foundation of the oven can be seen in the lower left corner. Compare with Figure 3.

In the long-house, House 22 (Figure 5 *cf* the plan in Figure 3), part of the wall was extremely well preserved and facilitated a detailed examination of the method of construction. This section of wall could be mapped at two levels, showing the change in the orientation of the individual turves from one level to the other, as shown in Figure 6. This method of construction, which resembles the bonding of a brick wall, no doubt helped to make the wall more stable and indicates that the turf walls are the result of a sophisticated building technique. This particular bonding technique is not seen in all turf houses, but in all examples the wall consists of two or more rows of rectangular turves.

Turf houses in Thy

Turf houses in Denmark have a history that begins more than a thousand years before the medieval turf houses of Sjørring and elsewhere. In the major part of the Early Iron Age, between approximately 400 BC and AD 400, turf-built long-houses dominated the form of house construction in Thy, where they are known from many settlements (*eg* Bech 1985; Kann Rasmussen 1968; Kaul 1999). This wall-construction, however, went out of use around AD 400, and for more than 600 years, during the Germanic Iron Age

and the Viking Age, all long-houses known from the area had post-built walls, as was the case in the rest of Denmark. From around 1050 turf-built houses reappear and exist side by side with houses with post-built structures.

There are important differences, however, between the turf houses of the Early Iron Age and those of the medieval period. The prehistoric turf houses followed the normal building-scheme for Early Iron Age houses in Denmark and were three-aisled with inner dimensions that often extended to 5 x 15 m, and had centrally-placed open hearths, normally located at the western end, while the eastern end was occupied by a byre. Moreover, the building technique of the turf wall was also fundamentally different. Where the medieval houses consisted of rectangular turves, mostly 30-60 cm long, in some cases placed in alternating directions and laid in bond, prehistoric houses had walls made of oblong turves around 1 m long, laid side by side at a right angle to the direction of the wall (Kann Rasmussen 1968: 140). This basic difference in construction, viewed together with the considerable gap in time between the two turf-building periods, seems to preclude the idea of a direct continuity between the turf walled houses of the Early Iron Age and those of the Early Medieval in the region of Thy.

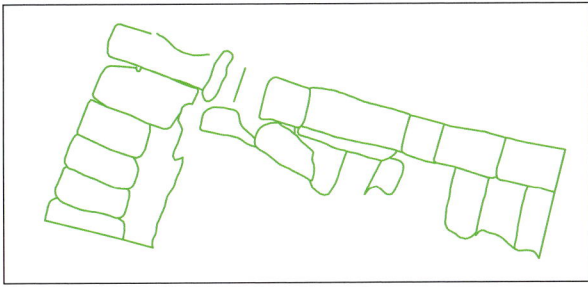

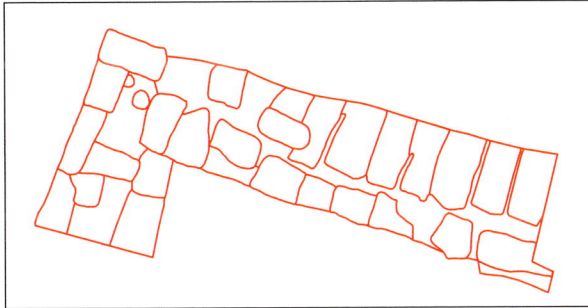

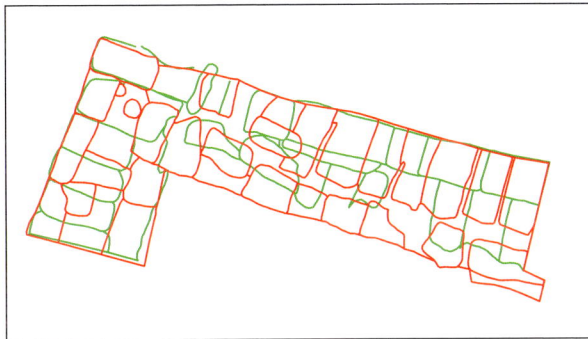

Figure 6. Turf wall in house 22 from Sjørring mapped at two levels, showing alternating orientation of turves. Compare with Figures 3 and 5. The green turves were on top, the red ones below. The third map shows the two levels combined.

Why turf-houses – or why not?

Turf-houses may be considered the perfect construction solution in an open and windy area where wood is a scarce building resource. This has been the case in Thy since prehistoric times. From the time of the Single Grave Culture, around 2800 BC, the forests of Thy have been under growing pressure, due no doubt to land-clearing and grazing caused by the farming communities of the area. Figure 7 shows a pollen diagram from lake Ove in the southern part of Thy, which demonstrates that Thy was heavily deforested by in the Bronze Age.[5]

It is only during the last 150 years that the extent of forestation has changed materially, thanks to extensive tree planting in the dune areas along the North Sea coast. Given this evidence, it is not surprising that the inhabitants of Iron Age Thy turned to other building materials like turves for their house-walls. There was plenty of turf available from heath and grasslands, and the thick turf walls must have been found to be good insulators, thereby also reducing the consumption of fuel for heating. The question is rather, why did this stop? As noted above, nothing in the pollen diagrams points to a rise in local resources of wood that could be used in the post-built house-walls of the following 600 years. At the present time, the source of the wood used in house-building in Thy during the Germanic Iron Age and the Viking Age cannot be determined. It seems however, that this shift in construction technique reflects cultural influences rather than newly-available building resources (see Kaul 1999: 65).

So why, around AD 1050, did new forms of turf house reappear in Thy, employing a fairly standardized plan? The re-discovery of this construction method may reflect an ongoing shortage of building timber, as reflected in the pollen diagrams. However, houses with post-built walls continued to exist side by side with the turf-houses, with no clear indication of difference in the economic or social status of the household. The supplies of wood for building therefore cannot have dried out, or at least not completely. The appearance and reappearance of turf houses in the prehistoric and medieval times must be seen in the context of the natural environment. However, as this development shows, the construction of turf houses cannot be explained by environmental determinism, and environmental factors must therefore also been understood in the context of cultural and historical factors.

External influences

The reappearance of the turf-house as an established and fairly standardized phenomenon with no immediate local predecessors might point to its re-introduction as part of a wider cultural 'package' whose origins were outside the region. Two areas

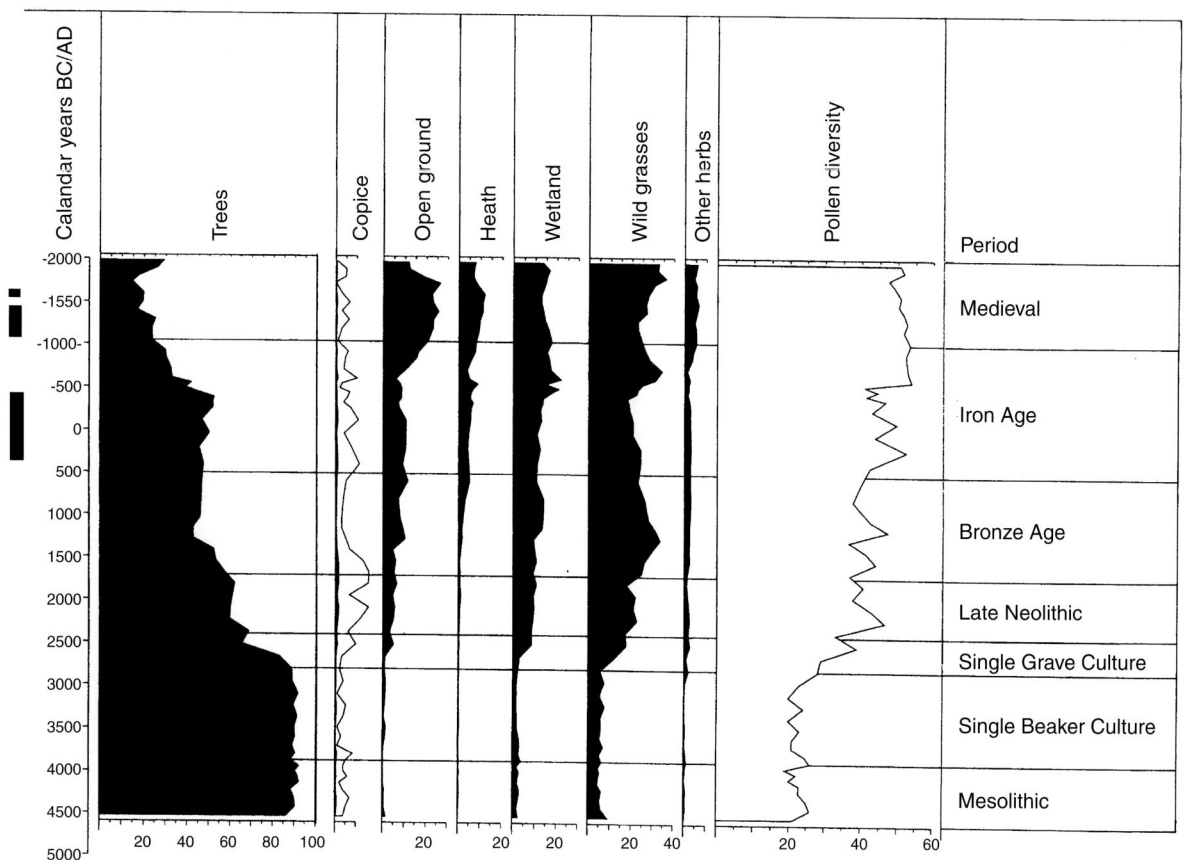

Figure 7. Regional pollen diagram from lake Ove in the southern part of Thy. After Andersen 1995 and Bech 2003. To the left the two periods of turf-building are marked, in the Iron Age and the medieval period respectively. It is obvious that the intervening centuries with wooden houses did not coincide with a rise in tree pollen values.

offer themselves as possible sources of inspiration. One is the North Atlantic, where turf houses were common from the Viking Age onwards in Iceland, Greenland and the Faroe islands (Myhre et al 1982). The other is the North Sea coast of Germany and the Netherlands, where turf-built houses occur from the 5th century onwards (*eg* Gerrets & De Konig 1999; Kersten & La Baume 1958; Segschneider 1998; van Giffen 1940).[6]

Turf houses have a tendency to look very similar, due to the characteristics and the limitations of the building material. If one looks at the turf-building technique in detail, however, the similarity between the walls of the medieval houses of Thy and some of the houses from the Dutch and the German North Sea coast is striking. In comparison, the North Atlantic turf-houses were built with a different technique,

where a double-faced turf wall was filled out with earth and rubble (Gestsson 1982). An example of a close resemblance in turf-building technique with the medieval houses from Thy shows the Dutch *terp* of Leens (van Giffen 1940). The walls of the turf-built houses in this site, dating from the 7th to the 10th century, show exactly the same construction of rectangular turves placed with different orientations. Another close parallel to some of the walls from Thy is seen at the German site Lembeksburg from the 9th-10th century on the island of Föhr (Kersten & La Baume 1958: 91, 231ff). Even though many details are still unclear, these and other examples in our opinion justify the assumption that the reappearance of the turf houses in the Middle Ages in Thy is due to an external influence, most likely coming from the south along the west coast of Jutland.

Conclusion: a regional building practice?

The extent to which the medieval turf houses of North West Jutland can be seen as a regional phenomenon is another question. As mentioned in the introduction and illustrated in Figure 1, these houses today are almost exclusively known from western Jutland, especially the region of Thy and the island of Mors, with the one exception from Tårnby on the island of Amager. In a few medieval castles, turf walled buildings have also been excavated (Engberg & Frandsen 2011: 36; Hyldgård 1988). This North Western distribution makes sense in view of the natural environment of the area, which in the medieval period was windy and had little tree cover. However, conditions of preservation must also be taken into account, since the identification of turf houses is entirely dependent on the existence of a preserved culture layer. In the subsoil, all that remains of these houses are the holes from the single row of central posts. The culture layer therefore must somehow be protected against destruction by modern cultivation – either by a protecting layer of wind-blown sand, as was the case at the afore-mentioned site of Fjand, or by later deposits of soil as a result of agricultural practices, as was the case at Sjørring and several other sites in Thy and in Mors (above). In the example of Tårnby the turf wall was preserved by later settlement deposits. The two former conditions may be said to be typical of Western Jutland and no doubt lie behind the many sites with turf houses in this area. On the other hand it is clear that if turf houses had been common in the medieval towns, traces ought to have been found in the many cultural strata found there. This does not seem to be the case, but may simply be due to turf houses being a rural form of building. The question cannot be answered fully at this time, but there are indications that turf houses should be viewed as a regional phenomenon in Denmark, and characteristic of Western Jutland. In order to confirm or disprove this hypothesis future research is needed. This involves a large degree of awareness in all excavations where conditions are favourable for the preservation of turf walls, in order to decide if the present distribution gives a true picture of conditions in the past. In excavations of turf houses it is important that sufficient resources be available for the time-consuming excavation work as well as C14-datings, macrobotanical and soil analysis etc. Only in this way is it possible to procure evidence of a microclimate, environment and economy with a view to obtaining a comprehensive view of the house-type, its function and milieu. Analysis of existing material from excavated locations would be an important starting point towards acquiring a better understanding of the conditions which influenced life in the medieval turf houses.

Notes

1. THY 3471, locality no. 110305-264. Campaigns: 1995-1996, 1997-1998, 2008.
2. Personal communication from Gurli Meyer, Norges geologiske undersøkelse.
3. Unpublished report by Arne Jouttijärvi, Heimdal Archaeometry, in the museum.
4. Identification by curator Jens-Christian Moesgaard, The National Museum of Copenhagen.
5. 15-20% of the tree-pollen in the diagram should be considered foreign pollen transported by the wind from other regions (Andersen 1995: 41).
6. Turf-built houses from the Early Iron Age similar to those from North West Jutland are also known from the island of Sylt (Kossack et al 1975).

References

Andersen, S.T. (1995) Pollenanalyser fra Ove Sø. In: *Geobotaniske undersøgelser af kulturlandskabets historie. Pollenanalyser fra gravhøje og søer i 1994. Danmarks Geologiske Undersøgelse*, eds. S.T. Andersen, & P. Rasmussen, 37-55. Kunderapport nr. 12. København: Miljøministeriet. Danmarks Geologiske Undersøgelse.

Bech, J.-H. (1985) The Iron Age Village Mound at Heltborg, Thy, *Journal of Danish Archaeology* 4, 129-146.

Bech, J.-H. (2003) The Thy Archaeological Project – Results and Reflections from a Multinational Archaeological Project. In: *Diachronic Settlement Studies in the Metal Ages*, ed. H. Thrane, 45-60. Aarhus: Jysk Arkæologisk Selskab.

Carelli, P. & P. Kresten (1997) Give Us This day Our Daily Bread. A Study of Late Viking Age and Medieval Quern Stones in South Scandinavia, *Acta Archaeologica* vol. 68, 109-138.

la Cour, V. & H. Stiesdal (1957) *Danske Voldsteder Fra Oldtid og Middelalder. Thisted Amt.* København: Nationalmuseet.

Engberg, N. & J. Frandsen (2011) *Valdemar den Stores borg på Sprogø*. Højbjerg: Wormianum.

Gerrets, D.A. & J. De Konig (1999) Settlement development on the Wijnaldum-Tjitsma terp. In: *The excavations at Wijnaldum* Volume 1, eds. J.C. Besteman et al, 73-124. Rotterdam: A.A. Balkema.

Gestsson, G. (1982) Brugen af sten og tørv i de islandske huse fra landnamstid til nyere tid. In: *Vestnordisk byggeskikk gjenom to tusen år: Tradisjon og forandring fra romertid til det 19. Århundre/ West Nordic Building Customs from the Roman Period to the 19th Century (with English summary)*, eds. B. Myhre et al, 162-172. AmS-Skrifter 7. Stavanger: Arkeologisk Museum i Stavanger.

van Giffen, A.E. (1940) Een systematisch onderzoek in een der Tuinster wierden te Leens, *Jaarverslag van de Vereenigung voor Terpenonderzoek* 20-24, 26-115.

Henningsen, H. (2000) Middelalder i Fjand, *KUML. Årbog for Jysk Arkæologisk Selskab*, 151-198.

Hyldgaard, I.M. (1988) Hedegård – et træbygget borganlæg fra 1300-tallet, *hikuin* 14, 253-260.

Kann Rasmussen, A. (1968) En byhøj i Thyland, *Nationalmuseets Arbejdsmark* 1968, 137-144.

Kaul, F. (1999) Vestervig – an Iron Age Village Mound in Thy, NW Jutland. In: *Settlement and Landscape*, eds. C. Fabech & J. Ringtved, 53-67. Aarhus: Jysk Arkæologisk Selskab.

Kersten, K. & P. LaBaume (1958) *Vorgeschichte der Nordfriesischen Inseln*. Die vor- und frühgeschichtlichen Denkmäler und Funde in Schleswig-Holstein, bd. IV. Neumünster: Karl Wachholtz Verlag.

Kossack, G. et al (1975) Zehn Jahre Siedlungsforschung in Archsum auf Sylt, *Bericht der Römisch-Germanischen Kommission* Band 55, 1974. II Teil.

Liebgott, N.-K. (1989) *Dansk Middelalderarkæologi*. København: G.E.C. Gads Forlag.

Mikkelsen, P. et al (2008) Tæbring, NW Denmark, AD 600-1100. An archaeological and archeobotanic study, *Acta Archaeologica* 79, 79-109.

Myhre, B. et al (eds.) (1982) *Vestnordisk byggeskikk gjenom to tusen år: Tradisjon og forandring fra romertid til det 19. Århundre/ West Nordic Building Customs from the Roman Period to the 19th Century (with English summary)*. AmS-Skrifter 7. Stavanger: Arkeologisk Museum i Stavanger

Olsen, A.-L.H. (2005) Af tørvehusets saga, *Skalk* 2005 (4), 20-27.

Segschneider, M.G. (1998) Zur Besiedlung der nördlichen nordfriesischen Küstenlandschaft in der Wikingerzeit. In: *Beretning fra det 17. tværfaglige vikingesymposium*, ed. Dietrich Meier, 77-85. Kiel: Forlaget Hikuin og Afdeling for Middelalder-arkæologi, Aarhus Universitet.

Steensberg, A. (1952) *Bondehuse og Vandmøller i Danmark gennem 2000 år*. København: Hassing.

Svart Kristiansen, M. (2005) Bygninger. In: *Tårnby. Gård og landsby gennem 1000 år*, ed. M. Svart Kristiansen, 163-264. Jysk Arkæologisk Selskabs Skrifter 54. Højbjerg: Jysk Arkæologisk Selskab.

Aaby, B. & P.B. Vegger (1996) Tykke muldlag fortæller om brug af tørvegødning, *Arkæologiske udgravninger i Danmark* 1995, 30-39.

Islands Across the Sea – Aspects of Regionality in the Norse North Atlantic Diaspora

Mogens Skaaning Ravnsbjerg Høegsberg

Abstract

The paper explores the building customs of the Greenland Norse in comparison with the building customs on the other North Atlantic islands, particularly Iceland. The established house typology of Norse Greenland, established in the 1940s, is reviewed, and it is argued that the typology established by Danish archaeologist Aage Roussell in the 1940s is problematic, from both a terminological and analytical viewpoint. In light of later findings in both Greenland and Iceland it is argued that the architectural developments in the two countries may not be as different as has previously been believed and that the differences between the architectural solutions across the North Atlantic may best be understood in the light of the study of regionality.

Introduction

This paper will address ideas first developed in a research project on the cultural identity of the Greenland Norse and their dwellings (Høegsberg 2009a). The material cultures of Viking Age and Medieval Norway, Faroe Islands, Iceland and Greenland are, broadly speaking, highly similar, although there are of course also differences between them. However, attempting to explain these comparisons and contrasts purely in the light of identity issues may overlook important factors that were at work when, from the beginning of the 9th century, Norse settlers set out to make new homes on the different islands across the North Atlantic. This paper therefore studies these cultures within the framework of 'regionality studies', which offer a more open-ended approach where regional differences may be explained in a variety of ways, including functional explanations.

The North Atlantic settlements and regional differences

The North Atlantic islands were settled by Norsemen in the 9th and 10th centuries: The Faroe Islands at some point in the early 9th century, Iceland in 871 plus/minus a year or two and Greenland in the 980s (Arge 2000: 156; Arneborg & Seaver 2000: 282; Vésteinsson 2000: 164). While the settlements on the Faroe Islands and in Iceland endured, the Greenlandic settlements eventually died out in the late Middle Ages.

The settlers brought with them an economic system based on pastoral farming in a dispersed settlement pattern focused around single farmsteads. This was supplemented by various other activities such as fowling, fishing, sealing and hunting. The precise strategies employed by the settlers depended on the island in question as the settlers adapted their modes of living to varying climates, ecologies and topographies of the different islands and island groups (the Faroe Islands is an archipelago with 18 islands). Greenland, for example, had large indigenous terrestrial mammals such as caribou, which was not the case in the Faroe Islands or Iceland (Buckland 2000; McGovern 2000). Whereas the Greenlanders soon came to rely heavily on seal, this was not the case in Iceland and the Faroe Islands, where the settlers instead engaged in fishing which, in turn, appears to have been negligible in Greenland (McGovern 2000). While the basic economic system was therefore superficially the same, there were definite regional differences in the subsistence strategies employed in different areas. In the long term, this had major consequences as may be exemplified by Iceland and Greenland.

Regional differences in subsistence strategies and resource use emerged gradually over time, since it would appear that both the late 9th-century settlers in Iceland and the late 10th-century settlers in Greenland attempted to establish farming systems very similar to the ones they knew from their homelands. The Icelandic settlers seem to have been inspired by Norwegian farming systems (although a contingent of the settlers appears to have come from the British Isles), while the Greenland settlers transplanted the farming system from Iceland to Greenland.

One significant difference was that the settlers of the North Atlantic appear to have engaged much less in cereal growing than Norwegian farmers, although cereal was probably grown in both Iceland and Greenland (and probably to a larger extent in the Faroe Islands) (Øye 2005: 363; Vésteinsson 2006a: 101; Henriksen 2012: 176f). The composition of the animal stock was more or less the same across the North Atlantic and comprised pigs, cattle, sheep and goats.

Zooarchaeological investigations clearly indicate that while the Icelanders quickly reduced both the number of cattle and pigs, the Greenlanders continued to rely on their resource-demanding cattle although they did quickly phase out pigs (McGovern 2000: 332). The Greenlanders' continued reliance on cattle must not be understood as evidence that Greenland was more suitable for cattle than Iceland. Rather, it appears to reflect the persistence of old ideas about the proper composition of animal stock,

to the point where even very small and marginally-situated farms such as farm W48 in the Western Settlement appear to have had at least one or two heads of cattle (McGovern 2000: 333).[1]

The use of marine resources reveals even greater differences. Whereas the Icelanders engaged in substantial fishing as early as the 9th and 10th centuries, fish apparently played an almost imperceptible role in Norse Greenland, where fish bones are rare in excavated middens, despite the abundance of both fresh and saltwater fish in the locality (McGovern 1992: 195). Although zooarchaeologists agree that fish played a larger role in the Greenlandic subsistence economy than the evidence of the middens suggest, they assert that neither pre- nor post-depositional attrition can account for the sheer paucity of fish bones in Greenland. Fishing cannot, therefore, have played a major role in the Greenlandic economy (McGovern 1992: 196).

These differences in resource use have yet to be explained. To a certain degree it may have something to do with availability, seal being far more abundant in Greenlandic waters than in Icelandic. Still, this cannot be the only explanation for the conspicuous absence of fish in Greenlandic middens. Another possible explanation may be connected with the manpower required to engage in substantial fishing activities – manpower which the Greenlanders may instead have directed at sealing. These examples reflect a broader pattern of marked regional differences in the economic systems of the various North Atlantic islands.

The dwellings on the North Atlantic islands

Turning to the dwellings on the North Atlantic islands, such marked differences are lacking, just as they are in the artefact assemblages. In fact, despite some variation, the differences between the dwellings of particularly Iceland and Greenland may turn out to be very small indeed.

An important factor to note here is the shared use of building materials. Having no proper forests, the primary building material of Iceland and Greenland was turf, combined with some stone, especially in Greenland. Timber could be, and was, imported from Norway, but not in quantities that made timbered buildings feasible. Instead, imported timber was probably reserved for roof constructions, interior panels etc. Driftwood was also utilized when possible, but the large supply of driftwood that would have been available to the settlers on their arrival was soon depleted.

While turf is an excellent building material in the North Atlantic climate, it is, of course, not nearly as flexible a material as wood. Consequently, a certain likeness is bound to develop between the dwellings of the different islands, due simply to the use of the same building materials. Also, it should be remembered that most of the Greenland settlers originated in Iceland and therefore initially carried shared cultural memories of Icelandic forms of architecture with them to Greenland. It is therefore not surprising that the differences in building styles only manifested themselves over time. The same was true in the Faroe Islands, where the earliest dwellings were longhouses of a similar type to those in use in contemporary Scandinavia (Arge 2000: 157). In Iceland, the picture is less clear. Here, it would seem that longhouses in the Scandinavian tradition did not prevail until the mid to late 10th century (about 100 years after the landnám), after which longhouses became dominant (Vésteinsson 2006b: 116ff). At the time of the Norse landnám in Greenland in the 980s it would seem that the dwellings in both the Faroe Islands and Iceland were very similar, not only to each other but also to Scandinavian Viking Age longhouses with either curved or straight long walls (Arge 1991: 109; Vésteinsson 2006b: 116).

The primary work on the houses of Norse Greenland is still Aage Roussell's thesis *Farms and Churches in the Mediaeval Norse Settlements of Greenland* (Roussell 1941). In spite of later findings which cast doubt on some of Roussell's conclusions, his typology remains influential. Roussell divided the Greenlandic dwellings into three types: the longhouse, the passage house and the centralized house (Roussell 1941: 137). Roussell defined the types as follows: the longhouse (type I) was a house "with one or more rooms"; the passage house (type II) was a house "with rooms in

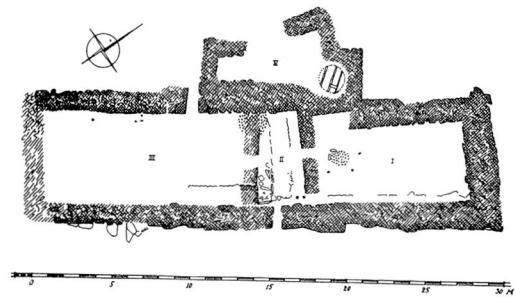

fig. 1 a
V 51

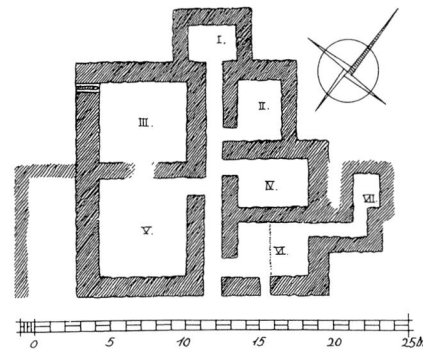

fig. 1 b
Ø 2

Figure 1. Aage Roussell's three Greenlandic house types. From the top: A longhouse, exemplified by the dwelling at ruin group V51 (Sandnes); a passage house, exemplified by the dwelling at ruin group Ø2 and a centralized house, exemplified by the dwelling at ruin group V54. After Andreasen 1981: 180.

rows behind one another and connected by one or more passages"; and finally the centralized house (type III) was a house "where dwelling and livestock premises are in the same block, which usually is of type II" (Roussell 1941: 137) (Figure 1).

The longhouse

As will be evident from Figure 1, Roussell's longhouses do not correspond with what most archaeologists understand by a longhouse in the Scandinavian

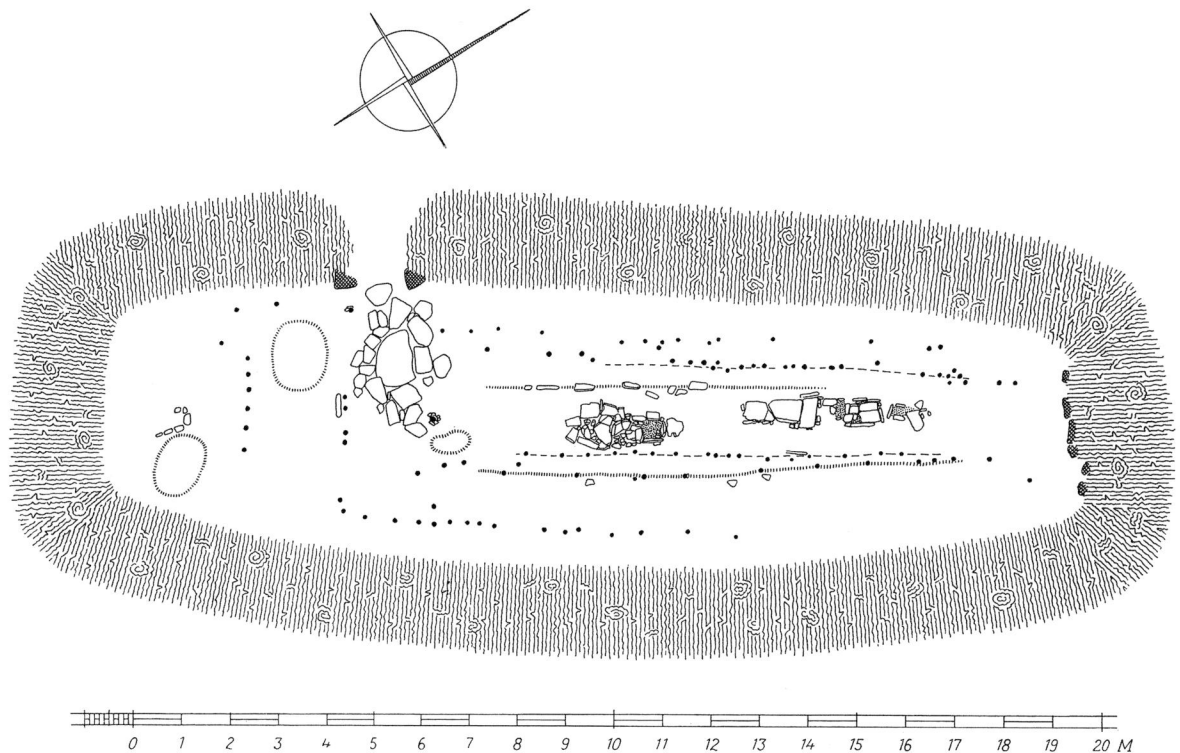

Figure 2. Longhouse excavated at Ísleifsstaðir in Borgarfjarðasýsla, Iceland, 1939. After Stenberger 1943: 158.

sense, *ie* a building with contiguous long walls, a contiguous roof construction based on roof-bearing posts and perhaps subdivided into more than one room by walls of wood (*eg* Schmidt 1994: 45ff; Vésteinsson 2006b: 116). This is the type of longhouse that dominated Iceland at the time of the settlement of Greenland (Vésteinsson 2006b: 116ff).

Contrary to this, Roussell's longhouses do not necessarily have contiguous long walls, a fact which has consequences for the roof construction. While examples of buildings with roof-bearing posts have been found, in many cases it is likely that each room had its own roof construction and in some cases it must be considered certain, for example at the farm E20, which is used by Roussell as an example of the type (Roussell 1941: 150). Furthermore, in Roussell's longhouses, room divisions are made out of thick walls of turf, as in Figure 1. Roussell interpreted the Greenlandic longhouses as a variation on a theme: a Greenlandic attempt to emulate typical Scandinavian longhouses such as the ones we also know from Iceland (Figure 2), but in light of the differences just

mentioned, as well as later findings, the term may be misleading.

More recent research has demonstrated that longhouses which correspond closely with buildings excavated in Iceland were also built in Greenland in the early years of the settlements there. This is the case with the earliest phases of both farm E17a and The Farm Beneath the Sand, and remnants of longhouses with curved long walls have also been found at E29a (Albrethsen 2003: 99-101). It also should be noted that these buildings lack the heavily accentuated room divisions that exist in Roussell's longhouses (Figure 3).

Roussell's longhouses should be understood in the context of the development of late Viking Age and early medieval houses in Europe, Scandinavia and Iceland, which featured more rooms and more accentuated room divisions within them. The particular North Atlantic expression of these buildings is likely to be a consequence of using turf as the primary building material, resulting in complexes that are actually composed of a number of individual build-

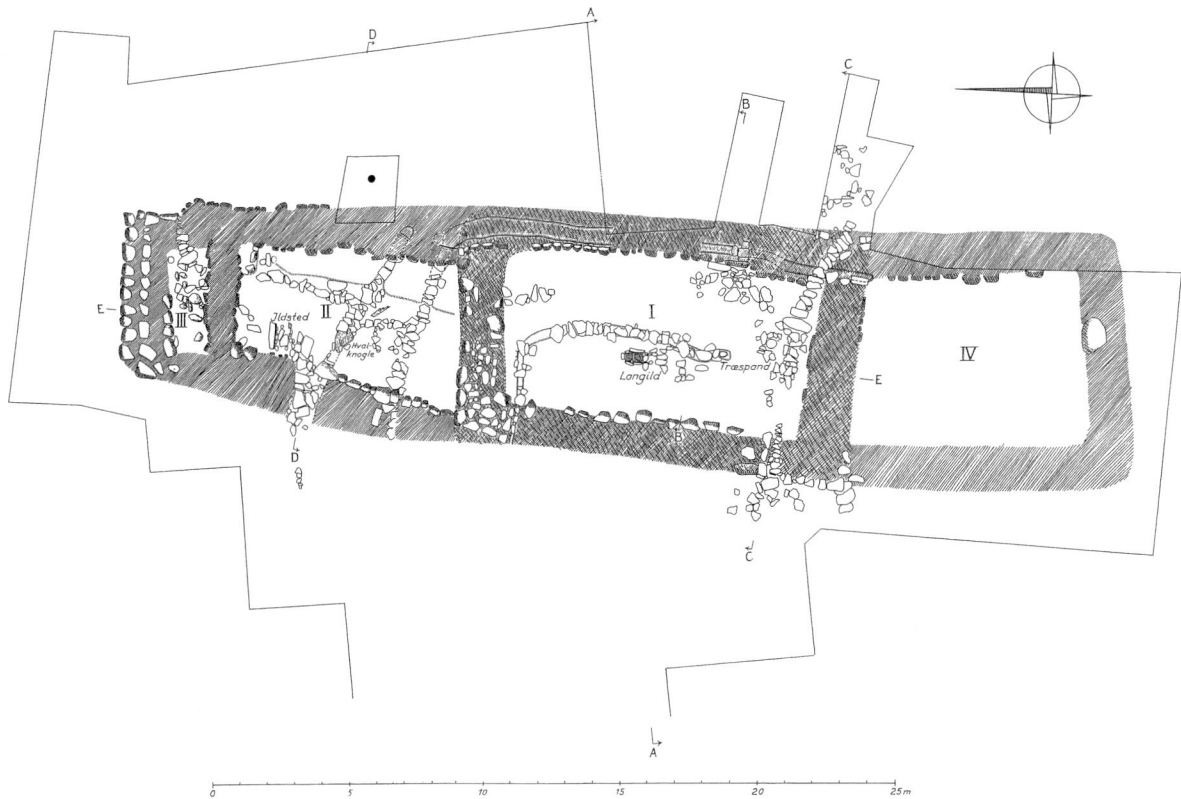

Figure 3. Plan of the final phase of the dwelling at ruin group Ø17a in the Norse Eastern Settlement in Greenland. The large room in the middle is the oldest phase of the dwelling and was originally a longhouse with straight long walls such as the one excavated at the Farm Beneath the Sand in the Western Settlement. After Vebæk 1993: 13.

ings with their own roof construction, set closely together, rather than being a number of rooms under a single roof.

That the developments in Iceland and Greenland were similar is exemplified by two houses: the well-known Icelandic dwelling at Stöng, excavated in 1939, and a Greenlandic house from the Eastern Settlement, E71 (Figure 4) (Roussell 1943: 78; Vebæk 1992: 30). While they are not physically identical, their spatial layouts are highly similar. This highlights the need to look beyond architectural appearance towards spatial organisation in the analysis of houses. The dating of these two examples is debated. There has been an ongoing discussion over the dating of Stöng. Initially, it was given a relative dating, based on the tephrochronological dating of the volcanic eruption that laid waste to Þjórsárdalur. This eruption was first dated to 1300, but later revised to 1104 (Dugmore et al 2007: 2). Following an excavation in the early 1980s, Vilhjálmur Örn Vilhjálmsson

pointed out inconsistencies in the dating, based on artefactual evidence, and argued that Þjórsárdalur was likely abandoned sometime in the 13th century and not necessarily as the result of one single catastrophic volcanic eruption. Still, the 1104-date for the destruction of Þjórsárdalur remains widely accepted. It is certain that Stöng was built before 1300 and it may be even earlier, dating before 1104 (Dugmore et al 2007: 1-3).

As for the Greenlandic example, no precise dating can be given either. The excavation was conducted in 1948, before stratigraphic excavation became the norm in Greenland, and there are few datable artefacts from the site. However, the presence of double sided bone combs at the site suggests that it was in use at least into the 13th century, although the excavator believed the site to have been abandoned in the 12th century, based on carbon dating of a number of mouse bones found at the site (Vebæk 1992: 107f).

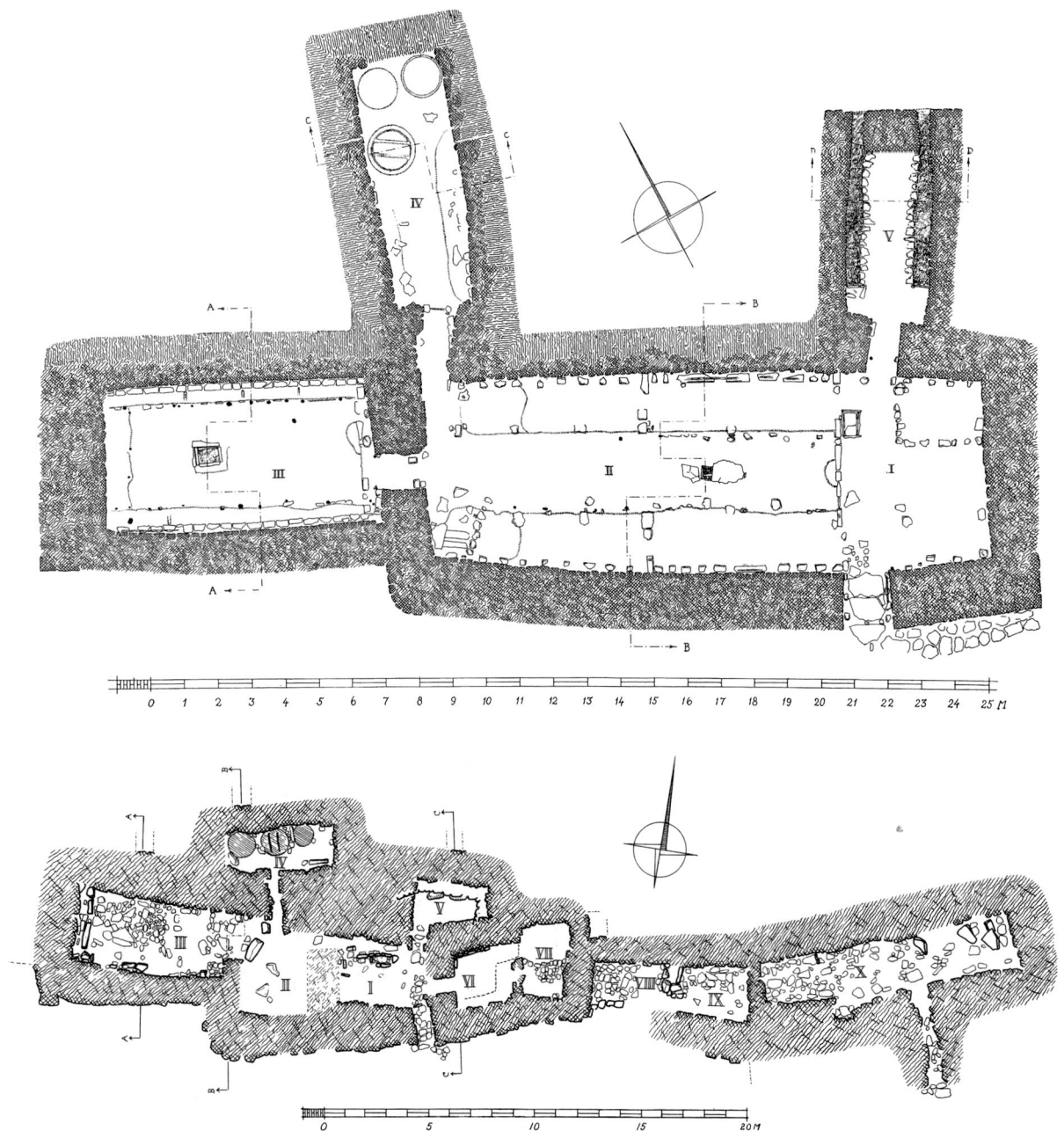

Figure 4. Plans of the dwellings at Stöng, Iceland (top) and ruin group Ø71 in the Eastern Settlement of Greenland. While the two dwellings are not identical, there are clear structural similarities. After Roussell 1943:78 & Vebæk 1992: 30.

For the purposes of my argument about the general development of architecture in Greenland and Iceland, the exact dating of Stöng and E71 are not of paramount importance, but obviously a solution to the dating debate would be welcome. The important point is that dwellings in both Iceland and Greenland during the 12th and 13th centuries seem to have followed a similar trend towards more segregated spaces within houses.

Another example which supports the hypothesis that Greenland and Iceland followed the same general trend is the Icelandic proto-passage house at Gröf and the Greenlandic dwelling at ruin group W51 (Sandnes), both dating to the 14th century (Figure 5). This tripartite division, featuring an entrance room in the centre, which gives access to larger rooms at either side is also known from Norway in both rural and urban settings from the 11th century onwards

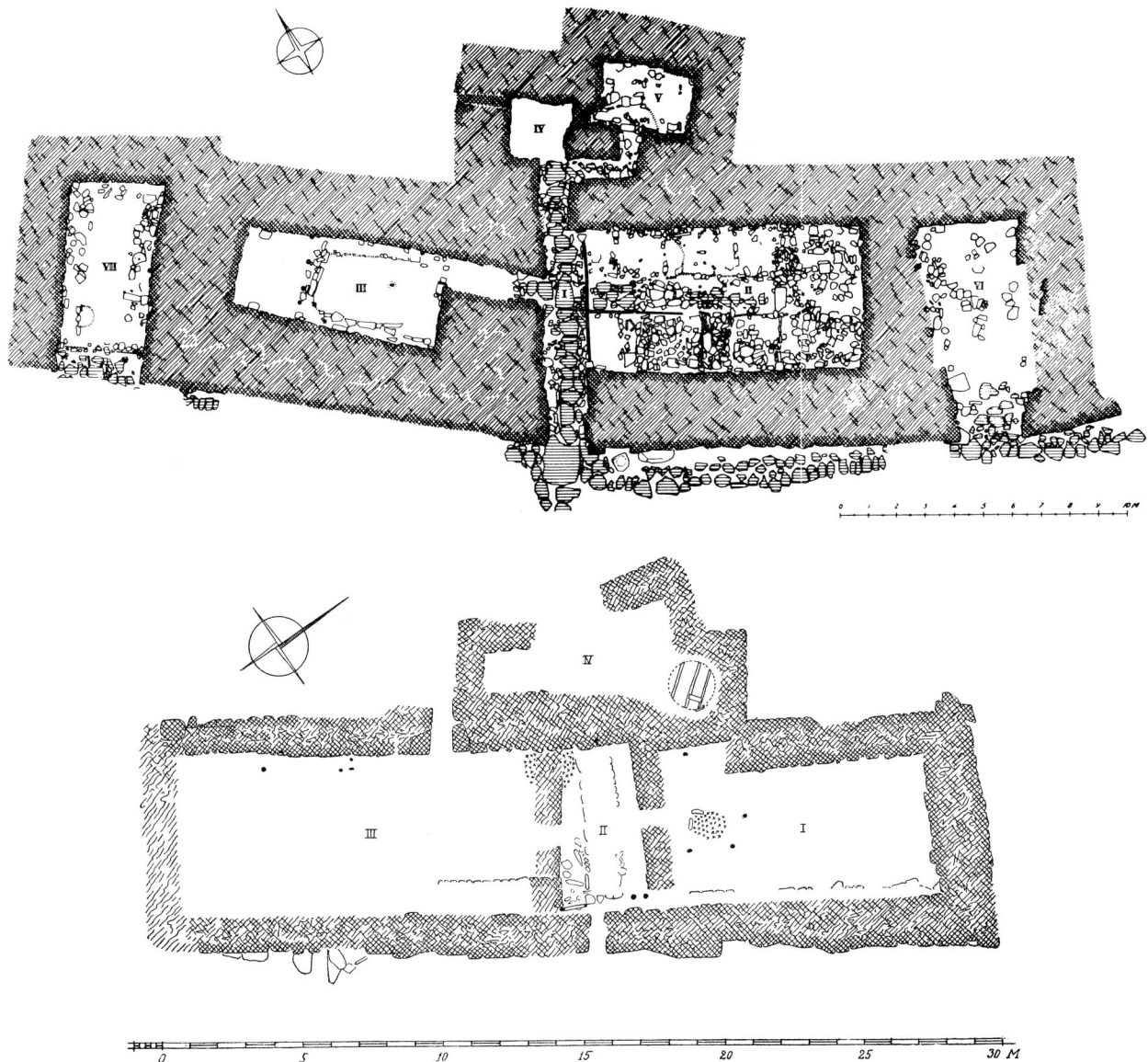

Figure 5. Plans of the dwellings at Gröf, Iceland (top) and ruin group V51 (Sandnes) in the Western Settlement of Greenland. At Gröf, a passage separates the two main rooms and a separate building has been added at either end of the complex. At Sandnes, the two main rooms are separated by a wider passage and there are no extra structures at either end. Otherwise the two are remarkably similar. After Ágústsson 1982: 258 & Roussell 1936: 31.

(Christophersen 1994: 184; Fett 1989: 34; Martens 1973: 55ff). While the idea that this layout was developed in Iceland or Greenland without inspiration from Norway cannot be completely dismissed, it seems more likely that it originated in Norway and was transmitted subsequently to the North Atlantic. It is impossible to know at present whether this layout reached Greenland by way of Iceland (or vice versa) or was transmitted to both Greenland and Iceland directly

from Norway. More excavated examples of the building type and better dating evidence is needed.

In both Iceland and Greenland buildings such as these are typically seen as the first step towards the development of the passage house, and this is where the beginnings of a divergence between the houses of Iceland and Greenland can be observed. It is also the place where conventional terminology becomes problematic.

The passage house

The term 'passage house' is primarily used to describe buildings from post-medieval Iceland where passage houses were in use in some parts of the country until the mid-20th century. The term is apt, since one of the defining features of the passage house is a long passage, usually running the depth of the building complex, providing access to most of the individual buildings that make up the complex (Figure 6).

Aage Roussell's defined the passage house as one "with rooms in rows behind one another and connected by one or more passages"; in contrast to the 'centralized house' (type III), "where dwelling and livestock premises are in the same block, which usually is of type II".

We may immediately disregard Roussell's qualifier "usually" in his definition of the centralized house, since *all* his examples of this type were passage houses in the morphological sense. The only difference between the two types is the presence or absence of one or more rooms for animals. From a morphological point of view it can therefore be argued that we are dealing with only one type, namely the passage house – a term which may be appropriate for the post-medieval and modern Icelandic examples, but appears less appropriate for the Greenlandic material.

The term is misleading because there are only two good examples of Greenlandic passage houses. The first, at ruin group E2, was excavated in 1894 by Daniel Bruun who was quite aware of post-medieval Icelandic buildings, having read Valtyr Guðmundsson's 1889 book *Privatboligen paa Island i Sagatiden* (which can be translated as *The Icelandic Dwelling in Saga Times*). In this book, Guðmundsson established a building typology for Iceland, based on descriptions in the sagas as well as his knowledge of contemporary Icelandic farm houses.

Although Bruun was a conscientious excavator, it is possible that his observations were somewhat affected by his knowledge of Guðmundsson's book. At least no other Greenlandic passage house corresponds as well with the Icelandic post-medieval passage house as the one at E2. The only other building that comes close is the dwelling at ruin group W8, excavated in the 1930s by Aage Roussell.

However, looking at the entirety of the material, and insofar as we can trust the excavation plans, the Greenlandic houses which Roussell termed passage houses are not as much organized around a passage

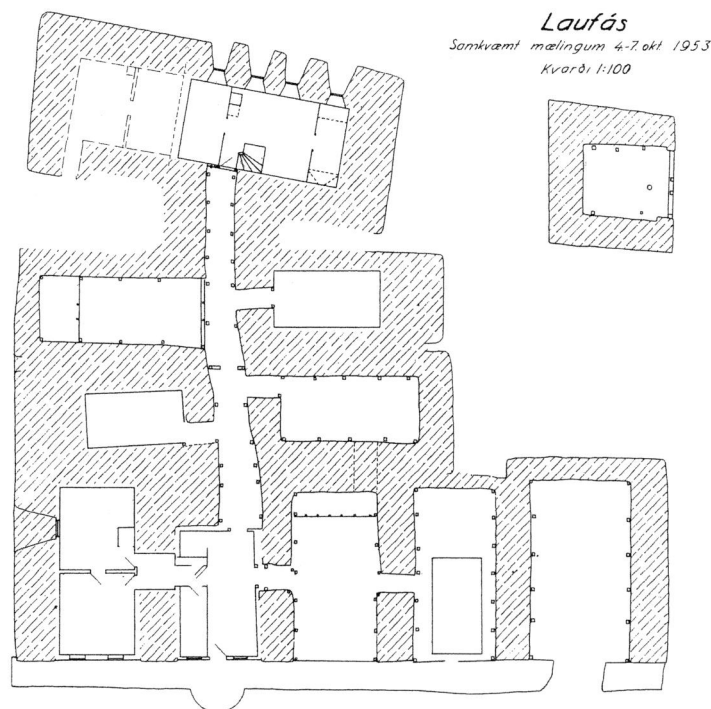

Laufás
Samkvæmt mælingum 4-7 okt. 1953
Kvarði 1:100

Figure 6. The final phase of the Icelandic passage house Laufás (1876) as it may be seen today in Eyjafjörður, North Iceland. Note how the passage runs the depth of the building and provides access to the majority of the rooms. After Ágústsson 1982: 265.

as they are around traffic being conducted directly from room to room (or, more appropriately, from building to building). A couple of examples are the dwellings from ruin group E29 and W53c (Nørlund & Stenberger 1934: 72; Roussell 1941: 171).

Unfortunately there are some problems connected with these buildings. Most of these complexes were excavated in the 1930s with little or no attention paid to stratigraphy and very little focus on how the dwellings developed over time. We can take it almost for granted that many of the excavation plans of these complexes represent more than one phase, making the existing material difficult to interpret. The excavation of The Farm Beneath the Sand in the 1990s revealed a large building complex which had gone through an extremely complicated development, expanding and contracting from phase to phase (Berglund 2000: 297).

A second problem relates to dating, because we do not know exactly when these large building complexes began to develop in Greenland. What we do know is that the different Greenlandic house types do not represent a linear chronological development, contrary to what Roussell believed. While Roussell is not entirely clear on the matter, it would appear that he viewed the different house types as replacements for each other, developed as the Norse Greenlanders adapted to Greenlandic conditions. That is, the longhouse was replaced in an evolutionary sequence by the passage house which was finally superseded by the centralized house (Roussell 1941: 241f). Later excavations have shown that the development of large passage house complexes such as for instance The Farm Beneath the Sand could happen over a long period, as a continuous process from a Viking Age longhouse into a passage house with animal premises without Roussell's intermediate phase which would have been a passage house without animal premises. Also, carbon dates have demonstrated that houses such as W51 (Sandnes), belonging to Roussell's oldest type, the longhouse, were still being built in the 14th century (Høegsberg 2009b: 98-100), at a time where, according to his hypothesis, it ought to have fallen out of use. Consequently, Roussell's neatly linear model for the development of house types which allowed for the relative dating of sites,

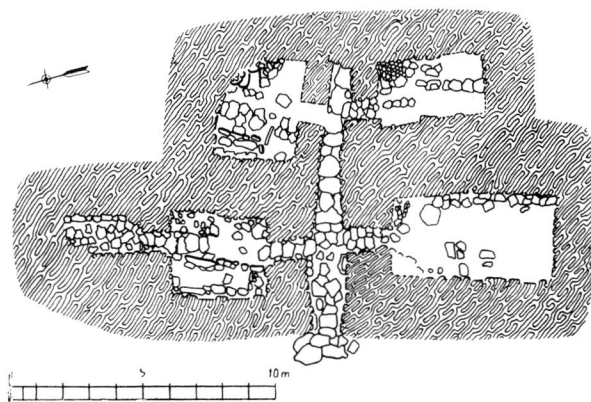

Figure 7. The dwelling at the Icelandic farm Forna-Lá. In its spatial layout with the central passage that provides access to most rooms in the dwelling, Forna-Lá is a clear precursor to the later and much larger passage house complexes in Iceland. After Ágústsson 1982: 259.

based solely on the type of dwelling, has been proven erroneous.

A third problem is that we lack comparative material from Iceland. Currently, there is only one published medieval building with which to compare the Greenland material. The large complexes excavated at Bessastaðir, Storaborg and Viðey may turn out to be extremely important, but unfortunately these have yet to be published (Vésteinsson 2004: 81).

The one medieval example of an Icelandic passage house we do have is Forna-Lá, dated to between circa AD 1450 and 1550 (Eldjárn 1951: 108). Another farm, Sandártunga, is probably a century later, from the second half of the 17th century, but otherwise very similar to Forna-Lá (Eldjárn 1951: 114). Both houses appear to be typological precursors to the later and much larger passage house complexes in Iceland which are very well known from the 19th and 20th centuries but which may go as far back as the 16th century (Ágústsson 1982: 261-265). A salient feature of both Forna-Lá and Sandártunga is the clear layout of individual buildings on either side of a central passage (Figure 7).

Comparing these Icelandic passage houses with the Greenlandic complexes that have come to be described using the same term indicates that the Icelandic examples are laid out more regularly. This factor alone suggests that we should not use the same term for the Greenlandic buildings. But there is another reason, too, namely the chronological differences between these buildings. As the material presents itself today, the first Icelandic examples of the proper passage house date to after circa 1450, while most, if not all, the Greenlandic 'passage houses' are of necessity older – the Norse Greenlandic settlements were abandoned at the latest sometime in the second half of the 15th century.

It is possible that the large Icelandic complexes at Bessastaðir, Storaborg and Viðey are the proverbial 'missing link' between Iceland and Greenland. From a morphological point of view, they may have more in common with the Greenlandic 'passage houses' than we currently appreciate. The development toward the passage house proper in Iceland could be a refinement that occurred in Iceland in the late Middle Ages, but was never implemented in Greenland because the settlements there were abandoned before such a development occurred.

At the moment, it is impossible to know whether, given time, the Greenlandic 'passage houses' would have developed into something more regularly laid out, such as the Icelandic passage houses. It may be that I am attempting to impose an idea of similarity on the building cultures of Greenland and Iceland more than the evidence currently suggests. For now, the large Greenlandic 'passage house' complexes appear to be unique to Greenland. As far as we know, Icelanders never reintroduced the accommodation of animals within complexes also inhabited by humans.

On the other hand, since Aage Roussell wrote his thesis in 1941, new excavations in both Greenland and Iceland have produced results that challenge Roussell's marked emphasis on the difference between the building cultures of Greenland and Iceland (Roussell 1941: 206, 212, 241f). Longhouses of the same type as those found in Iceland have been identified in Greenland; a building such as E71 in Greenland bears striking similarities to Icelandic dwellings of the so-called Þjórsárdalur-type, eg Stöng (Figure 4), and a building such as Gröf contradicts Roussell's claim that the tripartite layout seen at W51 was unique to Greenland.

Interestingly, complexes – so-called multi-room houses – which are very similar to the Icelandic and Greenlandic passage houses have begun to be identified in Arctic Norway as well, particularly in the Finnmark region, giving further rise to the question of how different the North Atlantic building cultures really were (Amundsen et al 2003).

The driving forces behind the large agglomerated complexes in Greenland, Iceland and Norway are not understood, and several different possibilities have been proposed. However, the appearance of relatively similar complexes in widely different areas where regional differences are known to exist, makes it tempting to seek answers in differences in climate, ecology and resource use. Neither of these factors would have been identical in Arctic Norway, Iceland or Greenland, yet they were perhaps similar enough to provide the impetus for building such large complexes.

An important feature is that the individual buildings in these complexes are relatively small and consequently would have been easy to heat. In arctic regions where fuel was not abundant, this could certainly have been a motivating factor, and in Greenland it might explain why there appears to be more of the large agglomerated complexes in the more northerly Western Settlement than in the Eastern Settlement. The smaller units that comprise these complexes would also have been easier to roof than the larger units that make up other house types, such as the longhouse. Moreover, collecting a large number of buildings together would also serve to reduce the amount of turf needed for building materials. This was an important resource for animal fodder, cutting large quantities of turf could result in major problems of erosion. There are of course other possible answers as to why complexes such as these developed in the North Atlantic areas, including the economic strategies employed at the farms. This has particularly been suggested for the Greenlandic variants, which links the building type to the amount of available grassland as well as to the economic focus of the farm (Andreasen 1981).

This line of thinking stresses that the agglomerated complexes of Norse Greenland are primarily found in inland areas or in very small niches on the coast of the Greenlandic fjords where quality grazing land was scarce and where the farms may have focused on either sealing or reindeer hunting and with less domestic animals than on other, better situated farms (Andreasen 1981: 183). Following Andreasen, the reason for condensing dwelling and outbuildings into one large complex was simply a lack of space. Furthermore, it could also be argued that by reducing the number of individual buildings and the necessary pathways between them, farmers could also reduce the destruction or disturbance of grazing areas. These ideas need to be explored further and backed up by studies in both Iceland and Norway.

As mentioned, there is one real difference between Greenland and the other areas which needs to be explained, and that is the introduction of animal premises into the same complex where humans lived. This is the case with the majority of the Greenlandic examples of the large agglomerated complexes. It may simply have been another expression of resource conservation: by incorporating one or more buildings for animals into the complex, the Norsemen did not have to build a free-standing byre with its large consumption of turf for insulating walls. Another consideration may have been purely practical: having the animals close at hand, the farmer did not have to go outside the dwelling to a free-standing byre in order to tend to the animals in the deep cold of the Greenlandic winters. But Icelandic farmers must have confronted many of the same problems without adopting this solution. This could be yet another example of regionality, perhaps on several levels: between Greenland and the other North Atlantic islands, but also within Greenland itself. It appears that the large complexes that also housed animals were more prevalent in the Western Settlement than in the Eastern Settlement. Is this again a reflection of intra-regional differences which we do not yet understand?

Why regionality?

In the final analysis, there are certainly differences in the physical layout of the dwellings of Greenland, Iceland and Norway, but there are also marked similarities between them. How much weight should we assign these differences, which may reflect functional adaptation to the specific conditions of environment, rather than cultural, or conceptual norms? After all, the Greenlandic and Icelandic passage houses as well as the examples from Arctic Norway share the same basic idea of a number of individual buildings agglomerate into large complexes. And Roussell's Greenlandic longhouse appears to be based on the very same ideas that in Iceland led to the construction of houses such at that at Stöng.

I do not wish to question the importance of materiality or to suggest that the physical differences which can be detected were not meaningful to the people of the past. But having analyzed the dwellings as well as substantial artefact types from Norse Greenland in the light of identity studies, what stands out are not the differences between these societies, but rather the similarities. While there are differences in both the dwellings and in the artefact material, these differences are much less apparent than their similarities. Even though we are dealing with societies on islands separated by large stretches of the North Atlantic, the material differences between Greenland, Iceland, the Faroes and Norway are no more striking than some of the differences that may be detected in different regions of a much smaller and geographically-integrated country such as Denmark. That is not to say that regional differences could not be significant in terms of *eg* identity or that the Norwegians, the Faroese, Icelanders and Greenlanders did not think of themselves as "their own people".

The importance that has been assigned in the past to the uniqueness of the Greenlandic 'centralized house' is therefore not commensurate with the overall picture. This suggests that the Norse societies in the North Atlantic are more fruitfully studied as regions within the same culture and that the great distances between them should not be over-interpreted as automatically producing widely separate cultures. From a material point of view there was a much larger affinity across the 3000 kilometres of the North Atlantic than there was across the barely 1000 kilometres from, for example, Denmark to France.

The geographical locations of the different North Atlantic islands naturally forced the settlers to adapt, since climate, local ecological conditions, topography etc were distinctive. Although this gave rise to variations in the material and cultural expressions of these societies, just as is apparent in the different regions of Norway, Denmark or any other country of Viking Age and medieval Europe. However, the material cultures of these peoples are strikingly similar. This is perhaps unsurprising. The diaspora communities in the North Atlantic were, at least in a cultural sense, rooted in the same place, namely Scandinavia. The Greenland settlers set out from Iceland which had itself, like the Faroe Islands, been settled primarily by Norwegians. And contrary to the settlements established by *eg* Danes in the British Isles and Normandy, the North Atlantic islands had no indigenous populations into which the settlers could ultimately be assimilated or encultured.[2] Furthermore, the settlers on the North Atlantic islands relied on contact and trade with Norway – and with each other – in order to obtain important goods that they could not procure themselves. This would further have strengthened the cultural ties in the region. The importance of kinship and familiar ties, so poignantly stressed by the Icelandic sagas, must not be underestimated either. Vast distances or not, blood relations mattered and must have ensured a continuing interest in maintaining contact from Norway in the east all the way across to Greenland in the west.

The idea that self-contained geographical entities, such as islands, or even lines on a map must necessarily give rise to a sense of self and produce a separate and easily identifiable culture has long since been abandoned in both anthropology and archaeology. Yet a tendency to project modern conceptions about nationhood and ethnic identities backwards in time lingers. It is scarcely necessary to point out that this is hopelessly anachronistic, but in spite of the best intentions, predetermined ideas produced by our own time often insinuate themselves with great subtlety into studies of the past. This paper has argued that the houses and settlements on the North Atlantic islands are best studied as regions within a shared basic culture and that this approach will widen rather than limit the avenues of investigation into the differences and similarities that characterize the Norse North Atlantic diaspora.

Notes

1. The designations W and E, used throughout this paper, are Anglicisations of the Danish V and Ø, designating West (Danish: 'Vest') and East (Danish: 'Øst'). Since the late 19th century until the 1980s, Norse farms in Greenland were given a number, and the prefix W or E was used to designate farms in the Western Settlement and Eastern Settlement respectively. While Greenlandic antiquarian authorities have adopted a new numbering system for archaeological sites, the old system is still almost universally used by archaeologists working with the archaeology of Norse Greenland.

2. The Inuit of Greenland were not present in South Greenland when the Norse arrived, and while the Inuit slowly inched closer to the Norse settlements over the course of the Middle Ages, nothing suggests later assimilation by Norsemen into the Inuit culture.

References

Ágústsson, H. (1982) Den islandske bondegårds udvikling fra landnamstiden indtil det 20. århundrede. In: *Vestnordisk byggeskikk gjenom to tusen år: Tradisjon og forandring fra romertid til det 19. Århundre/ West Nordic Building Customs from the Roman Period to the 19th Century (with English summary)*, eds. B. Myhre, B. Stoklund & P. Gjærder, 255-268. AmS-Skrifter 7. Stavanger: Arkeologisk museum i Stavanger.

Albrethsen, S.E. (2003) The Early Norse Farm Buildings in Western Greenland: Archaeological evidence. In: *Vinland Revisited: the Norse World at the Turn of the First Millennium*, ed. S. Lewis-Simpson, 97-110. St. Johns: Historic Sites Association of Newfoundland and Labrador.

Amundsen, C., J. Henriksen, E. Myrvoll, B. Olsen & P. Urbanczyk (2003) Crossing Borders: Multi-room houses and Inter-ethnic Contacts in Europe's Extreme North, *Fennoscandia archaeologica* XX, 79-100.

Andreasen, C. (1981) Langhus-ganghus-centraliseret gård, *hikuin* 7, 179-184.

Arge, S.V. (1991) The landnám in the Faroes, *Arctic Anthropology* 28:2, 101-120.

Arge, S.V. (2000) Vikings in the Faeroe Islands. In: *Vikings: The North Atlantic Saga*, eds. W.W. Fitzhugh & E.I. Ward, 154-163. Washington D.C.: Smithsonian Books.

Arneborg, J. & K. Seaver (2000) From Vikings to Norsemen. In: *Vikings: The North Atlantic Saga*, eds. W.W. Fitzhugh & E.I. Ward, 281-284. Washington D.C.: Smithsonian Books.

Berglund, J. (2000) The Farm Beneath the Sand. In: *Vikings: The North Atlantic Saga*, eds. W.W. Fitzhugh & E.I. Ward, 295-303. Washington D.C.: Smithsonian Books.

Buckland, P.C. (2000) The North Atlantic Environment. In: *Vikings: The North Atlantic Saga*, eds. W.W. Fitzhugh & E.I. Ward, 146-153. Washington D.C.: Smithsonian Books.

Christophersen, A. (1994) Gård og grunn. In: *Kaupangen ved Nidelva*, eds. A. Christophersen & S.W. Nordeide, 113-212. Trondheim: Riksantikvaren.

Dugmore, A.J., M.J. Church, K. Mairs, T.H. McGovern, S. Perdikaris & O. Vésteinsson (2007) Abandoned Farms, Volcanic Impacts, and Woodland Management: Revisiting Þjórsárdalur, the "Pompeii of Iceland", *Arctic Anthropology* 44:1, 1-11.

Eldjárn, K. (1951) Tvennar bæjarrústir frá seinni öldum, Árbók hins Íslenzka Fornleifafélags 1949-50, 102-119.

Fett, T.M. (1989) Bygninger og bygningsdetaljer. In: *De arkeologiske utgravninger i Gamlebyen, Oslo 6: Hus og gjerder*, ed. E. Schia, 15-92. Oslo: Universitetsforlaget.

Guðmundsson, V. (1889) *Privatboligen på Island i sagatiden, samt delvis i det øvrige Norden*. København: Høst.

Henriksen, P.S. (2012) Agriculture on the edge. The first finds of cereals in Norse Greenland. In: *Challenges and solutions: Northern Worlds – Report from workshop 2 at the National Museum, 1 November 2011*, eds. H.C. Gulløv, P.A. Toft & C.P. Hansgaard, 174-177. Copenhagen: The National Museum.

Høegsberg, M.S.R. (2009a) *Materiel kultur og kulturel identitet i det norrøne Grønland* (Material culture and cultural identity in Norse Greenland). PhD thesis, Aarhus University.

Høegsberg, M.S.R. (2009b) Continuity and Change: The Dwellings of the Greenland Norse, *Journal of the North Atlantic: Special Volume* 2: *Norse Greenland: Selected Papers from the Hvalsey Conference 2008*, 82-101.

Martens, I. (1973) Gamle fjellgårder fra strøkene rundt Hardangervidda, *Universitetets Oldsaksamling Årbok* 1970-1971, 1-84.

McGovern, T.H. (1992) Bones, Buildings, and Boundaries: Palaeoeconomic Approaches to Norse Greenland. In: *Norse and Later Settlement and Subsistence in the North Atlantic*, eds. C.D. Morris & D.J. Rackham, 193-230. Glasgow: University of Glasgow.

McGovern, T.H. (2000) The Demise of Norse Greenland. In: *Vikings: The North Atlantic Saga*, eds. W.W. Fitzhugh & E.I. Ward, 327-339. Washington D.C.: Smithsonian Books.

Nørlund, P. & M. Stenberger (1934) *Brattahlid*. Meddelelser om Grønland 88:1. Copenhagen: C.A. Reitzels Forlag.

Roussell, Aa. (1936) *Sandnes and the Neighbouring Farms*. Meddelelser om Grønland 88:2. Copenhagen: C.A. Reitzels Forlag.

Roussell, Aa. (1941) *Farms and Churches in the Mediaeval Norse Settlements of Greenland*. Meddelelser om Grønland 89. Copenhagen: C.A. Reitzels Forlag.

Roussell, Aa. (1943) Stöng, Þjórsárdalur. In: *Forntida gårdar i Island: Meddelanded från den nordiska arkeologiska undersökningen i Island sommaren 1939*, ed. M. Stenberger, 72-97. Copenhagen: Munksgaard.

Schmidt, H. (1994) *Building Customs in Viking Age Denmark*. Copenhagen: Bergiafonden.

Stenberger, M. (1943) Ísleifsstaðir, Borgarfjarðarsýsla. In: *Forntida gårdar i Island: Meddelanded från den nordiska arkeologiska undersökningen i Island sommaren 1939*, ed. M. Stenberger, 145-170. Copenhagen: Munksgaard.

Vebæk, C.L. (1992) *Vatnahverfi: An inland district of the Eastern Settlement in Greenland*. Meddelelser om Grønland: Man & Society 17. Copenhagen: Kommissionen for Videnskabelige Undersøgelser i Grønland.

Vebæk, C.L. (1993) *Narsaq – a Norse landnáma farm*. Meddelelser om Grønland: Man & Society 18. Copenhagen: Kommissionen for Videnskabelige Undersøgelser i Grønland.

Vésteinsson, O. (2000) The Archaeology of Landnám. In: *Vikings: The North Atlantic Saga*, eds. W.W. Fitzhugh & E.I. Ward, 164-174. Washington D.C.: Smithsonian Books.

Vésteinsson, O. (2004) Icelandic Farmhouse Excavations: Field Methods and Site Choices, *Archaeologia Islandica* 3, 71-100.

Vésteinsson, O. (2006a) Making a living – what did they live on? In: *Reykjavík 871 ±2: Landnámssýningin. The Settlement Exhibition*, ed. B. Sverrisdóttir, 98-107. Reykjavík: Reykjavík City Museum.

Vésteinsson, O. (2006b) The building and its context. In: *Reykjavík 871 ±2: Landnámssýningin. The Settlement Exhibition*, ed. B. Sverrisdóttir, 116-121. Reykjavík: Reykjavík City Museum.

Øye, I. (2005) Farming and farming systems in Norse societies of the North Atlantic. In: *Viking and Norse in the North Atlantic: Select Papers from the Proceedings of the Fourteenth Viking Congress, Tórshavn, 19-30 July 2001*, eds. A. Mortensen & S.V. Arge, 359-370. Tórshavn: Føroya Fróðskaparfelag.

PART 3

Houses, Homes and Social Strategies

Houses and Households in Viking Age Scandinavia – Some Case Studies

Sarah Croix

Abstract

Excavated houses form the primary source material for investigating the daily life of rural communities in Viking Age Scandinavia. Although the exact composition of the household is difficult to determine, its activities and the choices made regarding comfort and physical setting give some hints about its members' roles and relations. Taking as a point of departure houses from South Scandinavia and the limitations of this material for discussing functional space, the analysis of spatial distribution of domestic activities is facilitated through a comparison of selected examples from Norway and Iceland.

Introduction

Houses and households stand traditionally within the frame of inquiry of anthropology (Blanton 1994), but in the last two decades have increasingly been included in archaeological research agendas (Allison 1999; Benjamin 1995; Kent 1990; Parker Pearson & Richards 1994; Samson 1990) and also in the field of Viking and medieval studies (Beattie, Maslakovic & Rees Jones 2004; Boyd 2009; Milek 2006; Kowaleski & Goldberg 2008; Roesdahl 2003; Roesdahl 2009; Roesdahl & Scholkmann 2007). The connection between houses and households has been considered as one of the structuring elements of daily life, resting on the dynamic relationship between architectural forms and human beings.

Spatial organization in Viking Age houses has already been the object of a number of studies, which focused on access and circulation as organizing and regulating interactions between inhabitants and guests, based on the opposition of private and public spaces. Late Iron Age aristocratic houses, the 'halls', have received particular attention (Herschend 1998, especially 167-172), as being the place where chieftains organized large feasts to reward their retainers or celebrate the cult, thus using the hall as a public space for social representation and the gathering of a large amount of people (idem; Stamsø Munch 2003).

More recently, this approach has also been applied to houses of lower status, based on the argument that not only aristocratic households would receive guests (Beck 2010: 81f; Mikkelsen, Moltsen & Sindbæk 2008: 80), as Old Norse written sources emphasize the importance of hospitality in Viking times (Milek 2006: 206, with reference to Page 1995). Milek (2006), Boyd (2009) and Beck (2010) used spatial syntax analysis as established by Hillier and Hanson (1984) to establish patterns of movement through the house and the plot from the perspective of a visitor, in order to enlighten the relationship between inhabitants and strangers.

Thus, even the living room of a simple farm house could temporarily become a 'hall' in the functional sense, namely the setting for certain social activities. This definition of the 'hall', which will be used in the following paper and which is normally mostly employed by philologists, should be distinguished from the 'hall' of the archaeologists describing architectural features, such as large buildings or their vast central room.

In the present article, the everyday functions of dwelling areas and their multiple purposes will be considered in order to explore how domestic space was arranged to serve the daily, practical needs of inhabitants, on the basis of archaeological rural settlements from modern-day Denmark compared with selected examples from Norway and Iceland. As noted by Holger Schmidt (1994: 82), "the large common dwelling room did not exclusively denote the affluence and standing of the owner, since obviously it was first and foremost an expression of how the occupiers utilised their home". In other words, a house was primarily planned to accommodate the life of a household, after a certain number of cultural and social standards defining what a 'proper' house should be like, had been met.

Spatial organization can be related to many practical and social aspects, the interaction between inhabitants and guests being but one of them. The dynamics of the Viking Age household relied mostly on the relationships between men and women, parents and children, and perhaps masters and servants. Thus, spatial arrangements and domestic facilities will be considered as a reflection of the organization of household life, both at a practical and social level.

The Viking Age household

In general terms the household can be defined as "a group of people co-residing in a dwelling or residential compound, and who, to some degree, share house-holding activities and decision making" (Blanton 1994: 5). For the Viking Age, not much is known about the composition of the household or the number of its members. In previous research inferences have been made from later sources, including Icelandic sagas (Meulengracht Sørensen 1993: 27-33), early medieval provincial laws (Øye 2002: 255f) and late medieval population registrations (Johansen 1982: 60f), by measuring the dimensions of farm buildings (Donat 1980: 133; Myhre 1982: 213) or their number (Näsman 2009: 108). However, commemorative inscriptions, carved in runes on stones, provide contemporary evidence to investigate family relations which in all likelihood were the basis of household composition. There is evidence for farms run jointly by a man and a woman, who were husband and wife (Hassmyra stone, Vs 24, Sawyer 2000: 60) and may have considered each other as equal partners in this enterprise (Randbøl stone, DR 40; Moltke 1985: 296-299) (Sawyer & Sawyer 1993: 169). Runic inscriptions also reveal close bonds between parents, children, brothers and sisters (Sawyer & Sawyer 1993: 168). Inscriptions naming more than three or four children in one family are rare (ibid: 170).

The composition of peasant households in Carolingian northern France is better documented and gives a valuable point of comparison for enlightening the dynamics of household structure in Viking Age Scandinavia. Carolingian estate inventories registered the inhabitants of their tenant farms, revealing that most households were composed of a couple and their two to three children (Devroey 2003: 63-65, 72; Herlihy 1985: 56-78; Ring 1979). This pattern would of course be variable, depending for example on the age at which children would leave – or not – their parents' house; the size of the land – there seems to be a correlation between large amount of cultivated land and more children; and the high mortality rate, also in adult years, leading to periods of widowhood and the possibility of remarriage. It is likely that the Carolingian estate inventories did not register everyone, especially those who were not relevant for the economic management of the estate – grand-parents, the ill and disabled, domestic servants. The hereditary tenancy system on these estates implied that in some cases two families (fathers and sons) would live on the farm for a few years (Ring 1979: 15-20), but this is not necessarily applicable to independent farms. These two families could then be considered as one, extended household, in the sense of a shared residential and economic unit, although one can wonder how many rooms and buildings were used for dwelling.

It seems thus likely that, as in other contemporary agrarian communities, the Viking Age household varied according to inheritance and transmission customs. A low overall life-expectancy also implied its frequent redefinition. Both in Viking Age Scandinavia (Thedéen 2009: 62f) and in Carolingian France (Garver 2007: 126-130), an early death was often met, caused by accident or illness, by starvation or epidemics, at war, at sea or during childbirth. As the example from Hassmyra underlines, a farm was run jointly by a man and a woman, and the loss of one of the partners would ask for his or her replacement. The frequency of remarriage is occasionally hinted at by the rune-stones, and few couples would have shared their entire lives together.

Determining whether households based on nuclear families included other members is problematic. Slavery existed in Viking Age Scandinavia (Brink 2012). It is for example attested on the Danish rune-stone from Hørning (DR 58; Moltke 1985: 316) which unfortunately does not mention whether the freed slave Toki was regarded as a member of his master's household or resided in the same dwelling compound. Apart from this unique example, dependents are absent from the runic evidence. As in other pre-industrial societies, it is likely that the number of hired hands, domestic servants or slaves varied according to the status of the household, its economic needs and resources (Vésteinsson 2006: 122).

Thus, the Viking Age household should be described as a variable group of individuals, in numeral and structural terms, with the nuclear family at its core and together with an undetermined range of dependents.

The house: potential and limitation of the archaeological material

In the archaeological material from Viking Age Scandinavia, buildings with dwelling functions, *ie* houses, are generally identified from a number of criteria: their dimensions – they are often the largest building on the settlement unit; their quality – they are often the better and more strongly built; their location – usually in the middle of the unit; and typological comparison. Furthermore, their finds evidence is often richer than other buildings, and they are equipped with a hearth. This is not, however, an absolute criteria considering that it has not been preserved in many instances.

Understanding the spatial organization of these houses is challenging primarily because of the limitations of preservation conditions. With the exception of a few examples in Norway and Iceland, where

the lower parts of the walls may have left a mark in the landscape, and some very well-preserved finds from urban contexts (for example in Hedeby, see Schietzel 1984: 135-158), no sign of an elevation has been preserved in Viking Age houses from Southern Scandinavia. Even their ground level, including floors and associated fixtures, and the upper part of the holes which were used to support the timber construction have very often been truncated.

These regional differences can be explained by the subsequent use of abandoned sites, which suffered more heavily in modern day Denmark from agricultural cultivation, but also by different building traditions. Apart from timber, Viking Age houses in Norway and Iceland used earth, turf and stones for the construction of the walls which, when they collapsed, would have preserved the internal features beneath them, while Danish houses were mostly built of timber and wattle-and-daub.

Nevertheless, post-holes allow us to reconstruct house plans to a fairly reasonable degree, as well as identifying the position of entrances and internal partitions. For this reason, the archaeology of houses in South Scandinavia has mainly focused on construction techniques (Schmidt 1994), chronology (Hvass 1993) and typology (Skov 1994) although a more functional or social approach (Kaldal Mikkelsen 2003; Mikkelsen, Moltsen & Sindbæk 2008) is possible. Information about room partition and position of entrances allows spatial analysis, although this is limited again by the lack of surviving elevations and our inability to identify other kinds of ephemeral partitions such as curtains, screens, and perhaps lofts or upper floors.

Identifying the function of rooms or specific areas is also highly problematic in South Scandinavia. Ploughed-out floor layers took with them lost or abandoned items, production debris and refuse, which would have been deposited as a result of various activities. Fill from post-holes or wall trenches are often the only contexts which can securely be related to the occupation of a house, although the information they provide, most often in the form of a few potsherds, some unidentified iron fragments and perhaps a spindle whorl, is meager. However, well-preserved floor layers do not necessarily reveal rich

House	Nb of rooms	Central fire place	Platforms	Activities heated room	Activities unheated room	References
Aggersborg D (8th-10th c.)	4	x		Cooking (suspension structure); feasting (?); weaving	Food preparation (?)	Gjøstein Resi 1979-1980; Näsman 1980; Roesdahl 1986:67; Schmidt 1994:50; Sindbæk pers. comm. (Dec. 2010); Croix 2011a; Croix 2011b; Roesdahl, Sindbæk & Pedersen (forthcoming)
Borg in Lofoten I:1a (8th-10th c.)	4	x (2)	x	Feasting (+ gold-foiled figures); carving of soapstone objects; small scale metal working (?); weaving		Herschend & Kaldal Mikkelsen 2003: 62-66, 73-74; Holand 2003a:136-137; Holand 2003b; Johansen, Kristiansen & Stamsø Munch 2003:143-145; Stamsø Munch 2003
Fyrkat 2S and 4N (late 10th c.)	3	x	x (2S)	Soapstone potsherds; weaving		Olsen & Schmidt 1977: 174-176; 179-181; Roesdahl 1977:29-32, fig. 237
Hviding (late 10th c.)	3	?			Metal working	Schmidt 1994:58
Omgård Aiib (9th c.)	2	x			Cereal grinding	Schmidt 1994:48; Nielsen 1980:184
Omgård Aiv (late 10th c.)	3	?			Metal working	Nielsen 1980:194
Omgård Axlvi (late 10th c.)	3	x		Small scale metal working?		Nielsen 1980:194
Sædding III (10th c.)	5	x (2)	x (?-W dwelling)	Metal working (E dwelling)		Stoumann 1980:106-110; Schmidt 1994:68
Tæbring I (11th c.)	2	(x)			Food preparation	Mikkelsen, Moltsen & Sindbæk 2008:97; 101
Tæbring VII (9th-10th c.)	2	x			Food preparation?	Mikkelsen, Moltsen & Sindbæk 2008:97
Vorbasse CCIII (9th c.)	3	(?)		Weaving	Cereal grinding?	Schmidt 1994:45; Hvass 1980: 144-147
Vorbasse CII (late 10th-11th c.)	3	x			Metal working (forge pit)	Hvass 1980:159-161
Vorbasse CVI (late 10th-11th c.)	3	x		Metal working (central fire place)		Hvass 1980:159-161

Table 1. Main examples of Danish Viking Age houses discussed in this article + Borg in Lofoten I:1a (Norway), with references. Their identification is based on the literature, except for Omgård Axlvi which was interpreted by Nielsen (1980:194) as a workshop; however, the construction of the house, of Fyrkat type, its central fire place and its position in the middle of the farmstead rather indicates that it is a dwelling. Information about Vorbasse CCIII was supplemented by the plans and find list formerly available on the online archive Arena (/d1http://ads.ahds.ac.uk/arena/archlist.cfm?T=b&ID=uk). These files have now been removed and have been kindly provided to the author without modification by Mads Holst.

artefact material, which may have been displaced from its original deposition context by a number of factors, during the occupation of the house and subsequently; various scientific techniques can palliate to this lack of information, such as the analysis of microstratigraphy and microscopic residues in floor deposits (Milek 2006: 27-29).

The number of South Scandinavian houses for which it is possible to identify plan, organization and circulation as well as activity areas is thus fairly limited. The following analysis will only be based on some significant examples (see Table 1 and Figure 1), whose interpretation will be supplemented by the evidence from better preserved house sites from Norway and Iceland.

Features and functional organization in Viking Age houses

Needless to say, many daily activities on a farm, which functioned as the basic residential and economic unit in Viking Age Scandinavia, would have taken place outside the house – in various functional buildings, outdoors, in the fields and pastures etc. In the present article I will, however, only focus on the activities taking place inside the house, which represent a very small fraction of the daily tasks of a Viking Age household.

In the earlier part of the period (8th-9th century), the Viking Age house in South Scandinavia belonged to the Iron Age longhouse type (Kaldal Mikkels-

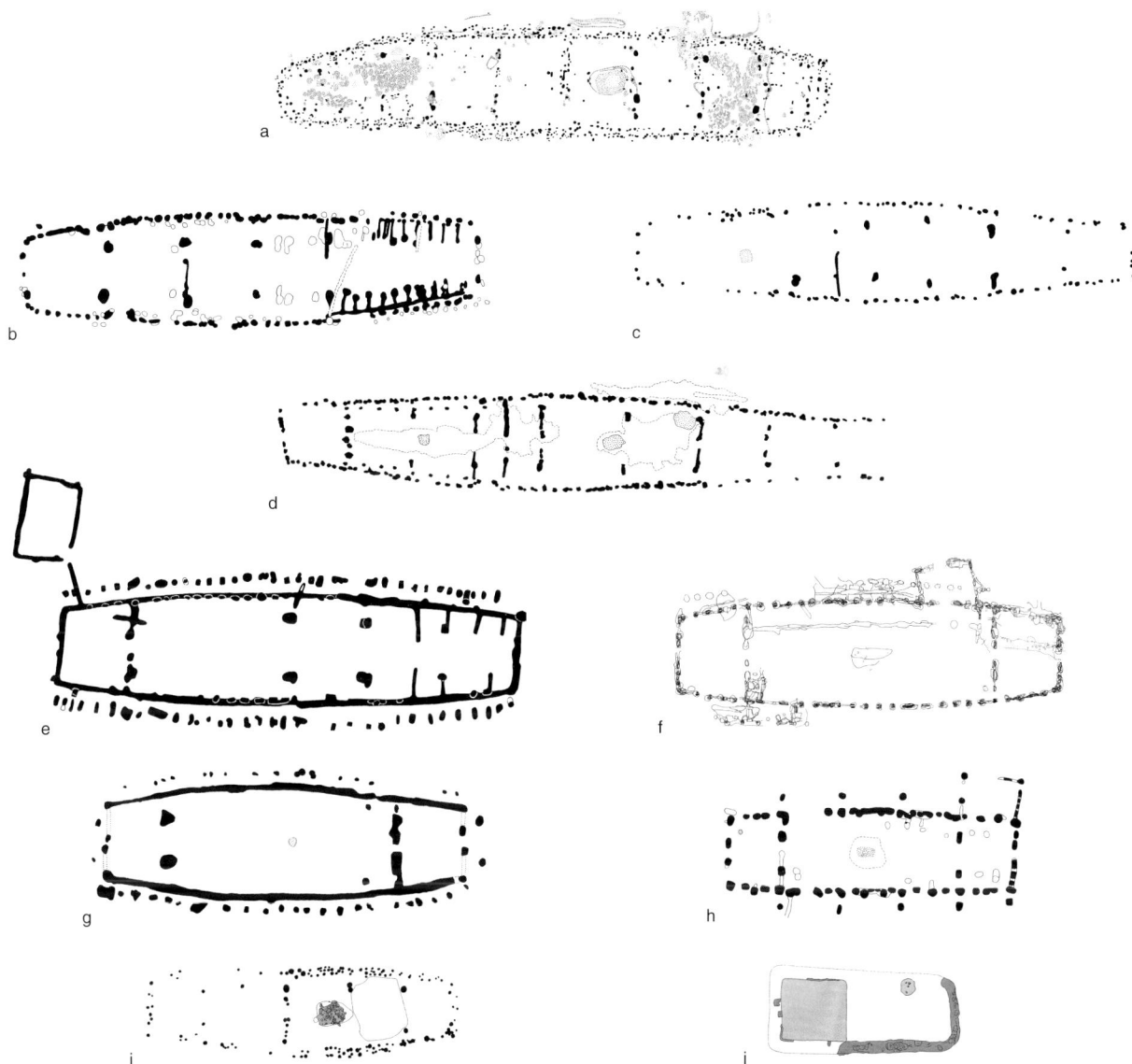

Figure 1. Plans of the main examples of Danish Viking Age houses discussed in the text, drawn to scale. a. Aggersborg D; b. Vorbasse CCIII; c. Omgård Aiib; d. Sædding III; e. Hviding; f. Fyrkat 2S; g. Omgård Axlvi; h. Vorbasse CII; i.-j. Tæbring VII & I. Plans a.-e. and g.-h. after Schmidt 1994; f. after Olsen & Schmidt 1977, figure 119; i.-j. re-drawn after Mikkelsen, Moltsen & Sindbæk 2008: figures 12 & 18.

en 2003: 78f), also known in Norway (Myrhe 1980: 371-374) as well as the Netherlands and North-West Germany (Hamerow 2002: 22-25). It was generally composed of a byre and a dwelling section, which was itself sub-divided into several rooms (up to 6-7). These were positioned in a row and connected by doors in the middle of the partition walls, and hosted various functions – storage, food processing, workshop etc. A high degree of room division was, rather expectedly, characteristic of larger houses, for example Aggersborg D or Borg in Lofoten I:1a (Norway), where they are usually connected to larger farms with a more complex economy (Myhre 1980: 371).

In the course of the Viking period this model tended to disappear, marked by the gradual detachment of the byre from the house and a diminution of the number of rooms. Houses with two rooms are known, one being equipped with a hearth, as well as tripartite houses of the so-called Trelleborg type, with a large dwelling room freed of roof-bearing posts and flanked on both sides by a gable room. These are found in Denmark (Kaldal Mikkelsen 2003: 78f), but also in Norway and Iceland (Milek 2006: 98; Myhre 1980: 358-370). While the primary function of the byre is rather obvious, the activities taking place in the dwelling section deserve particular attention.

The main dwelling room is usually interpreted as that equipped with a central hearth. It can be located in the middle of the house or at the opposite end from the byre (Schmidt 1994: 45-48). Most houses had only one room with a central hearth for example Aggersborg D or Fyrkat 2S, with a few exceptions. At Sædding, a 36 m long house (III) with a possible 10 m long byre to the east comprised two dwelling areas of exact same size and layout; each was equipped with a central heated room and framed by two rooms in the gable.

A similar situation is known in Norway from a number of longhouses, for example at Arstad (end 8th-mid 12th century) (Stamsø Munch 1983), Moi in Aust-Agder (c 900-1200) (Reitan 2011) and Borg in Lofoten I:1a. These three houses present a similar internal organization, namely two living rooms with central hearth. At Borg and Moi, about a third of the house is occupied by a byre and, although no diagnostic evidence is mentioned in the publication, similarities in layout suggest that the corresponding room at Arstad may have had the same function. At Borg, where the evidence is the richest, the two heated rooms seem to have hosted different functions. Room A (c 160 m²) has been interpreted as an ordinary living room (Herschend & Kaldal Mikkelsen 2003: 65) although in situ finds provide scarce evidence for metal working near the hearth, as well as for soapstone working and storage or repair of fishing gear. Room C (c 120 m²) has been interpreted as a hall, meant to receive guests and perform the cult as well as hosting family life and various domestic activities (Herschend & Kaldal Mikkelsen 2003: 65f). All in situ evidence for cooking and textile working has been found there, as well as for banqueting (or any social event involving the use of glass beakers and Tating ware jugs). It has also delivered most evidence for the manufacture of soapstone objects.

The situation at Sædding and Borg in Lofoten differ in several ways. The exact symmetry in the plan-

Figure 2. The heated room at the reconstructed Vorbasse farm house near the Fyrkat fortress in Hobro. Photo Margaret Stephensen 2010.

ning of the two heated rooms at Sædding indicates that this house was used by two households of equal standards, while the relation between room A and C at Borg seems more problematic. In situ finds are much more numerous in room C (138 items) than in A (30 items), a situation partly due to excavation methods (Holand 2003a: 131-135), but the fact that no in situ evidence for cooking and textile production was found in A may indicate that domestic life was fairly limited there. Perhaps it was used only for crafts, storage, food preparation and the like.

In all cases, it is worth emphasizing the 'central' role of the hearth both functionally and spatially (Figure 2). It was the principal indoor cooking facility and source of light, with perhaps a few lamps and a vent (Kaldal Mikkelsen 2003: 83). It was also the main heating system, although of a limited efficiency, its horizontal radiation at floor level diminishing rapidly when moving away from it (Beck et al 2007: 142-145). Difficulties in keeping the main living room warm can perhaps explain why it could rarely be entered directly from outside, using instead entrance rooms, porches or other windbreakers for access (Schmidt 1994: 84).

Its position also made of the hearth a defining architectural element. Indeed, it was not only positioned in the middle of the main living room, but often at the centre of the building as well. The slight curve of the long walls, a characteristic feature of Viking Age houses, implies that the hearth was generally located where the building was the widest. This position would have allowed more people to gather around it, to eat, talk, work, and play than if it was located along a wall, as seen for the same period at Tæbring I.

The central hearth was also a visual focal point: it could be seen by everyone and from there it was possible to see everyone. This quality has been interpreted by Rebecca Boyd as facilitating control over the rest of the household for the woman cooking by the hearth (Boyd 2009). However, it is difficult to imagine women stirring stews all day long, as cooking in cauldron or other kind of vessel would require minimal attention and would have allowed them to work on other tasks in the same room – for example weaving. Food was certainly a source of power for those controlling it in Viking Age Scandinavia. Perhaps control over food resources was more explicitly expressed by its distribution than its preparation, for example through the serving of meals.

Until the end of the 10th century, the architecture of Viking Age houses, with a roof resting on internal pairs of load-bearing posts, would have divided the heated room into three aisles. The presence of earth or wooden platforms along the long walls has been identified in several instances and throughout the Viking world (Milek 2006: 98; Schmidt 1994: 84f), making the central aisle slightly lower. Even when the evolution of the roof construction allowed the removal of the internal posts, this three-aisled system with platforms was retained, as seen in some houses at the ring-fortresses, for example Fyrkat 2S.

This raised position would have created fairly comfortable areas for working, sitting and other activities, as it would be warmer than the central aisle, which was lower and more subject to drafts, and consequently reserved for circulation and activities performed around the hearth (Roesdahl 2009: 277). The difference in height may have given the impression of distinct spaces. As mentioned earlier, further partitions, such as curtains, or even mental boundaries, may have existed, but the fact that they cannot be identified represents an important limitation in trying to discuss whether a concept of privacy existed and how it was physically managed in the arrangement of the dwelling areas. This is particularly problematic for discussing the function of these platforms, as it is commonly assumed that they were used for sleeping (Olsen & Schmidt 1977: 132; Vésteinsson 2006: 123). Without partition, such as wall beds or alcoves, or even curtains, one could conclude that privacy was not a major concern in sleeping arrangements in Viking Age Scandinavia, which may well be erroneous.

Living areas as activity areas

It is also in the dwelling room that, when the circumstances of abandonment and preservation conditions permit, most evidence for activities is normally found. The most common evidence is that of food preparation and consumption in the form of vessel fragments, of ceramic or soapstone, as well as burnt and unburnt animal bone fragments. Structures to hang cooking pots over the central hearth are also known, for example at the ring fortresses (Olsen & Schmidt 1977: 132), Aggersborg D but also in Iceland at Aðalstræti (Milek 2006: 163).

Special consumption practices, in terms of diet (animal bones) and use of luxury vessels (glass beakers) are also visible in high status houses (Tissø, Jørgensen 2003: 189; Gotfredsen 2006; Aggersborg D); at Borg in Lofoten I:1a and Slöinge II-III (Sweden, Lundqvist & Arcini 2003: 53f, 58f, 82), such glass beaker fragments were found in association with gold-foiled figures, which perhaps indicate their use during cultic feasts. Personal items, of practical (knives, whetstones) or ornamental (beads, brooches) purpose are also found, as well as evidence for pastime in the form of gaming pieces and, much more rarely, musical instruments.

Various economic activities are also represented, among which metal working and textile production are the most frequent. The first is attested at Omgård Axlvi, Vorbasse CVI and Sædding III. Textile production, including spinning and/or weaving, is rather frequent in South Scandinavian houses, for example at Fyrkat 2S and 4N, Aggersborg D and Vorbasse CCIII, as well as in Norway (Myhre 1980: 367) and Iceland, where textile tools are among the best represented artefact categories in Viking Age houses (Milek 2006: 121).

The lack of diagnostic features and artefacts often leads to interpret additional unheated rooms, located in the gables or between the living room and the byre as storage rooms, although evidence for specific functions is sometimes found. Food preparation seems to have held an important position in the spatial organization of houses, since it is indeed an activity which would have required a lot of space (Roesdahl 2009: 277). Cooking pits and barrels are rather frequent in the gable rooms of Icelandic houses, and are generally interpreted in relation to dairy production (Milek 2006: 125f); cereal grinding using hand-rotating querns is attested at Omgård Aiib and perhaps also at Vorbasse CCIII. The location of this activity in a specific room might indicate that several elements of cereal processing were performed there.

In Tæbring, the clay floor in the eastern part of house VII is reminiscent of the stone lining of the eastern room of Aggersborg D, which may have been the basis for a clay floor. House VII (9th-10th century) is fairly similar to house I (11th century) at the same site, in which a clay-floored room to the east has been identified on the basis of ecological data as a space for vegetable and, to a lower extent, meat preparation (Mikkelsen, Moltsen & Sindbæk 2008: 92-101). The eastern room of Aggersborg D has also revealed evidence for food preparation in the form of several soapstone potsherds. It is thus possible that both in Aggersborg D and Tæbring VII, gable rooms with clay floor, which would have been easier to keep clean than earth-beaten floors, were annexes used for food preparation. The use of unheated rooms as workshops is also fairly common (Schmidt 1994: 87), including metal working, especially noticed for the late Viking Age at Hviding, Vorbasse CII and Omgård Aiv.

The presence of metal working and textile production in the main dwelling building, and particularly in the heated living room, deserves special attention. Indeed, these two activities are usually considered as taking place in separate buildings. The association between sunken-featured buildings (SFBs) and textile production is proverbial; they offered particularly good conditions for weaving wool and hemp, in terms of light, temperature and milieu, and have been found on specialized production sites, such as

Næs (Møller Hansen & Høier 2000) but also on landing sites (Ulriksen 1998) or assembly sites (Nørgård Jørgensen, Jørgensen & Gebauer Thomsen 2011). SFBs used as weaving huts are also found in small numbers on village farmsteads such as at Vorbasse (Hvass 1980: 147-149), Omgård (Nielsen 1980: 185) or Sædding (Stoumann 1980: 111f). Evidence for textile production in dwelling rooms remains more limited than in SFBs. This difference might be due, partly, to preservation conditions, the deep-plough being hardly able to reach the circa 50 cm deep floor layer of SFBs. Also, the distribution of loom weights inside houses presents several source-critical issues and can only be used to identify a weaving area in a few cases (Figure 3). Loom weights have been found in several post-holes of house CCIII at Vorbasse, indicating that a loom was probably standing when the building burnt down. These post-holes are concentrated in the western part of the house, including post-hole 108 which was the richest in finds (2 complete and 4 fragments), and functioned as part of the partition wall between the central and the western rooms, thus associating the finds from post-hole 108 to the north-west corner of the central room. In Aggersborg D, a few loom weight fragments of burnt clay were found scattered across the main dwelling room, four along the northern wall and two in the rest of the room. The house was sealed by a dark layer, presumably from the burning of the house, and there is no evidence of a previous occupation in that specific area. It seems fairly likely that, as at Vorbasse, the loom may have been standing in the house when it burnt down, and that the distribution of the fragments reflects the original location of weaving activities.

Outside Denmark, the position of the loom can be determined with a little more precision. At Aðalstræti, the loom probably stood at floor level, between the platform and the partition wall near the south-west entrance, diagonally opposite the main entrance (Milek 2006: 161-163, 191). A similar position in the innermost part of the heated room can be seen at Storrsheia 2 in Norway (Myhre 1980: 344f; Petersen 1933: 43-45). At Borg in Lofoten I:1a, the loom was positioned on a platform by the middle of the north wall, facing the hearth, and at a short distance from the north-west corner of the room, where imported

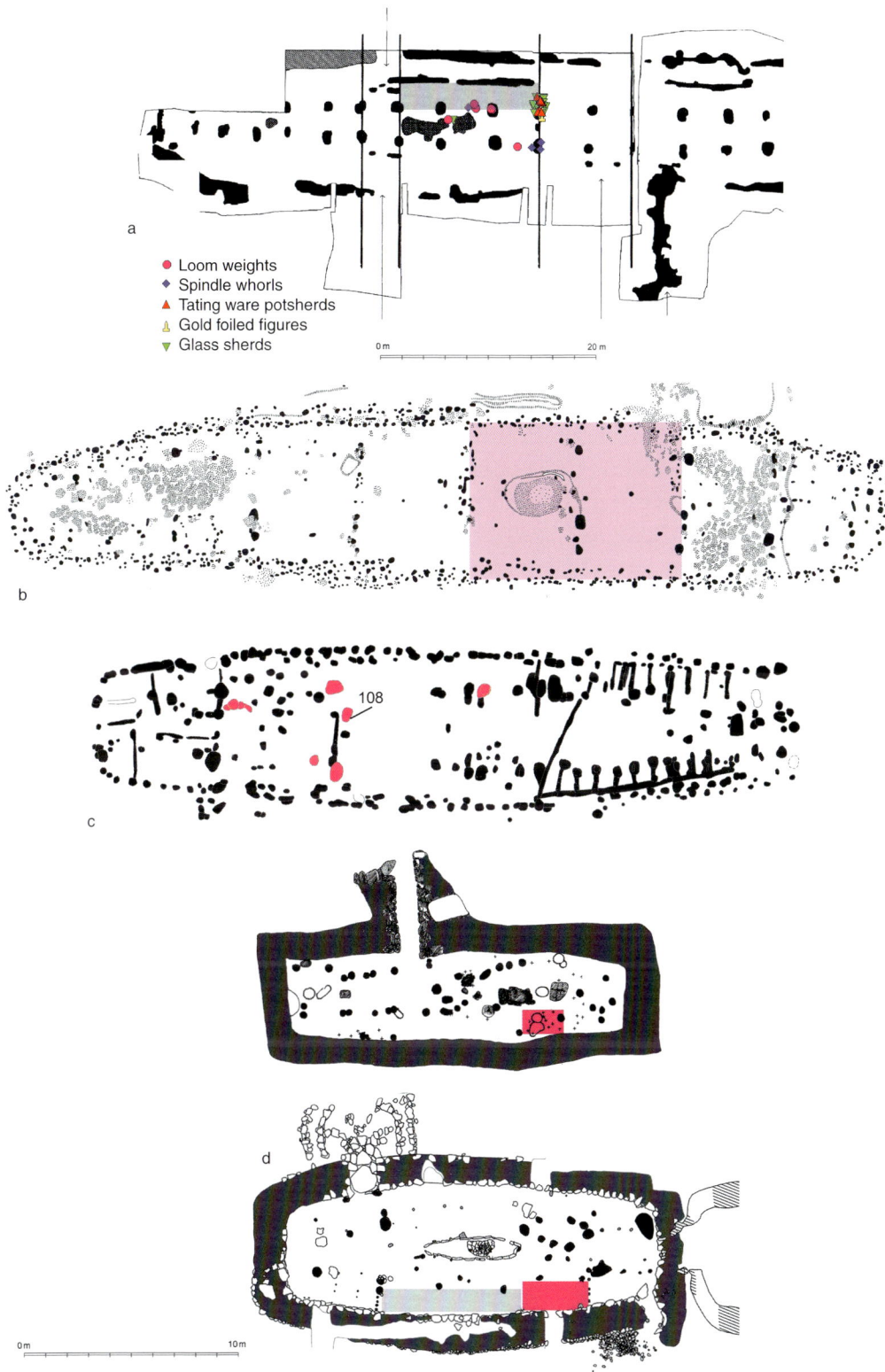

Figure 3. Comparative house plans showing the distribution of loom weights (complete or fragmented) and the possible location of a weaving loom (in pink) across the entrance to the house in the main dwelling room. For a. prestige finds are also indicated (see legend) and for a. and e., the location of the platform (in grey). a. Borg in Lofoten I:1a; b. Aggersborg D; c. Vorbasse CCIII; d. Storrsheia II; e. Aðalstræti. a. after Herschend & Kaldal Mikkelsen 2003: 52, figure 6A.12; b. after Schmidt 1994: 51; c. after online archive Arena (see note in table 1); d. after Petersen 1933, plate XLVIII; e. after Roberts 2004: 18. Modifications by the author, e. redrawn after Milek 2006: figure 3.42.

vessels, including Tating-ware jugs, glass beakers and other precious items were kept and/or displayed; a connection between weaving and prestige objects, namely glass beaker fragments and gold-foiled figures, is also known from another chieftain site, Slöinge II-III (Lundqvist & Arcini 2003: 53f, 58f, 82).

In all cases, the location of the loom in the main dwelling room indicates that weaving was an integrated part of domestic life, while its exact position seems to have varied according to the layout of the heated room and a number of practical considerations. Indeed, a corner position opposite the main entrance would have been warmer and more protected from drafts, dirt and other people's movements. A weaving loom is also a rather large implement and it may have been considered advantageous to keep the area around the hearth for other activities. From a more social perspective, it can hardly be argued that this 'corner position' was meant to seclude women involved in textile production. Rather, the presence of the loom in the main living room emphasizes the integration of this activity into the life of the household, along with those who wove. The example from Borg in Lofoten, supported by the finds from Slöinge, also shows that not only weaving was not considered as an activity to be hidden but that it was also particularly exposed in upper class context (Croix 2011b: 119-121).

Metal working is usually associated to specialized buildings, too. However, a number of examples presented above attest that it could also take place inside houses. When found by the central hearth of the main dwelling room, evidence for metal working should perhaps be considered as reflecting a later phase of occupation, although the stratigraphic information (or the lack thereof) hardly helps deciding on the matter, and that small-scale non-ferrous metal working could virtually be performed by any hearth. On the other hand, the example of Hviding, where the tripartite layout of the so-called Trelleborg type was modified in order to accommodate the forge in a special room between the central heated room and the eastern gable room, indicates that metal working taking place next to the dwelling areas while these were in use was conceivable. In this light, there is no reason to assume that evidence for metal working

found in gable rooms of house Aiv in Omgård or house CII in Vorbasse reflect a secondary use considering that, as in Hviding, this activity was physically secluded from the main living room.

The case of Sædding house III remains puzzling. Indeed, the dangers of locating a forge pit in a corner of the dwelling room seem considerable. It is thus interesting to notice that, when forges were integrated in houses at Vorbasse and Omgård in the Late Viking Age, though in the gable rooms, metal working seems to have had a particular importance on these sites. Around house III at Sædding a number of features related to metal working have been found, leading to interpret this complex as belonging to a smith (Stoumann 1980: 108-110). Perhaps the presence of facilities for iron working in houses should be connected to the role of this activity for the status and economy of the household and of those who performed it, which prevailed over the nuisances it generated (risk of fire, smell, dirt) for the functional organization of space.

Conclusion

In this article I have tried to discuss some aspects of household life on the basis of domestic features and activities documented archaeologically in a number of selected Viking Age houses. Our lack of knowledge regarding the composition of the household and the general low degree of preservation of archaeological buildings from this period, especially in South Scandinavia, represent the main limitations for a research topic which remains more accessible to ethnographers and anthropologists. Although limited, contemporary evidence indicates that Viking Age households were composed of members of different ages (parents/children, perhaps grand-parents), genders (men/women), to which should probably be added ranks (masters/servants).

The archaeological material found in a house can be considered as representing the entire household, but the activities which are the easiest to identify, namely textile production and metal working, are also those which were respectively performed by women and men.[1] On the other hand, both written and archaeological sources from the Viking Age are too scarce to identify the attribution of activities according to rank and age. The problems encountered when trying to determine the function of a room, and consequently the identity of the people using it, are also considerable, and one can only hope that in the future well preserved sites will be the object of such a detailed study as the one conducted by Karen Milek for Aðalstræti, for example.

The open central hearth seems to have played a major role in household life, its position at the centre of the main living room and of the house emphasizing its significance for the definition of domestic space. One can thus wonder how houses equipped with two rooms with central hearths should be interpreted. Helena Hamerow (2002: 24) suggests that it could indicate "multiple family households (...) linked by kinship or marriage under one roof", while other interpretations, such as a 'summer' and a 'winter' living room or for use by people of different status ('master' family/servants) are also possible. As shown with the examples of Sædding and Borg in Lofoten, the archaeological evidence hardly allows choosing one interpretation rather than the other.

Another interpretative gap concerns the dimensions of houses as a reflection of household size (Perez 1998: 6). Great regional and chronological variations of the surface under roof are known, largely conditioned by the presence or absence of a byre. As mentioned earlier, larger buildings with a high degree of room partition are often associated to wealthier sites, and size differences in contemporary houses within a same region may be used to investigate social stratification. The composition of the household may well have been conditioned by the factor of wealth, but as it has been shown a lot of space in houses was used for various activities, some being extremely space-consuming such as food preparation and storage or large social gatherings. In this sense the main living room at Borg in Lofoten (120 m^2) and at Tæbring (25-30 m^2) (Mikkelsen, Moltsen & Sindbæk 2008: 103) certainly offered different possibilities, but what was considered suitable living conditions for families of different status cannot only be calculated on the basis of a number of square meters.

Several activities have been identified as taking place in the main dwelling room, equipped with a hearth, and in unheated living rooms, physically separated from the main domestic area. Although this variation may be based on practical concerns, it may also indicate the significance given to certain activities and their degree of integration, as for the individuals performing them, in the life of the household. This is for example the case for iron metal working in late Viking Age houses in Denmark: the danger presented by fire, smoke, and a forge pit in a house with, most likely, a number of children running and playing, was perhaps dealt with by locating this activity in a separate room outside the main dwelling area. Children are hardly detectable in the archaeology of Viking Age houses, and one can only wonder which solutions would have been found to prevent them, for example, from the risk presented by a 2 m long open hearth at floor level in the living room. Contrary to iron metal working, weaving does not present any particular restrictions and can be performed wherever there is enough space to set up a loom.

In any case, spatial organization in Viking Age houses remains fairly simple and offers relatively little opportunities for segregation. Clearer functional and social differentiations may be found when considering spaces between and within the other buildings composing the Viking Age farmstead. The removal of a number of activities from the house in the course of the Viking Age, and their scattering in separate buildings with distinct functions may have had an impact on the relations between household members and their interactions in daily life.

Notes

1. The gender division of activities is a question which deserves detailed investigation, as it cannot be assumed based on modern standards or pre-conceptions about Viking Age Scandinavia how this was established and performed. I addressed this question in my doctoral dissertation (Croix 2012); on the basis of contemporary evidence it appeared that only two activities could be securely attributed to men and women, namely metal working and textile production.

References

Allison, P.M. (ed.) (1999) *The Archaeology of Household Activities*. London: Routledge.

Beattie, C., A. Maslakovic & S. Rees Jones (eds.) (2004) *The Medieval Household in Christian Europe, c. 850-c. 1550. Managing Power, Wealth, and the Body*. Turnhout: Brepols.

Beck, A.S. (2010) *Døre i vikingetidens langhuse. Et forsøg på at indtænke mennesket i bebyggelsesarkæologien*. Magister Artium thesis, Copenhagen University. [Downloaded 01.11.2011, http://bricksite.com/annasbeck]

Beck, A.S. et al (2007) Reconstruction – and then what? Climatic experiments in reconstructed Iron Age houses during winter. In: *Iron age houses in flames: testing house reconstructions at Lejre*, ed. M. Rasmussen, 134-173. Lejre: Historical-Archaeological Experimental Centre.

Benjamin, D.N. (ed.) (1995) *The Home: Words, Interpretations, Meanings, and Environments*. Brookfield: Ashgate.

Blanton, R. (1994) *Houses and Households: A Comparative Study*. New York: Plenum Press.

Boyd, R. (2009) The Irish Viking Age: A Discussion of Architecture, Settlement Patterns and Identity, *Viking and Medieval Scandinavia* 5, 271-294.

Brink, S. (2012) *Vikingarnas slavar. Den nordiska träldomen under yngre järnålder och äldsta medeltid*. Stockholm: Atlantis.

Croix, S. (2011a) Jeg ved en væv, *Skalk* (6), 7-9.

Croix, S. (2011b) Status, Gender and Space on High Status Settlement Sites from the Viking Age, *Arkæologi i Slesvig / Archäologie in Schleswig*. Sonderband "Det 61. Internationale Sachsensymposium 2010", 113-122. Neumünster: Wachholtz Verlag.

Croix, S. (2012) *Work and space in rural settlements in Viking-Age Scandinavia – gender perspectives*. PhD thesis, Aarhus University.

Devroey, J.-P. (2003) *Economie rurale et société dans l'Europe franque (VIe-IXe siècles). Tome 1: Fondements matériels, échanges et lien social*. Paris: Belin.

Donat, P. (1980) *Haus, Hof und Dorf in Mitteleuropa vom 7. bis 12. Jahrhundert: archäologische Beiträge zur Entwicklung und Struktur der bäuerlichen Siedlung*. Berlin: Akademie Verlag.

Garver, V. (2007) Old Age and Women in the Carolingian World. In: *Old Age in the Middle Ages and the Renaissance. Interdisciplinary Approaches to a Neglected Topic*, ed. A. Classen, 121-141. Berlin: De Gruyter.

Gjøstein Resi, H. (1980) Klæberstenskar og hvæssesten. Unpublished manuscript, forthcoming in: *Aggersborg i vikingetiden. Landbebyggelsen og borgen*, eds. E. Roesdahl, S. Sindbæk & A. Pedersen. Højbjerg: Jysk Arkæologisk Selskab & Nationalmuseet.

Gotfredsen, A.-B. (2006) Jagt og husdyrbrug i sen jernalder og vikingetid på stormandssædet ved Tissø, *Beretning for Kalundborg og Omegns Museum* 2005. [Downloaded 01.11.2011, http://www.kalmus.dk/Sidehistorier%20 og%20program06/Jagt%20og%20husdyr.pdf]

Hamerow, H. (2002) *Early Medieval Settlements. The Archaeology of Rural Communities in Northwest Europe 400-900*. Oxford: Oxford University Press.

Herlihy, D. (1985) *Medieval Households*. Cambridge/London: Harvard University Press.

Herschend, F. (1998) *The Idea of the Good in Late Iron Age Society*. Occasional Papers in Archaeology 15. Uppsala: Department of Archaeology and Ancient History, Uppsala University.

Herschend, F. & D. Kaldal Mikkelsen (2003) The main building at Borg (I:1). In: *Borg in Lofoten. A chieftain's farm in North Norway*, eds. G. Stamsø Munch, O.S. Johansen & E. Roesdahl, 41-76. Trondheim: Tapir Academic Press.

Hillier, B. & J. Hanson (1984) *The Social Logic of Space*. Cambridge: Cambridge University Press.

Holand, I. (2003a) Finds collection and documentation, distribution and function. In: *Borg in Lofoten. A chieftain's farm in North Norway*, eds. G. Stamsø Munch, O.S. Johansen & E. Roesdahl, 131-140. Trondheim: Tapir Academic Press.

Holand, I. (2003b) Glass vessels. In: *Borg in Lofoten. A chieftain's farm in North Norway*, eds. G. Stamsø Munch, O.S. Johansen & E. Roesdahl, 213-231. Trondheim: Tapir Academic Press.

Hvass, S. (1980) Vorbasse. The Viking Age Settlement at Vorbasse, Central Jutland, *Acta Archaeologica* 50, 137-172.

Hvass, S. (1993) Bebyggelsen. In: *Da klinger i muld ... 25 års arkæologi i Danmark*, eds. S. Hvass & B. Storgaard, 187-194. Århus: Århus Universitetsforlag.

Johansen, O.S. (1982) Viking Age farms: Estimating the number and population size, *Norwegian Archaeological Review* 15 (1–2), 45–69.

Johansen, O.S., K. Kristiansen & G. Stamsø Munch (2003) Soapstone artefacts and whetstones. In: *Borg in Lofoten. A chieftain's farm in North Norway*, eds. G. Stamsø Munch, O.S. Johansen & E. Roesdahl, 141-158. Trondheim: Tapir Academic Press.

Jørgensen, L. (2003) Manor and Market at Lake Tissø in the Sixth to Eleventh Centuries: The Danish 'Productive' Sites. In: *Markets in Early Medieval Europe, Trading and 'Productive' Sites, 650-850*, eds. T. Pestell & K. Ulmschneider, 175-207. Macclesfield: Windgather Press.

Kaldal Mikkelsen, D. (2003) Boligfunktioner i vikingetidens gårde. In: *Bolig og familie i Danmarks middelalder*, ed. E. Roesdahl, 77-87. Højbjerg: Jysk Arkæologisk Selskab.

Kent, S. (ed.) (1990) *Domestic architecture and the use of space: an interdisciplinary cross-cultural study*. Cambridge: Cambridge University Press.

Kowaleski, M. & P.J.P. Goldberg (eds.) (2008) *Medieval domesticity: Home, Housing and Household in Medieval England*. Cambridge: Cambridge University Press.

Lundqvist, L. & C. Arcini (2003) *Slöinge 1992-1996: undersökningar av en boplats från yngre järnålder*. Göteborg: Institutionen för arkeologi, Göteborgs universitet.

Meulengracht Sørensen, P. (1993) *Saga and Society. An Introduction to Old Norse literature*. Odense: Odense University Press.

Mikkelsen, P., A.S.A. Moltsen & S. Sindbæk (2008) Tæbring, NW Denmark, AD 600-1100. An Archaeological and Archaeobotanic Study, *Acta Archaeologica* 79, 79-109.

Milek, K.B. (2006) *Houses and Households in Early Icelandic Society: Geoarchaeology and the Interpretation of Social Space*. PhD thesis, University of Cambridge.

Moltke, E. (1985) *Runes and their origin, Denmark and Elsewhere*. København: Nationalmuseets Forlag.

Myhre, B. (1980) *Gårdsanlegget på Ullandhaug I. Gårdshus i jernalder og tidlig middelalder i Sørvest-Norge*. AmS Skrifter 4. Stavanger: Arkeologisk Museum i Stavanger.

Myhre, B. (1982) Settlements of Southwest Norway during the Roman and Migration Periods, *Offa* 39, 197-215.

Møller Hansen, K. & H. Høier (2000) Næs – en vikingetidsbebyggelse med hørproduktion, *KUML*. Årbog for Jysk Arkæologisk Selskab, 59-89.

Nielsen, L.C. (1980) Omgård, A Settlement from the late Iron Age and the Viking Period in West Jutland, *Acta Archaeologica* 50, 173-208.

Näsman, U. (1980) Perler, rav og glas. Unpublished manuscript, forthcoming in: *Aggersborg i vikingetiden. Landbebyggelsen og borgen*, eds. E. Roesdahl, S. Sindbæk & A. Pedersen. Højbjerg: Jysk Arkæologisk Selskab & Nationalmuseet.

Näsman, U. (2009) Jernalderens driftsformer i arkæologisk belysning. In: *Danske landbrugslandskaber gennem 2000 år fra digevoldinger til støtteordninger*, eds. B.V. Odgaard & J. Rydén Rømer, 99-116. Aarhus: Aarhus Universitetsforlag.

Nørgård Jørgensen, A., L. Jørgensen & L. Gebauer Thomsen (2011) Assembly sites for Cult, Markets, Jurisdiction and Social Relations. Historic-ethnographical analogy between North Scandinavian church towns, Old Norse assembly sites and pit house sites of the Late Iron Age and Viking Period, *Arkæologi i Slesvig/Archäeologie in Schleswig*, Sonderband "Det 61. Internationale Sachsensymposium 2010", 95-112. Neumünster: Wachholtz Verlag.

Olsen, O. & H. Schmidt (1977) *Fyrkat. En jysk vikingeborg. I. Borgen og Bebyggelsen*. København: Det kongelig nordiske Oldskriftselskab.

Page, R.I. (1995) *Chronicles of the Vikings: Records, Memorials and Myths*. London: British Museum Press.

Parker Pearson, M. & C. Richards (eds.) (1994) *Architecture and Order – Approaches to Social Space*. London/New York: Routledge.

Pesez, J.-M. (1998) Marqueurs sociaux et indicateurs économiques en archéologie rurale. In: *RURALIA II, Památky archeologické – Supplementum 11*, ed. J. Klápště et al, 5-8. Praha: Archeologický ústav.

Petersen, J. (1933) *Gamle gårdsanlegg i Rogaland*. Oslo: H. Aschehoug & Co.

Reitan, G. (2011) Moi – ett jorde, én gård, mange faser? Fra bronsealder til vikingtid og middelalder i Bygland, Setesdal, *Viking* 74, 165-191.

Roberts, H. M. (ed.) (2004) *Excavations at Aðalstræti, 2003*. Reykjavik: Fornleifastofnun Íslands.[Downloaded 08.11.2011, http://www.nabohome.org/uploads/fsi/FS243-00162_Adalstraeti_2003.pdf]

Ring, R.R. (1979) Early Medieval Peasant Households in Central Italy, *Journal of Family History* 4(2), 2-25.

Roesdahl, E. (1977) *Fyrkat. En jysk vikingeborg. II. Oldsagerne og gravpladsen*. København: Det kongelig nordiske Oldskriftselskab.

Roesdahl, E. (1986) Vikingernes Aggersborg. In: *Aggersborg gennem 1000 år. Fra vikingeborg til slægtsgård*, eds. F. Nørgaard, E. Roesdahl & R. Skovmand, 53-93. Herning: Poul Kristensens Forlag.

Roesdahl, E. (2009) Housing culture: Scandinavian perspectives. In: *Reflections: 50 Years of Medieval Archaeology, 1957-2007*, eds. R. Gilchrist & A. Reynolds, 271-288. Leeds: Maney Publishing.

Roesdahl, E. (ed.) (2003) *Bolig og familie i Danmarks middelalder*. Højbjerg: Jysk Arkæologisk Selskab.

Roesdahl, E. & B. Scholkmann (2007) Housing culture. In: *The Archaeology of Medieval Europe. Vol. 1. Eighth to Twelfth Centuries AD*, ed. J. Graham-Campbell with M. Valor, 154-180. Aarhus: Aarhus University Press.

Roesdahl, E., S. Sindbæk & A. Pedersen (eds.) (2014, forthcoming) *Aggersborg i vikingetiden. Landbebyggelsen og borgen*. Højbjerg: Jysk Arkæologisk Selskab & Nationalmuseet.

Samson, R. (ed.) (1990) *The Social Archaeology of Houses*. Edinburgh: Edinburgh University Press.

Sawyer, B. (2000) *The Viking-Age Rune-Stones. Custom and Commemoration in Early Medieval Scandinavia*. Oxford: Oxford University Press.

Sawyer, P. & B. Sawyer (1993) *Medieval Scandinavia: From Conversion to Reformation, circa 800-1500*. Minneapolis: University of Minnesota Press.

Schietzel, K. (1984) Die Baubefunde in Haithabu. In: *Archäologische und naturwissenschaftliche Untersuchungen an ländlichen und frühstädtischen Siedlungen im deutschen Küstengebiet vom 5. Jahrhundert v. Chr. bis zum 11. Jahrhundert n. Chr. Vol. 2: Handelsplätze des frühen und hohen Mittelalters*, eds. H. Jankuhn et al, 135-158. Weinheim: Verlag Chemie.

Schmidt, H. (1994) *Building customs in Viking Age Denmark*. København: Poul Kristensen.

Skov, H. (1994) Hustyper i vikingetid og tidlig middelalder. Udviklingen af hustyper i det gammeldanske område fra ca. 800-1200 e.Kr., *hikuin* 21, 139-162.

Stamsø Munch, G. (1983) Et hustuftområde fra vikingtid på Arstad, Nordland. In: *Hus, gård og bebyggelse. Föredrag från det XVI nordiska arkeologmötet, Island 1982*, ed. G. Ólafsson, 133-146. Reykjavík: Þjóðminjasafn Íslands.

Stamsø Munch, G. (2003) Borg as a pagan centre. In: *Borg in Lofoten. A chieftain's farm in North Norway*, eds. G. Stamsø Munch, O.S. Johansen & E. Roesdahl, 253-263. Trondheim: Tapir Academic Press.

Stamsø Munch, G., O.S. Johansen & E. Roesdahl (eds.) (2003)

Borg in Lofoten. A chieftain's farm in North Norway. Trondheim: Tapir Academic Press.

Stoumann, I. (1980) Sædding. A Viking Age Village near Esbjerg, *Acta Archaeologica* 50, 95-118.

Thedéen, S. (2009) A desirable, deceitful or disastrous death. Memories of men and masculinities in late Viking Age runic inscriptions. In: *From Ephesos to Dalecarlia. Reflections on body, space and time in medieval and early modern Europe*, eds. E. Regner, C. von Heijne, L. Kitzler Åhfeldt & A. Kjellström, 57-82. Stockholm: Historiska Museet / Stockholms Universitet.

Ulriksen, J. (1998) *Anløbspladser. Besejling og bebyggelse i Danmark mellem 200 og 1100 e.Kr.* Roskilde: Vikingeskibshallen i Roskilde.

Vésteinsson, O. (2006) Life in the Hall. In: *Reykjavík 871 ± 2. Landnámssýningin. The Settlement Exhibition*, ed. B. Sverrisdóttir, 109-123. Reykjavík: Reykjavík City Museum.

Øye, I. (2002) Landbruk under press, 800 – 1350. In: *Norges Landbrukshistorie I, 4000 f. Kr. -1350 e. Kr.*, eds. B. Myhre & I. Øye, 214-477. Oslo: Det Norske Samlaget.

Opening Doors – Entering Social Understandings of the Viking Age Longhouse

Anna S. Beck

Abstract

Since the longhouses of Trelleborg were first excavated in Denmark, Viking Age longhouses have been studied typologically. However, such typological approaches have a range of inherent problems as, in seeking to identify similarities in the material, they tend to downplay variation and simplify the process behind their development. This limits our ability to understand the longhouse in its original context. A new approach to understanding the development of the Viking Age longhouse is presented here, where each single building element is studied in its own right. To illustrate the potential of the new approach, a study of doorways in the Viking Age longhouses is presented. The study reveals a close connection between the construction of the doorway and the development of a cultural ideal of hospitality in Viking Age society. The study demonstrates that the development of the longhouse is a complex process in which the longhouse, its inhabitants, and contemporary cultural ideals play important roles. The paper concludes that to further understand the development of the Viking Age longhouse, future studies should look for a common idea of 'the good life' reflected in longhouses, rather than trying to fit the material into a range of pre-defined standard forms of house.

Introduction

In this paper, I will discuss the perspective that previous typological studies have presented on the development of the Viking Age longhouse in Denmark and the problems this perspective creates in understanding the processes behind their development. The inspiration for this paper comes from my Magister Artium thesis[1] *Doorways in Viking Age longhouses. An attempt to re-insert humans into settlement archaeology* (Beck 2010). The thesis explored the construction and context of doorways in Viking Age longhouses in Sealand and Scania. From this study, the limitations of traditional approaches were revealed and a new understanding of the longhouse as a dynamic structure developed; a result that has important consequences for future archaeological studies of longhouse development in Denmark.

Problems with the typology of Viking Age longhouses

The first longhouses dated to the Viking Age were found in excavations at Trelleborg (in Sealand) in the 1930s and 1940s (Nørlund 1948). The excavations clearly demonstrated that the longhouses belonged to a radically different building tradition from the standard three-aisled Iron Age longhouses known at the time (Hatt 1938). The longhouses at Trelleborg had curved instead of straight walls, slanting outer posts (buttresses) in line with the walls, and doorways placed towards the end, instead of in the middle of the longhouse, and had only two pairs of roof-bearing posts in each end of the house instead of pairs of posts running in the whole length of the house. Rapidly, the 'Trelleborg-house' was interpreted as representing the standard house of the Viking Age.

Since then, the number of excavated longhouses has increased exponentially because of an increased excavation activity and the introduction of mechanised open area excavation (Becker 1981; Fabech et al 1999). The question of how the Trelleborg-house fits into the evolution of the longhouse from prehistory and into the Middle Ages has continued to be central to the study of the Viking Age longhouse. To answer this question, several typologies covering the period have been made either based on single sites (Christensen 1987; Jørgensen & Eriksen 1995; Stoumann 1981; Waterbolk 1994), regional studies (Artursson 2005; Ethelberg 2003; Fraes Rasmussen 1994; Hansen 1998; Tesch 1993) or in studies covering larger areas (Christensen 1973; Foged Klemensen 1991; Herschend 1989; Hvass 1993; Schmidt 1994; Skov 1994).

In their broad outline and approach, these different typological studies are surprisingly similar. All seek to define a sequence of standard houses; usually including the Trelleborg-house. The development is then presented as a step-by-step evolution where one standard longhouse evolves into the next type. The Trelleborg-house is fitted into this sequence as a natural step in the development from the three-aisled Iron Age longhouse to the one-aisled longhouse of the Middle Ages (Figure 1). With this traditional typological method, the development appears to be an inevitable, standardised process with little space left for variation. The change in building tradition is explained as a functional or technological response to the introduction of new building techniques. This traditional typology is rarely questioned by Danish archaeologists, even though it has a range of problems inherent in it.

One problem with the traditional typological method is that it downplays the range of variation in the material by elevating the different standard houses to a 'kind of typological law' (Artursson 2005). In reality, the longhouses are extremely varied through the last part of the Iron Age and the Viking Age. Moreover, during the Viking Age, both longhouses resembling the traditional three-aisled Iron Age longhouse (eg Carlie & Artursson 2005: 229), one-aisled longhouses (eg Söderberg 2005), longhouses with a mix of two- and three-aisled constructions (eg Tornbjerg 1998), Trelleborg-houses (eg Nilsson 1976)

as well as a range of other constructions continue to be found at sites contemporary in date. This variation can also be exemplified by listing some of the standard houses defined by the typological studies: the Sædding-house (both an early and a late type), the Trelleborg-house, the Vilslev-house, the Margrethehåb-house, the Bulagergård-house, the Tornmark-house, the Hviding-house, the Toftegård-houses – all named after the site where this specific type of house construction was found. That these specific house types – even the Trelleborg-house – rarely are found outside the original site underlines that the typologies have been neglecting the variety of longhouses in the Viking Age (Wranning 1999).

Working with house typology in this way has its background in the tradition of typology itself. In Danish archaeology, the study of typology is deeply rooted and goes back to the beginning of modern archaeology (Trigger 1989). The typological study of longhouses started with the finds of Early Iron Age longhouses in the beginning of the 20th century (Martens 2005). The method was developed on rather uniform Iron Age longhouses, where studying standard houses might be plausible. The problem comes when this approach is transferred directly to the study of the Viking Age longhouses, where the material is very different. Moreover, house typologies have been developed as a tool for dating houses rather than for studying the social and cultural processes behind their development. This has the consequence that – more or less consciously – the development of the longhouse has been simplified by focusing on similarities instead of variation in the material, because – broadly speaking – the simpler a typology is, the easier it is to fit new objects into it.

When the range of variation is not present in the typologies, it gives a simplified impression of the processes behind its development. The consequence is that the questions asked of the typology then tend to focus on chronological, technological and functional aspects of its development. Explanations of the development of the longhouse have in this way focused on technical explanations (the introduction of new building techniques) instead of investigating the social and cultural processes behind the development such as the question of *why* new building

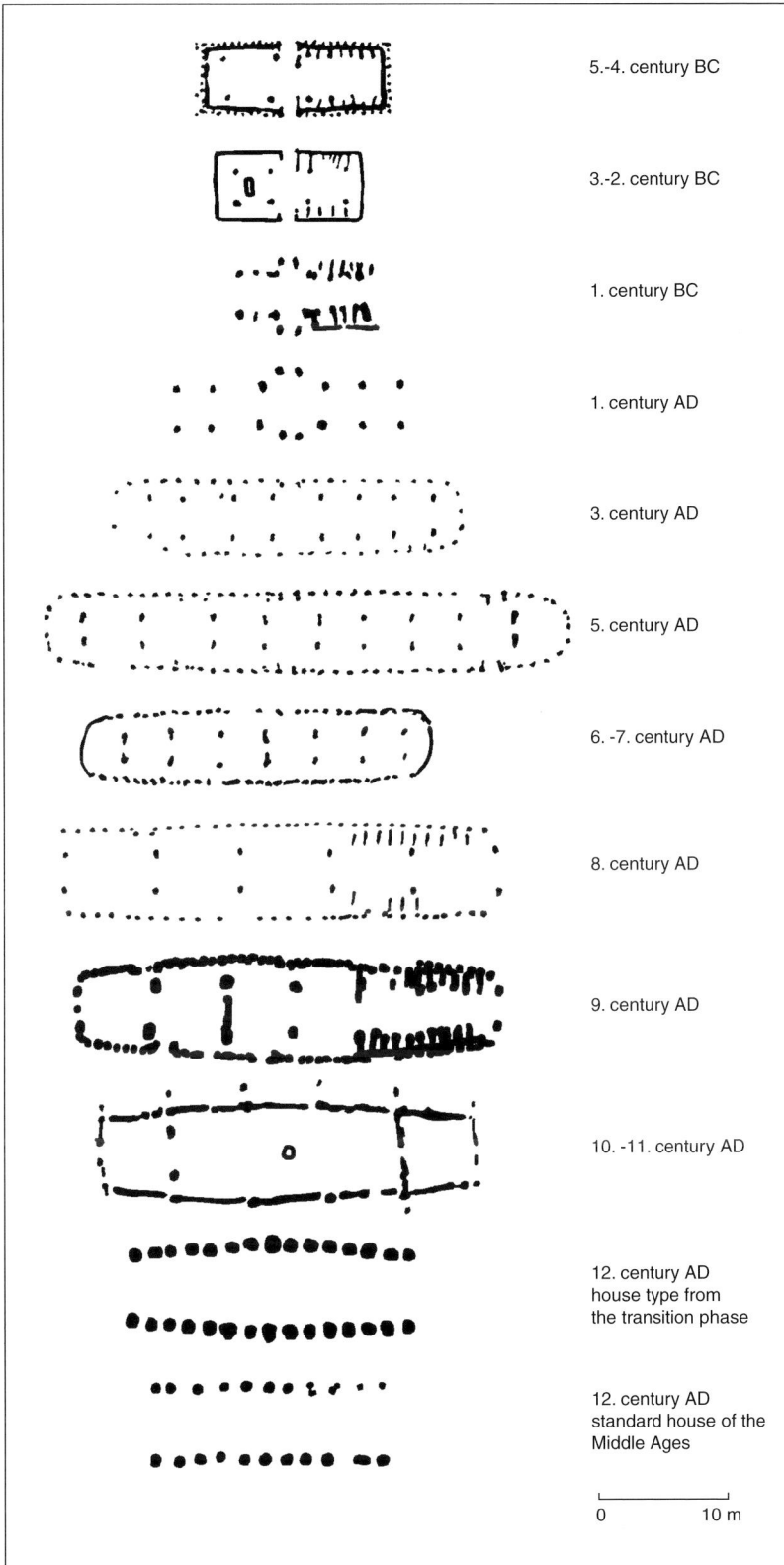

5.-4. century BC

3.-2. century BC

1. century BC

1. century AD

3. century AD

5. century AD

6. -7. century AD

8. century AD

9. century AD

10. -11. century AD

12. century AD
house type from
the transition phase

12. century AD
standard house of the
Middle Ages

0   10 m

Figure 1. An example of a house typology based on standard houses. After Rasmussen 1994: 77.

techniques were introduced after building according to the same tradition for more than 1000 years. The study of the longhouse and its development in a wider social and cultural context has therefore been limited by this traditional approach.

These problems call for a constructive debate about the development of a new approach to typological work. Instead of defining uniform standardised houses which in reality do not reflect the diversity of the material, a new approach should be able to handle both variation and similarities in the material and treat the development of the longhouse as a process reflecting the dynamics of the surrounding society. The remainder of this paper presents such an approach, based on recent research (Beck 2010).

Opening doors

In the archaeological record, the traces of a longhouse consist mostly of features dug into the ground. Only rarely are features preserved which shed light on the details of the building above ground level. From the scarce survival of material it can still be said that the longhouse is made up of a range of different building elements (walls, roof-bearing posts, doorways etc). Each building element can be constructed in different ways, and develops at its own pace. The variation of Viking Age longhouses seems to be based on the variation in the construction of each single building element and how they are combined rather than on a sequence of standard houses (Beck 2010: 43-45). This means that a house can both retain elements of the traditional Iron Age house (such as straight walls) but hold elements of the Trelleborg house as well (such as buttresses and a Trelleborg hall). Each building element and the context of which they are a part of can therefore be studied in its own respect. This is a constructive way of studying the development of the longhouse, taking both variation and similarities into account. This paper focuses on the potential of studying just one element of construction, namely doorways. Doorways are a prominent – though often neglected – building element that have an important role in the longhouse, but it seems likely that studying other building elements would yield equally interesting results. A typological study

was made of their construction, and the relationship between doorways and the longhouse itself was also investigated.

Studying doorways

In this study, the term *doorway* refers to both the actual construction (door posts, door, porch etc) and the openings which are framed by the door construction. The primary function of the door is to facilitate the movement of humans, animals and things, in and out of the house. The function of the door can also be to control this movement, because the door can be opened or closed (and locked), according to who has access and who does not. At the same time, the construction of the doorway controls the character and orientation of movement and in this way creates the framework for the experience and understanding of the longhouse by inhabitants and visitors.

The location of the doorway in the outer 'rim' of the house – on the edge between the house and its surroundings – means that the doorway defines the border between inside and outside, between public and private space and between house and exterior landscape. At the same time, the doorway also represents the link between these spheres. This makes the doorway an important focus in the house, and explains that doorways in cultures all over the world are connected to both symbolic meanings and conventions (Carlie 2004; Hoff 1997: 95; Rapoport 1969; Trumbull 2000; Van Gennep 1960). Meanings and conventions can be of practical, social, juridical or ritual character and be expressed as particular behaviour, rules, superstition and/or rituals associated with the door – such as when you knock on the door before entering a room, when the bride is carried over the threshold by her groom on their wedding night, or when a votive offering to protect the household is placed under the threshold. The construction of the doorway can in this way be influenced by other considerations than the purely functional.

In this way the door reflects how the original builders of, and dwellers within, the longhouse chose to organize their lives – both in relation with their physical world and in the relationship between

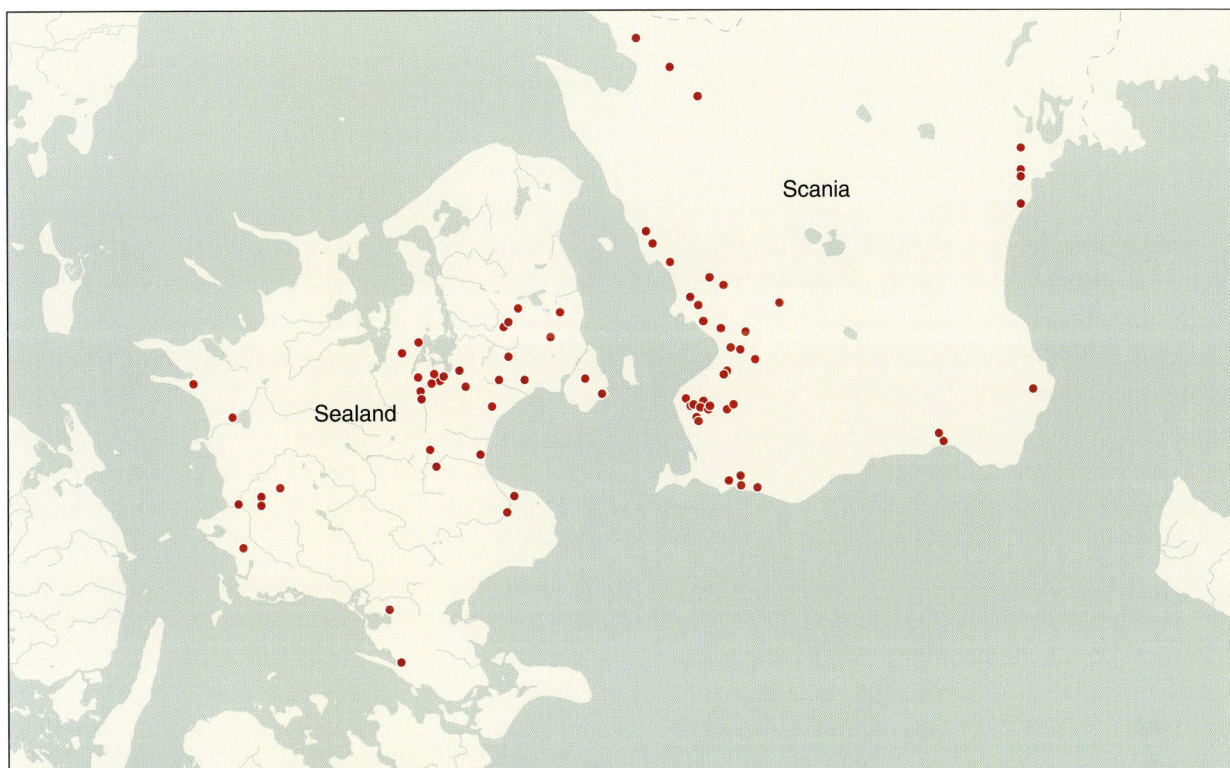

Figure 2. Map showing the distribution of the sites included in the study.

inhabitants and strangers as well as household and society. To understand the framework the doorway creates it is therefore necessary both to investigate the construction of the door and the context in which it is found.

Doorways in the Viking Age longhouse

The research presented in this chapter was executed as a regional analysis of a study area defined by Eastern Denmark (Sealand) and Southern Sweden (Scania). Within this area, data about all longhouses with preserved doorways dated to the Late Germanic Iron Age or Viking Age (600-1100 AD) were collected. Material from both published and unpublished excavations was included. The material contains longhouses from both high- and low-status sites, single farms and villages as well as living houses and outbuildings, to get as broad an insight into the material and the processes behind its development

as possible. The full material provides the possibility of an interpretation of a wider social context than if only the very well-preserved or very rich sites were studied. In all, information of 270 longhouses from 85 sites (41 on Sealand, 44 in Scania) was collected. The longhouses all had one or more doorways preserved, and in all 518 (outer) doorways were recorded (Figure 2). The data was synthesised in a database from which the following statistical analyses were derived.

The construction of the doorway

The doorways in the collected dataset have been reconstructed from evidence of features framing the doorway, as well as a corresponding lack of features matching the actual doorway. In the archaeological material, the most typical features that make up the doorway are postholes and ditches. Examples of stone pavements or trampling layers are also present, and in one case, the actual threshold and door posts had been preserved (Nilsson 1976). Within the dataset, there are examples of doorways consisting of just one feature and examples of doorways consisting of up to 12 features. The typical doorway consisted of between two and four features which were mostly traces of the door posts and further construction details around the door itself.

Investigating the construction of the doorway, two overriding principles emerged from an analysis of the relationship between the doorway itself and the surrounding walls. Either the doorway was an integrated part of the wall and was described as 'not enhanced', or the doorway stood out from the wall and was described as 'enhanced'. The actual construction that made the door 'enhanced' varied. Either the doorways had slanting outer posts which functioned as buttresses, or a porch, or the doorway could be recessed from the surface outer wall and the wall in itself made up a kind of enhancement (Figure 3). Alternatively,

the doorway could be enhanced by post constructions inside the house. The doorways in the collected material were categorized according to one of the construction principles (enhanced/not enhanced). The result from the studied material was that more than half of the doorways (58%) could be classified as 'enhanced' (Beck 2010: 55-68). Furthermore, enhancement of the doorways in different ways seemed to become more common during the Viking Age.

It can therefore be argued that making the doorway stand out from the wall was a new characteristic that was introduced to the longhouse in the Late Iron Age and Viking Age, as the doorway had been an integrated part of the wall in the Early Iron Age (Webley 2008). The enhancement of the doorway meant that it was separated from the rest of the house, and in this way defined as its own space – an entrance.

Figure 3. Two examples of marked doorways – a doorway with a porch on a reconstructed longhouse from Fyrkat (left) and a recessed doorway where the wall makes up a kind of enhancement on a reconstructed longhouse from Vorbasse (right), 10th-century sites in Westdenmark.

To understand why the enhancement of the doorways was introduced in the Late Iron Age and Viking Age, the context of the enhanced versus not enhanced doorways was further investigated. This was done by comparing the distribution of enhanced/not enhanced doorways (expressed in percentages) to some of the related features of the longhouse: specifically the location of the doorway in the house, the social status of the site and the organization of the longhouse itself.

In the Late Iron Age, the location of the doorways was no longer as regulated as it had been in the Early Iron Age (Beck 2010: 46-48). Doorways could both be located in the gables or in the longwalls of the house. In the longwalls, the doorways could both be located towards the middle or towards the ends of the longhouse. When comparing the distribution of enhanced/not enhanced doorways with the location of the doorway, it is clear that the distribution is very similar for the doorways in both the gable and the longwalls. This means that the location of the doorway could be considered to have had a minor, if any, influence on the enhanced form of the doorways.

The social difference of the settlements became more explicit during the Late Iron Age and Viking Age. During this period, the difference between the common farm and the rich magnate halls was expressed in both the size of the longhouses, the number of outbuildings and the quality and quantity of metal artefacts recovered from the site. Against this background, it would seem rather obvious that social status could be expressed by making the doorways more elaborate. However, a comparison of the distribution of the enhanced/not enhanced doorways with the size of the longhouses and the interpreted function of the longhouse (as a living house or outbuilding) respectively showed the same pattern as with the location of the doorways; neither had influence on whether the doorway was enhanced or not. A comparison of the distribution of enhanced/not enhanced doorways with the general social status of the site showed the same result.

Taking the analysis a step further, the distribution of the enhanced/not enhanced doorways was compared with the general layout of the longhouse. The general layout as defined here is based on the

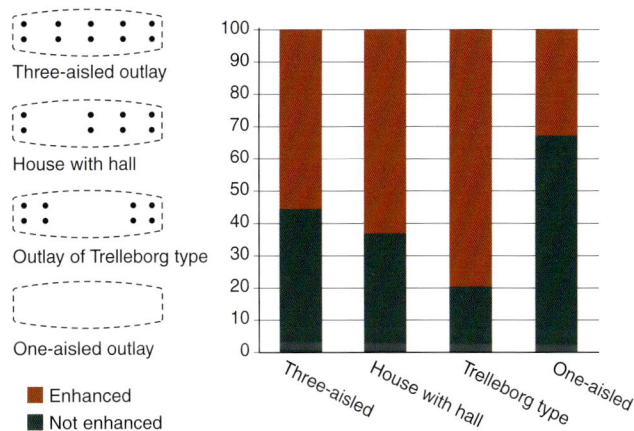

Figure 4. Diagram showing the distribution of enhanced and not enhanced doorways (N=518) in relation to the general outlay of the longhouse.

distribution of the pairs of posts in the roof-bearing posts (and should not be conflated with the traditional typologies or 'standard house types' discussed above). Four different types of layout were identified in the material: the three-aisled layout with pairs of posts placed at equal distance in the full length of the house; a variation of this layout is the three-aisled form where the distance between two pairs of posts somewhere in the construction are larger than the rest which creates one markedly larger room in the house (a hall); the layout of the longhouse with two pairs of roof carrying posts towards each end of the house and a large central hall as found in the Trelleborg-houses, and finally the one-aisled house with roof carrying walls and no inner posts (Figure 4). The comparison between the distribution of enhanced/not enhanced doorways and the layout showed certain differences between the distribution and the layout of the house. For the three-aisled longhouses the distribution was more or less 50-50, whereas for the three-aisled longhouses with a hall and especially for houses with Trelleborg-layout the enhanced doorways dominated over the not enhanced. For the one-aisled houses it was the other way around. In this way the investigation demonstrated that there was a connection between the enhanced doorway and the presence of a hall (Beck 2010: 78-80). This analysis was done across a broad chronological timespan including houses and doorways taken from the whole period under study. When executing the same

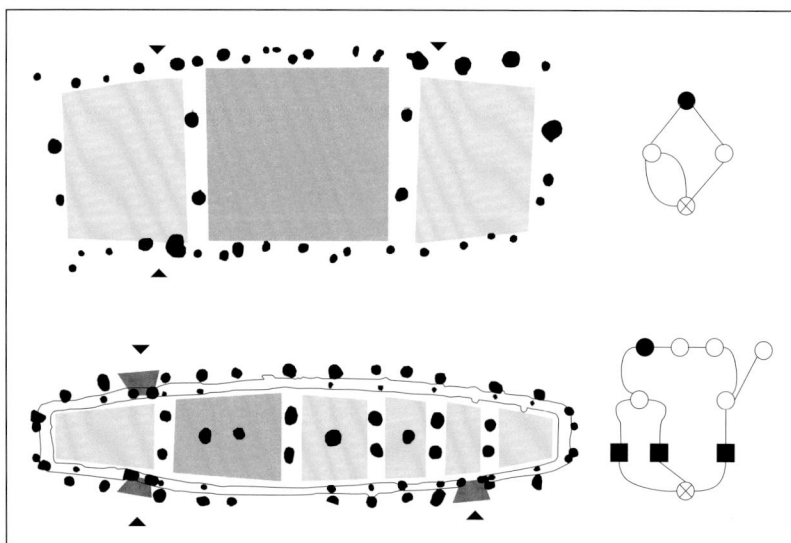

Figure 5. Examples of access analysis of two different longhouses with a hall – a low status site (upper) and a high status site (below). Please note that the longhouses are not reproduced in the same scale. Both gamma maps show that there is not direct access to the hall from the outside. Legend: Circle with a cross – 'outside'; black square – enhanced doorway; circle – room in the longhouse; black circle – hall. Lines mark the access routes. After Beck et al. 2005: 13 and Tornbjerg 1998: 223.

analysis for the older and younger Viking Age respectively, the connection between halls and enhanced doorways is even more apparent. As both halls and enhanced doorways become more common during the Viking Age, the connection gets more and more clear through the period.

The total number of doorways in each longhouse varies. In the material studied, there are longhouses with just one doorway and longhouses with up to seven doorways. The number of doorways and their location in relation to each other can show in more detail, how the longhouse is organized. The analysis of the data enabled an 'entrance pattern' to be defined for each longhouse based on the total number of doorways and their location. The entrance patterns could be grouped according to three overriding principles: either all the doorways were located towards the end of the longhouse; towards the middle of the longhouse; or a combination of these two principles. Comparing the distribution of the three principles of entrance patterns with the general organization of the longhouse, it is apparent that longhouses with a hall (either as one larger room or as a Trelleborg-hall) have doorways located towards the ends of the longhouse, whereas houses without a hall or with no inner posts have doorways located towards the middle of the house (Beck 2010: 79). As with the characteristics of enhanced and not enhanced doorways, the organization of the house – and the presence of

a hall – seems to have great influence on the general location of entrances.

To further investigate the relationship between the entrance pattern and the organization of the longhouse an access analysis of the best-preserved longhouses was carried out (Beck 2010: 69-83). The analysis can only be based on the room partitions which are recognizable in the archaeological record. It is possible that the house and the rooms within it were more segregated – not just by physical walls but also by ephemeral partitions or social conventions which have left no traces in the archaeological record. However, this cannot be taken directly into account in the analysis presented here. Access analysis produces a 'gamma map' – a graphical presentation of the access to the house and the movement between the rooms in the house. Each room or spatial unit is described as a symbol on the map and the access routes are presented as lines (Hillier & Hanson 1984). After this process, the map is justified according to the perspective of a common 'outsider' or visitor. Every room in the longhouse can be assigned a depth value according to the minimum number of steps that must be taken to access that particular room. A step is defined as the movement from one room to another in the map. With the analysis it is possible to look for general patterns and compare the structures of access and the movement within the longhouses across a larger material.

The access analysis showed that the longhouse in general has a very simple organization (Figure 5). The longhouses are relatively open structures often with more than one doorway. There are generally few room partitions preserved and the layout appears relatively simple. Three steps are the largest number required to access the 'deepest' space in the longhouse. The room placed deepest in the structure is often the hall, and there is never direct access from the outside into the hall. The relationship between the doorway and the house seems in this way again to be depending on the organisation of the longhouse. Once again, the presence of a hall seems to be a structuring factor. It is also possible that the hall was further segregated by more ephemeral features such as screens or curtains, which are not preserved archaeologically, or by social conventions. If so, it further underlines the conclusion that the hall was a structuring factor in controlling access to, and movement within, the longhouse.

Enhancement of the doorways makes the distance between the house and its surroundings more profound, and accessing the house became more difficult through the introduction of this 'extra step'. The formalization and creation of more complex access routes into a house, especially where these were associated with accessing a hall, made it possible to exercise closer control over those entering and exiting domestic space. To walk in and out of the house became an activity requiring confidence and knowledge on the part of the inhabitant or the visitor. The social and cultural practice of walking in and out was in this way formalized and placed in a physical framework. Despite variation such formalization was particularly apparent where access was ultimately being provided to a hall.

Entering social understanding

In the analysis presented thus far, the hall has been defined as a room physically larger than other rooms at the farm. But the hall as a room also needs to be interpreted in connection with the idea of the hall as a social phenomenon (Beck 2010: 81-83). The phenomenon of the 'hall' has played an important role in the Viking Age research, and through the excavation of several high status sites through the 80s and 90s the study has become a field in its own right, where the archaeological and written sources are combined to investigate the phenomenon (eg Callmer 1997; Herschend 2001; Söderberg 2005; Walker 2007). Both the archaeological and the written sources indicate that the hall works as a room for social gatherings in connection with social and cultural events as banquets, weddings, ceremonies and religious events. The hall has in this way probably played an important role as the place where social connections were made and maintained.

The general formalization of the access and the introduction of a hall can be interpreted in connection with a principle of hospitality which was developed during the Viking Age. The principle of hospitality is in this connection meant in the widest sense of the word – as hospitality for travellers, entertainment for visiting friends and in proper banquets where neighbours, family and friends were invited. That hospitality played an important role in the society of the Viking Age can be deduced from frequent references in the sagas and Edda poems. A large section of Havamál, for example contains advice about how to behave as a host and as a guest at such occasions (Bø 1960: 338).

Through the formalization and the enhancement of the doorway it can be suggested that to invite and to be invited to enter the house also became an important social act in the society of the Viking Age. An important point to make in this context is that the enhanced doorways and the halls with which they are associated were not phenomenons that were restricted exclusively to the higher social classes. Both are also found on more ordinary farms which suggests that hospitality was a more widespread and general cultural ideal within Viking Age society. The creation of a hall might in this way not have a direct connection to the actual banquets but instead to the cultural ideal that 'a proper home has a hall for having guests'.

The dialectical nature of the relationship between the longhouse and contemporary cultural ideals also needs careful consideration. When a longhouse was built according to a certain ideal, the process at the same time reinforced and reproduced it, influencing the future design and construction of houses in the same community. The development of the longhouse can be interpreted as a form of recursive social practice (after Bourdieu 2005: 202f). This may explain an observation made during the course of research that there was a correspondence between the introduction of enhanced doorways and the introduction of the slanting outer posts (which acted as buttresses). The buttresses might not have been introduced with the purpose of enhancing the doorway per se, but they served to reinforce the ideal of enhancement, and may in this way have been incorporated into the cultural 'package' of hall-enhanced doorway design. Indeed, although it seems likely that doorways were built to enhance and develop the social practices associated with halls, the 'package' of enhanced doorways and halls is also difficult to disentangle chronologically and culturally. The construction of the longhouse in the Viking Age worked to confirm and maintain the cultural ideal of hospitality. In this way, the architecture of the longhouse and the material form of doorways can be argued to reflect a dynamic structuring of contemporary changing cultural ideals, closely linked to the people who built and inhabited them.

Conclusions

The paper took its point of departure in the problems with the traditional typological study of Viking Age houses, which neglects variation in the material and simplifies the processes behind its development. As a contribution to the debate, a new approach was presented. With the new approach, the typological development of the longhouse should no longer be focused on defining and studying standard forms of house plan, but rather on studying the longhouses on its own terms. This should be done by studying each single building element, its construction, the range of variation, the development of it and its relationship to the rest of the longhouse. The result should be related to interpretations of the surrounding society as well.

The approach was exemplified by a regional study of the doorways of Viking Age longhouses. This demonstrated that there was a close connection between the development of the doorway, the introduction

of the hall and the development of cultural ideals of hospitality. These elements influenced each other and became increasingly intertwined through the Viking Age, resulting in the long-term development of the longhouse. Within the material, there was evidence for variation alongside certain patterns. Such variation is an expression of the fact that the cultural ideal of hospitality was not a phenomenon which was exclusively related to a certain social class but a process that all people in Viking Age society – high as low in status – participated in, appropriated and adapted to their particular circumstances and building traditions. As the connection between enhanced doorways and halls became more apparent during the Viking Age it also shows that the ideal of hospitality became more dominant through the period. In this way, the inhabitants, the longhouse itself and the common ideals were in this way active actors in the process (Latour 2005). All inhabitants responded to a cultural ideal and participated in the development of the building tradition in a constantly-moving, complex process where ideals are confirmed or changed according to the needs of society.

What can be learned for future typological studies is, that instead of looking for the common idea of the longhouse in a technical sense we should look for the common idea of 'the good life' reflected in the house, as it is the ideals that are common rather than the minutiae of technical construction of the house. The result is that the longhouse is lifted from being treated as a neutral, static construction to be an active structure reflecting the dynamics of the surrounding society. Future typological studies should in this way not just work with the material traces of houses that we find, but also with the humans who once lived in them.

Note

1. Magister Artium is a Danish 6 year master programme.

References

Artursson, M. (2005) Böndernas hus. In: *Järnålder vid Öresund. Band 1. Specialstudier och syntes*, ed. A. Carlie, 76-161. Skånska spår – arkeologi längs Västkustbanan. Lund: Riksantikvarieämbetet.

Beck, A.S. (2010) *Døre i vikingetidens langhuse. Et forsøg på at indtænke mennesket i bebyggelsesarkæologien*. Magister Artium thesis, Copenhagen University, http://brick-site.com/annasbeck.

Becker, C.J. (1981) Viking-age settlements in western and central Jutland. Recent excavations. Introductory remarks, *Acta Archaeologica* 50, 89-94.

Bourdieu, P. (2005) *Udkast til en praksisteori – indledt af tre studier i kabylsk etnologi*. København: Hans Reitzels forlag.

Callmer, J. (1997) Aristokratisk präglade residens från yngre järnåldern i forskningshistorien och deras problematik. In:"*...Gick Grendel att söka det höga huset...*" *Arkeologiska källor till aristokratiska miljöer i Skandinavien under yngre järnålder*, ed. J. Callmer & E. Rosengren, 11-18. Slöinge projektet 1. Hallands Länsmuseers Skriftserie no 9/ GOTARC C. Arkeologiska Skrifter 17. Göteborg: Hallands länsmuseer.

Carlie, A. (2004) *Forntida bygnadskult.Tradition och regionalitet i södra Skandinavien*. Riksantikvarieämbetet. Arkeologiska undersökningar Skrifter 57. Stockholm: Riksantikvarieämbetet.

Carlie, A. & M. Artursson (2005) Böndernas gårdar. In: *Järnålder vid Öresund. Band 1. Specialstudier och syntes*, ed. A. Carlie, 162-245. Skånska spår – arkeologi längs Västkustbanan. Lund: Riksantikvarieämbetet.

Christensen, J.K. (1973) *Vikingetidens langhuse på Trelleborg, Aggersborg, Fyrkat og Nonnebakken*. København: Arkitektskolen.

Christensen, T. (1987) Krumvægshuset, *Skalk* 1987:1, 13-18.

Ethelberg, P. (2003) Gården og landsbyen i jernalder og vikingetid (500 f.Kr.-1000 e.Kr.). In: *Det sønderjyske landbrugs historie. Jernalder, vikingetid og middelalder*, eds. P. Ethelberg, N. Hardt, B. Poulsen & A.B. Sørensen, 123-373. Skrifter udgivet af Historisk Samfund for Sønderjylland 82. Haderslev: Haderslev Museum, Historisk Samfund for Sønderjylland.

Fabech, C., S. Hvass, U. Näsman & J. Ringtved (1999) 'Settlement and Landscape' – a presentation of a research programme and a conference. In: *Settlement and Landscape. Proceedings of a conference in Århus, Denmark, May 4-7 1998*, eds. C. Fabech & J. Ringtved, 13-28. Højbjerg: Jysk Arkæologisk Selskab.

Foged Klemensen, M. (1991) *Middelalderlige bondehuse. En diskussion af Axel Steensbergs husrekonstruktioner på baggrund af de senere års landsbyundersøgelser*. Højbjerg: Middelalderarkæologisk Nyhedsbrev.

Fraes Rasmussen, U. (1994) Middelalderhuse. Nyere undersøgelser ved Køge, *hikuin* 21, 65-84.

Hansen, A.B. (1998) *Vikingetidens huse – et kronologisk forsøg fra Københavnsområdet*. MA thesis, Copenhagen University.

Hatt, G. (1938) Jernalders bopladser i Himmerland, *Årbøger for Nordisk Oldkyndighed og Historie* 1938, 119-266.

Herschend, F. (1989) Changing houses. Early medieval houses types in Sweden 500 to 1100 A.D., *TOR* 22, 79-103.

Herschend, F. (2001) *Journey of Civilisation. The Late Iron Age View of the Human World*. Occasional Papers in Archaeology 24. Uppsala: Institutionen för Arkeologi och Antik Historia.

Hillier, B. & J. Hanson (1984) *The Social Logic of Space*. Cambridge: Cambridge University Press.

Hoff, A. (1997) *Lov og Landskab. Landskabslovenes bidrag til forståelsen af landbrugs- og landskabsudviklingen i Danmark ca. 900-1250*. Århus: Århus Universitetsforlag.

Hvass, S. (1993) Bebyggelsen. In: *Da klinger i muld.... 25 års arkæologi i Danmark*, eds. S. Hvass & B. Storgaard, 187-194. Århus: Århus Universitetsforlag.

Jørgensen, L.B. & P. Eriksen (1995) *Trabjerg. En vestjysk landsby fra vikingetiden*. Holstebro Museums række/ Jysk Arkæologisk Selskabs Skrifter XXXI:1. Højbjerg: Jysk Arkæologisk Selskab.

Latour, B. (2005) *Reassembling the Social. An Introduction to Actor-Network-Theory*. Oxford: Oxford University Press.

Martens, J. (2005) Skånsk huskronologi. In: *Järnålder vid Öresund. Band 1. Specialstudier och syntes*, ed. A. Carlie, 46-75. Skånska spår – arkeologi längs Västkustbanan. Lund: Riksantikvarieämbetet.

Nilsson, T. (1976) Hus och huskonstruktioner. In: *Uppgrävt förflutet för PKbanken i Lund. En investering i arkeologi*, eds. A.W. Mårtensson, 41-71. Archaeologica Lundensia Investigationes Antiqvitatibus Urbis Lundae VII. Lund: Kulturhistoriska Museet i Lund.

Nørlund, P. (1948) *Trelleborg*. Nordiske Fortidsminder. IV. Bind. 1. København: Nordisk Forlag.

Rapoport, A. (1969) *House form and Culture*. Foundations of Cultural Geography Series. Englewood Cliffs: Prentics-Hall Inc.

Schmidt, H. (1994) *Building Customs in Viking Age Denmark*. København: Poul Kristensen.

Skov, H. (1994) Hustyper i vikingetid og tidlig middelalder. Udviklingen af hustyperne i det gammeldanske område fra ca. 800-1200 e.Kr., *hikuin* 21, 139-162.

Stoumann, I. (1981) Sædding. A Viking-age village near Esbjerg, *Acta Archaeologica* 50, 95-118.

Söderberg, B. (2005) *Aristokratisk rum och gränöverskridande. Järrestad och sydöstra Skåne mellan region och rike 600-1100*. Riksantikvarieämbetet Arkeologiska Undersökningar Skrifter 62. Stockholm: Riksantikvarieämbetet.

Tesch, S. (1993) *Houses, Farmsteads and Long-term Change. A Regional Study of Prehistoric Settlements in the Köpinge Area in Scania, Southern Sweden*. Uppsala: Uppsala Universitet.

Tornbjerg, S.Å. (1998) Toftegård – en fundrig gård fra sen jernalder og vikingetid. In: *Centrala platser-centrala frågor. Samhällsstrukturen under järnålder*, eds. L. Larsson & B. Hårdh, 217-232. Acta Archaeologica Lundensia 8°:28. Stockholm: Almqvist & Wiksell International.

Trigger, B. (1989) *A History of Archaeological Thought*. Cambridge: Cambridge University Press.

Trumbull, H.C. (2000) *The Threshold Covenant or The Beginning of Religious Rites*. Kirkwood: Impact Christian Books.

Van Gennep, A. (1960) *The Rites of Passage*. Chicago: Chicago University Press.

Walker, J. (2007) The Ideology of the early medieval hall in the North Sea region. PhD thesis T4882, University of York.

Waterbolk, H. (1994) The origin of the Lejre house type. In: *Kongehallen fra Lejre – et rekonstruktionsprojekt. International workshop 25.-27. november 1993 på Historisk-Arkæologisk Forsøgscenter, Lejre, om rekonstruktionen af vikingehallen fra Gl. Lejre og et vikingemiljø,* eds. A.C. Larsen, 101-114. Teknisk Rapport 1. Lejre: Historisk-arkæologisk Forsøgscenter Lejre.

Webley, L. (2008) *Iron Age Households. Structure and Practice in Western Denmark, 500 BC-AD 200.* Jysk Arkæologisk Selskabs skrifter 62. Højbjerg: Jysk Arkæologisk Selskab.

"Þat var háttr í þann tíma" – Representations of Viking Age and Medieval Houses in *Grettis saga*

Teva Vidal

Abstract

The narrative of the early 15th-century Grettis saga, one of the last of the Icelandic Family Sagas to have been written, is replete with rich details concerning the construction and use of domestic buildings. Studying the representations of domestic architecture in the narrative suggests that material culture may indeed be represented accurately in medieval literature. The descriptions of buildings also reveal an awareness of time and place, for example differentiating Norwegian buildings from Icelandic examples. Significantly, certain deliberately antiquarian references suggest that the saga's authors were aware of the evolution of housing culture in the chronological interval between the time of writing and the early 11th -century setting of the narrative.

Introduction

The *Islendingasögur,* or Icelandic family sagas, are a group of tales that relate the deeds mainly of Icelanders and their Norwegian kin during the Viking Age, roughly situated between the 9th and late 11th centuries (see the published editions of the sagas in the Íslenzk fornrit collection and for the present case study of *Grettis saga,* Jónsson 1936). The written versions of the stories that have come down to us, however, date from the later medieval period, starting in the 13th century, and were therefore composed several centuries after the events they aim to depict. While this means that the historical veracity of the narratives is a matter of much debate (see for example Friðriksson 1994; Sørensen 1993), the sagas take place in a realistic setting; locations and landscapes that are still, in many cases, recognisable today. The level of detail and description that the saga writers employed leaves no doubt as to their desire to represent a 'real' world, one that would be familiar and believable to their intended audiences (Sørensen 2003: 265, 267). One element of setting which benefits from this attention to realistic detail is the depiction of houses and the material culture of domestic life. In a society that was mostly rural, the farm, with the house at its centre, constituted the core not only of everyday domestic life but also of the wider social world.

An exhaustive overview of the representations of houses in the entire corpus of the Icelandic family sagas (some 40 separate narratives with approximately 50 additional short stories, or *þættir*) would significantly enhance our understanding of living conditions in medieval Iceland as well as the medieval perception of the Viking-Age world. This has not been attempted since Valtýr Guðmundsson's doctoral thesis *Privatboligen på Island i sagatiden,* published in 1889. However, considering the significant advancement of both saga literature studies and archaeology since that time, it can be safely said that Guðmundsson's study is now outdated. More recent studies, namely Arnheiður Sigurðardóttir's *Híbýlahættir á miðöldum* (1966), have provided more modern and critical input to this question, although the material culture of the saga world is still a field of study which remains largely underrepresented in recent scholarship. In order to reveal the potential richness of this approach, this chapter focuses on the representations of the house as a physical construction in a sample from one saga, *Grettis saga* (Jónsson 1936; see also the translations by Fox & Pálsson 1974, Scudder 1998, and Scudder & Thorsson 2005). This is thought to be one of the last sagas to have been written, around the turn of the 15th century, though the events it describes are said to have taken place in the early 11th century (Byock 2009: 242-248; Scudder 1998: 49; Scudder & Thorsson 2005: xxxv-xxxvi). The saga provides rich descriptions of domestic interiors in Iceland and Norway which demonstrates the saga writer's awareness of the evolution of housing culture between the Viking Age setting of the narrative, and the time of recording in the medieval period.

Bjarg: A Case Study

The vast majority of domestic sites represented in the sagas are farms, consisting of a house, various outbuildings and a certain amount of land for agricultural exploitation immediately adjacent to the collected buildings. It is within this context that much of the narrative action takes place, and this chapter will therefore focus on descriptions of rural houses. In studying *Grettis saga* and other saga texts, it becomes evident that the amount of detail that is provided for any given domestic site is dependent on its importance to the plot. There appears to be a fairly simple logic behind this: there is little point in describing the layout of a farm's grounds or the internal construction of a house unless a segment of the narrative takes place there and detailed description becomes necessary to understand the narrative's progression. Indeed, there are few if any detailed descriptions of the physical world, either landscapes or constructed spaces, which are given gratuitously.

In *Grettis saga*, the reader's attention is attracted to the question of the layout of the house early in the saga, thanks to one particular passage that occurs in chapter 14 at the farm of Bjarg in Northern Iceland, the home of the main character Grettir Ásmundarson. This is the first description of a house in the saga, and it is conspicuous for purposefully providing a detailed portrait of the physical layout of the inside of the farm's main room (all translations by the author):

"Þat var háttr í þann tíma, at eldskálar váru stórir á bœjum; sátu menn þar við langelda á öptnum. Þar váru borð sett fyrir menn, ok siðan sváfu menn upp frá eldunum; konur unnu þar ok tó á daginn. Þat var eitt kveld, at Grettir skyldi hrífa bak Ásmundar, at karl mælti: "Nú muntu verða af þér at draga slenit, mannskræfan," segir hann. Grettir segir: "Illt er at eggja óbilgjarnan." Ásmundr mælti: "Aldri er dugr í þér." Grettir sér nú, hvar sótðú ullkambar í setinu, tekr upp kambinn ok lætr ganga ofan eptir baki Ásmundar."

"That was the custom in that time, that there were large fire-rooms on farms; people sat there near the long fires in the evening. There were tables placed there in front of the people, and afterwards people would go to sleep up from the fire; women also worked the wool there during the day. It was one evening, when Grettir was to scratch Ásmundr's back, that the old man spoke: "Now you should drag the laziness from yourself, you good-for-nothing," he said. Grettir said: "It's a bad thing to goad the stubborn." Ásmundr said: "There is never any spirit in you." Grettir saw where the wool-combs were lying on the bench, took one up and ran it down Ásmundr's back."

Ásmundr, Grettir's father, then jumps up in rage and tries to hit his son, and the episode continues to illustrate Grettir's childhood depravity. The details of spatial layout in this passage are required to make sense of the plot's action, but they are nevertheless quite rich and revealing of an extensive understanding of material space.

Firstly, the passage situates the action. We see that the episode is taking place at a farm (Old Norse:'bœr'). This is a word with a rather large semantic range and is used consistently in *Grettis saga* to refer to both the entire farmstead and specifically the farmhouse, as in this example. The reader is further situated inside the 'fire-room' (Old Norse: 'eld(a)skáli'). 'Skáli' is one of the two most common words in Old Norse used to describe the main room of a house, the other being 'stofa' (although 'skáli' can also sometimes refer to the entire building of the house and is the accepted generic term for a Viking Age house in modern Icelandic archaeology (Milek 2006: 88f)). It is important here to note that there is a later medieval divergence in the meaning of these two words, but that when referring to the main room of the house in the Icelandic family sagas, the terms are essentially synonymous (Sigurðardóttir 1966: 9-19; see also Águstsson 1979: 63-66; Stoklund 1993: 215). Both words occur frequently in this sense in *Grettis saga*. 'Stofa' is related to the English word 'stove' and suggests a heated room. In this case, the compound 'eldskáli' ('eldr' = fire) does the same thing and helps indicate the presence of a fire, and also that the fire is one of the defining features of the room. The fire itself is described as being a 'langeldr' or 'long fire', and descriptions elsewhere in the saga give further reference to it as a long open hearth situated in the middle of the room. Additional detail about the fire is provided in chapter 37 by one of Grettir's rivals, who utters the deliberately insulting and untrue statement that Grettir's father Ásmundr "died choked like a dog in the smoke of his main room's fire" ("hann kafnaði i stofureyk sem hundr"). This suggests that this was at least a plausible scenario and that the long fire is an open hearth without any means to help with the extraction of smoke.

The eldskáli is described as being a large room, and apart from the fire, the space is taken up by the 'set' ("hvar sótðú ullkambar í setinu"). These are the raised platforms that lined the walls of the main room. The fact that they are raised is suggested by their description when used for sleeping, as being 'up from' the fire ("upp frá eldunum"), above the level of the open hearth.[1]

This description also tells something of the daily activities that went on within the eldskáli. It is a communal space: meals are taken there, on removable tables (perhaps trestle tables), set up on or in front of the same platforms that were used for sleeping at night, and for resting at the end of a day's work. Although it is revealed in a plot-driven episode, the strange task of grooming that Grettir is given is a privileged glimpse at a very intimate level of daily

life as it may have gone on indoors. Similarly, the detail about wool working is required by the plot so that Grettir can have a carding comb with which to assault his father. However, it still gives an idea of the kinds of domestic industry that might take place inside the main room of the house.

Descriptions in time and space

The skáli / eldskáli as it is described in this passage corresponds, in its basic elements, to the main room of Scandinavian houses of the Viking Age, following the model of the three-aisled longhouse (Hamerow 2002:14-26; Johansen 1982: 51-53; Magnus 2002: 11-21; Milek 2006: 89-98; 113-123, 201; Myhre 2000: 37; Schmidt 1994). Of greatly varying lengths, these buildings were rectangular with their long walls bowed slightly outward. Their main room, as in *Grettis saga*, featured a long central open hearth, and raised platforms lining the long walls and occasionally across one of the gable walls. Along the edge of these platforms ran two parallel rows of posts supporting the weight of the roof, creating the three aisles that typified the construction. It was not unusual for these buildings to be divided into several rooms by the addition of partitions through the width of the house. In the Scandinavian homelands, longhouses often incorporated habitation for both humans and livestock, with a byre located at one end of the house. This feature is absent from Viking-Age houses in Iceland, where the byre was contained in a separate building, but houses did frequently have internal divisions of space most often delimiting rooms at the gable ends (Milek 2006: 98f, 123-125; Vésteinsson 2007: 157).

This basic design was prevalent throughout the Viking Age Scandinavian world and proved remarkably adaptable to the different local building materials and climatic conditions encountered throughout the North Atlantic migrations. In Iceland, this model could be manifest with utmost simplicity in the most basic structures, such as at the early/mid-Viking-Age house at Snjáleifartóttir, seen in Figure 1 (10th-11th century, Stenberger 1943; Milek 2006: 99, 327f). Although variation between individual buildings occurred, this house model persisted into the 11th

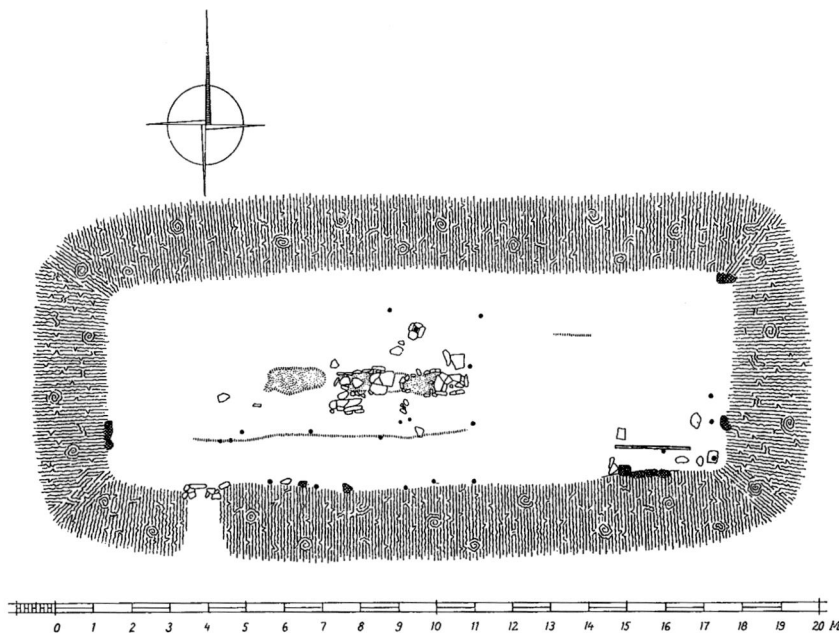

Figure 1. The 10th-11th century farm at Snjáleifartóttir, Iceland. © Stenberger 1943: figure 63.

century, which could easily fit with the chronological placement of the *Grettis saga* narrative.

The excerpt examined earlier, at Grettir's farm at Bjarg, is exceptional in character. The majority of house descriptions in *Grettis saga* are brief and are not introduced in any special way. An exception can be made here for the lengthy descriptions of houses, or rather of the destruction of houses which occurs during two very similar battles between Grettir and house-invading monsters (a revenant and a troll) at the farms of Þórhallsstaðir and Sandhaugar (chapters 35 and 64-65 respectively). Still, while these passages might be as detailed as the passage mentioned above at Bjarg, none of the other descriptions specifically explains how house features were constructed and used. These other descriptions also differ in character, and mention additional elements of the house, such as auxiliary rooms, passageways, and multiple entrances. The following excerpt from chapter 47, also at Grettir's home at Bjarg, serves to illustrate this:

"Hann gekk á bak húsum ok þær dyrr, er þar váru, því at honum váru þar kunnig göng, ok svá til skála ok at rekkju móður sinnar ok þreifaðisk fyrst fyrir."

"He [Grettir] went to the back of the house and to the door that was there, because the passage there was known to him. And so he went to the main room and to his mother's bed, feeling his way with his hands first."

Grettir is feeling his way because it is dark in the house. From this excerpt we gather that houses could have more than one entrance, and more importantly, that different parts of the house could be connected with passageways. While Viking-Age houses in Iceland could have more than one entrance (Milek 2006: 109-111), this description does not fit with the simplest model of housing described above. This new model is, however, contextually relevant. At this point it is important to remember the dating of *Grettis saga*: while the events it describes occur in the early 11th century, it is one of the latest of the Icelandic family sagas and is arguably thought to have been composed around 1400 (Byock 2009: 242-248; Scudder 1998: 49; Scudder & Thorsson 2005: xxxv-xxxvi). Late in the Viking Age (starting around the 12th century) the Icelandic house started to evolve. Rooms and annexes were added to the existing houses which already fit the basic model described above. These annexes were often perpendicular to the long axis of the house, and often interconnected with short passageways (Milek 2006: 130-134, 306). This would eventually lead to the development of late medieval multi-roomed 'passage-houses' and eventually into elaborate, centralised farm complexes of the late Middle Ages and early modern period (Andreasen 1981; Følstad 2003; Milek 2006: 46; Vésteinsson 2007: 157). The early stages of house expansion, with the inclusion of annexes on the basic house model, can be seen in the late-Viking Age house of Stöng (Figure

2), long thought to have been abandoned due to the eruption of Hekla in 1104, but whose latest phases of occupation have been recently re-dated to the 12th-13th centuries (Milek 2006: 328f; Roussell 1943). The medieval evolution of the house into what would become the passage house can be seen in the layout of the late 14th century (1362) house at Gröf (Figure 3) (Gestsson 1959). It is important to note, however, that there is no strict chronology to this evolution, as architectural rates of change are uneven and various construction techniques and styles show great overlap (Foged Klemensen 2003: 144f).

Further evidence of contextual precision relating to house construction can be seen in the description of the unnamed farm belonging to Þorfinnr Karsson on Haramsøy in Norway (chapter 19). This farm features a detailed description of a multi-level storehouse:

"Berserkir komu fram í þessu. Grettir mælti: "Göngum út, ok mun ek sýna yðr fatabúr Þorfinns." Þeir létu þat leiðask; kómu þeir at útibúri ákafliga stóru. Þar váru á útidyrr ok sterkr láss fyrir, þat var allsterkt hús. Þar var hjá salerni mikit ok sterkt ok eitt skjaldþili milli húsanna: húsin stóðu hátt, ok var nokkut rið upp at ganga... Hljóp hann (Grettir) ut ór húsinu ok greip í hespuna ok rekr aptr húsit ok setr láss fyrir. Þórir ok hans félagar ætluðu fyrst, at svarfazk myndi aptr hafa hurðin, ok gáfu sér ekki at. Þeir höfðu ljós hjá sér, því at Grettir hafði sýnt þeim marga gripi, þá er Þorfinnr átti; litu þeir þar á um stund... Hlaupa þeir á hurðina ok finna, at hon var læst; treysta nu a timbrveggina, svá at brakar í hverju tré. Hér kemr um síðir, at þeir fá brotit skjaldþilit, ok kómusk svá fram í gangrúmit ok þar út á riðit... "

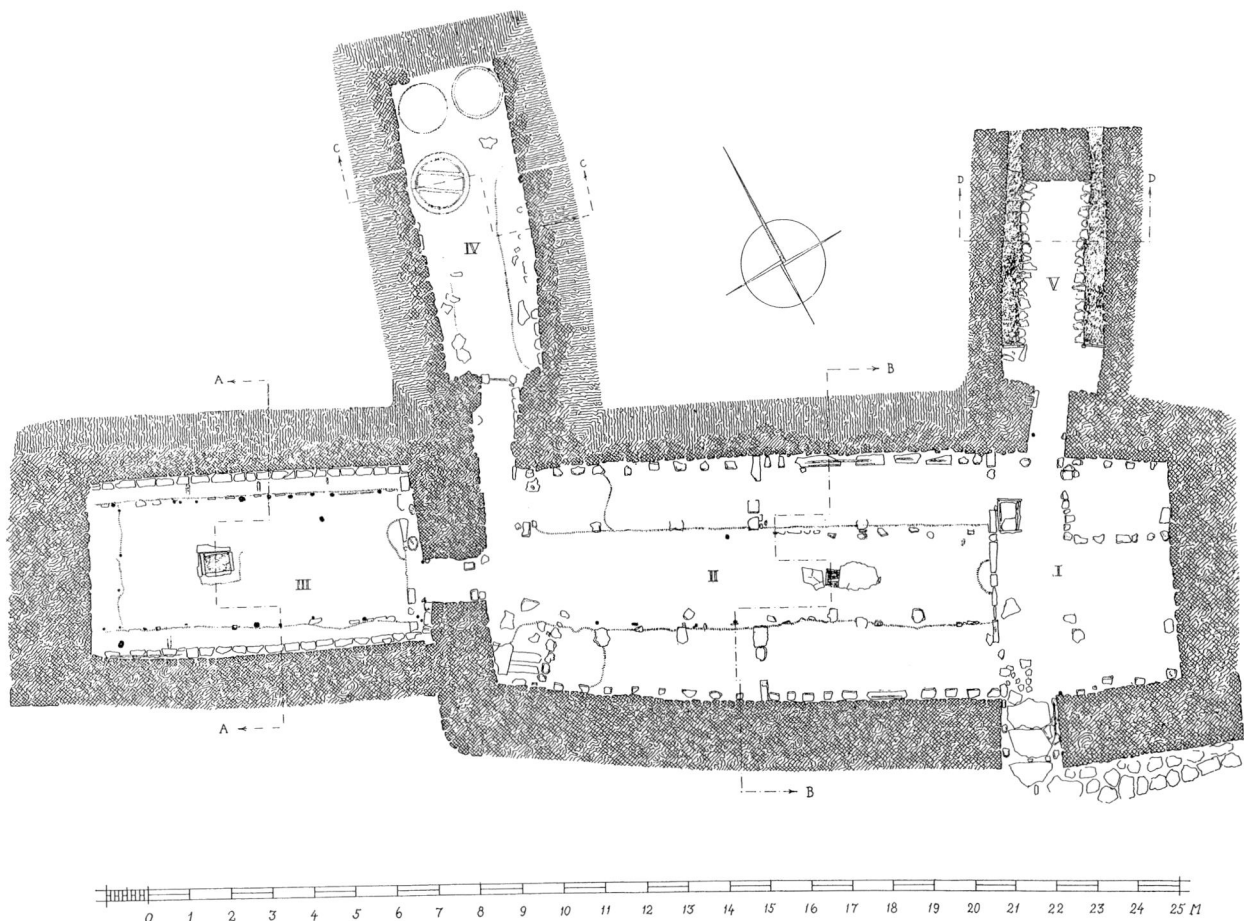

Figure 2. The 12th-13th century farm at Stöng, Iceland. © Roussell 1943: figure 7.

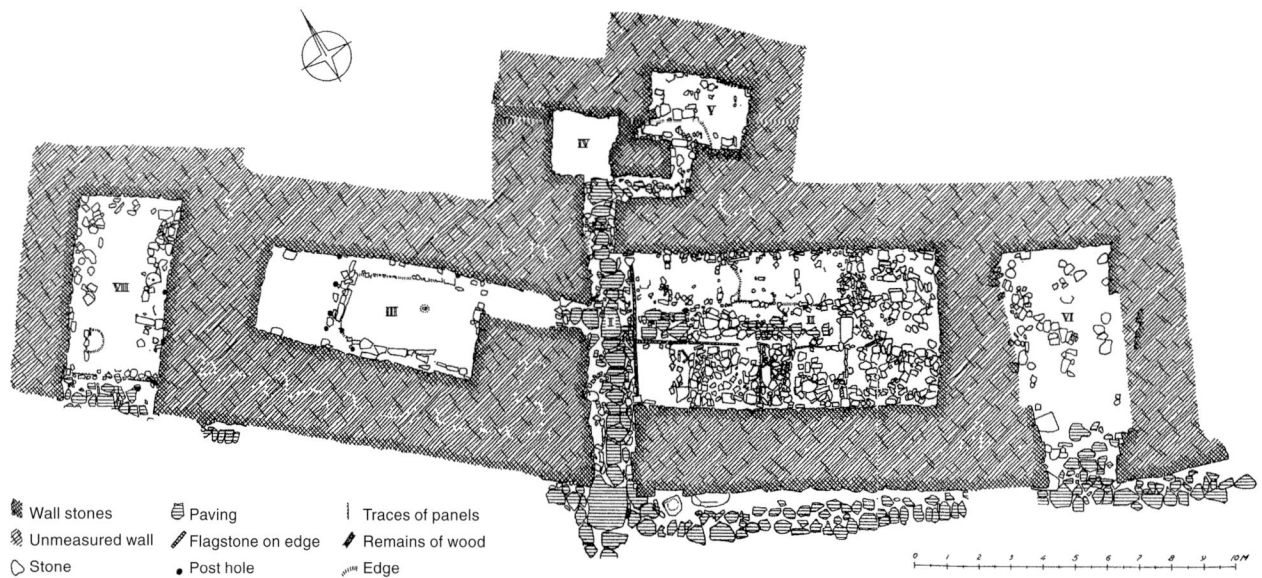

Figure 3. The 14th century farm at Gröf, Iceland. © Gestsson 1959: plate 2.

"The berserkers came forward at that [statement]. Grettir said: "Let us go out, and I will show you Þorfinnr's store of clothes." At that they let themselves be led, and they came to an exceedingly large outbuilding. There was also a strong lock on the outer door; it was a very sturdy house. Next to it was a large and sturdy privy, and there was a wooden partition wall between these parts of the house. The house stood high, and there were some stairs to go up to it... [Grettir] ran out of the house, seized the latch, slammed the door and set the lock on it. Þórir and his comrades thought at first that the door must have been knocked back, and they paid it no mind. They had a light with them, because Grettir had been showing them many treasures that Þorfinnr owned, and they looked around there for a while... They [the berserkers] ran to the door and found that it was locked. They now tried the strength of the timber [partition] wall, so that every board creaked. In the end, they managed to break down the partition wall, and so they came forward into the gallery and from there out to the stairs..."

This kind of multi-level storehouse, external to the main dwelling, was a Norwegian innovation from the beginning of the 13th century, and is therefore a properly medieval (not Viking Age) feature of the Norwegian rural farmstead (Stoklund 2003: 21-25, see also Landsverk 1988). An example of such a storehouse can be seen in the early-15th century loft from Heierstad, currently at the Vestfold folk museum in Tønsberg, Norway (Figure 4). This type of building was entirely absent in Iceland, which lacked the timber resources to build such impressive wooden structures. As has been seen, the medieval Icelandic solution to incorporating additional storage areas often came in the form of annexes to the main house.

The first appearance of the multi-level outbuilding in early 13th-century Norway coincided with the abandonment of the longhouse model. Even during the Viking Age, the interior space of the longhouse began to be cleared up by gradually eliminating the interior rows of roof-supporting posts and integrating the weight-bearing timbers into the walls (Hamerow 2002: 26; Hansen 2002; Schmidt 1994: 90-110). This construction was, however, unsuitable for the large longhouse model and led to the adoption of a new 'standard' house plan consisting of a smaller square or rectangular main room, built of wood in either stave or log construction, and heated with an open hearth or a flueless stove placed in one corner of the room or along a side-wall. The room's upper space was open to the roof-ridge, where a hole allowed smoke to escape and also served as the main source of light for the room. This house model adopted one of the former Viking Age names for the main room, the stofa, and is known by its derivative in various Scandinavian languages: stofa/stova/stuga/stue. This building technique (predominantly its stave-built version) was exported from Norway throughout the North Atlantic, contributing to the primacy of stave construction in medieval Icelandic building, and persisting in Faroese construction well into the 18th, and even 19th centuries (Christie 2002: 137-139; Stoklund 1993: 215; 1999: 83-86; 2003: 25-28).

The open upper space in the main room was necessary for rising smoke from the open hearth to gather and escape through the smoke-hole. This meant that heated rooms could not be divided by floors to incorporate upper levels. This feature of the medieval stofa seems to have remained unchanged even after the introduction of chimneys in the later medieval period (Christie 2002; Krongaard Kristensen 2003: 170f; Stoklund 1993: 212-214; 2002; 2003: 25). However, the medieval stofa often did have ceilings built over unheated rooms adjacent to the main room, becoming more frequent in the early modern period as of the 16th century (Svart Kristiansen 2003: 96). Viking age houses would have had to contend with the same problem of smoke in their heated rooms, and while it is not impossible that larger Viking Age longhouses may have had upper levels built over their unheated parts, especially at the gable ends away from the central hearth, there is no conclusive archaeological proof of this (Kaldal Mikkelsen 2003: 80). It does appear that the technique of building up, as with the multi-level outbuildings, was a medieval innovation.

Keeping with this pattern, Þorfinnr's Norwegian farm, in addition to having its raised outbuilding, has an upper level, a 'loft' (Old Norse: 'lopt') with a window, in which a beacon is lit to help the hero Grettir find his way back at night after routing a band of marauders (chapter 19):

"Húsfeyja lét kveikja ljós í inum efstum loftum við gluggana, at hann hefði þat til leiðarvísis; var ok svá, at hann fat af því heim, er hann sá ljósit."

"The housewife had a light lit in the upper loft by the window, so that he [Grettir] would have it as a guide, and it so happened that he found his way home when he saw the light."

Þorfinnr's farm therefore does fit the portrait of a medieval Norwegian farm complex, rather than a Viking Age longhouse.

Figure 4. The early-15th century loft from Heierstad, currently at the Vestfold folk museum in Tønsberg, Norway.

Back to Bjarg

It would appear that *Grettis saga* provides both Icelandic and Norwegian evidence of medieval house construction, and that the saga reflects the domestic material context of a medieval period of composition. Even more compelling evidence of this comes from the first excerpt mentioned above, which appeared to show an interior setting that was compatible with a standard Viking Age Icelandic house. Here, it is relevant to look not only at the material descriptions in the passage, but also the way it is introduced: "Þat var háttr í þann tíma", "That was the custom in that time". By specifying that this section describes the way houses were built in bygone times, the author is explicitly expressing a consciously-antiquarian chronological distance with the narrative's setting. The placement of the fire is especially singled out as unusual and needing explanation, and the detailed description of *how* the internal features of the skáli were used by its occupants suggests that such a physical layout might have been unfamiliar to a potential audience or reader at the time of the saga's writing, or at least at the time when the story was crystallised in the form we now have it.

Most of the other house descriptions in *Grettis saga*, both in Iceland and in Norway, create a portrait of the dwelling that reflects medieval innovations in housing culture. The fact that these descriptions are mentioned in passing, without special introduction and, significantly, without explicit markers of chronological distance or 'guides' for the use of internal space, suggests that the later-medieval house model was more contemporary, or at least more familiar, to both the saga writer and potential audience. There was therefore no need to explain what was obvious.

Those material details that are stated as unfamiliar, the layout of the skáli and its features such as the central open hearth and the set-platforms lining the walls, are all necessary to the plot itself in the passage where Grettir assaults his father. It would appear, then, that the plot sealed these architectural details into the story at an earlier stage, closer to the Viking-Age events depicted, and that this material setting is therefore part of the genesis of the *Grettis saga* narrative. The medieval saga writer cannot eliminate these unfamiliar elements, but is never-

theless able to explain them to a contemporary audience. This would appear to demonstrate a conscious awareness on the part of the writer of the evolution in housing culture over time, between the Viking-Age setting of the narrative and the later, medieval period of recording.

Conclusion

While the interaction between archaeology and text is a vast question worthy of much further exploration, the examples presented in this chapter, even from a single case study, are sufficient to demonstrate that the domestic material culture represented in the sagas is not a random or fictional fabrication. The descriptions of houses in *Grettis saga*, both for Iceland and Norway, appear to accurately reflect a medieval architectural context. The descriptions given almost in passing appear to give a portrait of an ordinary reality that would have been familiar to the saga's potential audience. Certain details of the plot, however, required a specific material reality to be expressed, possibly one originating in earlier incarnations of the saga. These material details were crystallised, by their importance to the plot, in a form that became, by the time of the saga's writing, potentially unfamiliar to the saga's audience, and thus needed to be explained.

This brief analysis of *Grettis saga* demonstrates that a reading of the sagas in the light of archaeology can be advantageous on several levels. For the saga-writer's craft and the study of medieval literature and its mechanisms of transmission, it can show how reliably the sagas might represent the material realities of the medieval society which created them. It can also show how the memory of the past might be anchored in material culture and how, in turn, these material memories of the past could be sealed within narrative. For the archaeology of housing, the evidence of physical structures as written in the sagas might help trace the evolution of housing culture. And perhaps most importantly, such a reading can inform us on the social importance of houses and domestic space in this society by filling the vestiges of domestic structures, the ruins provided by archaeology, with living characters whose daily activities both shaped, and were shaped by, the domestic space they occupied.

Notes

1. The term 'upp frá' is most likely to mean the vertical elevation above the fire itself, and not to an 'upper' or 'high' end of the room in terms of space that is coded and divided by social hierarchy. When such space is indeed referred to, it is in relation to the room's entrance and to the outside world: the more privileged space is farther within the room, 'innar', and the less privileged is closer to the door and to the outside world, 'útar'.

References

Ágústsson, H. (1978) Fjórar fornar húsamyndir, *Árbok hins Íslenzka Fornleifafélags* 1977, 135-159.

Ágústsson, H. (1979) Fornir húsaviðir í Hólum, *Árbok hins Íslenzka Fornleifafélags* 1978, 5-66.

Ágústsson, H. (1982) Den islandske bondegårds udvikling fra landnamstiden indtil det 20. Århundede. In: *Vestnordisk byggeskikk gjenom to tusen år: Tradisjon og forandring fra romertid til det 19. Århundre./West Nordic Building Customs from the Roman Period to the 19th Century (with English summary)*, eds. B. Myhre, B. Stoklund & P. Gjærder, 255-268. AmS-Skrifter 7. Stavanger: Arkeologisk Museum i Stavanger.

Andreasen, C. (1981) Langhus – ganghus – centraliseret gård. Nogle betragtninger over norrøne gårdtyper, *hikuin* 7, 179-184.

Byock, J., (trans.) (2009) *Grettir's Saga*, with skaldic verses by R. Poole, Oxford World Classics. Oxford: Oxford University Press.

Christie, H. (2002) The *stofa* in Nordic Building Tradition, *Collegium Medievale* 15, 127-140.

Foged Klemensen, M. (2003) Udgravede træhuse i danske byer ca. 800-1600 – konstruktion og indretning. In: *Bolig og familie i Danmarks middelalder*, ed. E. Roesdahl, 129-167. Højberg: Jysk Arkæologisk Selskab.

Følstad, E. (2003) Fra langhus til laftahus, *Årbok Nord-Trøndelag historielag* 78, 7-22.

Fox, D. & H. Pálsson (trans.) (1974) *Grettir's Saga*. Toronto: University of Toronto Press, reprint 2001.

Friðriksson, A. (1994) *Sagas and Popular Antiquarianism in Icelandic Archaeology*. Worldwide Archaeology Series 10. Aldershot: Avebury.

Gestsson, G. (1959) Gröf í Öræfum, *Árbók hins Íslenzka fornleifafélags* 56, 5-87.

Gestsson, G. (1982) Brugen af sten og tørv i de islandske huse fra landamstid til nyere tid. In: *Vestnordisk byggeskikk gjenom to tusen år: Tradisjon og forandring fra romertid til det 19. Århundre/West Nordic Building Customs from the Roman Period to the 19th Century (with English*

summary), eds. B. Myhre, B. Stoklund & P. Gjærder, 162-172. AmS-Skrifter 7. Stavanger: Arkeologisk Museum i Stavanger.

Guðmundsson, V. (1889) *Privatboligen på Island i sagatiden, samt delvis i det øvrige Norden*. København: Høst.

Hamerow, H. (2002) *Early Medieval Settlements. The Archaeology of Rural Communities in Northwest Europe 400-900*. Oxford: Oxford University Press.

Hansen, S.S. (2002) Scandinavian Building Customs – The Faroese Case and its North Atlantic Context, *Collegium Medievale* 15, 111-125.

Johansen, O.S. (1982) Viking Age Farms: Estimating the Number and Population Size. A Case Study of Vestvågøy, North Norway, *Norwegian Archaeological Review* 15, 45-69.

Jónsson, G. (ed.) (1936) *Grettis saga Ásmundarsonar*. Íslenzk fornrit vol. 7. Reykjavík: Hið Íslenzka Fornritafélag.

Kaldal Mikkelsen, D. (2003) Boligfunktioner i vikingetidens gårde. In: *Bolig og familie i Danmarks middelalder*, ed. E. Roesdahl, 77-87. Højberg: Jysk Arkæologisk Selskab.

Krongaard Kristensen, H. (2003) Planløsninger i byernes stenhuse. In: *Bolig og familie i Danmarks middelalder*, ed. E. Roesdahl, 169-192. Højberg: Jysk Arkæologisk Selskab.

Landsverk, H. (1988) Tradisjonar omkring bur og loft i norske gardstun, *By og Bygd* 32, 1-17.

Magnus, B. (2002) Dwellings and settlements: structure and characteristics. In: *Scandinavians From the Vendel Period To the Tenth Century: An Ethnographic Perspective*, ed. J. Jesch, 5-33. Woodbridge: Boydell/San Marino: Centre for Interdisciplinary Research on Social Stress.

Milek, K.B. (2006) *Houses and Households in Early Icelandic Society: Geoarchaeology and the Interpretation of Social Space*. PhD thesis, University of Cambridge.

Myhre, B. (1982a) Bolighusets utvikling fra jernalder til middelalder i Sørvest-Norge. In: *Vestnordisk byggeskikk gjenom to tusen år: Tradisjon og forandring fra romertid til det 19. Århundre/West Nordic Building Customs from the Roman Period to the 19th Century (with English summary)*, eds. B. Myhre, B. Stoklund & P. Gjærder, 195-217. AmS-Skrifter 7. Stavanger: Arkeologisk Museum i Stavanger.

Myhre, B. (1982b) Synspunkter på huskonstruksjon i sørvestnorske gårdhus fra jernalder og middelalder. In: *Vestnordisk byggeskikk gjenom to tusen år: Tradisjon og forandring fra romertid til det 19. Århundre/West Nordic Building Customs from the Roman Period to the 19th Century (with English summary)*, eds. B. Myhre, B. Stoklund & P. Gjærder, 98-118. AmS-Skrifter 7. Stavanger: Arkeologisk Museum i Stavanger.

Myhre, B. (2000) The Early Viking Age in Norway, *Acta Archaeologica* 71, 35-47.

Roussell, A. (1943) Stöng, Þjórsárdalur. In: *Forntida gårdar i Island: Meddelanded från den nordiska arkeologiska undersökningen i Island sommaren 1939*, ed. M. Stenberger, 72-97. Copenhagen: Ejnar Munksgaard.

Schmidt, H. (1994) *Building Customs in Viking Age Denmark*. trans. J. Olsen. Copenhagen: Poul Kristensen.

Scudder, B. (trans.) (1998) *The Saga of Grettir the Strong*. In: *The Complete Sagas of the Icelanders*, Vol. 2, ed. V. Hreinsson, Reykjavík: Leifur Eiríksson.

Scudder, B. (trans.) & O. Thorsson, (ed.) (2005) *The Saga of Grettir the Strong*. London: Penguin Classics.

Sigurðardóttir, A. (1966) *Híbýlahættir á miðöldum*. Reykjavík: Bókaútgáfa menningarsjóðs og þjóðvinafélagsins.

Sørensen, P.M. (1993) Historical Reality and Literary Form. In: *Viking Revaluations: Viking Society Centenary Symposium 14-15 May 1992*, eds. A. Faulkes & R. Perkins, 172-181. London: Viking Society for Northern Research/ University College London.

Sørensen, P.M. (2003) The Hall in Norse Literature. In: *Borg in Lofoten: A Chieftain's Farm in North Norway*, eds. G.S. Munch, O.S. Johansen & E. Roesdahl, 265-272. Arkeologisk skriftserie 1. Trondheim: Tapir/Lofotr Vikingmuseet på Borg.

Sørheim, H. (2003) Ildsteder og de første laftehusene. In: *Middelaldergåren i Trøndelag: Foredrag fra to seminar*, ed. O. Skevik, 91-125. Verdal: Stiklestad Nasjonale Kultusenter AS.

Stenberger, M. (1943) Snjáleifartóttir, Þjórsárdalur. In: *Forntida gårdar i Island: Meddelanded från den nordiska arkeologiska undersökningen i Island sommaren 1939*, ed. M. Stenberger, 98-112. Copenhagen: Ejnar Munksgaard.

Stoklund, B. (1982) Røgstue og glasstue: Boligutviklingen på Færøerne set i vestnordisk sammenhæng. In: *Vestnordisk byggeskikk gjenom to tusen år: Tradisjon og forandring fra romertid til det 19. Århundre/West Nordic Building Customs from the Roman Period to the 19th Century (with English summary)*, eds. B. Myhre, B. Stoklund & P. Gjærder, 218-230. AmS-Skrifter 7. Stavanger: Arkeologisk Museum i Stavanger.

Stoklund, B. (1993) On the concepts of *eldhus* and *stova*: The Faroese evidence. In: *Tools and Traditions: Studies in European Ethnology Presented to Alexander Fenton*, ed. H. Cheape, 211-217. Edinburgh: National Museums of Scotland.

Stoklund, B. (1999) North Atlantic Stave Constructions. In: *Grindbygde hus i Vest-Norge. NIKU-seminar om grindbygde hus, Bryggens Museum 23-25.03.98*, eds. H. Schjelderup & O. Storsletten, 82-87. NIKU Temahefte 30. Oslo: Norsk Institut for Kulturminneforskning.

Stoklund, B. (2002) The Riddle of the Stock-Stove Houses: An Attempt at an Explanation. *Collegium Medievale* 15, 141-153.

Stoklund, B. (2003) Andre veje til middelalderhuset – en filologisk-etnologisk tilgang. In: *Bolig og familie i Danmarks middelalder*, ed. E. Roesdahl, 15-29. Højberg: Jysk Arkæologisk Selskab.

Svart Kristiansen, M. (2003) Boligindretning i middelaldergårde. In: *Bolig og familie i Danmarks middelalder*, ed. E. Roesdahl, 89-99. Højberg: Jysk Arkæologisk Selskab.

Vésteinsson, O. (2007) The Icelandic House. In: *The Archaeology of Medieval Europe. Vol. 1. Eighth to Twelfth Centuries AD*, ed. J. Graham-Campbell with M. Valor, 157. Aarhus: Aarhus University Press.

Proper Living – Exploring Domestic Ideals in Medieval Denmark

Mette Svart Kristiansen

Abstract

Houses frame homes, households, and daily life, and it is reasonable to suggest that ideas of domestic space in medieval society, and ideas of how to live in an orderly and acceptable manner in the eyes of one's peers and oneself are reflected in domestic architecture, its layout, fittings, and ornaments. This paper addresses ideas of proper living in affluent rural and urban milieus in medieval Denmark, particularly as they are expressed through houses, inventories, and murals, and it also addresses current challenges in understanding the materialized ideas based on excavations and analysis of a very fragmented past.

Housing culture and homes, an outline of the research

Research on medieval domesticity and dwellings as social spaces and markers of social status has a long tradition in history, archaeology, and ethnology, and particularly in the last 20 years, this area of research has undergone rapid development. It has only briefly and with varying intensity, been addressed in medieval archaeology in Denmark.

In the late 19th to mid-20th centuries, there was a keen interest in domestic culture in Denmark. Archaeology as a professional discipline was developing rapidly, and excavations of rural and urban houses in the 1940s to 1960s generated new data and optimism about research on houses and homes. However, a new generation of researchers turned to other areas, and gradually abandoned the study of houses, homes, and households. Within archaeology, interests were now mainly focused on settlement and village structures, building construction methods and typologies. Owing to a combination of preservation, accessibility, and heritage legislation, and to the specific interests of the individual researchers, the period focus of work on houses has been pri-

marily on the Iron Age and the Viking Age (c 800-1050) and, to a lesser degree, the Early Middle Ages (in Denmark: c 1050-1150). The available data and research strategies have also promoted theoretical discussions on the communication of social stratigraphy within and between settlements. Of particular interest during the past few decades is the identification of Viking and early medieval manorial sites (eg Poulsen & Sindbæk 2011). In recent years, vigorous theoretical debates regarding the home, social space, and communication have prompted a new perspective on Danish research, particularly influenced by Anglo-Saxon studies. In particular, the Viking Age hall has attracted interest as a framework for the household, and a setting for a display of social space and power (eg Croix 2011).

When it comes to the Middle Ages, the archaeological data become more tenuous and the research accordingly more fragmented, as, unlike in many other regions of Europe, only a score of surviving medieval vernacular buildings are preserved in Denmark today. Questions related to the medieval house as home and social space have been raised, but at a quite preliminary level. In order to resurrect the interest in domestic culture, and provide a point of departure for new, interdisciplinary research embracing current trends in this field, Else Roesdahl outlined the research and important questions to be addressed in the anthology, *Bolig og Familie i Danmarks Middelalder* in 2003 ('House and family in medieval Denmark'), based on a collection of papers that took stock of studies by archaeologists, historians, ethnologists, art historians, and linguists, on selected aspects of private life and family structure, houses on farmsteads, in fortifications, and in towns, and domestic arrangements and furnishing. The anthology raises a series of important questions related to the social aspects of houses, and emphasizes the urgent need to 'get behind' the structures, for example, the interrelationship of house and home, the emergence and currency of particular urban or rural ideals of 'proper living', and the use of houses as vehicles for social strategies, by adapting to, or resisting new ideals and technical innovations (Roesdahl 2003a; 2003b).

This paper will outline some of the results, challenges, and questions raised by the research into domestic ideals regarding proper living, particularly those based on medieval buildings themselves, and raises some concerns regarding the data and the researcher.

Antiquarian prerequisites

All the preserved medieval buildings in Denmark are of late medieval origin, the oldest from the second half of the 15th century; all are from urban settings, and reconstructions of their layouts are often disputed. In the countryside, major and radical reconstructions of rural society, starting in the late 18th century and continuing today, left no medieval buildings standing. A few buildings containing medieval timber are rebuilt in open air museums. Written records, such as probate inventories, are also sparse, and more or less restricted to the elite. Therefore, to understand medieval domestic spaces and the underlying ideologies of the household and society, research depends extensively on archaeology.

A series of studies on medieval buildings, construction methods, layout and fittings and fixtures published as recently as the first decade of the 21st century demonstrates the need for basic archaeological outlines (*eg* Foged Klemensen 2001; 2003; Krongaard Kristensen 2003; Rensbro 2002; Roesdahl 2003c; Svart Kristiansen 2003). The data on medieval buildings fall into chronologically, regionally, and societally distinct groups: Viking and early medieval buildings throughout rural Denmark (Skov 1994), early and high medieval rural buildings from western Denmark (Foged Klemensen 2001), high and late medieval rural buildings from eastern Denmark (Rensbro 2002), excavated, predominantly wooden urban buildings (Foged Klemensen 2003), and preserved, late medieval brick urban buildings (Krongaard Kristensen 2003). The groups reflect the character of different excavation and preservation conditions in rural and urban areas, and emphasize the limitations of analysis across time, space, and social structure, in understanding similarities, differences, and patterns.

Most excavations in Denmark take place in open rural areas, where sites are ploughed up by heavy tilling. Usually, only structures in the subsoil are preserved, such as dug-in, roof-bearing posts, and information about the layout of buildings, as might be indicated by the position of partition walls, fireplaces, and other interior arrangement of the rooms is rarely preserved. This particularly affects high and late medieval buildings, which were often built on sills, and are therefore often not preserved in the archaeological record. In villages, deeply stratified farmsteads may be preserved under existing farms. In general these are not locations favoured by contractors, though there are exceptions, for example the village of Tårnby, south of Copenhagen, lying along the course of the highway to Sweden (Svart Kristiansen 2005a).

Urban excavations provide deeply stratified sites and preserved culture layers, but they are usually limited in size, usually cover less than one plot, and fully-excavated houses are rare (see also papers by Klinge and Thaastrup-Leth, this volume). In the urban milieu, we find a small number of quite rebuilt brick buildings, the majority from the 16th century; most were built by mayors, noblemen, and wealthy merchants. In towns, brick buildings seem to have been rather popular in the 15th-16th centuries, but in the 17th century they were replaced by richly decorated, timber framed buildings.

In 2003, Else Roesdahl explained the profound lack of discussion of the social aspects of houses in Denmark as being due to rescue excavations, which usually exposed only parts of houses, tofts, and plots, noting that basic knowledge and a certain overview were necessary, before further conclusions could be drawn (Roesdahl 2003a: 10). Today, ten years later, the situation has changed little. This reflects a second major influence, which is the form of heritage legislation in Denmark. It lacks basic financial support for research related to post-excavation analysis. Data are supposed to be archived for future research and funding. As a result, data are piling up, publication is rare, and where it occurs, it often focuses on standard data, such as constructions, layout, and structure (Holst & Svart Kristiansen 2011).

Past and present ideas of houses and homes, and a case study from the town of Næstved

Preserved buildings seem to be a suitable point of departure for discussions of houses, homes, and ideas of proper living. But all medieval houses in Denmark have been rebuilt and heavily restored, and the reconstruction of the original room partitions, doorways, and fireplaces is challenging. For example, five different reconstructions of the layout of The House of Rosenvinge in Malmö have been proposed, largely on the basis of analogy and hypothetical reconstruction rather than substantial empirical evidence (pers. comm. Hans Krongaard Kristensen). Indeed, it seems likely that many of the reconstructed layouts of Danish brick houses represent more accurately the current ideas of the researchers, rather than actual representations of a past reality, particularly when based on data that are sparse and uncertain.

Many of the preserved buildings are 'booths', rooms for rent (Danish: 'Boder'). Some of the old-

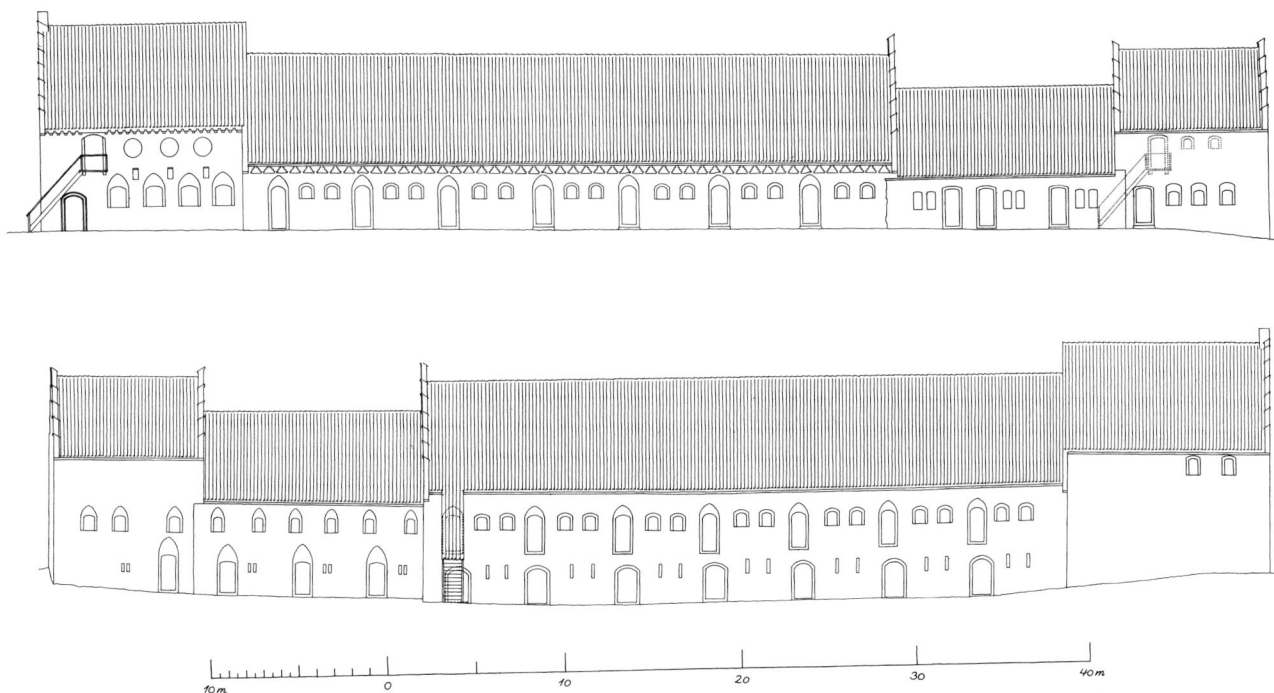

Figure 1. Medieval booths for rent, Næstved. Reconstruction c 1500, north and south. After Engqvist 1988a: 73 (detail).

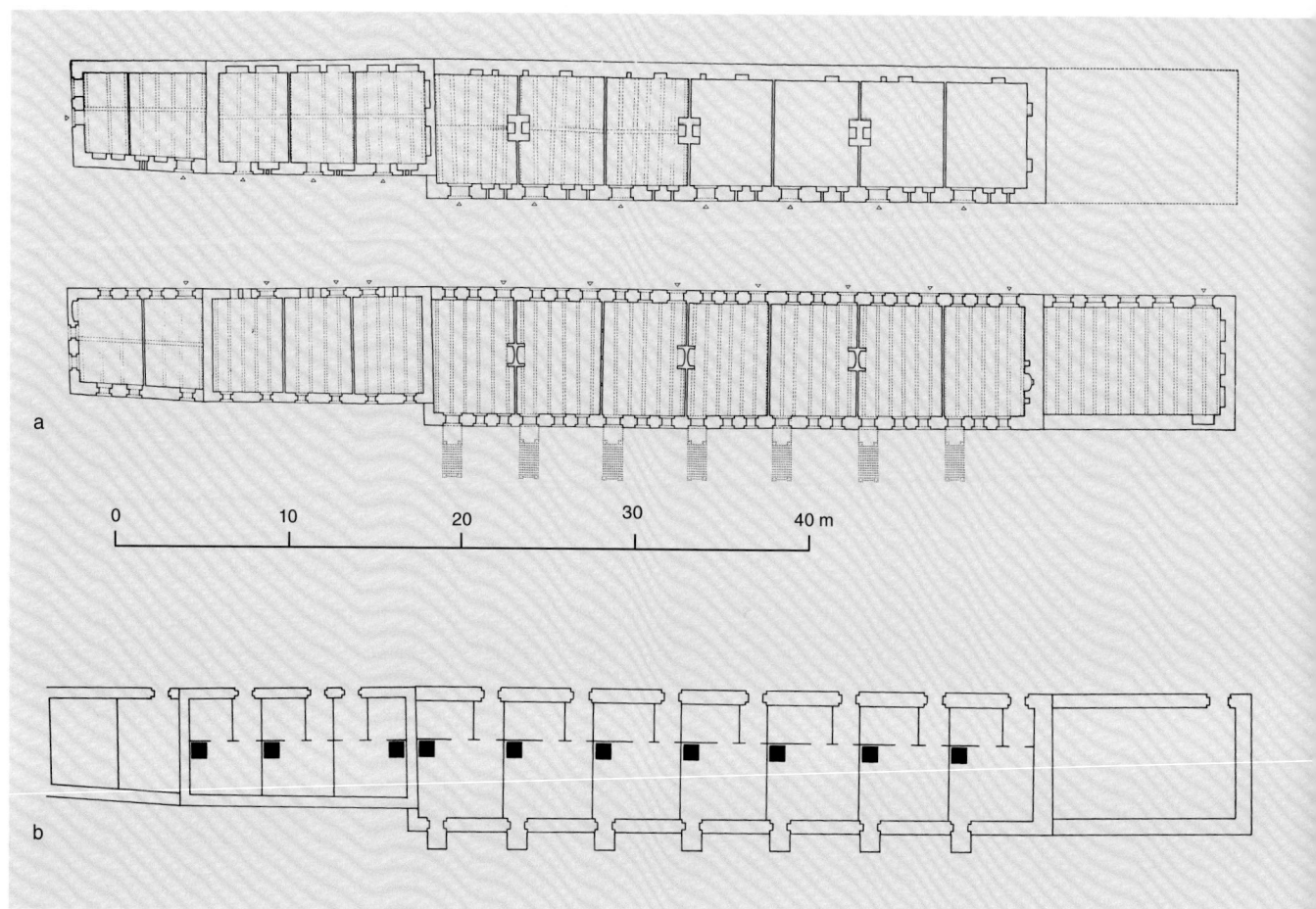

Figure 2. Mogens Tuesens Boder has three floors: a cellar with access from the deeper terrain to the south, facing the former harbour on the river Suså, an upper floor with access from the former churchyard to the north and to the south from a staircase, and a loft. Two different plans for the layout of the dwelling are suggested: a. reconstruction by Engqvist 1988; b. reconstruction and c. (page 153) detail by Birk Hansen. After Birk Hansen 2003: 198-199.

est, as well as best-preserved, are from the medieval town of Næstved (Figure 1). A row of various buildings is situated south of the church of Sankt Peder, from west to east: 'Vesthuset', 'Gotschalks Stenhus', containing three sets of rental accommodations. The next and oldest in the row dating probably from the mid-15th century, 'Mogens Tuesens Boder', was built by mayor Mogens Tuesen in Næstved, and donated to the church in 1484. It contained seven separate 'rents'. A further building, 'Latinskolen', c 1500, far to the east, was demolished in 1881 (Engqvist 1988a). The restoration history of these booths serves as an example of how divergent reconstructions of interiors often relate to different understandings of their social contexts over time (discussed in Birk Hansen 2003).

Previously, 'rents' or rental accommodation was regarded as poor lodgings and salesrooms used by artisans, and descriptions of the booths from 1888 and 1912 reflect this, with words like 'small', 'humble', and even 'for the homeless' used to describe them. These perceptions were probably fostered by the poor state of the buildings in this period. This understanding of the complex, supported by a misreading of the medieval deeds, formed the basis for understanding of the buildings' analysis and restoration (Birk Hansen 2003: 194ff). In the 1960s, this gave way to the identification of service hatches in Gotschalks Stenhus, based on the incorrect presumption that this part of the complex was identical with the 'booths for bakers', known from a writ-

Chamber

Vestibule

Sitting room

c

0   1   2 m

1596, the layout of one of the booths was described as divided by 'old partitions' into three rooms: a small vestibule, a chamber, and sitting room, and an 'old' tile stove was renovated (Varming 1988: 86). These partitions were recovered during the restoration, but dated to *c* 1600 by the architect H.H. Engqvist (Engqvist 1988b). Birk Hansen argues that the layout described in 1596 probably was the original 15th-century arrangement, and that this solution was designed as a draught-prevention measure between the doors to the north and the south. Birk Hansen argues that it was perhaps easier for previous scholars to interpret a cold and draughty, one-room living space as belonging to a family in 'humble' social conditions rather than those of a higher social level (Birk Hansen 2003: 197f). Engqvist's reconstruction of a chimney in each of the seven rental accommodations is also questioned, as it was based on traces of only one foundation between the two westernmost rents which may not even be part of the original structure, but rather a secondary addition. Nevertheless, the originally tile-covered floor would have allowed constructions to be built on top of them, and the removal of partitions and floor surfaces may also have swept away evidence of alternative heating systems.

In Birk's reconstruction, the 'old partitions' are suggested as being original, the fireplace and chimney are positioned to the west in all the rental accommodations, and a tile stove fuelled from the adjacent room is suggested as being situated in the chamber. Birk's reconstruction has also met with critique: how old were the 'old partitions'? If they were original they would be 100 years older than any of the other known surviving examples from more prominent buildings. The smoke-free parlour became an important element in the new, more partitioned layout of homes, as seen in late 16th and early 17th century urban houses (Engqvist 1989; Krongaard Kristensen 2003: 189). A partition in two might be a stronger possibility (Krongaard Kristensen 2003: 182).

One might add that Birk's reconstruction may also be partly biased by modern judgements regarding the inconvenience and discomfort of smoke and draughts, which are very culturally specific (Grenville 1997: 155f), and may partly be affected by the

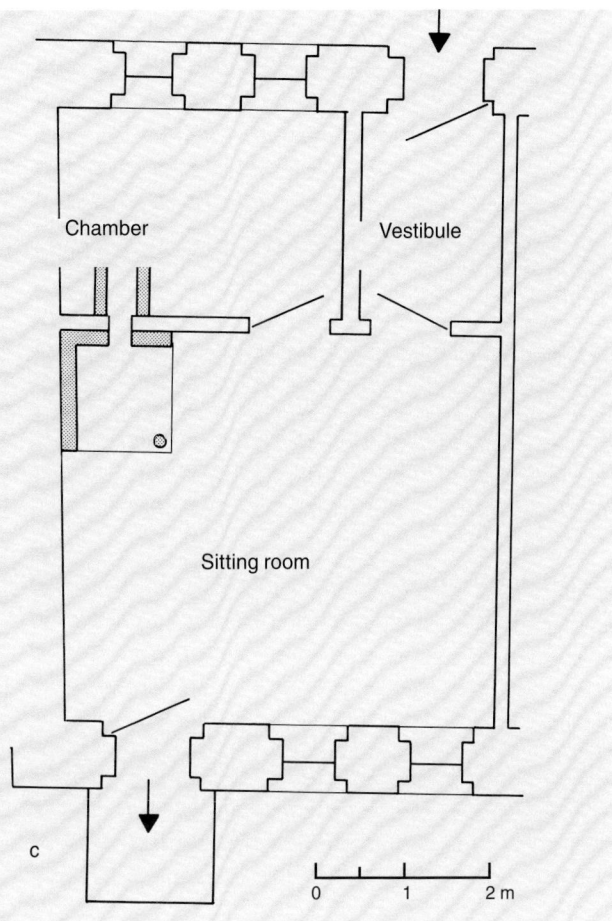

ten record, and a misinterpretation of fragments of bipartite, flat-arched window openings as evidence to support this association (Engqvist 1988a: 23f). In the 1970s, Mogens Tuesens Boder were restored, and the layout reconstructed as one large room and a chimney shared by two rental accommodations (Figure 2a).

Today, we have quite another perception of rental accommodations: Mogens Tuesens Boder are regarded as having been good quality lodgings for the well-off bourgeoisie, priests, and lesser gentry. From the analysis of deeds of gift, we know they were built so that the rents could pay for services in the church; clearly, the tenants were expected to have a good income, and to pay a substantial rent. New ideas regarding their higher status, and reinterpretations of the data have established a more elaborate layout, suggested by Palle Birk Hansen (Figure 2b-c). In concept of the German breech loader, a stove built with decorated tiles, for heating a smoke-free 'Stube'. In Danish homes, however, the implementation of new ideas regarding lighting, heating, and interior decoration, provided by combinations of windows, (tiled) breech loader, ceilings, and elaborate furniture, as we know them to have been integrated in the 16th-17th-century Renaissance home, is not yet fully understood, and the emphasis on the inconvenience of smoke, and on the Stube being a fully-integrated concept in Danish homes, may be misleading. The tiled stove used as smoke oven is known from contemporary illustrations, and this could be the case in Næstved as well. 'The old tile stove' referred to at Mogens Tuesens Boder in 1596 could have been fired as a smoke oven beside the chimney in one large room, offering a steady and fuel-efficient form of heating, whilst the fire in the fireplace provided light, a solution known from the prominent 17th-century Baroque castle, Skokloster, in Sweden, for example (Eriksdotter 2013).

Ideas about ordering people – the house plan

The house communicates a set of ideas shared by the household and community through the way it orders people and everyday activities. Medieval society was profoundly religious and hierarchical, and one might expect this to be a highly-integrated part of ideal household living. The study of relationships of spatial structures and hierarchical arrangements of symbolic spaces mapping feudal social relations has a long tradition in England, where the tripartite hall in particular, with its upper and lower ends, and its distinct communication of status and hierarchy in houses across all levels of society has catalyzed discussions (Gardiner 2000; Grenville 2008; Johnson 2010; Kowaleski & Goldberg 2008; Pearson 2005). Interestingly, this apparently clear organization of social space is not apparent in medieval Danish houses. This could be explained by differing research traditions that take their points of departure in the homes of the elite and those of 'the common people', respectively (but see Giles and Tankard's

notes of caution about the ideal and the reality of this apparently 'universal' plan, this volume). This could also be related to a past reality, where hierarchy might have been communicated by the positioning of human actors alone or communicated by architectural details in the above-ground parts of the standing building itself. It is known from ethnological evidence from many parts of Europe that farm houses of the 19th and 20th centuries framed a strict hierarchy based on gender and age, household and visitors, in a given room. This was clearly supported by the furnishings, and sometimes indirectly indicated by particular beams in the ceiling, or other marks legible to the initiated (Grenville 2008: 104; Stoklund 2003: 93ff). On ceremonial occasions these underlying norms needed to be reinforced precisely, though they might be ignored on a daily basis by the multiple uses of household space. In an archaeological context, this would not be revealed.

The absence of a distinct, dominant form of domestic architecture, except for that of the houses of the elite, has resulted in a largely-absent scholarly attention to the hierarchy in Danish medieval houses and homes, in contrast to the prominent architecture of the earlier Viking hall. Halls with central hearths were a prominent feature of the Viking Age tripartite house, as well as a particular southern Jutlandic early medieval house type (11th century) with partial aisles (Danish: 'Udskudshus'). This type of hall had a wagon room to the west, and to the east a chamber, or perhaps room for storage. Some buildings also had a passage separating the wagon room and the hall. In one instance, at the seminal excavations of the site at Østergård in 1995-2001, conducted by Anne Birgitte Sørensen, posts at the end of the house have been identified as the remains of an exterior staircase to an upper floor, as in the large, representative hall in the German 'Saalgeschosshaus', or to an upper chamber, as in the later Wealden houses (Sørensen 2011: 118-124). This distinctive architecture, and particularly the Viking hall, has highlighted the ways in which Viking buildings could be used to structure and reinforce social hierarchy (Roesdahl 2009: 272).

Urban and rural Danish houses from the 13th to 15th centuries had one to three rooms; four rooms appear less usual, but that might be due to the lack of data. Not until *c* 1600 was the house divided into additional rooms, usually a separate kitchen and a smokeless heated room. Many (late) medieval merchants' and artisans' houses comprised just two rooms, with a workshop, salesroom, or office in the front, and a private room for cooking, sleeping, and all other domestic activities at the rear (Engqvist 1989; Foged Klemensen 2003; Krongaard Kristensen 2003, also see Klinge, this volume, on houses in Aalborg, in which the development of room functions from the high to the late medieval house may be observed). Some exceptionally well-preserved houses provide information on interior arrangements; a few selected examples are mentioned below (Figure 3).

A 13th-century tripartite house in the town of Viborg (Figure 3a) was lined with benches in the western chamber (the upper end?), and heated by a breech loader fuelled from the larger living room, with a central, open hearth in the middle. The eastern room, also furnished with a central hearth (and with possible services at its lower end), was not fully excavated (Krongaard Kristensen 1987: 79). An entrance to the living room must have stood just outside the limits of the excavation.

Some of the best-preserved evidence of rural houses from the 13th and 14th centuries comes from excavations in the village of Tårnby, where houses appear to have had three or four rooms. One of the houses from the 13th century (Figure 3b) had a hearth in the western room (which was not fully preserved); the other rooms were used for different sorts of storage and food preparation, and one of the rooms was totally covered in a thick layer of herring bones. Features along some of the walls indicate the positions of large chests or benches, as in the easternmost room. Some, but not all doors can be identified, and the lack of entrances from the courtyard and access between the rooms remains a central unresolved problem in our understanding of the hierarchy of the building (Svart Kristiansen 2005b: 216-221, 242-245).

In the village of Hejninge, a burned-out house from the 14th or 15th century also left detailed surviving evidence (Figure 3c). The house had three, or possibly four, rooms. To the west was a chamber heated by a hearth in the corner, and insulated by a ceiling of mud-plastered rafters. A platform in the floor might have indicated the position of a bed in the north-western corner; the southern part of the room was not preserved. This was adjacent to an entrance area, open to the rafters. A dirt floor which was markedly different from the clay floor in the adjacent living room, indicates that this area was defined, either symbolically or physically, by a partition. The living room had two phases of hearths and ovens in its south-eastern corner, and was also ceiled by mud-plastered rafters (above which were found grain storage areas). To the east was yet another chamber, perhaps a service room; there were no traces of ceilings (Steensberg 1986: 44-50). This sequence of rooms seems to conflict with the idea of 'upper' and 'lower' end of the building.

The final example is from the early 16th century, when the cross-passage house developed in the urban elite milieu (Figure 3d). Today, this particular plan is represented by a few stone houses from the 1520s to 1530s, the best-preserved examples of which are in Malmö. The plan presents the most complicated layout of a medieval house, with an entrance from a central hall with access to rooms on either side. An external or internal staircase led to a second floor, and a series of private chambers. In the House of Rosenvinge, a large chamber, probably for reception of guests and public activities, was originally heated by a fireplace with a chimney in a back corner, later by a breech loader fuelled from the kitchen in an adjacent wing. Niches in the walls indicate the presence of built-in cupboards. At the other side was a salesroom with a large opening to the front, and a smaller private chamber to the rear, heated by a fireplace with a chimney in a corner, and with access to a latrine. On the second floor were private chambers, and a large room which may have been used for a variety of functions, including entertaining guests (Krongaard Kristensen 2003; Rosborn 1987). The large room on the ground floor indicates the presence of a 'high end' access to which had to be negotiated. The heating in a back corner may indirectly indicate the position of a table, and the light from the open fire, later a tiled stove, probably decorated in splendid and colourful motifs, presented a visual focal point within the room.

Figure 3. Examples of different house plans in medieval Denmark (ordered chronologically): a. Viborg, town. Store Sct. Peder Stræde, 13th century, three rooms, after Krongaard Kristensen 1987: 79; b. Tårnby, village. Main house A21, 13th century; four rooms, green features are modern pits, after Svart Kristiansen 2005b: 218; c. (page 157) Hejninge, village. Main house Farm IX, phase C, 14-15th century; three or four rooms, 'Lerforhøjning' = platform for a bed in the western chamber; 'Ildsted (ovn)' = hearth (oven); 'Åben tagstol' = open to the rafters; 'Stegers' = living room; 'Forrådskammer' = service room. After Steensberg 1986: Pl. VIII, authors translation; d. (page 157) Malmø, town. House of Rosenvinge, built 1534, a two-storey, double house with a central hallway plan in the ground floor, after Rosborn 1987: 295 (detail).

Most house plans do not offer distinct architectural evidence for a structural or spatial hierarchy, though the houses per se might be loaded with meaning and accommodate hierarchically-graduated spaces. Without the evidence of the standing buildings, or the three dimensional reconstruction of two dimensional, and usually quite data-poor house plans, it might be tempting to appropriate and apply the tri-

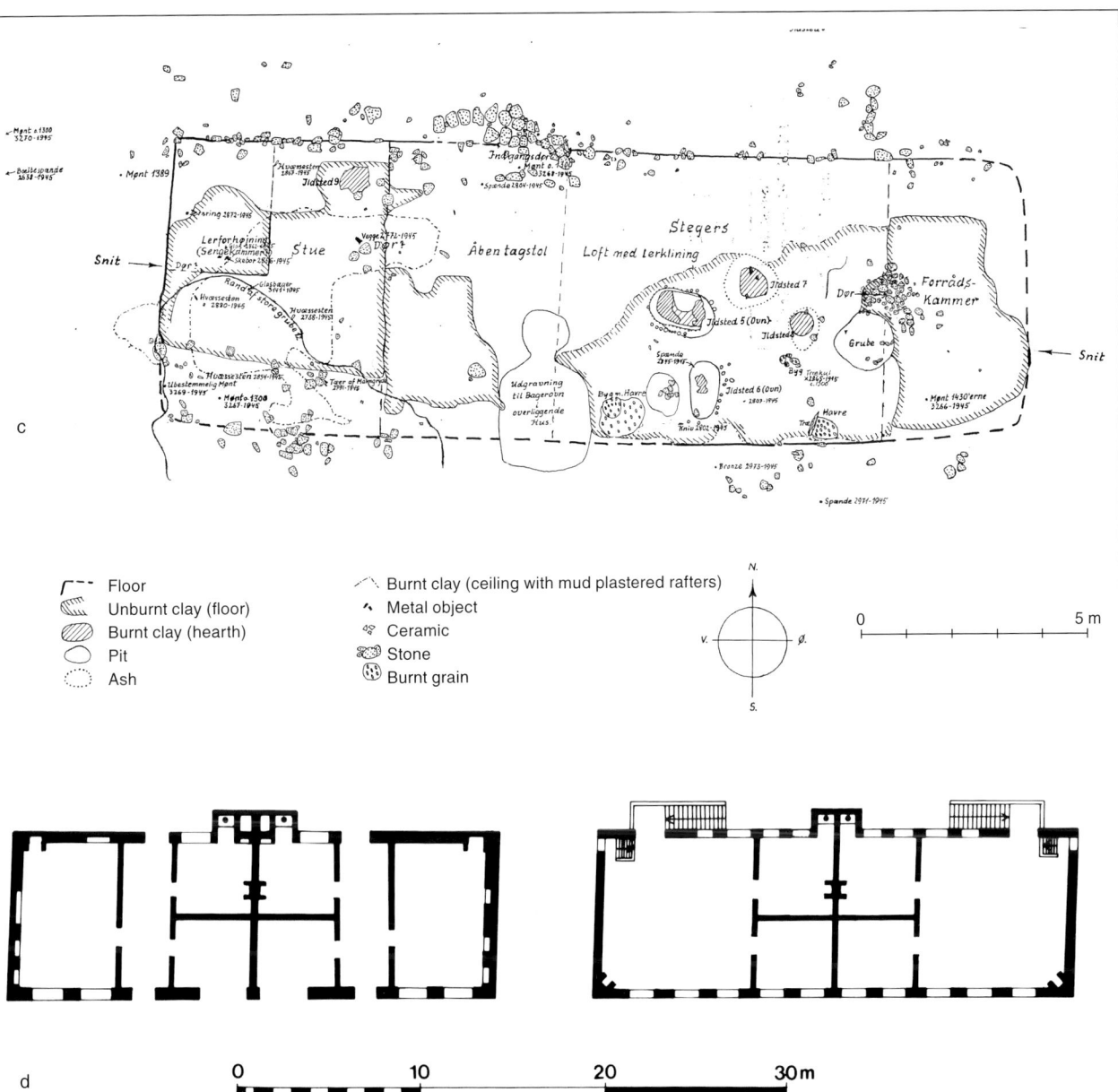

Legend:

- Floor
- Unburnt clay (floor)
- Burnt clay (hearth)
- Pit
- Ash
- Burnt clay (ceiling with mud plastered rafters)
- Metal object
- Ceramic
- Stone
- Burnt grain

partite model of English hall-houses to the Danish tripartite house plans. But the physical resemblances of form do not necessary result in the production of the same meanings. This can be demonstrated using a very different topography in the house from Hejninge. As argued by Jane Grenville, we cannot assume that 'social organization can be simply "read off"…, that social relations are somehow solidified or reified in spatial relations. In fact, of course, very different social systems might be represented in similar access patterns' (Grenville 1997: 20). The houses in Figure 3 reflect the organization of society, pluralities of urban and rural identities, as well as regional and socio-economic differences. To understand how these buildings were perceived by different kinds of medieval audiences requires new and sufficient data from a variety of disciplinary sources.

Ideas about ordering people – fireplaces and heating

Most of the examples referenced in this article have central, open hearths, but fireplaces, ovens and stoves had many possible positions in the house, and a peripheral position, in a corner or by a wall, dominates (Foged Klemensen 2003: 142ff). The various solutions for heating, cooking, and lighting defined different movement patterns and working areas in the rooms, and must have ordered social spaces as well.

Chambers heated by a breech loader are known from as early as the 12th century in urban contexts (see Klinge, this volume; also present in the predecessor to the house in Viborg Figure 3a, Krongaard Kristensen 1987: 79). In the second half of the 16th century, the breech loader, now built with beautiful decorative tiles, was widespread in the homes of artisans, merchants, and the elite, while their adoption in rural milieus still needs to be examined. Indeed, a focus on the until recently widely-ignored late medieval and Renaissance features in Danish archaeology might provide a more detailed and diverse picture of regionality and adoption in different social milieu (Kristiansen 2003). This could further the understanding of the strategies behind the adoption and adaption of heating technologies, and their social implications for the household, for example, the nascent division of servants and family members in the Late Middle Ages.

In the post-medieval period, the arrangements of hearths and heating became increasingly regionally distinct in rural households. In western Denmark, the living room was still heated by an open fire under a chimney, in front of which the housewife cooked as in the Middle Ages, while housewives in the eastern and northern parts of the country were cooking standing under a large chimney centrally situated in the house (Stoklund 1969). Excavations at the 16th-century fishing site where these two house types are identified side by side (Berg, Bender Jørgensen & Mortensøn 1981: 186ff). The presence of these different solutions in the same milieu ought to make us reflect on how ideals of proper living emerged and developed, and the extent to which they supported regionally different, gendered spaces.

Ideas of homes – the written records

The house was an 'engine of social practice, rather than a mere reflection of it', and also used deliberately in social strategies, for example, to signal distinctive forms of urban and rural identities (Christophersen 2001; Grenville 2008: 97; Stoklund 2003: 96ff with references). Written records and pictorial sources, and, on rare occasions, even preserved furniture, add important perspectives to interiors and fittings of medieval houses and homes.

Probate inventories give information on interiors, comfort, and 'must haves', mainly from wealthier, late medieval urban households and those of the clergy, though rural homes also are represented indirectly, in complainants from peasants whose homes had been looted. Apparently, Danish homes followed the Northern and Western European trends in furniture culture, for example the introduction in the 14th century of new types of furniture such as cupboards and folding tables (Poulsen 2003: 39ff; Roesdahl 2003c). The only particularly Scandinavian element convincingly identified is a particular type of Nordic bed with prominent extensions on the bedposts, known from pictorial evidence (murals), and this particular element appears to have ancient roots, as related forms are evident in beds from the Oseberg and Gokstad Viking burials (Haastrup 2003: 215f; Roesdahl 2003c).

The comparison of records from different social milieus provides insight into quite different urban and rural housing cultures. The urban home contained a rich variety of furnishings, while the rural house was sparsely furnished, usually with one or several beds. The movable bed was the most common piece of furniture, firmly tied to family, lineage, and social obligations (Poulsen 2003: 39ff). Different settings may mirror different sets of values, and this may be substantiated by analysis of the more extensive English records: for peasants, the 'household' section of inventories accounts for only a small part of the total value of the estate, frequently a quarter or less of all goods accounted for (livestock and grain), while the opposite was true of the bourgeoisie (Goldberg 2008). In the inventories often associated with hangings and coverings, cushions were strictly related to the urban sphere, until the end of the 15th century. Jeremy Goldberg has recently suggested that the differences in the nature and prevalence of such objects might reflect particular strategies for communicating prosperity to social peers. In the relatively permeable urban house, which functioned as the site of manufacture and trade, and a setting for encounters with a broad range of visitors and business contacts, cushions were a means of communicating wealth and leisure, while the rural house was primarily for the family, and therefore less permeable. Here, wealth was communicated through livestock and agricultural investment (Goldberg 2008), in Denmark – at least in the past few centuries – by the size of dung heaps. Research on the archaeological material on Scanian farmsteads (in southern Sweden, during the Middle Ages a part of Denmark) might supports the existence of a rural seclusion and privacy through the structural development of the farm layout, concluding with the closed, four-winged farm (Thomasson 2005: 113-117).

Ideas of homes – the pictorial records

While inventories enumerate material objects in normative records, the ideas of a proper life may be found in pictorial sources, in Denmark primarily as late medieval murals in parish churches. The murals were, firstly, symbolic representations of religious events based on ancient iconographic traditions and a northern European pictorial set world, but they took their points of departure in their surroundings, and presented scenes recognizable to the audience. Therefore, murals were, secondly, representations of the world of people's imagination, interpreted and visualized by the individual painter (Bolvig 1994: 112-116).

It is impossible to infer much from Danish murals, regarding interiors, fittings, and homely settings (Haastrup 2003). They communicated in a particular grammar quite different from the contemporary triptychs from the Netherlands and Northern Germany. For example, the intimate setting so elaborately emphasized in The Annunciation, on the altarpiece

of Mérode, in the murals in Sulsted Church, dating to 1420s, one of the more elaborate Danish examples, is reduced to only a few requisites and symbols, a pars pro toto: an ornamented table covered by a cloth, and a book in Mary's hand identify the scene as being indoors, further stressed by a building behind Mary, and a 'floor' line. On rare occasions, the murals provide glimpses of elaborate beds, chairs, books on desks, benches, and laid tables, as well as cradles, chairs and stools, and cooking equipment, usually in relation to scenes involving Mary and Christ, and in scenes depicting Adam and Eve.

It has been argued that the murals expressed ideas and world views at the level of the community and the benefactors who paid for them, and in the 15th to 16th centuries, this primarily meant the growing classes of well-off and self-aware peasants and artisans. Several murals depict scenes of Eve and Adam at work, transformed into confident, late medieval peasants: Eve spins, surrounded by an abundance of children hanging onto her breast and in her skirt, some lying in a cradle. Adam cheers on spirited horses preparing a field, and thinks of breakfast, or supper. In their own grammar, the murals present another dimension of ideal living, not defined by worldly goods, but by the importance of the family and home, as well as the work of men and women founded by God (Bolvig 1994: 112-116).

Reflections

There are some indications that different groups within medieval society held both shared and specific ideas of living, of domestic habitus. Medieval society was profoundly patriarchal and hierarchical, and this formed the basis for society as a whole, and for social relationships. But within this shared framework, different classes in society and upper and lower orders had different needs and opportunities, and had different instruments for expressing this in their houses and homes. How these social differences were realized, appreciated, and expressed in medieval Denmark is not yet clear, though it is apparent that a distinct, bourgeois ideology of domesticity emerged during the Middle Ages, as did a class of self-confident peasants.

When it comes to houses, their communication of ideas of proper living and social values among peers, and their communication with other groups in society, we still need a firmer basis for identifying differences and shared elements, in order to discuss urban and rural ideas about living, regional differences, integration of new technologies, and the use of architectural details, for example. Artefacts, which have not been addressed in this paper, are critical to the research, and in some instances more suitable for research than the buildings themselves; while buildings are fixed expressions of ideas, and in time become fossilized, and sometimes even fossilizing structures, artefacts relate tightly to the family, expressing its wealth, its strategic position within particular social identities, and sensitivity to particular ideals, for example, specific dining and drinking cultures.

The interrelationship of ideas, social practices, and their materiality is complex. Furthermore, ideas do not necessarily have material expressions, but have immaterial dimensions as well: former ideas of proper living are not fully translatable in today's archaeological context, as they are passed on as materialized dimensions of lived lives without the feelings, relationships, memories, and smells of a home, and only as those particular materialized dimensions preserved in an archaeological context. Unfortunately, the Danish written and pictorial records cannot provide an insight into the intangible; to a great extent, we must rely on records from other parts of Europe. Drawing analogies when it comes to the better-preserved data in general may be useful in formulating research questions, but we must be aware of diverse cultural, material, and regional differences. To move forward, and for Danish archaeology to contribute to these questions from its own point of departure requires an overview of the unpublished archaeological data in the museum archives, but it also requires a focus on relevant research questions, to understand the messages communicated by the position of a hearth, a subtle indication in a floor layer, of the position of a partition wall or a door. For most houses, only the roof supporting posts are preserved, and archaeology must challenge the data as they stand.

References

Berg, H., L. Bender Jørgensen & O. Mortensøn (1981) *Sandhagen. Et langelandsk fiskerleje fra renaissancen*. Rudkøbing: Langelands Museum.

Birk Hansen, P. (2003) Boderne i Næstved – middelalderlig boligkultur i praksis. In: *Bolig og Familie i Danmarks Middelalder*, ed. E. Roesdahl, 193-205. Højbjerg: Jysk Arkæologisk Selskab.

Bolvig, A. (1994) *Bondens billeder. Om kirker og kunst i dansk senmiddelalder*. København: Gyldendal.

Christophersen, A. (2001) Bóndi, bæjarmaðr, burghere. Om folk, hus og fremveksten av urban identitet i norske byer ca 1000-1700. In: *Från stad till land. En medeltidsarkeologisk resa tillägnad Hans Andersson*, eds. A. Andrén, L. Ersgård & J. Wienberg, 51-62. Lund Studies in Medieval Archaeology. Stockholm: Almqvist & Wiksell International.

Croix, S. (2011) Status, Gender and Space on High Status Settlement Sites from the Viking Age, *Arkæologi i Slesvig / Archäeologie in Schleswig*. Sonderband "Det 61. Internationale Sachsensymposium 2010", 113-122.

Engqvist, H.H. (1988a) Bygningernes datering. In: *Boderne i Næstved*, 74. Næstved: Miljøministeriet Planstyrelsen.

Engqvist, H.H. (1988b) Mogens Tuesens boder. A. De tre vestlige boder før restaureringen. In: *Boderne i Næstved*, 35-39. Næstved: Miljøministeriet Planstyrelsen.

Engqvist, H.H. (1989) Bebyggelsesmønstre og bygningstyper i danske byer i årene mellem 1480 og 1630, *Købstadmuseet 'Den Gamle By' Årbog 1988-89*, 1989, 25-71.

Eriksdotter, G. (2013) Did the Little Ice Age Affect Indoor Climate and Comfort? Re-theorizing Climate History and Architecture from the Early Modern Period, *The Journal for Early Modern Cultural Studies* 13/2, 24-42.

Foged Klemensen, M. (2001) *Huskonstruktioner i tidlig middelalderlig landbebyggelse. En kritisk vurdering af udviklingsteorier og terminologi samt en analyse af udgravede hustomter i Jylland ca. 1100-1300*. Nyhedsbrevets ph.d.-afhandlinger og specialer, Ny række, bind 12. Højbjerg: Middelalderarkæologisk Nyhedsbrev.

Foged Klemensen, M. (2003) Udgravede træhuse i danske byer ca. 800-1600 – konstruktion og indretning. In: *Bolig og familie i Danmarks middelalder*, ed. E. Roesdahl, 129-167. Højbjerg: Jysk Arkæologisk Selskab.

Gardiner, M. (2000) Vernacular Buildings and the Development of the Later Medieval Domestic Plan in England, *Medieval Archaeology* 44, 159-179.

Goldberg, P.J.P. (2008) The fashioning of bourgeois domesticity in later medieval England: a material culture perspective. In: *Medieval Domesticity. Home, Housing and Household in Medieval England*, eds. M. Kowaleski & P.J.P. Goldberg, 124-144. Cambridge: Cambridge University Press.

Grenville, J. (1997) *Medieval Housing*. The Archaeology of Medieval Britain. London: Leicester University Press.

Haastrup, U. (2003) Interiørfremstillinger i danske kalkmalerier – og forlæg. In: *Bolig og familie i Danmarks middelalder*, ed. E. Roesdahl, 213-222. Højbjerg: Jysk Arkæologisk Selskab.

Holst, M.K. & M. Svart Kristiansen (2011) Mellem mål og midler. Strategier, programmer og den arkæologiske udgravningspraksis, *Arkæologisk Forum* 24, 10-13.

Johnson, M. (2010) *English Houses 1300-1800. Vernacular Architecture, Social Life*. Harlow: Pearson Education Limited.

Kowaleski, M. & P.J.P. Goldberg (eds.) (2008) *Medieval Domesticity. Home, Housing and Household in Medieval England*. Cambridge: Cambridge University Press.

Kristiansen, O. (2003) Danske kakkelovne og deres billedprogrammer i 1. halvdel af 1500-tallet. In: *Bolig og familie i Danmarks middelalder* ed. E. Roesdahl, 259-282. Højbjerg: Jysk Arkæologisk Selskab.

Krongaard Kristensen, H. (1987) *Middelalderbyen Viborg*. Århus: Centrum.

Krongaard Kristensen, H. (2003) Planløsninger i byernes stenhuse. In: *Bolig og familie i Danmarks middelalder*, ed. E. Roesdahl, 169-192. Højbjerg: Jysk Arkæologisk Selskab.

Pearson, S. (2005) Rural and urban houses 1100-1500: 'Urban adaption' reconsidered. In: *Town and Country in the Middle Ages. Contrasts, Contacts and Interconnections, 1100-1500*, eds. K. Giles & C. Dyer, 43-63. The society for medieval archaeology monograph 22. Leeds: Maney Publishing.

Poulsen, B. (2003) Privatliv i middelalderens huse. In: *Bolig og familie i Danmarks middelalder*, ed. E. Roesdahl, 31-45. Højbjerg: Jysk Arkæologisk Selskab.

Poulsen, B. & S.M. Sindbæk (eds.) (2011) *Settlement and Lordship in Viking and Early Medieval Scandinavia*. Turnhout: Brepols.

Rensbro, H. (2002) *Bygninger på landet. Middelalderhuse i Østdanmark 1200-1600. Indsamling og analyse af arkæologisk udgravede bygninger*. Nyhedsbrevets ph.d.-afhandlinger og specialer, Ny række, bind 14. Højbjerg: Middelalderarkæologisk Nyhedsbrev.

Roesdahl, E. (2003a) Boligkultur – et forsømt forskningsområde. In: *Bolig og familie i Danmarks middelalder*, ed. E. Roesdahl, 9-13. Højbjerg: Jysk Arkæologisk Selskab.

Roesdahl, E. (ed.) (2003b) *Bolig og familie i Danmarks middelalder*. Højbjerg: Jysk Arkæologisk Selskab.

Roesdahl, E. (2003c) Møbler og indretning. In: *Bolig og familie i Danmarks middelalder*, ed. E. Roesdahl, 223-246. Højbjerg: Jysk Arkæologisk Selskab.

Roesdahl, E. (2009) Housing culture: Scandinavian perspectives. In: *Reflections: 50 years of medieval archaeology, 1957-2007*, eds. R. Gilchrist & A. Reynolds, 271-288. Leeds: Maney Publishing.

Rosborn, S. (1987) Medeltida stenhus i Malmö, *hikuin* 13, 283-300.

Skov, H. (1994) Hustyper i vikingetid og tidlig middelalder. Udviklingen af hustyperne i det gammeldanske område fra ca. 800-1200 e. Kr., *hikuin* 21, 139-162.

Steensberg, A. (1986) *Hal og gård i Hejninge: En arkæologisk undersøgelse af to sjællandske gårdstomter*. Det Kongelige Danske Videnskabernes Selskab, Historisk-Filosofiske Skrifter 11. København: Munksgaard.

Stoklund, B. (1969) *Bondegård og byggeskik før 1850*. København: Dansk Historisk Fællesforening.

Stoklund, B. (2003) *Tingenes kulturhistorie. Etnologiske studier i den materielle kultur*. København: Museum Tusculanums Forlag & University of Copenhagen.

Svart Kristiansen, M. (2003) Boligindregning i middeldergårde. In: *Bolig og familie i Danmarks middelalder*, ed. E. Roesdahl, 89-99. Højbjerg: Jysk Arkæologisk Selskab.

Svart Kristiansen, M. (2005a) Udgravningen i Tårnby landsby – resultater/Excavations in the village of Tårnby – results. In: *Tårnby. Gård og landsby gennem 1000 år*, ed. M. Svart Kristiansen, 11-62. Jysk Arkæologisk Selskabs Skrifter 54. Højbjerg: Jysk Arkæologisk Selskab.

Svart Kristiansen, M. (2005b) Bygninger. In: *Tårnby. Gård og landsby gennem 1000 år*, ed. M. Svart Kristiansen, 163-189. Jysk Arkæologisk Selskabs Skrifter 54. Højbjerg: Jysk Arkæologisk Selskab.

Sørensen, A.B. (2011) *Østergård. Vikingetid og middelalder*. Skrifter fra Museum Sønderjylland, vol. 5. Haderslev: Museum Sønderjyllands Forlag.

Varming, J.C. (1988) Stenhusenes historie efter reformationen. In: *Boderne i Næstved*, 75-101. Næstved: Miljøministeriet Planstyrelsen.

Form and Function in the Late Medieval Rural House

– An example from the Weald and Downland Open Air Museum, Sussex

Danae Tankard

Abstract

In late medieval England the houses of the wealthier peasantry and those of the aristocracy were built to a standard plan, with a central open hall, residential accommodation at the 'upper' end and service rooms at the 'lower' end. Archaeologists have typically interpreted the spatial hierarchies displayed in these houses as a reflection of the social hierarchies that operated within them. This chapter argues that whilst this was undoubtedly the case in aristocratic households, peasant households were less hierarchically ordered. An alternative interpretation of the domestic plan is offered here, based on a division of the house into perceived 'clean' and 'dirty' ends.

Introduction

This chapter reviews ideas about the organisation of space within the late medieval rural house in the UK, using a reconstructed house in the collection of the Weald & Downland Open Air Museum as an example. The Weald & Downland Open Air Museum, which first opened in 1970, is located in West Sussex, in the south of England. It is a distinctive type of open air museum, consisting of a collection of nearly fifty reconstructed buildings dating from the thirteenth to the early twentieth centuries which are set out across a 40-acre site.[1]

The house which forms the focus of analysis in this chapter is called Bayleaf (Figures 1 and 2). It was originally located in the parish of Chiddingstone in Kent and was built in two phases. The earliest part, which has been tree-ring dated to 1405-1430, consisted of an open hall and service end. This was probably attached to an earlier structure, which stood where the upper end bay now stands. The upper end bay, which gives the building its present form,

has been tree-ring dated to 1505-1510. Bayleaf is the most important building in the museum's collection. It forms part of the museum's only complete farmstead and it was the first exhibit house to be fully furnished. From 2002 it has been 'served' by a late fifteenth or early 16th-century detached kitchen, which was originally located in the adjoining parish of Sundridge. The kitchen is the location of much of the museum's live interpretation – visitors can observe food being cooked, talk to the interpreters and taste the food.

Before discussing Bayleaf in detail it is worth revisiting current understandings of the main social divisions of rural society in medieval England. The primary social categories were the aristocracy and the peasantry. Each of these was in turn subdivided by wealth and status. The aristocracy were divided into the upper and lower aristocracy, the latter comprising the gentry. By the 15th century the peasantry were divided into three layers: an upper rank

Figure 1. Bayleaf as reconstructed at the Weald & Downland Open Air Museum.

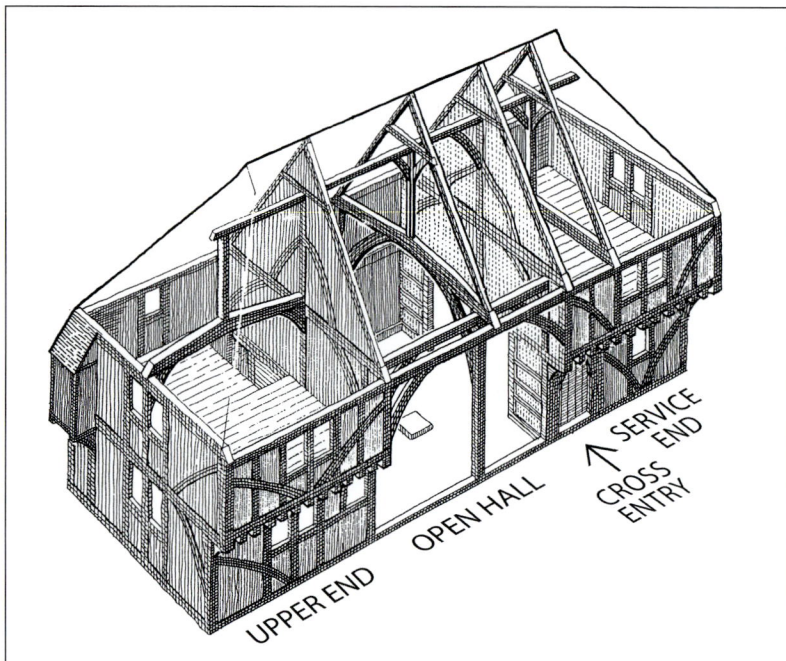

Figure 2. Cutaway plan of Bayleaf. By Richard Harris.

of yeoman, a middle category of husbandman and a lower rank of labourer. Although late medieval society was stratified and hierarchical, there was also a considerable degree of social mobility (Dyer 1989: 10-26; 2003: 358). The occupants of Bayleaf were yeomen, farming about 100 acres. They held their farm on a long lease from the gentry 'manor' (or estate) of Bore Place which in the late 15th century and throughout the 16th century was owned by a succession of eminent London lawyers (Tankard 2012: 59, 62f).

The late medieval domestic plan

As a building type Bayleaf is significant because it represents a domestic plan which was in widespread use in rural England from about 1200 to about 1500. The fundamental elements of this plan are a central open hall with a chamber at one end and a service room or rooms at the other, the latter typically separated from the hall by a cross entry or cross passage. For some peasant houses this represented the full extent of the living accommodation but larger peasant houses like Bayleaf had first-floor chambers at either end of the house. Many peasant houses had detached kitchens or bakehouses together with a range of agricultural buildings depending on the extent of their farming activities. The same tripartite domestic plan is evident in aristocratic houses, but they typically had a greater number of residential rooms at the chamber end and a range of attached and detached service rooms at the service end (Gardiner 2000). There were smaller peasant houses comprising one or two rooms, but it is the tripartite house plan that has received the most scholarly attention (Dyer 1994; Field 1965).

The century between 1150 and 1250 was crucial to the emergence of this house plan (Gardiner 2000). According to Mark Girouard there were 'centripetal' forces at work during this period affecting both buildings and the way people lived in them, which effectively fused the hall into the physical and social centre of the medieval house (Girouard 1978: 30). The fully-evolved tripartite domestic plan embodied a clear spatial hierarchy, with private living accommodation at the upper end and services at the lower end. The hall itself was not an undifferentiated space. In larger houses the upper end was given a structural emphasis by the raised dais on which the 'high' table would be located and a moulded beam or a canopy to frame those seated there, and even in smaller houses the upper end might have decorative timber framing, such as a dais beam and arch braces. In interpreting the cultural significance of this domestic plan archaeologists and historians have typically seen it as a reflection of a social hierarchy in which certain household members had a more privileged status than others. Richard Harris has observed that "the hall was evidently a 'hierarchical' space, mirroring the hierarchies of society: the servants at the lower, service, end; the cross-passage entrance; the screen; the 'lower bay' of the hall; the fire; the 'upper bay' of the hall, with the high table; and the private apartments entered from the upper end" (Harris 2006: 32). Mark Gardiner has described the hall as "not merely a room, but a hierarchical space with places for the owners of the house and for their servants and guests according to their status. It provided a stage on which one of the central events of the day, the formal rituals of the serving and consumption of food could take place" (Gardiner 2008: 38). Most recently, Matthew Johnson has written that the hall "structured the movement of people from one end of the house to the other and displayed different ranks of people much as a stage displays the bodies of the actors. The head of household, sitting in the middle of the bench at the upper end, was the first to sit down; in this way, the arrangement of the hall structured even the temporal rhythm of movement. Households at relatively humble social levels shared in this everyday rhythm: the smallest hearth was placed in a hall which, however humble, was still open to the roof, still had upper and lower ends, and around which different family members sat in a hierarchical pattern" (Johnson 2010: 73). The assumption that underlies each of these quotations is that the structural hierarchy of the late medieval domestic plan was matched by hierarchical patterns of social behaviour which were common to both aristocratic and peasant households. What I would like to suggest in this chapter is that peasant – or more specifically yeoman – households were both structurally and functionally different to those of the aristocracy and produced different patterns of social behaviour.

Living in the medieval house

Historians have been able to reconstruct daily life within the aristocratic household in considerable detail because of the quantity of documentary, literary and pictorial evidence that survives (Dyer 1989: 27-108; Girouard 1978; Woolgar 1999).[2] The great house was a symbol of the lord's power and prestige from which he was expected to dispense lavish hospitality to all ranks of society, from the guests at his table to the poor at his gates. The size and composition of the household varied with the status and income of the lord – between twelve and thirty for a rich knight to as many as 400 for a king – and its members were strictly stratified (Dyer 1989: 50f). The hierarchical structure of the household matched the spatial hierarchy of the house, with the lord and his family at the upper, residential, end and the servants at the lower, service, end. In between was the hall, described by Girouard as the "supreme expression of power, ritual, wealth and hospitality" (Girouard

1978: 30). The daily rhythm of the household surrounded the lord in a continuous round of ritual, both secular and religious, from getting up in the morning to going to bed at night.

The most elaborate and lengthy rituals were associated with mealtimes. Servants entering the hall from the service end would have seen the lord and lady seated at the centre of a high table which might be raised on a dais and framed by a canopy. Other members of the household and any guests were seated according to complex rules of precedence either at the high table or at low tables set down either side. Tables, cupboards and buffets were covered with expensive cloth and loaded with plate; drink flowed in abundance and more food was served than could possibly be eaten. Not surprisingly, these were *consuming* households. In the late 13th century Joan de Valence spent at least two-thirds of her domestic outgoings and about forty per cent of her income on food and drink and in the early 16th century almost all the food consumed by the Earl of Northumberland's household was bought at market rather than produced on his extensive estates (Girouard 1978: 26; Woolgar 1999: 111).[3] They were also essentially *masculine* households. The only women found in them apart from the lord's wife and his daughters were the gentlewomen who kept them company, their personal servants and nurses (Girouard 1978: 27).

This chapter now examines the social and economic characteristics of the late medieval yeoman household and the evidence for how a house like Bayleaf might have functioned on a day-to-day basis. In contrast to the detail available for aristocratic households, there is a marked paucity of evidence for 'middling' households and much of the best evidence is from the 16th century – a 'transitional' century which is usually seen as marking the end of the medieval period and the start of the early modern period and which, in architectural terms, is especially significant because it saw the gradual disappearance of the open-hall house (Johnson 1993: 64-88; 2010: 89-94).

Peasant households were different from aristocratic households not only in size but also in structure. Historians have calculated an *average* late medieval peasant household size of between 4.5 and 5 people. Of course these figures disguise wide variations: wealthier households were larger because they tended to have more surviving children as well as resident servants. We know that in 16th-century Chiddingstone, where Bayleaf was originally located, yeoman households could be relatively large, at between eight to ten people including one or two female servants. Households were typically nuclear, consisting of a husband and wife and their children, although more complex, multi-generational families were not unknown (Tankard 2012: 71f). They were also nominally *patriarchal*, with all those resident in the house – wife, children and servants – subject to the authority of the male householder, who was also its legal head. However, household work strategies meant that during the day the wife was effectively in charge of the household's management, whilst the husband was out in the fields (Flather 2007: 39-93).

At the start of this chapter I described yeomen as forming the upper band of the peasantry – below the gentry but above husbandmen and labourers. Their farms were relatively large – 80 acres or more – allowing them to produce a large, marketable surplus, and requiring them to employ non-family labour (Dyer 2003: 358). If we want to define their social characteristics more closely we can turn to a work by William Harrison called *The Description of England*, first published in 1577. According to Harrison yeomen had "a certain pre-eminence and more estimation than labourers and the common sort of artificers, and these [ie the yeomen] commonly live wealthily, keep good houses, and travail to get riches". Harrison's observation that yeomen 'travail to get riches' distinguishes them from the gentry, since yeomen typically farmed the land themselves rather than earning rental income from it. Through a combination of hard work, thrift and social ambition some yeomen were able to buy enough land from 'unthrifty gentlemen' to set their sons up as landlords rather than tenant-farmers, effectively allowing them to enter the ranks of the gentry (Harrison 1994: 94-123).[4]

One of the characteristics which Harrison considered distinguished yeomen from the gentry was that they had servants who 'get both their own and part of their master's living', in contrast to the 'idle servants' of gentlemen. What he means is that yeomen's servants were essential to the economic livelihood of their master, rather than merely reinforcing his social status. In the countryside most adolescents entered some form of service in their early teens – boys working as farm labourers and girls as domestic servants. What historians usually describe as 'life-cycle' service was an essential preparation for adult life – a rural equivalent to urban trade and craft apprenticeships. Whilst in service these young men and women lived and worked alongside their masters and mistresses and were subject to the same behavioural regulation as the householder's older children – in other words, they became part of the householder's family for the duration of their employment (Gilchrist 2012: 114; Wrightson 2002: 32-34). Probate inventory evidence from the late 16th century shows that some of the larger yeoman houses had a separate servants' room but in most houses the female servants probably slept alongside the family, perhaps sharing a bed with the children or sleeping on a truckle bed in the same room as the householder and his wife (Figure 3) (Tankard 2012: 74f).[5]

The complex round of ritual and ceremony that surrounded the head of the aristocratic household was made possible not only by his wealth but by the fact that he did not have to work for a living – the daily rhythm of the household was essentially dictated by the leisured lifestyle of the family. In contrast, in a yeoman's household everyone, except

the youngest children, was expected to be economically productive. We can get some idea of what this meant in practice by looking at a husbandry manual by Thomas Tusser which was first published in 1557 as *A hundred good points of husbandry* and expanded and reprinted in 1573 as *Five hundred points of good husbandry united to as many of good huswiferie* (McRae 2002: 146-151; Tusser 1984). This included, amongst other things, a monthly check-list of things to do around the farm, the farmer's daily diet and the duties of the housewife. Tusser's descriptions of the respective duties of the husband and wife are largely pragmatic and reflect the widely-held view that marriage was an economic partnership. During the day whilst the husband was out in the fields with his labourers the wife was left in sole charge of the house and household. Her duties, which began on rising at four or five in the morning and ended when the household went to bed at nine or ten at night, included looking after her children, baking, brewing, cooking, washing, sewing and mending. She worked alongside her domestic servants, and was responsible for their supervision. The housewife's activities also took her away from the house – she tended poultry, milked cows and sowed and harvested flax and hemp; she also took her produce to market to sell (Tusser 1984: 159-177).[6]

There is little evidence for elaborate mealtime ritual in the household Tusser describes; he suggests that

Figure 3. Bayleaf, bedchamper at upper end. Photograph WDOAM Archive.

Figure 4. Bayleaf, upper end of hall. Photograph WDOAM Archive.

it is better to leave a table bare rather than to cover it with a cloth which is going to get dirty and urges the housewife to make sure that the farm labourers have enough to eat – too little and they will not have enough energy to work; too much and they will become lazy (Tusser 1984: 170f). Tusser makes it clear that whilst the farmer should be hospitable to his neighbours and charitable to the poor, unrestrained largesse, of the sort seen in aristocratic households, was not only inappropriate, but potentially ruinous. The farmer should live within his means. Tusser's depiction of the lack of pretension in the yeoman household provides a useful contrast to Chaucer's much-quoted description of the franklin in *The Canterbury Tales*, whose hall table was laid 'all day' and whose meat and fish were as plenteous as snow. Rather than seeing this as an admirable quality, contemporaries are likely to have interpreted it as a sign of social pretension and wastefulness (Figure 4) (Chaucer 1998: 10).[7]

The most useful type of document for looking at domestic culture in the yeoman house is the probate inventory – a list (usually by room) of the moveable goods that the testator had in his or her house shortly after death. However, Kent probate inventories do not survive in any numbers before 1565 and there are none at all for the parish of Chiddingstone. A sample of 100 Kent probate inventories dating from 1565 to

1566 was examined by the museum's former research director, Richard Harris, as part of the research that underpinned the furnishing and reinterpretation of Bayleaf in the late 1980s but, as he noted, none of them provided an exact match with a house like Bayleaf (Centre for Kentish Studies, PRC 10/1/88-100). By the 1560s, of course, many medieval houses were being adapted by the insertion of a chimney stack and the ceiling over of the open hall (Johnson 1993: 64-88; 2010: 89-94). But it is reasonable to assume that some of the houses in these inventories still had their open halls. Halls were always the first room to be listed in an inventory, confirming their importance within the house. But what do their contents tell us about their use? At this date halls contained a limited range of furniture – typically a table and a bench, one or two chairs, stools and a cupboard. An element of social display was provided by painted wall hangings, cupboard cloths and pewter and latten-ware. However, many of the listed items were entirely functional: cooking equipment indicates that halls were used for cooking even in houses which had internal or external kitchens; some halls contained items connected with the occupants' economic activities such as hand tools and spinning wheels; cradles in halls suggest a pragmatic solution to childcare in a busy household. Overall, the evidence suggests that in a house like Bayleaf the open hall was a multi-func-

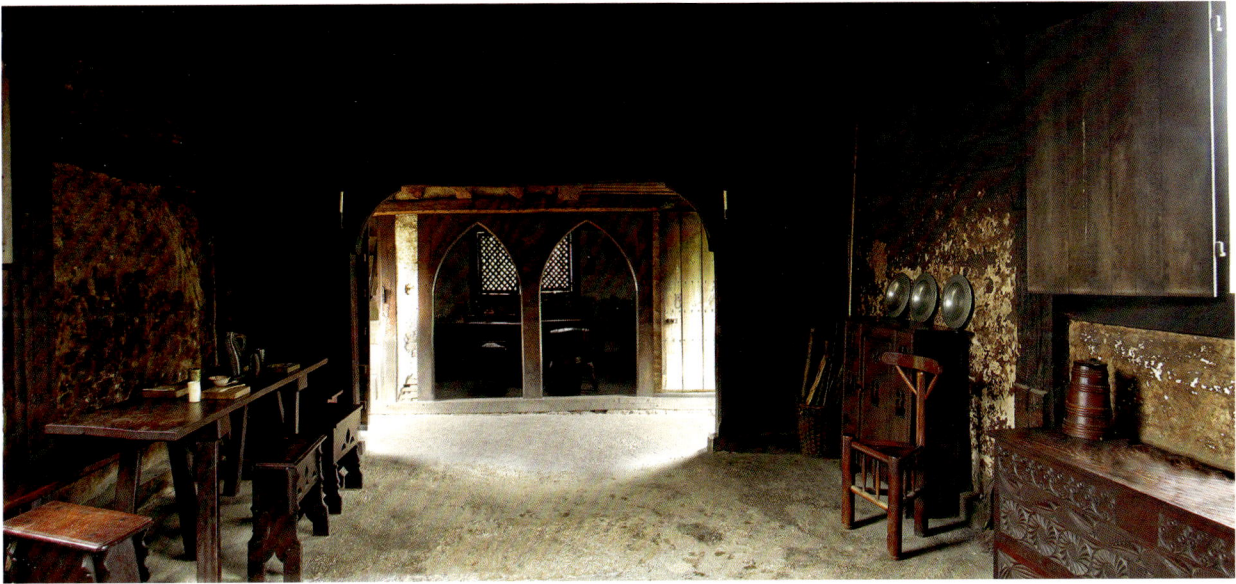

Figure 5. Bayleaf, lower end of hall, cross passage and service rooms. Photograph Richard Harris.

tional space: it was where the family ate and social-ised but it was also a working room at the centre of a busy and productive household. If we take into account the diverse range of service rooms that are recorded in these inventories – including kitchens, milkhouses, brewhouses and bakehouses – along-side the literary evidence of Harrison and Tusser, it is clear that yeoman households were primarily geared towards production (Figure 5). Whilst some of this would have been for domestic consumption, much of it would have been for the market. This highlights one of the fundamental differences between houses of yeomen and those of the aristocracy: the former *produced* whilst the latter *consumed*.

What I would like to emphasise is that yeomen households functioned differently from aristocratic households for both practical and ideological rea-sons: not only was the yeoman incapable of follow-ing the elaborate ritual of the aristocratic household, he would have had little interest in doing so. In this sense, whilst the tripartite domestic plan itself might be rigidly hierarchical in its structural principles, the domestic culture it contained – at least at this social level – was not. In contrast, there appears to be little evidence for spatial or social segregation in a house like Bayleaf and where segregation did take place it

was more likely to be between older and younger members of the household – the householder and his wife and the servants and the children – rather than on the basis of gender or social status.[8]

An alternative interpretation of the late medieval domestic plan

This chapter has argued that the apparent common-ality of the late medieval domestic plan should not be interpreted as evidence of a commonality of domestic culture between aristocracy and the wealthier peas-antry. But that leaves unanswered the question of why tripartite open-hall houses with distinct upper and lower ends remained in use for so long. To assume that this house plan had no cultural significance at all would be disingenuous. However, it is possible to offer an alternative interpretation of this phenome-non, drawing on literary evidence and contemporary medical theory rather than buildings alone.

In 1540 an anonymous treatise was published in London entitled *Book for to Learn a Man to be Wise in building his House for the Health of his Body* which offered the prospective house-builder advice on where to situate a new house and how to lay out the house and its ancillary buildings. The treatise is usually associated with the physician and medical writer, Andrew Boorde, who incorporated it into his *Compendious regiment, or, dietary of health*, first published in 1542. The advice contained in the treatise reflected the contemporary belief that infectious diseases were transmitted by corrupt or polluted air. There were many things that could cause such corruption – the author identified "the influence of sundry stars, and standing waters, stinking mists, and marshes, carrion lying long above the ground, much people in a small room lying uncleanly, and being filthy and sluttish" (Boorde 1870: 236). The south wind, according to the author, "does corrupt and does make evil vapours"; in contrast, the east wind was "temperate, frisk, and fragrant", the west wind was "mutable" and the north wind "purges ill vapours". All these factors needed to be taken into account when siting your house: it should be built on stony or gravelly ground, or on a hill or hillside, away from stagnant water, and with its main range facing east and west. When locating rooms and ancillary buildings, the author was similarly concerned to keep anything that might cause contagion away from the main living areas. So, the parlour should be 'annexed' to the head of the hall, with the buttery and pantry at the lower end. Additional service rooms – the cellar, kitchen, pastry-house and larder-house should be set below the buttery and pantry, in other words, at the opposite end of the house from the 'head of the hall' and the parlour. The 'houses of easement' (*ie* toilets) and all ancillary buildings connected with 'dirty' activities, such as the stables, slaughter-house and dairy, should be detached from the house and set at a reasonable distance from it (Boorde 1870: 237-239).

Like most late medieval advice literature, it is evident that the author was addressing an elite; he envisages the house having, amongst other things, a chapel, a moat, a "fair garden", a fish pond, a "park replete with deer and conies", a dove house and a bowling alley (Boorde 1870: 238f). Yet in their bare essentials his design principals are consistent with the layout of the typical open-hall house like Bayleaf: in this scheme the segregation of space within and beyond the medieval house is based on the need to separate the 'clean' living areas – the upper hall and the parlour – from the 'dirty' and potentially contagious service areas – the buttery, pantry and kitchen. Although the author does not mention it specifically, the location of the hearth effectively demarcates the clean/dirty boundary.

It could be argued that the author's interpretation of the layout of the medieval house merely reflects his desire to fit a standard house plan into a *regimen sanitatis* and that in any case it comes at the very end of the period of the open-hall house. Moreover, despite the derivative nature of much medical writing of this period, a *Book for to Learn a Man to be Wise in building his House for the Health of his Body* and the *Compendious regiment, or, dietary of health* which incorporated it, appear to be the only English texts to attempt this kind of linkage between house design and the occupants' health. But that does not mean that they should be discounted as curiosities. In an essay published in 1994, drawing on contemporary sociological theory, John Schofield suggested that medieval and Tudor London houses owed their organisation, in part, to what he described as "an axis of perception of *clean:dirty*", with external privies and kitchen blocks located at some distance down the garden or yard for properties with open space. Where privies had to be incorporated into the structure of the house because of lack of outside space they were typically placed at a distance from the main living rooms (Schofield 1994: 201-205). In other words, Londoners were concerned to keep dirt and bad smells as far away from their living accommodation as possible. The same is as likely to be true of country dwellers: the *clean:dirty* axis makes perfect sense as an organising principle for the late medieval open-hall house.

We should also not overlook the perceived health benefits of the open hearth. Fire purified and dried out the air, thereby counteracting potentially fatal miasmas. Plague – the scourge of late medieval Europe – was frequently blamed on corrupt air. In *A little book for the pestilence* first published in England in 1485 the author recommends that those wishing to avoid it should keep their houses clean and "make clear fire of wood flaming": in this instance the fire needed to be smokeless, a point made more clearly by Boorde who observes that the fire should be "of clear burning wood or charcoal without smoke" (Furnivall 1870: 291).[9] However, smoke (especially when fragranced with herbs and spices like juniper, rosemary or frankincense) had restorative properties for those suffering from a variety of ailments although its efficacy was dependent on the nature of the illness and the humoral composition of the patient; smoke, as Boorde points out, is 'evil' for those who are asthmatic, 'short winded' or 'lacking breath' (Boorde 1870: 290f, 297).

Coincidentally, in a recent essay on the origins and evolution of the two service rooms at the lower end of the medieval house – the buttery and pantry – Mark Gardiner suggested that the desire to separate 'wet' and 'dry' materials within the house might be related to the spread of knowledge about humoral theory in the thirteenth and fourteenth centuries (Gardiner 2008: 62f).[10] It would be stretching the argument too far to suggest that medieval medical theory can explain the origins of the tripartite house plan but it may – at least in part – account for its longevity.

Conclusion

The spatial organisation and architectural detail of a house like Bayleaf can tell us a certain amount about the domestic culture of its occupants. We can see that the upper end of the hall was perceived by those who lived in it to be the 'best' end. The separation of upper-end living chambers from lower-end service rooms tells us that householders thought it appropriate to isolate 'living' and 'working' activities. We can deduce that within the house there was a distinction between areas that were more 'public' (the lower end of the hall, accessed by the cross entry) and those that were more 'private' (upper-end chambers and any second-floor chambers). But what else can these features tell us about how men and women lived in their houses?

The limited amount of documentary evidence for medieval peasant domestic culture has led to what might be described as an 'architectural determinism', that is, that the obvious structural hierarchies of the tripartite house both reflected and *dictated* hierarchical patterns of domestic behaviour. Mark Gardiner

and Matthew Johnson have both described the open hall as a 'stage' displaying the bodies of the 'actors' (*ie* the inhabitants). But to extend the metaphor, the only 'play' that appears to be sufficiently complete to 'perform' to a modern audience is that written for aristocratic households. Inevitably, therefore, the peasant (or more accurately, yeoman) house is seen as functioning in the same way as the aristocratic house. It has been the intention of this chapter – drawing on a variety of evidence – to suggest that it did not. An alternative explanation for the layout of the medieval house has been offered, suggested by a little-known 16th century text that linked medical theory to model house design: the lower end of the house was used for 'dirty' activities; the upper end was used for 'clean' activities. This pragmatic interpretation has merit and should certainly be considered alongside other explanations for the longevity of the late medieval domestic plan.

As this chapter has pointed out, the 16th century is frequently seen as 'transitional', marking the end of the medieval period and the start of the early modern period. In architectural terms, it was significant because it witnessed the gradual disappearance of the open-hall house. Why the open hall fell finally and permanently out of favour in the 16th century is contested.[11] Attempts to relate it to specific social, cultural and economic changes are interesting, and sometimes provocative, but in the end never entirely persuasive (Johnson 1993). To our minds the advent of the 'closed' house, with its central or axial chimney stacks, fully-floored upper storey and the increasing use of window glass led to a rapid improvement in living conditions. Some contemporaries were not so sure. To William Harrison the improved houses had turned men of 'oak' into men of 'willow' – the implication being that greater domestic comfort was effeminising English men. In particular, Harrison saw the demise of the open hearth as undermining the health of the nation. In his words:

"Now have we many chimneys, and yet our tenderlings complain of rheums, catarrhs, and poses [colds]. Then we had none but reredoses [fire screens], and our heads did never ache. For as the smoke in those days was supposed to be a sufficient hardening for the timber of the house, so it was reputed a far better medicine to keep the goodman and his family from the quack [hoarseness] or pose, wherewith as then very few were oft acquainted." (Harrison 1994: 276).

Acknowledgements

I should like to thank Richard Harris for commenting so carefully on both conference paper and chapter and for allowing me to reproduce his cutaway plan of Bayleaf.

Notes

1. The Museum is located in Singleton, West Sussex. The website address is http://www.wealddown.co.uk.
2. It should be noted that the bulk of the evidence is for the households of the upper aristocracy; the households of the lower aristocracy, or gentry, are less well documented.
3. Joan de Valence was Countess of Pembroke (d. 1307). Her properties included Goodrich Castle and Pembroke Castle.
4. Harrison's chapter 'Of degrees of people in the commonwealth of England', from which this description is taken, is based on an earlier work by Thomas Smith called *De Republica Anglorum*, first published in 1551 (Cornwall 1988: 8-10).
5. Evidence for where servants slept in 'middling' status households tends to be anecdotal. In a deposition given to the Court of Chancery in 1534 a female servant called Faith Carter gave evidence about the paternity of the child of her former mistress. She said that she had overheard her mistress and her lover discussing the pregnancy whilst she and her fellow servant, Alice Byrd, were 'lying together in their bed by the bedside of their said mistress ...' (TNA C24/1 Hall v Bulstrode). See Flather 2007: 39-74 for a discussion of servants' position within the household during the early modern period.
6. For a more detailed examination of rural women's work during this period see J. Whittle (2005).
7. *All* literary sources should be carefully analysed alongside other evidence rather than taken as factual descriptions of normative practices.
8. For a nuanced analysis of social organisation within the household for a slightly later period see Flather 2007: 39-74.
9. Knutsson's work is lifted in its entirety from the plague tract of John Jacobus written c.1364. Extract printed in Horrox, 1994: 173-177 (quote from p. 176).
10. For an explanation of humoral theory see Rawcliffe 1995: 29-57.

11. The decline of the social significance of the hall was a gradual one. According to Girouard, in aristocratic houses 'the great hall was past its prime by 1400', as the lord and his most important guests retreated into private parlours to eat (Girouard 1978: 30-33). See also Woolgar 1999: 145f.

References

Primary sources

Anon. (1540) *Book for to Learn a Man to be Wise in Building his House for the Health of his Body*. London.

Boorde, A. (1870) *The First Book of the Introduction of Knowledge made by Andrew Bord*, ed. F.J. Furnivall. Early English Text Society, extra series, 10.

Chaucer, G. (1998) *The Canterbury Tales*, ed. D. Wright. Oxford: Oxford Paperbacks.

Harrison, W. (1994) *The Description of England*, ed. G. Edelen. New York: Dover Publications Inc.

Horrox, R. (ed.) (1994) *The Black Death*. Manchester: Manchester University Press.

Knutsson, B. (1485) *Here Begins a Little Book the which Treated and Rehearsed Many Good Things Necessary for the Infirmity and Great Sickness Called the Pestilence*. London.

Tusser, T. (1984) *Five Hundred Points of Good Husbandry*, ed. G. Grigson. Oxford: Oxford Paperbacks.

Secondary sources

Cornwall, J.C.K. (1988) *Wealth and Society in Early Sixteenth Century England*. London: Routledge.

Dyer, C. (1989) *Standards of Living in the Later Middle Ages: Social Change in England, c.1200-1520*. Cambridge: Cambridge University Press.

Dyer, C. (1994) English peasant buildings in the later middle ages (1200-1500). In: *Everyday Life in Medieval England*, ed. C. Dyer, 133-165. London: Hambledon Continuum.

Dyer, C. (2003) *Making a Living in the Middle Ages: The People of Britain 850-1520*. London: Penguin.

Field, R.K. (1965) Worcestershire peasant buildings, household goods and farming equipment in the later middle ages, *Medieval Archaeology* 9, 105-145.

Flather, A. (2007) *Gender and Space in Early Modern England*. Woodbridge: Boydell Press.

Gardiner, M. (2000) Vernacular Buildings and the Development of the Later Medieval Domestic Plan in England, *Medieval Archaeology* 44, 159-179.

Gardiner, M. (2008) Buttery and pantry and their antecedents: idea and architecture in the English medieval house. In: *Medieval Domesticity: Home, Housing and Household in Medieval England*, eds. M. Kowaleski & P.J.P. Goldberg, 37-65. Cambridge: Cambridge University Press.

Gilchrist, R. (2012) *Medieval Life: Archaeology and the Life Course*. Woodbridge: The Boydell Press.

Girouard, M. (1978) *Life in the English Country House*. New Haven & London: Yale University Press.

Harris, R. (1978, 2006) *Discovering Timber-Framed Buildings*. Princes Risborough: Shire Publications Ltd.

Johnson, M. (1993) *Housing Culture: Traditional Architecture in an English Landscape*. London: University College London Press.

Johnson, M. (2010) *English Houses 1300-1800. Vernacular Architecture, Social Life*. Harlow: Pearson Education Limited.

McRae, A. (2002) *God Speed the Plough: The Representation of Agrarian England, 1500-1660*. Cambridge: Cambridge University Press.

Rawcliffe, C. (1995) *Medicine and Society in Later Medieval England*. Stroud: Sutton Publishing Ltd.

Schofield, J. (1994) Social perceptions of space in medieval and Tudor London houses. In: *Meaningful Architecture: Social Interpretations of Buildings*, ed. M. Locock, 189-206. Aldershot: Avebury.

Tankard, D. (2012) *Houses of the Weald and Downland: People and Houses of South-East England c.1300-1900*. Lancaster: Carnegie.

Whittle, J. (2005) Housewives and servants in rural England, 1440-1650: evidence of women's work from probate documents, *Transactions of the Royal Historical Society* 15, 51-74.

Woolgar, C.M. (1999) *The Great Household in Late Medieval England*. New Haven & London: Yale UP.

Wrightson, K. (2002) *Earthly Necessities: Economic Lives in Early Modern Britain, 1470-1750*. London: Penguin.

A House is Not Just a Home
– Means of Display in English Medieval Gentry Buildings

Jill Campbell

Abstract

This paper is a study of the architectural design and exterior display in a series of gentry houses in 14th and 15th century England. The study commences by thinking about the emergence of the gentry as a distinct community within early modern England. It then explores the ways in which these groups sought to display their new-found wealth and status through a series of architectural devices. These included the use of geometrical principles and symmetry in the design and planning of houses and the creation of a distinctive profile of the house, using features such as gables and stair turrets. The paper ends by calling for further research to establish the language, or codes of emerging gentry architecture in late medieval England.

Introduction

Late medieval England was an era of increasing social mobility amongst the upper levels of society. The period saw a large growth in the number of families who had risen in material wealth and consequently in status. The appearance of new aspirants to social position presented a challenge for the already wealthy. They needed to demonstrate their established status and reinforce their position. For those aspiring to higher status it was also necessary to display their new wealth, for the position of this group of *nouveaux riches* was not stable. Social prestige was demonstrated through particular dress, hospitality, titles and courtly positions, but also through investment in houses. The houses of the *nouveaux riches* were designed so that they displayed, both internally and externally, the identity and status of their owners through the use of particular architectural devices. They were built on a scale comparable to, and often surpassing those belonging to the long-established families. This interaction between the physical environment and material culture enabled the gentry to present their position in society by imitating patterns of display exhibited by those at the top of the social scale. Status found expression through material culture and architecture, and houses were one of the most conspicuous statements of elite identity during the period (De Clercq et al 2007: 31).

In the last twenty years, the type of medieval building that has received the most scholarly attention in the UK is the castle. Considerable analysis and reinterpretation has revolutionised the way in which these medieval buildings and the landscape surrounding them were viewed. Rather than seen as purely defensive, the martial elements have been recognised as part of an architectural language of display, often reinforced by a carefully designed landscape (Coulson 1990; 1992; Johnson 2002: 19-33; Liddiard 2005: 10; Taylor et al 1990: 155-57). Rather surprisingly, buildings of lesser status have not received the same attention or re-evaluation. This is particularly odd when it is accepted that they were also used as indicators of wealth and status. It is possible that this is because many of the 1500 or so surviving medieval houses remain in private hands, and so are more difficult to examine in detail (Emery 2011: 3). Excavated examples are often overlooked by architectural historians, yet works by Grenville (1997) and Johnson (1993; 2010) have shown the importance of studying both standing and excavated medieval buildings within a broader framework, incorporating other forms of evidence such as documentary, literary or landscape evidence (Giles 2000: 1).

Design in medieval buildings

In order to formulate a meaningful discussion, it is important to define of the term *design*. Harvey has discussed the problem of the meaning of the word, particularly in reference to works of art, as authorities have disagreed as to the person who performed the function of the designing (Harvey 1958: 55). The Oxford English Dictionary defines the noun 'design' as *'a plan or scheme conceived in the mind and intended for subsequent execution'* and the verb 'to design' as *'to form a plan or scheme of; to conceive and arrange in the mind; to originate mentally, plan out, contrive; to sketch, delineate, draw; to fashion artistically'*. Harvey suggested that these two definitions fall into two groups; the 'abstract' which is essentially the *mental* plan and the 'concrete', which centres round a tangible sketch or drawing (Harvey 1958: 55). In this paper, the term *design* will be taken to mean that the plan and architectural details were contrived; they had developed from a mental plan into something tangible.

Architectural history suggests that having a building suitable for the status of the owner and the use of architectural devices such as geometry and symmetry, are the product of the post-medieval period inspired by the Renaissance, yet classical literature tells us this began much earlier. For example the Roman writer and architect Vitruvius discussed the notion of *decor*, which described how a building should be suitable to the status of the builder, and the Greek philosopher Aristotle who examined the connection between display and duty (Cooper 1999: 13). In Europe, Vitruvius was regularly cited in philosophical and technical manuals from the 9th century. His work supplied medieval scholars with terms such as proportion and symmetry, as well as providing formulations for aesthetics and proportion (Eco 1986:

29). It is probable that the definition of symmetry in the Middle Ages was similar to the way Vitruvius understood the concept. In Book 1 Chapter 2 of his *Ten Books on Architecture*, he described symmetry as:

"a proper agreement between the members of the work itself and relation between the different parts and the whole general scheme, in accordance with a certain part selected as standard...symmetry may be calculated from the thickness of a column, from a triglyph, or even from a module" (*Ten Books on Architecture*, 14).

In other words, rather than being a mirror image, it was more the general keeping of proportion between parts of a building, in accordance with their uses. It will be argued in this paper that in the houses at gentry level, the creation of a sense of symmetry in the Vitruvian definition was important.

One of the difficulties of the late medieval domestic plan is that the axis of symmetry runs along the length of the building. A visitor approaching the front of the building saw a markedly asymmetrical arrangement of rooms, windows and doors, due to the hierarchical plan. The late medieval domestic building followed a 'typical' hierarchical plan. The principle of status differentiation was certainly formalised by *c* 1350 and must have been the basic 'given' that informed builders. The layout was tripartite, consisting of a central open hall, with the services at one end and the chamber or solar at the other. The entrance to the hall was via the cross-passage, which was most commonly separated from the hall by a screen. Opposite the screen was normally a wall, which had either two or three doors. At sites where there were only two doors, these would have led to the buttery and pantry. At sites where there were three doors, the central doorway would have led to the detached kitchen. The hall was the formal space in the house, commonly heated by an open hearth, often found in the centre. The hall would have been used as a place to eat, sleep, as a chamber and as a place for business. While the symmetrical plan supplanted the hierarchical one during the 16th century (Cooper 1999: 75-81), in the medieval period it remained important that the interior of the house could be read from the exterior.

During the Middle Ages, the internal hierarchy and layout of houses was reflected in the disposition of doorways and windows in the exterior elevation of these buildings. A visitor approaching a medieval house would have been able to identify the different internal elements from exterior architectural features. For example, the high end of the hall was often illuminated by a large, often oriel, window, while the low end was not. This changed from the 16th century onwards, as the number of rooms grew, and building design increased in complexity; it was no longer possible to recognise 'polite' rooms from the exterior. By the late 16th century a distinct ideal of architecture had emerged, resulting in a widening gulf between 'polite' architecture, and the architecture of everybody else (Johnson 2010: 124). Externally, the post-medieval house was more difficult to read. It is likely that the growth of symmetry is closely linked with this development of illegibility (Cooper 1999: 75). During the course of this paper the author will seek to argue that the idea of symmetry as defined by Vitruvius can be identified during the 15th century. We can begin to see a subtle move away from the traditional medieval tripartite plan to a more balanced façade, with the use of gables,

fenestration and rooflines. This is not to say that the medieval builders were rigidly using absolute symmetry, but were creating a balance of design.

It is well established that the architecture of the 16th century was 'designed' (Cooper 1999), and it would be odd if the architecture of 15th-century England had been any different. The argument could also be applied *ad absurdam* and it could suggest that the same must have applied in 14th century, and therefore the 13th century.

It has now been accepted that many medieval buildings, such as cathedrals, were designed using relatively simple geometric measurements. The ratio of √2 or 1:4142 is so commonly found in high-status medieval buildings that it has been argued to be the rule in the design in the large buildings of post-Conquest England (Fernie 1994: 111). Fernie has shown that the √2 ratio can be recorded in at least seven cathedrals in England, though it probably was used at almost all of them. Fernie's calculations, unlike Goodyear's, are extremely precise as he measured from the same point each time, either the inside edge, outer edge or mid-point of the wall. A similar approach was also adopted at the survey of Salisbury Cathedral (Wiltshire). The survey of the excavated foundations of Old Sarum, the Norman cathedral, showed that the building was designed

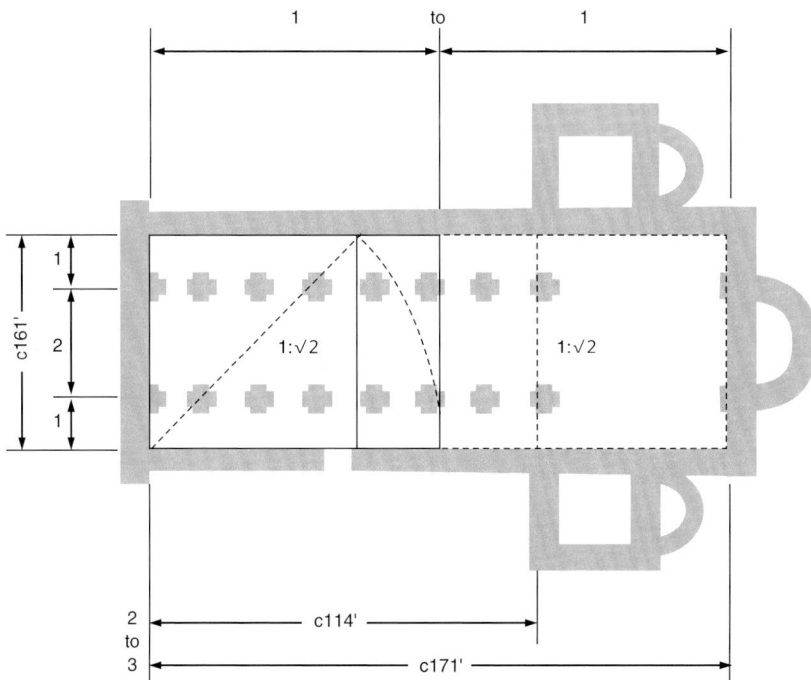

Figure 1. Plan of Old Sarum cathedral in the later 11th century showing geometrical design. After Cocke & Kidson 1993: 73.

using the ratio 1:2 (Figure 1). The plan showed that the church was a rectangle of 1: √2, two thirds of which formed the nave and one third the choir. This was emphasised once the square transepts were added (Cocke & Kidson 1993: 72). The example of Old Sarum showed that although the cathedral was laid out using geometry, the plan was actually quite simple. Drawing upon this argument, Fernie proposed that is likely that the same systems used for laying out churches were also applied to the areas around them. For most towns, the evidence is too tenuous to warrant investigation, though Bury St Edmunds (Suffolk) is an exception to the rule. The regularity of the street plan makes it clear that the town was laid out geometrically and probably in conjunction with the abbey church, since the axes of the church and town are aligned (Fernie 1998: 12-14; Lilley 2000; Lilley et al 2007: 289). As geometrical design can be seen in towns and in churches and cathedrals, it is likely that secular buildings were also laid out this way, applying the same techniques. The rectangular hall is similar in design to the nave of a church. It seems possible that the same techniques were applied in domestic structures as those in cathedrals and towns.

Geometrical design can also be seen in low-status buildings. A study of barns in Essex suggested that the plan and elevation were designed geometrically, using a modular system. This was first pointed out by Gibson (1994), who discovered that there was a ratio of 1:2 between the transverse and diagonal alignments of the arcade posts at the Cressing Temple barns. Smith (1996: 188-192) developed this argument, showing that the ratio 1:2 can be found in the circle-based medieval rectangle (Figure 2) and that this shows that there may be a geometrical construc-

tion behind the plan. Smith and Gibson established that the plans of both barns derived from intersecting circles (Gibson 1994: 183f; Smith 1996: 190-92). The radius of the first circle provides a measurement that is then repeated throughout the construction. The geometry used in the barn was the medieval rod equivalent to 16½ feet or 5.03 m. The advantage of using this type of geometry is the precision, whether the design was planned on a tracing floor or on site. We might suggest that if medieval architects were designing barns, it is likely that they were also planning high-status houses.

Geometrical design in gentry houses: the example of Hextalls

The site of the Manor of Hextalls is located 1½ km north of the village of Bletchingley, Surrey. The site began as a hunting lodge for the keeper of the deer parks at Bletchingley in the later 13th century. A new, larger chamber was built in the early 14th century, and this was retained until the house was abandoned. The arrival of the Hextall family in the mid-15th century saw the development of a new winged hall-house and detached kitchen (Figure 3). This was further developed during the Tudor period, before the house was demolished in the mid-16th century (Poulton 1998: 28).

The phase of the manor of Hextalls discussed here dates from *c* 1450, and coincides with the arrival of the Hextall family (Poulton 1998: 32). This phase is particularly important as a study of the plan demonstrates that the house was clearly laid out using the medieval rod system; suggesting that it was staked

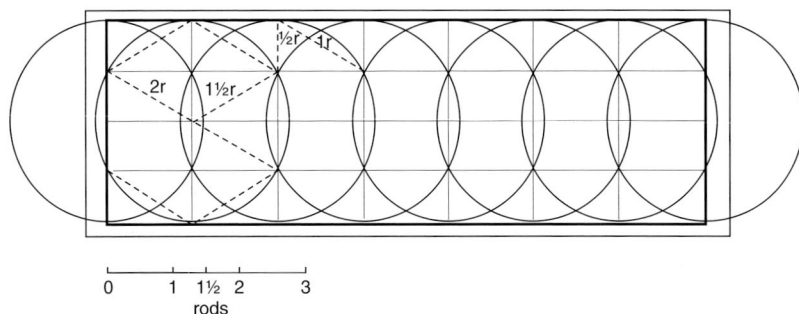

Figure 2. Plan of Barley Barn, Cressing Temple, derived from 6 intersecting circles and 2 half-circles with a radius of 1 ½ rods. After Gibson 1996: 183.

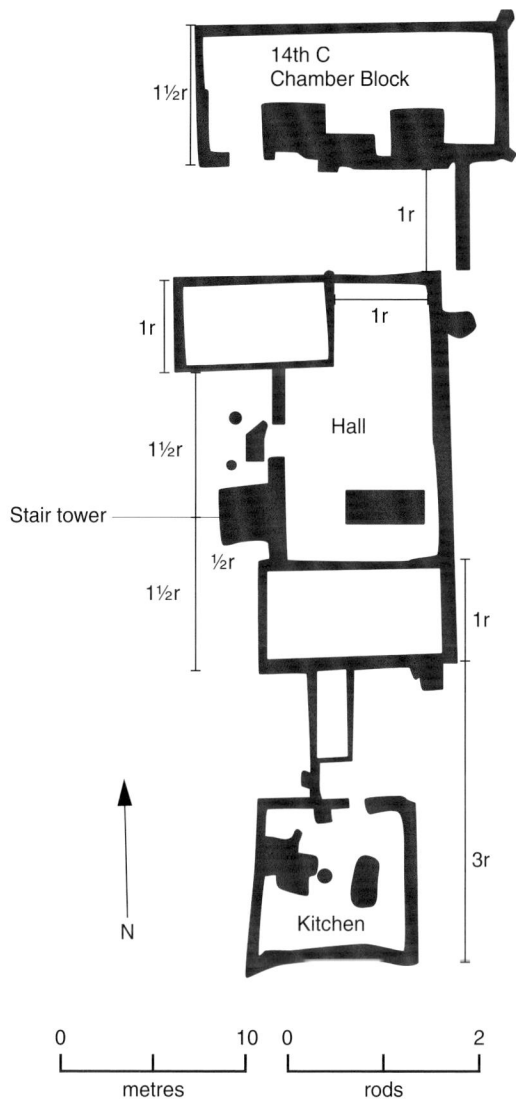

Figure 3. Plan of manor of Hextalls (Surrey) showing medieval rod measurements. After Poulton 1998: 182.

out the position of windows, doors and supporting columns. It has also raised the possibility that these sites were designed by architects or master masons. It is likely that proto-architects, such as Henry Yevele, were commissioned to design the plans, but that the construction work was sub-contracted to others as can be seen at Cooling Castle. A contract and receipt from Colling, dated 1382 suggested that it was the contractors Wreck and Sharnhale who built the body of the castle, yet payment was only made to them on the basis of the measurements which were certified by Yevele (Harvey 1944; 1987: 361f). This suggests that the gentry were concerned with design principles within the plan and elevation of the property; this can be seen in the way the building was laid out, but can also be seen in other ways such as through the use of symmetry.

Problems of symmetry

As has been shown, it is clear that geometry, symmetry and the fundamental principles of design were important to medieval architects. The use of symmetry to balance a façade in building design has its origins in the 15th century not in the post-medieval period; this can be seen in Great Chalfield Manor, Wiltshire. The house was built in the late 15th century by Thomas Tropnell, who emerged from relatively obscure gentry origins, to a position of great wealth founded on the cloth industry. The plan of the house is relatively straightforward, a central hall flanked on either side by two cross-wings with an offset porch (Figure 4). Yet the tripartite plan was designed in a way that it created a sense of symmetry; perhaps this house can be seen as a transitional building in the design and thought process? This is due to the centrality of the hall between the two cross-wings, and the fact that the porch is mirrored by another projection. Interestingly, the mid-point of the façade is the window at the high end of the hall, which would have emphasised the importance of that end (Cooper 1999: 60-64). The façade also made a clear social statement at a time when there was a growing emphasis on domestic comfort. The prominence of the porch and centrality of the hall invited hospitality, the chimney stack which would

out on the ground by the masons prior to construction. As indicated in Figure 3, the distance between the hall house and the chamber block to the north, and the kitchen to the south, was laid out using this system. The hall house itself was also laid out using the rod, indicated by the fact that the width of the stair tower measures half a rod, and the chamber blocks are both 1 rod in width. The results from Hextalls suggest modularity and regularity within the building plan, which implies design and perhaps the use of professional craftsmen. It is impossible to construct any complex building without using geometry. It is essential in creating right angles, for working

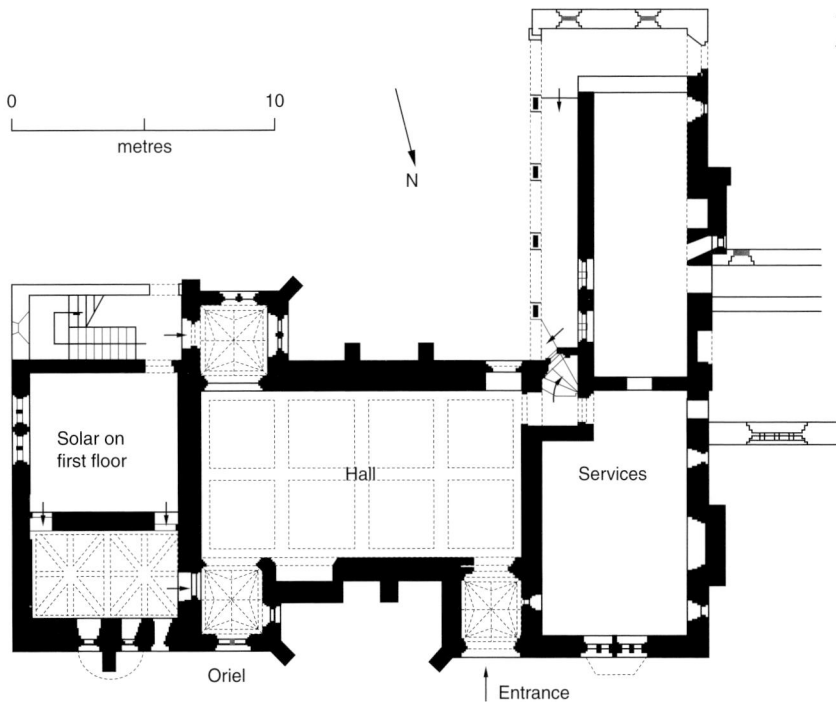

Figure 4. Plan of Great Chalfield Manor. After Cooper 1999: 60.

have suggested warmth, and the bays at the high end of the hall which would have indicated privacy (Emery 2006: 570). A house like Great Chalfield Manor is very obviously designed consciously as a whole: there is a clear equilibrium between symmetry and status, and so it can be argued that a balanced building must have been 'designed'. The design consequences of symmetry are clear, but often the motivation behind it, is not.

The use of gables to create a sense of balance can be recognised at both archaeological and standing sites. At Great Chalfield Manor, for example, the porch matches its balancing projection in height, but also the upper windows are mirror images, as are the diagonal buttresses. Ockwells Manor, Berkshire, is a typical example of the late medieval 'H'-shaped plan, consisting of a hall, two projecting cross-wings and a porch. The chamber and oriel window at the high end of the hall are slightly smaller than the cross-wing and porch at the low end, without being pedantic about symmetry in the modern sense. The windows and decoration are slightly different; clearly to demarcate the high and low ends, but the exterior is still clearly balanced. The matching pro-

jections were built at the same height, though the projection at the high end was slightly larger. The larger gable emphasises the conflicting aims of balance: to achieve a degree of symmetry while still signalling the distinction between the high and low ends (Figure 5).

Gables were also used as a device to dominate the skyline. This would have drawn the eye of the visitor upwards, which would have made the building appear taller. Drawing the focus of the visitor up would have emphasised the architectural detail such as the more elaborate windows at the upper levels, which demarcated the more high-status rooms. It would also have drawn the attention to the roof, which may also have been decorated. The crest of the ridge was often capped with shapes such as knife cut or moulded triangles (Cherry 1991: 195).

Some early 16th-century houses approached the problem of symmetry by playing down the differences between the high and low end. For example, at Barrington Court, Somerset, the porch was placed at the centre of the plan. To the right of the porch was the hall and cross-wing while to the left were the services and another cross-wing. Apart from a slightly larger window at the high end of the hall, it is not really possible to understand the internal arrangements from the exterior. The plan was still not symmetrical but it creates a uniformity and external balance (Cooper 1999: 75). Hextalls manor is another variation on this principle. The house followed the H-shaped plan, with one cross-wing only projecting 1 m from the hall. It was different to Ockwells Manor in that it used earlier buildings and ancillary structures to create a long linear range. The linear plan was created with the retention of the 14th-century detached stone chamber-block, and attaching the kitchen to the services by a pentice, all of which were constructed on the same alignment. The square foundations to the south of the entrance to the hall, and built at the same time, were very probably for a stair tower. After the 15th century, many buildings had staircases which projected from the side of the building (Wood 1965: 333). Stairs found at the low end of the hall, are often small and cramped. Hextalls is unusual in that its main stair tower was located at the front and centre of the building rather than at the junction of the hall and cross-wing.

The stair tower provided access to the first-floor chambers above the cross-wing (Poulton 1998: 181). The position of the stair tower at the front and centre of the building was unusual at this date (Wood 1965: 333). Analysis of the plan (Figure 3) suggested that it was to provide an alternative central axis, to be the focus for visitors who approached the house. The stair tower is exactly at the mid-point between the north wall of the earlier stone chamber block, and the south wall of the kitchen. This argues that the 15th-century modifications must have been planned, in order to create this mid-point. It also suggests that at sites where it was not possible to create a balanced façade using gables, an alternative might be sought.

Why houses were important for gentry display

Gentility during the 15th century was not something that was based on indisputable social criteria, and that once gained was never lost. Rather, those who claimed gentility during this time were part of a fluid society, where social meaning and status could change. Maddern (2005: 31) suggested that in order to be part of this community, the gentry were 'acting out a role'. This could mean showing the appropriate hospitality or building a house that displayed the right kind of message. Hall, in her study of the houses

Figure 5. Ockwells Manor, Berkshire. Photo: author.

of 17th-and 18th-century Gloucestershire, found that it was very difficult to distinguish between the houses of the lesser gentry and yeoman. However, she did observe that particularly on the western edge of the county, where there is very little freestone, stone mullions were a positive indicator of status. This is because houses of the gentry used stone mullions, while the yeoman had mullions made of wood, and so were distinguished visually (Hall 1991: 13).

Building was often inspired by competitive determination to provide proof of prosperity and social standing to all who saw it, and equally, it showed intelligence to those who were capable of understanding architecture (Airs 1999: 4-6). In a nation where power and authority were vested in the owners of land, houses were a public expression of dominance by the gentry (Cooper 1999: 3). This applied when the lord was in residence, and while he was away, as the house served as a permanent reminder on the landscape of his power and position. The gentry were not a homogenous class; they ranged in wealth and importance from knights, who were just below the peerage receiving often over £100 a year, to those gentlemen at the opposite end of the scale who may have received as little as £5 per annum. This would, of course, have had a considerable impact on what someone of gentry status could have afforded in terms of the size of the house, materials, and the sophistication of architectural features and detail used.

Houses in late medieval England were therefore clearly used as an expression of identity. Appearance and the way in which status was presented were fundamental to the late medieval gentry, in all aspects of their lives. They aspired to social and financial success, and rather than attempting to show differing tastes to the nobility, would have emulated them, only limited by their resources (Tolley 2005: 179). Giles (2000: 8) suggested that the archaeology of identity must 'be based on the premise that identities are constructed through an internal-external dialectic of identification between the individual and society.' She further argued that individual identity is always socially constructed, and can therefore be used to bring together the lived experience and social structures of medieval society. Ownership of land and expression of 'gentle' behaviour by the

mid-15th century, no longer automatically qualified an individual to the highest social status, though it would still have marked them out as privileged. This is in part due to the unstable language used by medievalists to describe this class, but also due to the increased stratification of the upper ranks of society, particularly when the nobility were restricted to peerage (Radelescu & Truelove 2005: 2).

One of the most radical changes in the lives of the aristocracy in the later Middle Ages involved their patterns of residence. Medieval households of the upper classes had been peripatetic, sweeping through the countryside in elaborate carriages with their possessions, as depicted in the *Luttrell Psalter*. This was not only for political and administrative purposes, but to allow the nobility to show themselves in areas of their rule, increasing their sphere of influence while consuming the surplus produce from their lands. The growth of the market for agricultural produce during the 13th century negated the need to travel to different estates to use the resources efficiently, resulting in the number of houses owned by upper class families falling (Dyer 1989: 99). This can be seen in the houses owned by the crown; in the early 14th century Edward II owned twenty-five houses but by the late 15th century Henry VII owned just ten.

Cooper (1999: 7) has suggested that it was the great noblemen that would have been involved in extravagant display. Yet, more than ever, the gentry would also have been committed to display, particularly as the mercantile class became more prosperous, and adopted the trappings of gentry status (Tolley 2005: 180). As part of the concept of gentry, visual culture became a key issue, to ensure that they were not confused with the lower social orders. This was shown through dress, heraldry, hospitality and buildings, both religious and secular. Tolley (2005: 178) has proposed that the gentry followed the trends set by the houses of the nobility. The result of living in a fewer number of houses was that expenditure could be concentrated on those buildings, to achieve the necessary scale of magnificence.

It was quality rather than quantity that the gentry of the 15th century strove for. The rise in the number of fixtures such as fireplaces and chambers suggests there was an increase in desire for comfort and privacy. There was also less emphasis on defensibility, a rise in the use of symmetry and in the choice of materials used, such as the increase in the use of brick and glass, which were still regarded as prestigious at this time (Dyer 1989: 100). Athelhampton Hall (Dorset) was built by the Martyn family during the 15th century. The house was built with considerable style, with the unusual buttresses, oriel window and porch and very high-status roof, but is also known for its stained glass windows (*Cal. Pat. Rolls: 1494-1509*, 43; Cooke 2010: 6; Emery 2006: 488; Wood 1965: 113). The survival of 15th- and 16th-century glass in a domestic context is not unusual, particularly in chapels. However, figural or historiated glass appears to have been less common in non-royal domestic settings, and when it is found, it is often restricted to the oriel window (Marks 2006: 96f; Woodforde 1954: 27f). The oriel only really became viable once glass had become readily available. It was then used by the upper classes as a vehicle for conspicuous consumption, to show that they could afford to purchase glass and to display it. The lights in the oriel and hall at Athelhampton, contained heraldic glass which displayed the marriage alliances of the Martyn family to the de Loundres, de Pydele, de Clevedon, Faringson, Cheverell, Daubeny, Kelway and Wadham families. The same can also be seen at Ockwells Manor (Berkshire): heraldic glass was used to display the arms of patrons, friends and family, while also demonstrating social and financial success.

Conclusion

This study set out to show that gentry houses of the 14th- and 15th-century England were designed using architectural devices to display status on the exterior of their homes. The paper explored the use of symmetry and geometry at a sample number of sites and began to recognise elements of design in the plan and elevation. The results hint at the fact that there was a growing concern amongst the upper classes of the late medieval period regarding design and that we as scholars should begin to rethink the concepts of design, and look for evidence of symmetry and other architectural devices through which status was displayed.

The central problem with existing research is that almost all of the literature depicts the 16th century as the watershed for architectural design in gentry houses (Cooper 1999; Howard 1987). The development of formal, external symmetry was a fundamental trend of the post-medieval period as was the level of involvement and interest from the builders in the design of their houses. In-filling the façade with gables or creating a central axis were all used to create a sense of balance and suggest symmetry. It is possible that presenting a balanced outward face was important in the medieval period, and was not exclusive to the post-medieval period. Without doubt, there are many more architectural devices that were used by medieval builders, but they have yet to be recognised. Architectural historians have begun to understand some of the more subtle messages of display, such as privacy and the role of gender, but these messages are not easy to decipher. In the past, it is likely that these subtle messages were understood and taken for granted. These include how these buildings were intended to be seen, and how they portrayed contemporary attitudes, social organisation and tastes. These statements may have been clear at the time of their construction, 'but to whose language we may have lost the code' (Cooper 2002: 28).

References

Primary sources

HMSO (1913) *Calendar of Patent Rolls 1266-72*. London: His Majesty's Stationery Office.

HMSO (1914-1916) *Calendar of the Patent Rolls 1485-1509; 1494-1509*, 2 vols. London: His Majesty's Stationery Office.

The Ten Books on Architecture by Vitruvius, trans. M. H. Morgan New York, 1914.

Secondary sources

Airs, M. (1999) *The Tudor and Jacobean Country House: A Building History*. Stroud: Alan Sutton Publishing.

Cherry, J. (1991) Pottery and Tile. In: *English Medieval Industries*, eds. J. Blair & N. Ramsay, 189-210. London: Hambledon Press.

Cocke, T. & P. Kidson (1993) *Salisbury Cathedral: Perspec-*

tives on the Architectural History. London: Her Majesty's Stationary Office.

Cooke, P. (2010) *Athelhampton House and Gardens*. Dorchester: Athelhampton House.

Cooper, N. (1999) *Houses of the Gentry 1480-1680*. London: Yale University Press.

Cooper, N. (2002) Display, Status and the Vernacular Tradition, *Vernacular Architecture* 33, 28-33.

Coulson, C. (1990) Bodiam Castle: Truth and Tradition, *Fortress* 10, 3-15.

Coulson, C. (1992) Some Analysis of the Castle of Bodiam, East Sussex. In: *Medieval Knighthood IV. Papers from the Fifth Strawberry Hill Conference 1990*, eds. C. Harper-Bill & R. Harvey, 51-107. Woodbridge: Boydell Press.

De Clercq, W., J. Dumolyn & J. Haemers (2007) "Vivre Noblement": Material Culture and Elite Identity in Late Medieval Flanders, *Journal of Interdisciplinary History* 28 (1), 1-31.

Dyer, C. (1989) *Standards of Living in the Later Middle Ages: Social Change in England c.1200-1520*. Cambridge: Cambridge University Press.

Emery, A. (2006) *Greater Medieval Houses of England and Wales 1300-1500* Vol. III Cambridge: Cambridge University Press.

Emery, A. (2011) Introductory Reflections after Greater Medieval Houses of England and Wales. In: *The Medieval Great House*, eds. M. Airs & P.S. Barnwell, 1-30. Donington: Shaun Tyas.

Fernie, E. (1994) Architecture and the Effects of the Norman Conquest. In: *England and Normandy in the Middle Ages*, eds. D. Bates & A. Curry, 105-16. London: Hambledon Press.

Fernie, E. (1998) The Romanesque Church of Bury St Edmonds. In: *Bury St Edmunds: Medieval Art, Architecture, Archaeology and Economy*, ed. A. Gransden, 1-15. Leeds: Maney Publishing.

Gibson, A. (1994) The Constructive Geometry of the Thirteenth-Century Barns at Cressing Temple, *Essex Archaeology and History* 25, 107-12.

Giles, K. (2000) *An Archaeology of Social Identity: Guildhalls in York, c.1350-1630*. BAR British Series 315. Oxford: Archaeopress.

Goodyear, W.H. (1910) Recently Published Measurements of the Pisa Cathedral, *American Journal of Archaeology* 14 (4), 434-49.

Grenville, J. (1997) *Medieval Housing. The Archaeology of Medieval Britain*. London: Leicester University Press.

Hall, L. (1991) Yeoman or Gentleman? Problems in Defining Social Status in Seventeenth- and Eighteenth-century Gloucestershire, *Vernacular Architecture* 22, 2-19.

Harvey, J. (1944) *Henry Yevele c.1320 to 1400: The Life of an English Architect*. London: B. T. Batsford.

Harvey, J. (1958) Mediaeval Design. *Transactions of the Ancient Monuments Society* 6 pp. 55-72.

Harvey, J. (1987) *English Mediaeval Architects: A Biographical Dictionary Down to 1550*. Gloucester: Alan Sutton Publishing.

Howard, M. (1987) *The Early Tudor Country House: Architecture and Politics 1490-1550*. London: George Philip.

Johnson, M. (1993) *Housing Culture: Traditional Architecture in an English Landscape*. London: University College London Press.

Johnson, M. (2002) *Behind the Castle Gate: From Medieval to Renaissance*. London & New York: Routledge.

Johnson, M. (2010) *English Houses 1300-1800. Vernacular Architecture, Social Life*. Harlow: Pearson Education Limited.

Liddiard, R. (2005) *Castles in Context: Power, Symbolism and Landscape, 1066 to 1500*. Macclesfield: Windgather Press.

Lilley, K.D. (2000) Mapping the Medieval City: Plan Analysis and Urban History, *Urban History* 27 (1), 5-30.

Lilley, K.D., Lloyd, C.D. & S. Trick (2007) Designs and Designers of Medieval 'New Towns' in Wales, *Antiquity* 81, 279-93.

Maddern, P.C. (2005) Gentility. In: *Gentry Culture in Late Medieval England*, eds. R. Radulescu & A. Truelove, 18-34. Manchester: Manchester University Press.

Marks, R. (2006) *Stained Glass in England During the Middle Ages*. London: Routledge.

Poulton, R. (1998) *The Lost Manor of Hextalls Little Pickle, Bletchingley*. Surrey: Surrey Archaeology Unit.

Radelescu, R. & A. Truelove (2005) Introduction. In: *Gentry Culture in Late Medieval England*, eds. R. Radulescu & A. Truelove, 1-17. Manchester: Manchester University Press

Ruskin, J. (1865) *Seven Lamps of Architecture*. New York: John Wiley.

Smith, L. (1996) The Geometrical Designer at Cressing Temple, *Essex Archaeology and History* 27, 188-92.

Taylor, C., P. Everson & R. Wilson-North (1990) Bodiam Castle, Sussex, *Medieval Archaeology* 34, 155-57.

Tolley, T. (2005) Visual Culture. In: *Gentry Culture in Late Medieval England*, eds. R. Radelescu & A. Truelove, 167-83. Manchester: Manchester University Press.

Wood, M. (1965) *The English Mediaeval House*. London: Ferndale Editions.

Woodforde, C. (1954) *English Stained and Painted Glass*. Oxford: Clarendon Press.

Unpublished theses, reports, and other works

Mann, J. *Serendipity, Paradox and Irony: The Peculiar Career of William Henry Goodyear (1846-1923)*. Paper presented to the Collins-Kaufmann Symposium, Columbia University 29th March 2007, 1-23.

Smoke Houses and Entrepreneurship in Two Rural Villages of Medieval Scania, Örja and Skegrie

Adam Bolander

Abstract[1]

During the last few years two medieval 'smoke houses' have been excavated in Örja and Skegrie, two villages situated in the western parts of Scania, Sweden. Their comparative study has revealed several similarities between the two smoke houses, regarding their physical appearance and functional aspects, which appear to be distinctive features of a smoke house. This paper advances the hypothesis that the smoke houses in Örja were run by farmers situated on an adjacent farm site or a village co-operative and are evidence not only of a distinctive form of specialized production, but also of early medieval entrepreneurship and enterprise. Estimations based upon the sampled fish bone material suggest that a considerable amount of fish had been handled in the smoke houses. The most remarkable feature of both houses was a clay-filled ditch which had been dug along the inside of the walls of each building, which is likely to have been used as a solid and dry pathway. Possible ritual deposits were identified in both houses. Elaborate hearths which had been modified several times indicated how the use of the buildings had changed over time. Finds of toll chips and lead seals are indications of regional contacts and a link to the large international markets in the southern parts of Scania, the Scanian fairs (Swedish: 'Skånemarknaderna'), which further emphasized the extent of the enterprise. The artefacts recovered from two clay-lined pits in Örja, further strengthen this proposed connection.

Introduction

In 2007, a medieval rural settlement was excavated in Skegrie. One of the buildings was interpreted as a smoke house, based on its distinctive features and fish-enriched floor layer. A few years later, in 2010, a parallel example was excavated in Örja, which revealed new information about the concept of a smoke house. The latter forms the main focus of this paper, while Skegrie is used for comparative purposes. The aim is to compare the two buildings, highlighting similarities as well as differences between them, and to try to understand how production activities may have been organized and carried out. A primary concern is the identification of

definitive or distinctive features of smoke houses. Another crucial question is whether the archaeological material can be used to reveal information on the extent and nature of the production process, the commercial aspect of such enterprises and wider networks and interactions in which its users were involved. Both smoke houses were excavated using a single context method, as practised by UV Syd (Larsson 2003). Parts of the rich osteological and archaeobotanical materials were sampled for further analysis. The sites are fully comparable regarding excavation technique, documentation and levels of preservation.

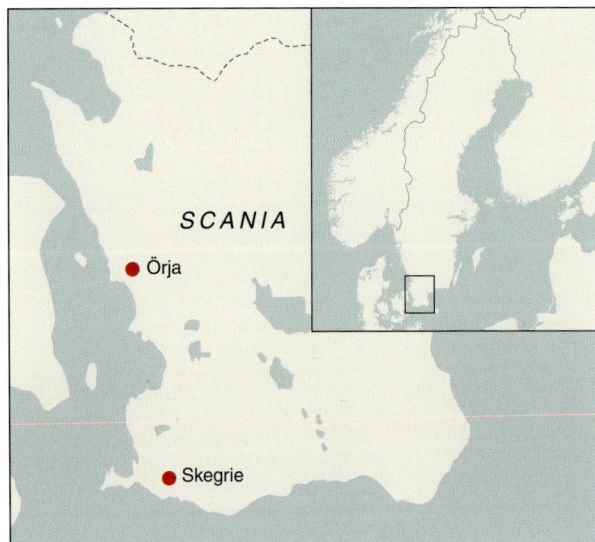

Figure 1. Map of Scania, with the two sites marked.

Setting

Örja village is situated in the northwestern part of Scania, a few kilometres from the coast and in the vicinity of the town Landskrona. Örja was established in the 11th century, even though there may have been an earlier land owning elite in the area, as indicated by the rune stone 'Örjastenen' (Moltke 1985). The area that was excavated affected the western part of the historical village, and in particular 4 farm sites numbered 1, 12, 20 and 16 on a map dated 1761. One particularly interesting feature was uncovered at farm site 12, namely a well-preserved smoke house, dated to the early 13th century. A parallel to the smoke house, with several similar features, was excavated in Skegrie village in 2007. Skegrie is situated in the southwestern part of Scania, not far from the coast or the town Trelleborg. The village was established the Early Middle Ages and is mentioned as existing in a written source dated to the the 12th century, which must be regarded as an early evidence (Skansjö 1983: 64, 83, 95) (Figure 1).

The smoke house in Örja

At farm site 12 particularly well-preserved remains of a building were excavated (Figure 2). Prior to the establishment of the actual building, *ie* during the Viking Age or the transition to the Early Middle Ages, there is evidence of activity which had involved the handling of a considerable amount of fish. The clearest evidence for this is a specific layer containing an enormous amount of fish bones and two adjacent clay-lined pits (Swedish: 'lerbottnar'). The presence of the latter is interesting, since clay-lined pits are usually intimately connected to, and associated with, the Scanian fairs (Swedish: 'Skåne-marknaderna'), which is a collective name for the medieval market places and trading sites along the southern and western coast of Scania. The most well-known market places were situated in Skanör/Falsterbo, Ystad and Malmö, where enormous amounts of herring were sold, of which most were transported to the Hanseatic towns. The commercial activity that took place in these large market places is often regarded as the beginning of a market economy, which in turn probably was a key factor for extensive urbanization during the Early Middle Ages (see Ersgård 2006). The fish market at the Scanian fairs was favoured by the fact that the church promoted the eating of fish during the long periods of Lent. A continuously-growing population during the Early Middle Ages was another factor that led to new food requirements, which further boosted the market and gradually led to a medieval sea fishing revolution (Barrett et al. 2011: 1517; Hildebrand 1983: 217f).

A number of clay-lined pits have also been found in agrarian settlements situated in the inland. The function of clay-lined pits has been the subject of considerable debate, resulting in two major interpretations. One interpretation is that they were connected to the practical processing of fish, such as their gutting or even the extraction of blubber (Stenholm 1981a; 1981b; 1981c). Lars Ersgård, however, argues that their function was more economic and symbolic than practical. He suggests that the clay-lined pits would have been physical markers validating the right of constructing a shed on a particular spot within the Scanian fairs, thus giving the participant the right to pursue in commercial actions under the protection of the King. Season after season people seemingly returned to the same fixed spots, where the clay-lined pits served as their land mark signalling their right to a particular piece of land. Following this hypothesis, it has been suggested that clay-lined pits found in agrarian settings may also have had a strong symbolic function. This is due to their sheer abundance on farm sites that were regulated and whose boundaries were marked out by trenches soon after the pits had been created. In this context the clay-lined pits may be interpreted as a first claim to a piece of land or estate (Ersgård 1988: 73; 2006: 51ff). Further connections to the Scanian fairs can be seen in the comprehensive material from farm site 12, where a toll chip was found by metal detecting of the area. Similar toll chips were used at the Scanian fairs as a receipt for a fee paid to the bailiff in order to attain rights for fishing, commercial activities or craftsmanship (Magnus 1555: 201; Rydbeck 1935: 48, 109ff).

On the actual site of the clay-lined pits in Örja and the associated layer rich in fish bones, a building constructed of wooden posts was erected during the 12th century. Fish-related activities clearly continued throughout this building phase. At the beginning of the 13th century the wooden posts were replaced by a solid framework of sill stones. The original layout of this sill house was unevenly separated into 4 rooms, with a slightly larger room covering central and eastern parts of the building. The structure measured around 22.5 m and the total indoor space amounted to 95 m². In the initial phase of the building at least 3-4 different hearths were used, even though they may not have been completely contemporary. They were all situated in different areas of the building and may also have served different purposes, even though it seems likely that their function in some way is related to the industrial use of the building. Although some of those engaged in processing fish within the building may also have used it as temporary dwelling quarters, there is little evidence to suggest it was ever a domestic space.

In the next phase, in the first half of the 13th century, some adjustments to the original design were carried out. A more spacious room was constructed in the centre of the building, as an earlier dividing wall was torn down, creating a floor area of 62 m². Furthermore, a hearth with an external fire chamber was constructed, and from now on appears to have been the centre of the house. Later alterations and adjustments of the house were made with respect to the hearth and the activities related to it. A greasy and thick floor layer began to accumulate, mainly consisting of charcoal, soot and ashes, also denoting the intense use of the hearth. Along the northern sill a wooden board walk was constructed, connecting what appears to have been an entrance with the western parts of the building. In addition, a wooden worktop based on a stone foundation was constructed close to the central hearth. In this phase, it is clearly evident that the building was functioning primarily as some type of specialized commercial enterprise, namely a smoke house.

Figure 2. The smoke house in Örja during excavation. Photo Karin Blom.

During the 14th and 15th centuries major alterations were made to the building (Figure 3). The hearth became more intricate in its construction, with a double external fire chamber and a re-designed heating chamber. The most radical change was the construction of a ditch, dug on the inside of the buildings' walls and immediately infilled with solid burnt and unburnt clay. The aim of creating this feature appears to have been to construct a compact and firm surface on which to walk, enabling the building's occupants or users to avoid stepping in the greasy accumulated floor layers, when it came to transporting materials around or simply working within the smoke house. Considering that work with fire and smoke also could have taken place on the floor outside the actual hearth, the clay filled ditch might also have served as a buffer zone to prevent fire from reaching the side walls. Further changes were made as the eastern dividing wall was moved, thereby creating a larger gabled room for storage. There are indications that the western part of the building was shortened by 5 m during this period. The earlier subsidiary hearths appear also to have lost their function or fallen out of use, leaving the central hearth as the sole source of fire in the building.

The floor layer, which had continuously accumulated through all three phases, consisted of multiple thin lenses of soot, ashes, charcoal, burnt clay and animal bones. It is possible that each lens represents a single smoke set (ie a smoking event). However, it seems likely that accumulated debris also may have been regularly removed from the building, leaving no archaeological traces. Therefore, what was left at the time of the excavation may not necessarily represent an unbroken stratigraphy, dating from the first use of the building until its demolition but simply the most recent phases of use prior to decommissioning or abandonment. Outside the building there were cultural layers containing burnt material. Initially they were interpreted as demolition layers by the excavators, but it may well be that some of the burnt material here was the result of clearance and cleansing of floor surfaces and rubbish between different smoke sets. Except for small fragments of sheep, pig and different fowl, the majority of the bone material from the floor layer consisted of vertebra, scales and bones of at least 10 different species of fish, consisting of herring, cod, haddock, plaice, flounder, short-spined sea scorpion, eel, garpike, perch and tuna. Herring, cod and flounder were the most well-represented species species and were all suitable for smoking. The NISP (number of identified specimens) count reached 211, which signals that an extensive amount of fish had been handled, considering that the analysed samples only equals a small percentage of the total floor layer. Based upon sampling, the total number of specimens in the preserved floor layer may be estimated to more than 4000. This material probably represents fish that for various reasons had been discarded and ended up on the floor. From this perspective the amount of fish processed was relatively high, which may indicate a specialized production for the market (Cardell in prep.).

Charcoal from different areas and sublevels of the floor layer was sampled and analysed and proved almost solely to consist of alder, with a minor content of oak. Alder is a type of wood traditionally used for smoking, due to its high energy efficiency and the fact that its smoke adds a characteristic flavour to the smoked fish. Contact with several modern-day smoke houses reveals that alder is still the most common wood used. No analysis of the charcoal from the hearths has yet been conducted, but could possibly add data to the interpretation of their function and internal relations with other features.

A brief look at the finds from the building yields evidence of a considerable number of tools, especially knives and whetstones, which further emphasizes the connection to some sort of specialized preparation activities, in this case the handling and processing of fish. A few finds of whorls and needles in the same context add complexity to the interpretation. It would be intriguing to link them to fish-related activities, as they could have been used in preparations of fish nets, the production of textile vessels or simply to string large quantities of fish for smoking. Of course these types of finds are also common evidence of household activities within rural farm sites. Five coins were found in the floor layer, all dated to early or mid 13th century and slightly concentrated to the northern part of the building. Apart from animal bones and the large quantities of fish bones,

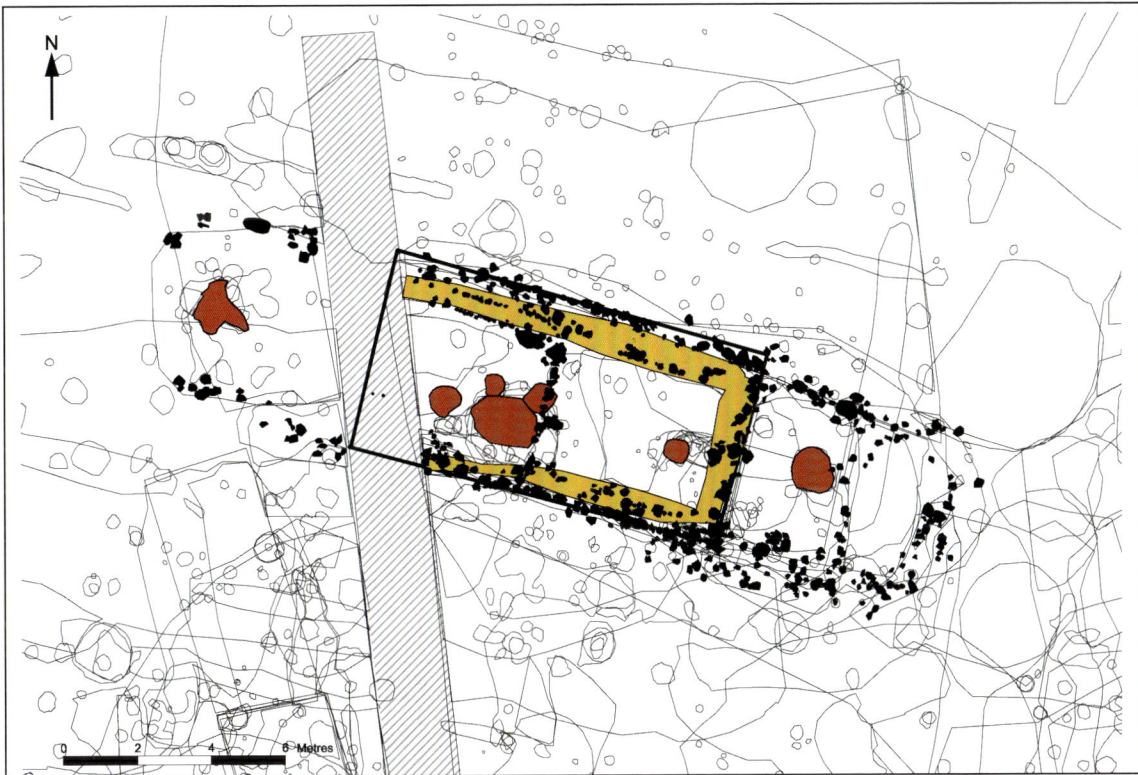

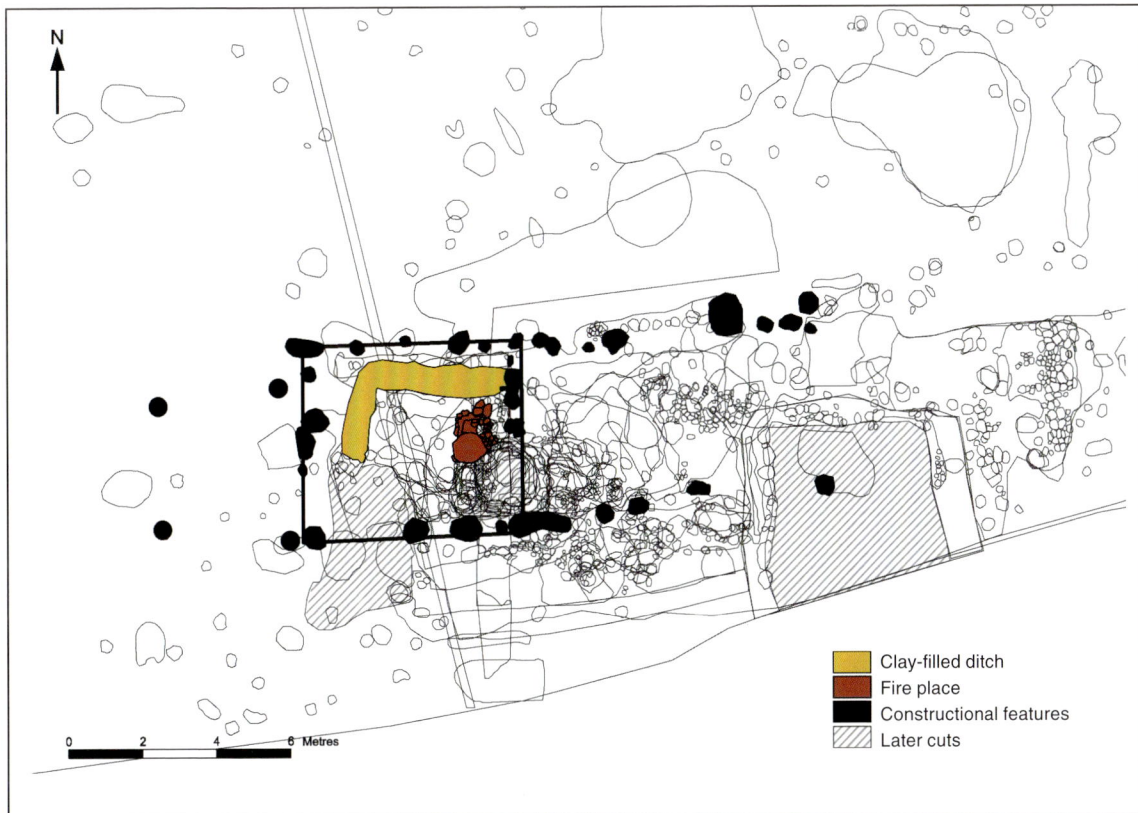

Figure 3. Overview of the two smoke houses. Upper: Örja, 14th-15th century. Lower: Skegrie, 13th-14th century. The grey line marks the parts of the building that had been used as a smoke house.

finds were mainly concentrated along the walls and especially along the northern wall. This fact supports the interpretation that the clay-filled ditch along the wall was used as a pathway or some kind of working surface. However there are alternative explanations for the location of these finds, which will be discussed below.

The smoke house of Skegrie

During a rescue excavation conducted in 2007 in Skegrie, in the vicinity of Trelleborg in the southwestern part of Scania, an interesting parallel to the smoke house in Örja was found (Schmidt Sabo 2008) (see Figure 3). This particular building had been in use during the 13th and 14th centuries and its construction was smaller, 5 x 18 m, and of rectangular shape. It was constructed of wooden posts and its western part had at some point been extended, adding an extra room, measuring 3.30 x 3.50 m. It would probably have been a storage room, alternatively some sort of heat saving entrance to the building. The central room of the building measured 4.6 x 5.0 m and had been the primary space for the smoking activities. The eastern room, which measured 4.65 x 8.0 m, was interpreted as a workshop or cooking house. It is possible that processing of plant fibre had taken place in this part of the building, since several cutting tools were found along with fibres. A possible interpretation is that this room had functioned as a small-scale brewery. A whetstone and a knife found in postholes where interpreted as votive offerings, along with a almost-complete skeleton of a sheep, which was found in a pit close to the wall of the workshop. The room where the smoking activity had taken place featured a hearth and two floor layers. The northern and western parts of the room were apparently bordered by a trench, which had been infilled with burnt clay. This seemed like a 'sill' of clay, approximately 0.40 m wide and 0.20 m high. Part of the material used in its construction appeared to have been re-used from an older demolished oven, since some of the clay pieces had a flat and sooty side. The floor layers had then accumulated in a way that resulted in a vertical contact surface to the clay sill. The main purpose of this structure was probably to prevent grease and soot

from reaching all of the available space in the room, but it also created a surface on which it was possible to walk and work without making contact with the greasy and probably slippery floor layer. The hearth was situated in the south-eastern part of the room in the centre of a circular pit, around 1 m wide. The sides of the pit had been covered with clay and it was filled with soot and charcoal. In front of the pit was a 1 x 1 m large stone construction, as well as a surface of unburnt clay, measuring 0.5 x 0.5 m. The hearth showed several structural phases, reflecting the adding of stone elements and refreshed clay surfaces.

The floor layer measured 3 x 3.7 m and was 0.2 m thick, consisting of multiple thin lenses. The layer contained black sand, burnt and unburnt clay, soot, charcoal, and burnt parts of plants. A considerable amount of bones, scales and vertebra from fish were found in the layer, as well as a strikingly large amount of other animal bones. Herring and cod were the most represented species, but eel and roach occurred as well (Cardell 2008: 55). On top of this layer was a similar layer, 0.1 m thick, connected to the later phases of the hearth. Some lenses proved to contain a rather stiff and dense mass, which had been intensely burnt, probably consisting of bark. It may reflect a cold smoking technique, where smouldering wood and bark were spread out over the entire floor. No analysis of the kind of wood that had been used for the hearth has yet been conducted. Macrofossil analysis showed that the floor layer barely contained any plant remains, so it is not likely that the room has been used for storing or drying cereals.

Finds from the smoke room consisted of a whetstone, ceramics and several iron objects that were severely corroded and affected by heat. Some of them may have been structural elements connected to the actual smoke construction. Nine objects found in the trench for the clay sill were of particular interest since they appear to have been deposited in a row, possibly as votive offerings. They consisted of a whorl, a humerus from a young horse, two whetstones, a fossil, a flint scraper, an iron handle, a handle from a redware pot and a whorl made out of amber. They were all placed in a structured manner and had clearly not ended up there by a coincidence. In addition, about 10 coins, dating from the beginning of the 14th century to AD 1360, were collected from the floor layer. Initially they were interpreted as having been lost accidentally in the day-to-day commercial activity of the building, but were later reconsidered to rather represent some sort of votive offering. Hypothetically, the purpose of these could have been to assure a successful smoke set, to add protection to the building or as a symbolic gesture to boost sales (Falk 2007: 24). Connections to the Scanian fairs was indicated by finds of toll chips, as well as lead seals, from parcels of textiles or clothing being shipped in *en mass* from Flanders (Rydbeck 1935: 110; Schmidt Sabo & Söderberg 2009: 23ff).

The excavation did not yield clear evidence of the location of living quarters within these sites. However, the excavated area was rather small, resulting in the identification of only a few of the structures which might be expected on this kind of site. The extension of excavations to the area immediately adjacent to the existing site would offer considerable potential to locate additional buildings associated with the farm complex, one of which would presumably be living quarters.

Discussion

The most striking similarity between the smoke house in Örja and the one in Skegrie, is the clay-filled trench, on the inside of the buildings' walls. That in Skegrie had obviously been built up like a wall, creating a buffer zone preventing fire from reaching the wooden walls. In Örja however, it seemed to have been dug as a regular trench that had been filled up only subsequently with demolition material. It must be pointed out that the trench became visible directly after the top soil had been removed and that the feature to some extent may have been affected by later land use. The need for a buffer zone was perhaps not so strong in Örja, since this building was based on a solid framework of sill stones. On the other hand, in both cases there seems to have been a need for a firm and dry area to walk, stand and work on, in order to avoid stepping on the greasy and slippery floor. They may also have facilitated the movement or transportation of small carts or barrows in and out of the building.

Another interesting aspect of these sites are the votive offerings of a flintscraper, a humerus from a horse and the fossil found in Skegrie. These were objects that appeared out of context but were deposited in a manner that suggested a ritual deposition rather than accidental loss. During the field work in Örja it was noted that several finds appeared close to the walls, mostly along the northern wall. These included a comb, needles, whetstones and knives. They appeared in no particular pattern, but their size suggested they were unlikely to have been lost accidentally, and they also appear to have been located close to the walls and in connection with the clay-filled trench. As the interpretation of the building as a smoke house became more and more convincing, the connection to the smoke house in Skegrie and the possibility that the finds may have been deposited in a similar ritual or votive manner seemed plausible. Equally, the coins discovered at Örja appear to parallel the finds of coins recovered from Skegrie. Once again it seems likely that they were as consciously deposited as votive offerings, to assure a successful smoke set or a thriving business. Such action is of course hard to prove and must, in both cases, remain a hypothesis.

The structure of the floor layers was strikingly similar between the two smoke houses. Both included accumulated with thin micro lenses consisting of burnt material, reflecting different sets of smoking. The buildings, however, also show several features that distinguish the two from each other. First, the smoke house in Skegrie was constructed of wooden posts, while that one in Örja had a solid framework of sill stones. The room that had been used for the actual smoking activity was considerably larger in Örja, differing more than 30 m², while parts of the building in Skegrie had been used for other activities.

The context and interpretation of the smoke houses

The Örja excavation revealed interesting information on the construction of a smoke house. At the same time it raised new questions regarding the immaterial aspects of the smoking activity and its organization

Figure 4. Three toll chips found in Örja (the one on the left) and Skegrie (the two on the right).

in a wider context. Some answers could possibly be embedded in the material of fish bones, which were extensively sampled from the floor layers. Analyses in progress will hopefully reveal information on the fishing strategies and the processing of the catch. For example we do not yet know if the residents at farm site 12 were involved in the entire process, from catching the fish to the final smoking. Furthermore, to run a smoke house would require a considerable amount of wood, which raises the question of who accumulated it and from where? Another interesting question is where and how the processed and smoked product accessed the market? Was this at the farm site itself, or was this transported to another local or regional market, and by whom? The connection to the Scanian fairs is evident from the toll chips that were found both in Örja and Skegrie, revealing that the people who ran the smoke houses were also directly involved in commercial networks and activities there (Figure 4). It is questionable whether we will be able to establish what particular action these toll chips actually represent. We can perhaps only guess whether the entrepreneurs from Örja and Skegrie commercialized their product at the Scanian fairs or rather bought fresh fish to bring back for processing and smoking.

Olaus Magnus has depicted the use of smoked, dried and salted products in his work over the Nordic peoples, which first was printed in Rome in 1554. He observed that smoked fish was often salted as well, in order to add preservation quality, which

further complicates the analysis of the handling of the products (Magnus 1555: 199). If that is the case in Örja and Skegrie, it would be most likely that the fish was salted directly after it had been caught, to be smoked later on. The soft and moist texture of fresh fish would make it somewhat easier to absorb the salt, while the drier and firm texture of smoked fish does not provide the same characteristics. Archaeological evidence of such a process is of course scarce, but could perhaps be acquired through an analysis of the anatomical distribution of the fish bones or a chemical analysis of soil composition. The floor layer in Skegrie was a lot greasier than the floor layer in Örja, which could suggest that salt had been used to a wider extent. The use of salt is known to extract fat from fish and meat, which during the smoking process could result in dripping and accumulating of large amounts of fat on the surface below.

Regarding the context of the smoke house at farm site 12 in Örja, an interesting observation can also be made. No dwelling building contemporary with the smoke house has been identified. This sparks a hypothesis that there might not have been any inhabitants on the farm site as the smoking activity was scaled up. In the 14th century, when the building was modified with the clay filled trenches, house 24, which was situated in the western parts of the farm site and interpreted as a possible dwelling building, appears to have been demolished. House 24 was then replaced by another building which was solely used for the drying and processing of flax. If it is really the case that no one was living on the farm site, at least for some period of time, one may wonder who actually ran the smoke house? A possible explanation would be that people from a neighbouring farm controlled and ran the activities on farm site 12, as well as controlling the use of the land attached to the farmstead. An alternative interpretation would be that both the smoking activity as well as the handling of flax, were carried out by a village co-operative. It is well known from written sources that handling of flax often was carried out by a cooperative and that the building used for that purpose was situated within the village structure (Talve 1960: 9f, 52). A similar way of organizing the work would possibly have been suitable for a smoke house as well. It is likely that these types of activities have been carried out on a seasonal basis, when the produce was in abundance and most cost-effective to process.

Summary

Two recent excavations in Örja and Skegrie uncovered buildings interpreted as smoke houses. On both sites the smoking activities seem to have been run on a commercial scale. In Örja, smoking seems to have started as a subsidiary income to the peasants living at farm site 12, whereas adjacent building structures show connections to ordinary agriculture. After a while the activity was scaled up, resulting in a switch of focus from agriculture to solely running the smoke house enterprise. Constructing such a large and solid building exclusively for smoking purposes indicates that it must have been financially viable. The length of time that the building was standing, the structural modifications being made, as well as the extensive floor layers which accumulated, indicate that the economic situation had been stable for a considerable amount of time, presumably occupying several people in the production process. Whether or not it was run by inhabitants of a single neighbouring farm or by a village co-operative, the smoke house must have been of considerable importance to those connected to it. The smoke house in Skegrie gives a slightly different picture, since the activities taking place within the building seem to have been somewhat more diverse. At Skegrie it seems clear that the inhabitants of the farm were running the smoke house, but that it was only one of the means by which its inhabitants derived an income. One part of the building had been used for some sort of craftsmanship, perhaps handling of plant fibres or even a small scaled brewery. In both cases, however, there is clear evidence of contact with the Scanian fairs and commercial networks.

The excavations in Örja and Skegrie have yielded new insights into the smoking of fish and the construction of smoke houses in a rural setting during the medieval period. It has to some degree been possible to denote the extent of the regional contacts of these enterprises. In both cases smoking activities have not been taking place merely to fulfil the need of a single or a few households but rather on a more commercial scale. The origin or development of a network of entrepreneurs with social and economic contacts appears to be emerging from this evidence. It may indicate the movement of those involved in such production from the status of peasant farmers to that of industrial entrepreneurs. This raises important questions about the production and organisation of such industries, evidence of which may emerge from further detailed analysis of these two sites as well as future excavations and research elsewhere.

Note

1. This paper is partly based upon a lecture held by Adam Bolander, Katalin Schmidt Sabo and Fredrik Strandmark.

References

Barrett, J.H., D. Orton, C. Johnstone, J. Harland, W. van Neer, A. Ervynck, C. Roberts, A. Locker, C. Amundsen, I. Bødker Enghoff, S. Hamilton-Dyer, D. Heinrich, A.K. Hufthammer, A.K.G. Jones, L. Jonsson, D. Makowiecki, P. Pope, T.C. O'Connell, T. de Roo & M. Richards (2011) Interpreting the expansion of sea fishing in medieval Europe using stable isotope analysis of archaeological cod bones, *Journal of Archaeological Science* 38, 1516–1524.

Cardell, A. (2008) Stinkande fiskrens och annat matavfall i gropar och golv. In: *Bronsålder på toftmark och medeltid på gård nr 12 i Skegrie*, UV Syd dokumentation av fältarbetsfasen 2008: 3. Arkeologisk slutundersökning 2007, ed. K. Schmidt Sabo, 52-58. Lund: Riksantikvarieämbetet UV Syd.

Cardell, A. (in prep.) Fisk för distribution och kött till husbehov. In: Örja 1:9. UV Syd Rapport, ed. K. Schmidt Sabo. Lund: Riksantikvarieämbetet UV Syd.

Ersgård, L. (1988) *Vår marknad i Skåne. Bebyggelse, handel och urbanisering i Skanör och Falsterbo under medeltiden.* Lund studies in medieval archaeology 4. Stockholm: Almqvist & Wiksell.

Ersgård, L. (2006) Lerbottnarna och det tidigmedeltida samhället. In: *Liljan. Om arkeologi i en del av Malmö*, ed. S. Larsson, 49-63. Lund: Arkeologiböcker.

Falk, A.-B. (2007) En grundläggande handling – byggnadssoffer och dagligt liv i medeltid. Licentiate thesis. University of Lund.

Hildebrand, H. (1983) *Sveriges medeltid. Landsbygden. 1st volume.* Malmö: Norstedts.

Larsson, S. (2003) *Handledning till stratigrafisk dokumentation och tolkning.* Lund: UV Syd.

Magnus, O. (1555) [reprint 1976] *Historia de gentibus septentrionalibus* (Swedish: Historia om de nordiska folken). Fjärde delen (sjuttonde till tjugoandra boken). 2nd edition. Östervåla: Gidlunds.

Moltke, E. (1985) *Runes and their origin, Denmark and Elsewhere.* Copenhagen: Nationalmuseets Forlag.

Rydbeck, O. (1935) *Den medeltida borgen i Skanör. Historik, undersökningar och fynd.* Skrifter utgivna av Kungl. humanistiska vetenskapssamfundet i Lund. XX. Lund: C.W.K. Gleerup.

Schmidt Sabo, K. (ed.) (2008) *Bronsålder på toftmark och medeltid på gård nr 12 i Skegrie.* Uv Syd dokumentation av fältarbetsfasen 2008:3. Arkeologisk slutundersökning 2007. Lund: Riksantikvarieämbetet UV Syd.

Schmidt Sabo, K. & B. Söderberg (2009) Skegrie – en by i förändring. In: *Dödens väg. E6 och arkeologi på Söderslätt.* Riksantikvarieämbetet UV Syd. Lund: Riksantikvarieämbetet UV Syd.

Skansjö, S. (1983) *Söderslätt genom 600 år. Bebyggelse och odling under äldre historisk tid.* Skånsk medeltid och renässans 11. Lund: C.W.K. Gleerup.

Stenholm, L. (1981a) Lerbottnar, *META* 1981:1, 36–38.

Stenholm, L. (1981b) Lerbottnar, *META* 1981:3–4, 59–60.

Stenholm, L. (1981c) Lerbottnar till belysning, *Ale* 1981:2, 17–30.

Talve, I. (1960) *Bastu och torkhus i Nordeuropa.* Nordiska Museets Handlingar 53. Stockholm: Nordiska Museet.

The 'Stube' and its Heating
Archaeological Evidence for a Smoke-Free Living Room between Alps and North Sea

Rainer Atzbach

Abstract

This paper discusses the concept of smoke-free heated living rooms between the Alps and the North Sea with a special focus on the tile stove. In the circum-Alpine zone, a new heating system was invented between the 8th and 11th century. It consisted of a clay cupola oven with inserted ceramic vessels and was mostly run as a 'breechloader' (the term is used throughout the article to describe an oven which is fired from an adjacent room). This provided not only a comfortable living room, but also tended to create a specific ground plan for the house – with a core of the heated 'stube' and an adjacent kitchen. In the 12th or 13th century, this concept was differentiated into an elaborated system of stube, kitchen, central corridor and unheated chambers. The tile stove and the corresponding ground plan spread, but was also modified, in the area between the Upper German speaking region and Southern Scandinavia until the 16th century.

"The German stove [Kachelofen] is by long odds the best stove and the most convenient and economical that has yet been invented. One firing is enough for the day; the cost is next to nothing; the heat produced is the same all day, instead of too hot and too cold by turns; one may absorb himself in his business in peace; he does not need to feel any anxieties of solicitudes about the fire; his whole day is a realized dream of bodily comfort.

The American wood stove, of whatsoever breed, it is a terror. There can be no tranquillity of mind where it is. It requires more attention than a baby. It has to be fed every little while, it has to be watched all the time; and for all reward you are roasted half your time and frozen the other half. It warms no part of the room but its own part; it breeds headaches and suffocation, and makes one's skin feel dry and feverish; and, when your wood bill comes in, you think you have been supporting a volcano."

Mark Twain 1891 (Twain 1923: 176)

Introduction

In archaeology, the distinction between a dwelling house and a subsidiary house is often defined by the existence of some form of permanent heating. Since mankind learned to light a fire, a central hearth has been the most important kind of heating in the home. Until the 19th century, in some regions until the present day, the presence of a fireplace in prestigious halls and a hearth in the kitchen was common. Both solutions have provided warmth, energy for preparing warm meals and – at least to some degree – lighting during the dark hours of the day. But there is rarely fire without smoke. On the one hand, smoke can be used for the conservation of food, esp. meat or grain; on the other hand this smoke is poisonous.

Until chimneys became common, smoke more or less freely streamed through all of the house protecting the wooden construction from vermin, but also causing dirt and disease, problems which are evident in developing countries still today (Ryhl-Svendsen et al. 2010; Skov & Fenger 2008; Skov et al. 2000). The easiest solution for dealing with smoke accumulating within the house is to build a chimney which leads the smoke out of house directly. But a chimney has two major disadvantages. Firstly, warmth disappears with the smoke; secondly, an effective chimney tends to pull sparks from the fire onto the own roof or that of the neighbour. The best way to prevent a fire from smoking and sparking is to enclose the flames completely which is addressed in technical kilns which feature a clay cupola. It is possible that the baking oven forms a missing link between kilns and more sophisticated heating systems. If the oven is run as a breechloader, *ie* fired from the adjacent room – usually the kitchen – where a funnel gathers the smoke, the step to a smoke-free heated living room is achieved. In this paper, the German word 'stube' will be used hereafter to refer to this kind of smoke-free heated living room, in the absence of an equivalent English term.

Two more refined systems provide a better solution for a smoke-free heated living room, which are also discussed in this paper: subfloor convection air heating in ancient construction traditions, and the tile-stove consisting of a clay body with inserted ceramic tiles constructed and fired as a breechloader (Bingenheimer 1998; Roth-Heege 2012: 22-35). Until today, the economic and ecological use of energy resources is a central question in society. Against this background, the Archaeology Section of Aarhus University is currently engaged in a research project entitled 'Housing Culture Between Climatic and Social Challenges in Medieval and Early Modern Europe' which beyond others explores the role of such stoves in heating the European house.

Subfloor convection air heating

This system is the oldest medieval form of smoke-free heating in Europe. Although styles varied as far as construction is concerned, the basic principle was

similar to the late 14th-century example discovered in the Bishop's castle at Forchheim in 1996 (Figure 1). The space under the floor of the room was either filled with stones, or by empty air channels, and heated by convection. A separate burning chamber, usually fired from a working place in the cellar or beyond the building, provides the heating core of this system. The stones or the walls of the channels respectively are heated by the fire in the burning chamber and act as a convection mass. After having been heated, they emit their energy to fresh, smoke-free air, which is then channelled into the room to be heated using outlets in the floor or in the walls. Elaborate systems dissipate the smoke from the fire through a chimney from the burning chamber out of the building, allowing these models to be fired permanently. In this case a thin but gas-proof wall that works as a heat-exchanger separates the fire from the convection mass. The earliest example is known from the castle Runneburg in Thuringia (Bingenheimer 1998: 133). Simpler systems like the one in Forchheim (Kohnert 2008) have to be run in two different phases for firing and for heating. In the first phase (Figure 1a), smoke and warmth is delivered directly through the convectional space while the outlets must be closed. In the second phase (Figure 1b), after the fire has been extinguished and the burning chamber cleaned, the outlets are opened and fresh air streams through the empty burning chamber and the convectional space heated into the room. An air convection heating system is easy to detect archaeologically, either through the identification of the characteristic remains of the fire chamber in the basement, outlets in the floor and even fragments of their closing lids. So far, about 500 systems have been identified in Central Europe, but this is probably only the tip of the iceberg (Bingenheimer 1998).

According to Bingenheimer's study, the air convection heating system is not to be regarded as a misunderstood or simplified medieval imitation of ancient Roman hypocaust, but rather represents a further stage in the development of this ancient technology; an antique example was discovered on the castellum Saalburg (1st century AD) by Jacobi (Jacobi & Cohausen 1897: Fig. 37). This special version of a hypocaust could be run as 'conventional' hypocaust

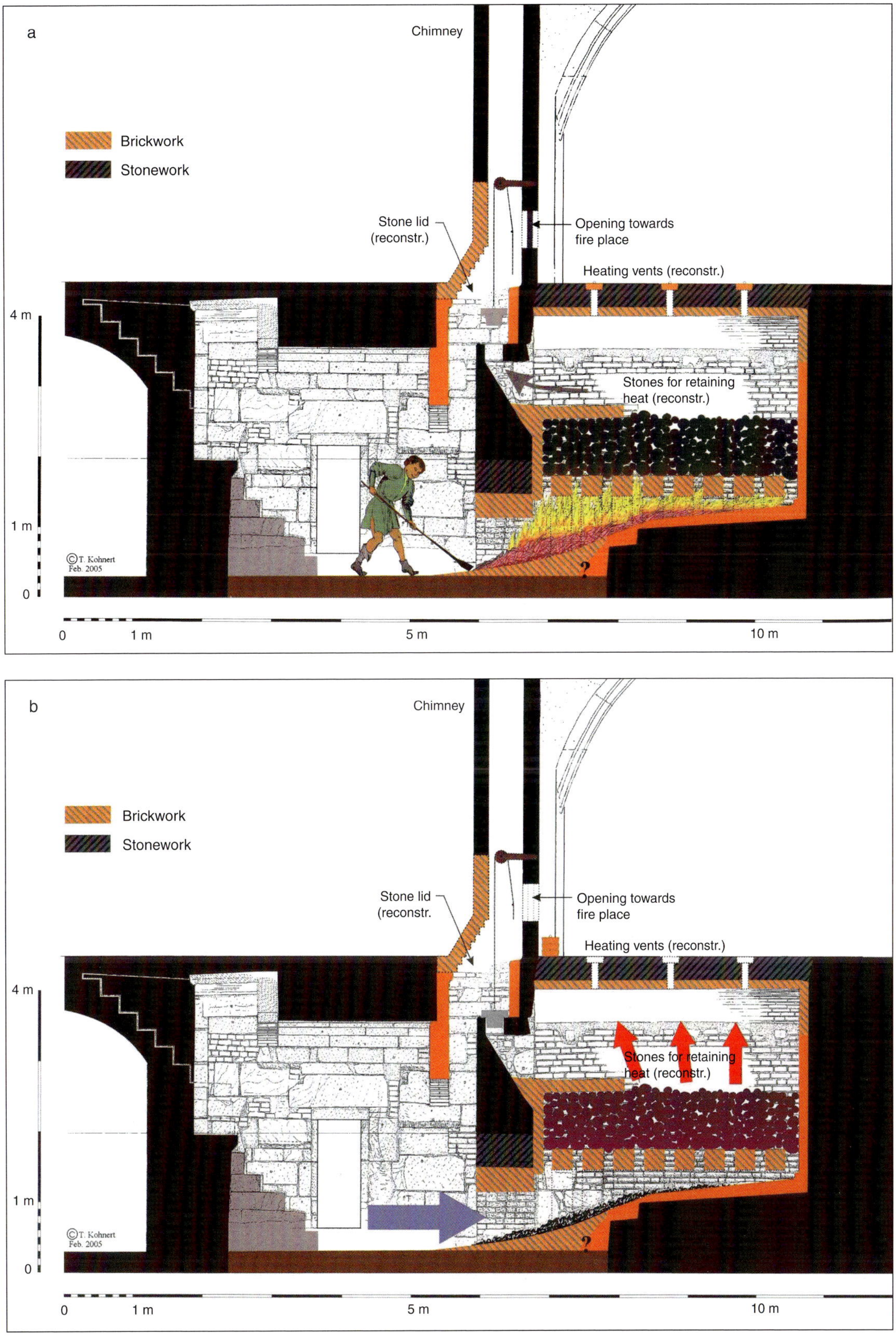
a
Chimney
Brickwork
Stonework
Stone lid
(reconstr.)
Opening towards
fire place
Heating vents (reconstr.)
Stones for retaining
heat (reconstr.)
4 m
1 m
0
©T. Kohnert
Feb. 2005
0
1 m
5 m
10 m
b
Chimney
Brickwork
Stonework
Stone lid
(reconstr.
Opening towards
fire place
Heating vents (reconstr.)
Stones for retaining
heat (reconstr.)
4 m
1 m
0
©T. Kohnert
Feb. 2005
0
1 m
5 m
10 m

Figure 1. Subfloor convection air heating, bishop's castle in Forchheim. a. the burning chamber heats the convection mass; b. fresh air streaming through the hot convection mass is heating the hall. After Kohnert 2008: 62-63.

with heated smoke streaming under the floor and through tubuli in the walls. A lateral opening in the wall and outlets into the rooms also facilitated its use in the medieval, indirect way after the fire had been extinguished. The structural difference between this ancient form of construction and its medieval successors was principally the lack of pillars made of flat tegula plates in the latter examples. Early medieval examples are shown on the St. Gall Monastery plan – drawn probably on the island Reichenau between 825 and 830 AD (Hecht 1983; Jacobsen 2002; online-version in high resolution: Frischer & Geary 2012). Several rooms were warmed by hypocausts here, whereas the majority of rooms were heated by simple hearths and fireplaces, mostly positioned in the corner of a room and frequently using a common chimney with an adjacent one in the next room as shown, for example, in the *'mansio abbatis'*. The building to the southeast of the church is heated by an air convection heating system, whose separate chimney is drawn and marked as *'evaporatio fumi'* on the plan. Until recently, this has been thought to be one of the earliest known examples of medieval air convection heating (Bingenheimer 1998: 46-53). The excavations on Reichenau – as the archetype for the plan – have discovered heating channels under the dormitory, too. In monastic contexts, smoke-free heating was primarily important for the work performed in the scriptorium and for the assemblies in the chapter house. In addition, this warm room also heated the dormitory above – as is indicated on the St. Gall plan *'subtus calefactoria domus/supra dormitorium'* (Sennhauser 1996: 296-298; Zettler 1988: 262f). In Cistercian monasteries, the calefactorium was usually the only heated room, mostly situated close to the refectory in the southern wing of a cloister. Most of these monastic calefactoria were warmed by an air convection heating (Binding & Untermann 1985: 61, 207). Apart from monasteries, further early examples are situated in representative ecclesiastical

Figure 2. Hypocaust heating palatium, Tilleda.

buildings, such as that in the Bishop's house at the cathedral castle in Minden, built around 1000 AD (Peine 2001: 43).

It seems likely that noble families became familiar with this technique whilst visiting their relatives living in a monastery or a convent – and became eager to use this comfortable way of heating in their own homes. It is not surprising to see the earliest secular examples under buildings on imperial castles in Quedlinburg, Werla and Tilleda in the 10th and 11th century AD. They belong to the older type of the hot air channelling system with a burning chamber on the outside of the building, primarily acting as heating for the assembly hall (Figure 2). In the 12th century, the later type with a stone filled camera as convection mass under the room to be heated was erected at the imperial castle in Goslar and at the ducal castle Dankwarderode in Brunswick (Bingenheimer 1998: 27-197; Dapper 2007; Feld 2006: 102). The construction principle is very similar to heating in bathrooms or houses, such as the castle Schlössel (Barz 2008; Tuchen 2001: 196).

This type of heating spread until the 14th century throughout Central Europe. It was not restricted to large halls and also came into use as heating for the lord's apartment at the castle of Rochlitz. Here, the Prince of Saxony installed an elaborate heating system in his private rooms around 1400 (Figure 3): In the corner of the complex, from the Querhaus to the Fürstenhaus, a subfloor heating with a burning chamber in the cellar and outlets in the first floor, was built. Its smoke was delivered through the wall into the adjacent room, where some type of tile stove as a reservoir for its warmth might have been positioned. This made it possible to warm at least two rooms with one source of heating (Reuther 2003; 2009). During the first (firing) phase, the tile stove was heated by the smoke from the burning chamber; during the second (convectional) phase, the room upon the hypocaust was heated through the outlets. Similar combinations of tile stove and air convection heating are known from the Castle of Marburg, Hesse, and from the Castle Neuenburg in Sachsen-Anhalt (Roth Heege et al. 2004; Schmitt 2007: 70; 2012: 106-108).

Bingenheimer (1998) has suggested that air convection heating was characteristic in the region

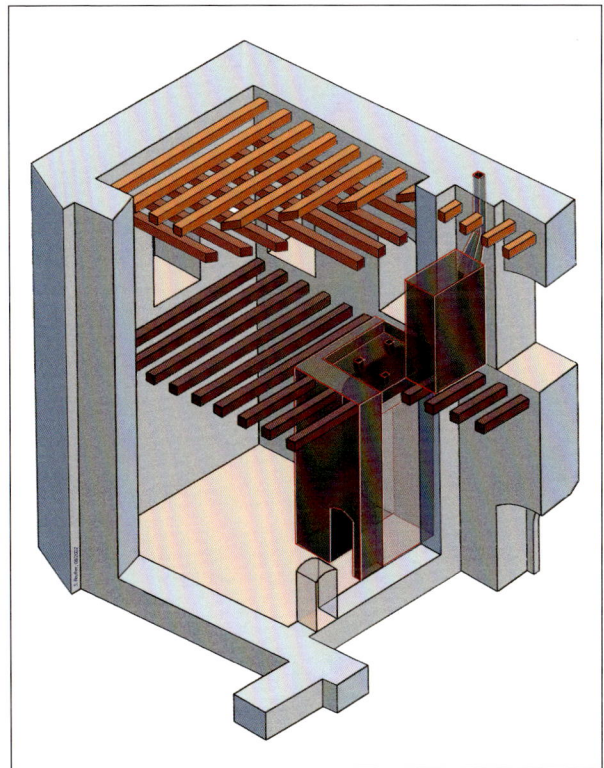

Figure 3. Hypocaust /tile stove hybrid on castle Rochlitz. After Reuter 2003: 117.

around the Baltic Sea, especially for dominions associated with the Teutonic Order. Indeed, nearly every Teutonic Order castle appears to have had such a heating system, but this may simply reflect the state of current research. The castles of the Teutonic Order have been in the focus of research for about 200 years (Biller 2001), and were used for early experimental archaeology. In 1822, Voß and Gersdorff commenced work on a remarkable experiment to heat the Winterremter, the winter refectory hall at the Teutonic Order's castle of Marienburg in Western Prussia. The Winterremter was built after 1310 and was equipped with a well-preserved subfloor air convection heating. Voß and Gersdorff fired this heating system and took measurements of the temperatures in the Winterremter. The air volume of this hall is about 9.100 m³. In the beginning of this tremendous experiment, the outer temperature was about 2.5 centigrade, the inner about 6.3 centigrade. The air streaming out of the outlets into the hall reached about 200 centigrade and heated the room air within

20 minutes up to 22.5 centigrade. By the next morning, the room had cooled down to 13.8 centigrade, but it was possible to reheat the room again up to 19 centigrade – simply by opening the outlets for one hour and without additional fire. The air streaming out still maintained a temperature of 147 centigrade – and even six days later, 46 centigrade (Ring 2001: 32; Voß & Gersdorff 1830). This experiment is a clear proof that a convectional air heating system does not provide only 'warm air', but is to be regarded as a highly efficient type of heating.

The Spanish traveller Pero Tafur described the importance of this heating system in Breslau during his travel through Central Europe in 1438. Evidently, he was not familiar with this kind of heating, because the ancient hypocaust system fell out of use on the Iberian Peninsula in the Early Middle Ages: "The country is […] cold. The chimneys and stoves do not give sufficient warmth; but there is another kind of stove for heating which they use. They make a fire beneath an upstairs room, and in the floor are covered holes, and they place seats above, also with holes in them. The people then sit down on those seats and unstop the holes and the heat rises between the legs to each one." (Tafur 1926: chapt. XXVI).

All known examples of air convection heating belong to upper social contexts such as monasteries, castles or patrician urban houses as examples from Uelzen, Lübeck und Lüneburg attest (Mahler 2001; Meyer 1989; Ring 2001). Evidently, this efficient and widespread heating system was still in use until the 16th century, such as the well-known example in Lüneburg townhall. The heating in the monastery Lüne, which was built in 1497, was renewed in 1663 and only stopped being used at the 17th century. In the monastery at Ebstorf the late medieval construction was renewed in 1671 before being finally replaced by a tile stove heating in 1689 (Ring 2001: 29-31). It is unclear why this system fell out of use. It is possible that it was found impractical to run a heating system from a distant room in the cellar. Moreover, it was easy to heat the room directly above the burning chamber, but it was growing difficult to warm remote rooms using funnels as at the castle of Rochlitz. Indeed, no air convection system is known with the burning chamber situated in an upper storey. This solution would have been not only structurally difficult, but – bearing in mind the danger of fire – it would have been possible only in stone buildings.

The tile stove

The second way to heat a room smoke-free is provided by the tile stove. Its body is made of clay, which serves as storage for warmth, whereas the integrated ceramic tiles are able quickly to conduct the heat into the room. This combination allows a room not only to be heated relatively quickly, but also for a longer period. In contrast to the open hearth which provides considerable but concentrated source of heat in a small radius around the fire, a tile stove produces a constant radiant heat. Once fired it warms a room for about 24 hours. The 'classical' tile stove is mostly run as a breechloader. This keeps the stube free of smoke. Basically, a breechloader can be serviced from each adjacent room or passage, but the most efficient combination is with the hearth to the rear, which makes it possible to preserve the embers after preparing meals safely. This efficiency is the core of a new concept of living in the late medieval house: the dwelling is differentiated into two adjacent rooms: the stube and the kitchen. A chimney is not necessary, the smoke might either stream free through the house, frequently the staircase is built close to the kitchen for that reason – or it is directed through a smoke stack into the roof. On its way, the smoke can be used to fumigate meat, fish or other foodstuffs.

The etymology of 'stube', 'stue' and 'dornse'

In philological research, the German word 'Stube', Danish 'stue' or English 'stove' (medieval latin: 'estuarium') was traditionally seen as closely related to a construed, but not recorded latin verb 'extufare', 'tufus' (= damp) which is interpreted as a clue to its relationship to 'bath' or 'bath room'. According to Joachim Hähnel's etymological study (1975), the word 'stube' in the context of 'living room' has been documented since the 10th century, an even earlier

Figure 4. Reconstruction of a Slavic smoke oven, Wollin. Photo Katrin Atzbach

record is known from Chur in 765 AD. Its use in the context of 'bath' does not appear before the 13th century – and might derive from the use of similar kind of heating in living room and bathroom. Hence, Hähnel reconstructs an origin in the Upper German speaking area from the word stem 'stubbe' (German), similar to 'stub' (Danish), which signifies a stub (preserving in English the same root) of a tree or a container made of wood, also used as an expression for a fire-retaining vessel – which still survives in English as 'stove' or German 'Stövchen' (= burner or rechaud). The common origin is the wooden, encapsulated construction in the house, known from the earliest upright preserved stube constructions in the zone Northern to the Alps (see below). Derivations of the term 'stube' are used throughout Germany, Northern Europe and England (Hähnel 1975: 328-333, 412-417).

Apart from the 'estuarium', which appears as a latinized version of 'stube' in 1170 (Helmold von Bosau), in the Low German language area and Southern Denmark, a second root is also in use. Variations on the word 'dornse', 'dorntze' are documented since 1270 (Halle an der Saale). The variation 'thürnitz', 'turniza' or 'Dürnitz' is documented since the 11th century in Southeastern Germany. Both versions are derived from the same Slavic root of uncertain ori-

gin used in the Slavic languages alongside the loan word 'izba', which again derives directly from 'stuba'. 'Dornse' primarily names heated living rooms in the area of the Hanseatic league between North Sea and Russia, whereas 'Dürnitz' is used as a synonym for 'Hofstube', *ie* a representative, heated hall on the ground floor in a castle (Hähnel 1975: 333-343).

Archaeological evidence for the 'stube'

In general, Europe is divided into a Western part with a mild climate consisting of Spain, England, France and Italy, which is dominated by fireplaces and hearths, and the Central and Eastern part from Switzerland to Russia, where several types of oven heating are in use (Figure 4). Eastern France, the BeNeLux-countries, Northern Germany and Scandinavia are a cross-over area, where the tile stove was adopted or transformed in the late medieval and post-medieval period (Stelze-Hüglin 1999: 12-44).

The use of oven heaters has a long tradition in Europe. In the Western Slavic area, stone and clay ovens have been known since the very beginning of the Slavic settlement in the late 6th-7th century, usually they were placed in a corner of the house

(Brather 2001: 99-101). Future research within the framework of the research project "Housing Culture" will explore the connection between these Slavic ovens and the Southern Scandinavian smoke ovens with clay cupolas. Both traditions used ovens serviced from inside the house. The earliest example of a Scandinavian smoke oven was documented at Hedeby, dendrochronologically dated in 870/882 AD, and Hedeby was situated in the transition zone between Danes, Slaves and Germans fostering the transmission of ideas and techniques between Central Europe and Scandinavia (Jankuhn 1986; Roesdahl 2009: 277-79). The Scandinavian smoke oven could also be run as a breechloader, as an example from Viborg proves which was fired from an adjacent room providing a smoke-free heated living room in the 12th century (Roesdahl 2004: 86-88). However, these ovens are constructed without tiles. The Slavic clay oven heating perhaps came in contact with Roman construction knowledge in the Alpine Zone. In late ancient Roman vaults in buildings, but also in kilns, ceramic vessels plugged into each other formed the wall. The earliest written source mentioning this kind of kiln made hundreds of 'caccabos' and placed 'in pisile' (MGH LL 1868: 179) derives from the Langobard kingdom in the 8th century. This pottery-based vaulting technique has been delivered in the circum-Alpine region until the Middle Ages, as an example of a pottery kiln in Winterthur, Switzerland, of the 14th century also demonstrates (Roth Kaufmann 1997: 473; Stelze-Hüglin 2004: 320), a similar constructed pottery kiln was recently excavated in Cottbus, dated into the 15th century (Wacker 2012: 325f). It is only a short step from these pottery vaulted kilns to a tile stove, thus the connection between both types is probable.

The earliest ceramic vessels which could be interpreted as beaker tiles – or as vaulting pottery – have been found in Alsace. They are dated into the early 8th century, while further findings from Northwest Switzerland and the Middle Neckar region belong into the 9th century (Roth Kaufmann 1997: 475; Stelze-Hüglin 2004: 325). Their cylindrical beaker shape typologically differs slightly from the well-known later examples of the 10th and 11th century, which were part of the oldest reliable tile stove

context from the castle Runder Berg close to Urach, Baden-Württemberg. On the castle of Frohburg, Kanton Solothurn in Switzerland, a tile stove with similar beaker tiles was excavated. It has been dated into the late 11th century (Kluge-Pinsker 1992: 215f). Both sites show the developed concept of two combined rooms, probably the one serving as a stube, the other as a kitchen. This is the earliest form of the medieval ground plan of houses in the Upper German speaking region. Apart from dislocated tiles, the first known urban tile stove in situ probably was a part of a similar ground plan in Winterthur, it was found in the remainder of a wooden building dendrochronologically dated from 1208 (Matter & Wild 1997: 79). Nevertheless, not every early tile stove was operated as a breechloader from the adjacent room: the earliest pictorial sources – in the Würzburg Psalter (1250/59) and on the wall painting in Rindermarkt 26, Zürich (dated to the early 14th century) – show openings on the front and thus some early tile stoves might have worked as a smoke oven at least until the early 14th century and possibly later (Stelze-Hüglin 2004: 322; Tauber 1980: 361).

In contrast to an air convection heating system that must be placed under the room to be heated, a tile stove widely is independent of subconstructions under the floor, apart from trimmed joists supporting the burden of the clay body and tiles. Thus, a tile stove can be lodged not only in the basement, but also in upper storeys. Apart from remains of the furnace itself, relics of the stube construction are the most important indicator for this heating system. Even in stone buildings, the earliest examples are erected as a wooden 'box' made of spruce wood, usually in a log construction between four corner posts. Since the 14th century, the outer face has been plastered with clay held by wooden pegs on the log surface (Bedal 2002). This box was mostly covered by a differentiated suspended beam and panelled ceiling, known as a 'Spunddecke' or 'Bohlen-Balken-Decke' in German. This construction forms a closed space above – under the floor of the next storey. This void primarily has an insulating function, but also can be filled with straw or simply rubbish. Although the earliest-preserved constructions were found in Regensburg and are dated from the 13th century (see below), the centre of this innovation is located in the Alps and in Suebia (Furrer 2002). It therefore seems likely that the construction of suspended ceilings or beam and panel floors with an additional board covering began in the 13th century in the Alps and spread, together with the innovation of the stube from there throughout Central Europe.

The oldest upright preserved examples of a stube have been detected in Untere Bachgasse 6 (dendrochronologically dated to 1264) and Wahlenstraße 8 (dendrochronologically dated to 1307), both located in Regensburg, Bavaria (Bedal 2002: 13; Kirchner 1988). Their ground plan corresponds to that of the oldest farmhouse in Southern Germany, the House from Höfstetten, built in 1368. Bedal coined the expression 'neunfaches Grundrissraster' (= ninefold ground plan), which is defined by three aisles and three bays. The stube usually is located in a corner of the first bay, sharing a wall with the kitchen, which either is placed in the adjacent aisle or in the central bay. This central bay works as traffic zone and gives access to all rooms. In multi-storey buildings, the staircase also is positioned here (Figure 5) (Bedal 1987: 44f).

The spread of the stube and the 'ninefold ground plan'

The stube as log construction is spread between Alsace, Switzerland, Tyrol, Bohemia, Bavaria, Suebia, Eastern Franconia, Thuringia, Sachsen-Anhalt and Saxony (Bedal 2002: 13-15). Since the 14th century, variations of the characteristic ninefold ground plan are common in Southern Germany, sometimes reducing the scheme to two aisles in three bays, *eg* in Geislingen an der Steige, Suebia (Cramer 1988: 356). In the Eastern part of Upper Bavaria, Keim has detected houses with a similar ground plan, but they were heated with a smoke oven until the 16th century (Keim 2002: 70f). Evidently, the concept of a smoke-free heated living room was invented before the 13th century and spread from the Alpine zone in all directions. In the Grand Est of France, the combination of kitchen and adjacent stube (French: 'poêle') was introduced starting in the Alsace before the 15th

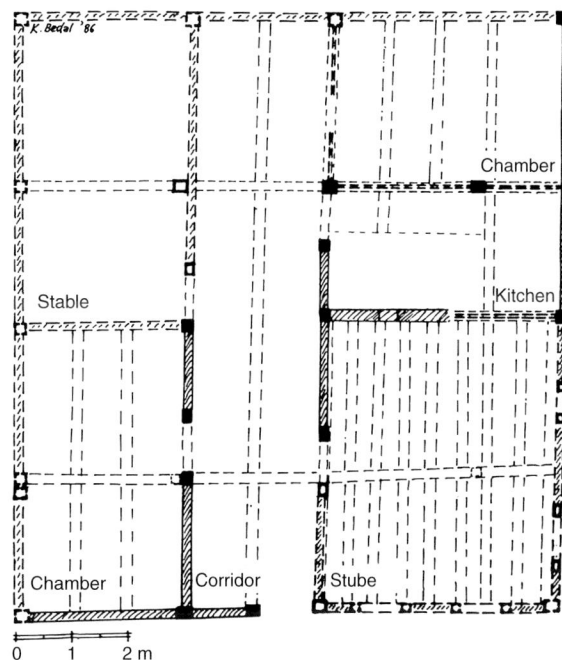

Figure 5. Ninefold ground plan. After Bedal 1987: 37.

century. It spread into Burgundy, Lorraine and Dauphiné by the 19th century. In contrast to the Alsace, the poêle does not work as an ordinary, everyday living room, but is used only during winter (Trochet 2006: 493-506).

The dissemination of the ninefold ground plan towards the North progressed slowly, although the tile stove heating itself had already reached the Baltic Sea in the 12th century (Hofmann & Schneider 2001). The Lower Mountain Range Zone did not take part in this ground plan development before the end of Middle Ages. In this area, medieval houses followed a different plan: the so-called Gothic hall house. In Limburg, Hesse, a group of late medieval citizens' houses have been preserved. The house Kolpingstraße 6/Bergstraße 7 was built in 1291. Originally, the ground floor and the first floor were timbered as a single storey structure, *ie* in high post construction (German: 'Ständergeschossbau'). The first two zones toward the street were filled by a great hall, while the last zone contained two sub-storeys, the lower one probably containing the stube. The hearth was situated in the great hall, while the staircase was located in front of the third zone and also worked as a funnel. The upper floor the house was subdivided into three bays, the central one probably with an opening into the roof (Altwasser et al. 1997: 61-115). This ground plan unites an older concept of living, the open hall with a hearth, and a differentiated concept consisting of three zones on the upper storey. We have no examples of older preserved standing urban or rural buildings in the Lower Mountain Range Zone, but excavations in Hesse have proven the existence of buildings that consisted only of one single room until the late 12th century, even in an upper social context, such as the manor house of Holzheim, close to Fritzlar, and the site of 'Krutzen' in Frankfurt am Main (Dohrn-Ihmig 1996: 66-76; Wand 2000: 90f). The subdivision of the upper floor into three zones is, however, known from imperial or baronial castles of the second half of the 12th century like the Pfalz Gelnhausen or the Wartburg castle (Großmann 2010). Further research is required to explore whether these upper class buildings either followed an older building tradition in the circum-Alpine region or represent the origin of this ground plan themselves.

What was probably an older concept of living in a big hall was common in the region between the Lower Mountain Range and Schleswig, known as the region of the 'Niederdeutsches Hallenhaus'. This derives from the longhouse of the 11th century that consisted of a hall with a central hearth and also accommodated livestock – usually in the lateral aisles (Reichmann 1991, Zimmermann 2002). Before the 15th century, a new development occurred. The ground plan was enlarged by an additional zone at the gabled end with the fireplace, the 'Kammerfach' (= chamber's partition). Frequently this zone is erected on a low cellar, and it is containing an 'upkammer', a stube with a tile stove adjacent to the kitchen zone and side chamber (Stiewe 2007: 73, 101).

In urban context, the Niederdeutsches Hallenhaus is built in a reduced version, the 'Dielenhaus'. Originally a big hall without compartments, in the 13th century, the Stube was constructed as a small, built-in room at the gabled end towards the street. This way of constructing compartments in the hall remained common until the end of the Middle Ages and thereafter. Like the 'Kammerfach' of the rural Hallenhaus, the stube could fill the whole width of

the house to the rear. These compartments may be heated by an air convection heating or a tile stove. In Lüneburg a house of the late 16th century was planned originally to be heated with a convection heating but was altered to accommodate a tile stove heating system during construction (Ring 2001: Abb. 2, Abb. 12).

Denmark was not reached until the 16th century by the differentiated ground plan concept consisting of a stube with a tile stove and adjacent kitchen and a central corridor as a traffic zone, which can be regarded as an adaptation of the ninefold ground plan (Danish: 'midtforstueplan') (Krongaard Kristensen 2004: 78f) . The earliest tiles are known from finds of the 13th century at the monastery of Sorø (Kristiansen 2008: 245-247). The medieval ground plan of Danish houses can be characterized as a linear scheme: since the 10th-11th century a house consists of a row of rooms, each one as wide as the house. The central room, the 'stue', is heated by a hearth, but in the late medieval period smaller, unheated annexes were added. Since the second half of the 16th century this linear scheme was differentiated: a corridor (named with the German word 'Diele') gave access to the group of 'dørns' (Stube) and adjacent kitchen at the front, and the 'pisel', a high status room with a hearth at the rear, in the tradition of the older 'stue' (Krongaard Kristensen 2004: 77f, Svart Kristiansen 2008: 117). The Northern part of Jutland seems to be reached not before the last decades of the 16th century, as the rebuilding of Vestergågade 9 in Aalborg shows in 1580 (Engqvist 1976: 185).

Archaeological witness for the process of innovation

The existence of a stube is unambiguously connected to stove tiles, *ie* a find of used tiles that show traces of smoke on the rear side clearly mark the former existence of a tile stove, whereas the find of unused tiles clearly mark the workshop of a stove maker and his kiln. Thus, it is possible to study the diffusion process of this innovation in the distribution of excavated tile deposits. Although the typological and chronological development of stove tiles has not yet

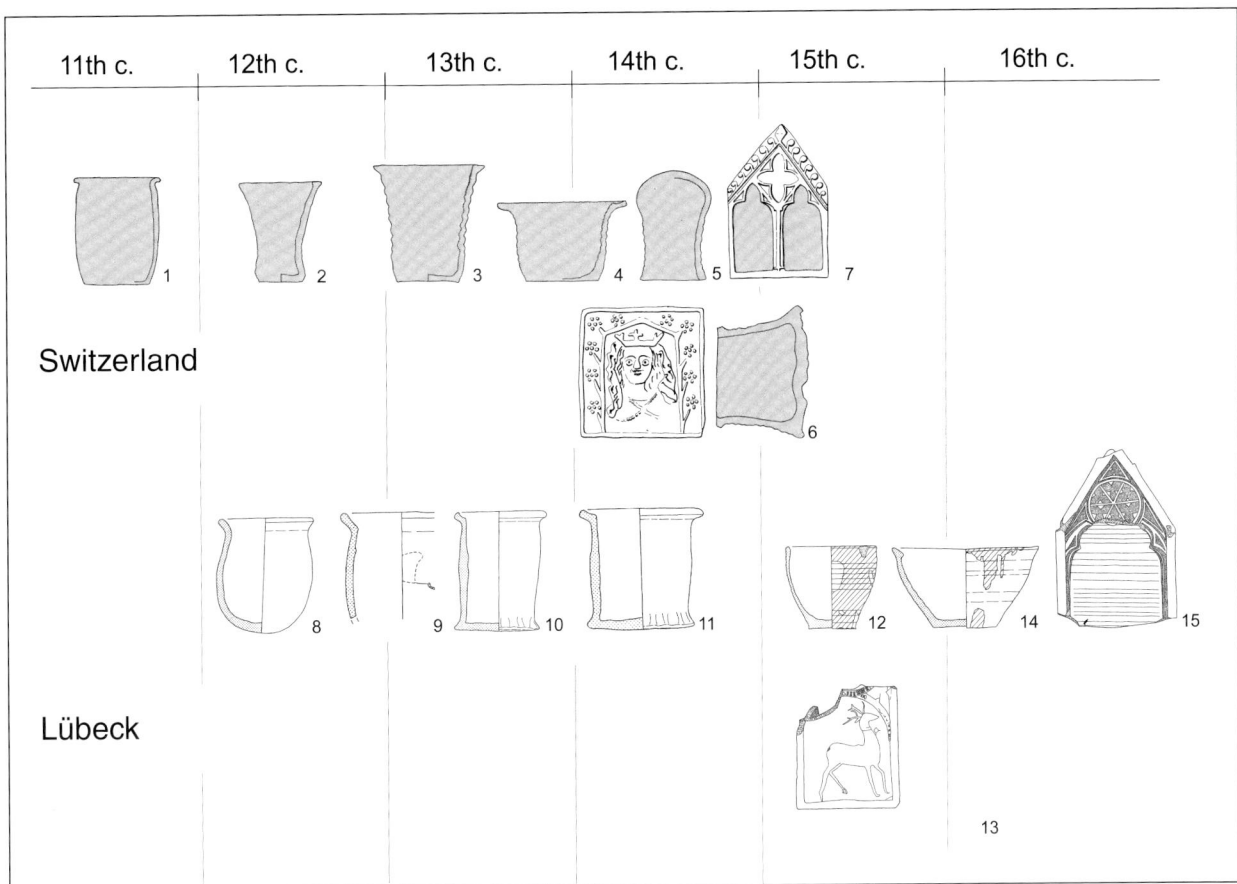

Figure 6. Typological development of tiles in Switzerland and Lübeck. Graph Katrin Atzbach, vignettes after Tauber 1980: 210 and Falk 2001: 67.

been established for all regions, several monographs describe its main features between Alps and North Sea. Franz (1969) and Liebgott (1972) have published systematic overviews from the art-historian point of view, Tauber's study (1980) put the focus on the Swiss tiles, Stelze-Hüglin (1999, summary 2004) published the material in the adjoined German region and Alsace, Harald Rosmanitz is working on his doctoral thesis about the southern Lower Mountain Range area. Hallenkamp-Lumpe (2006) and Henkel (1999) covered Westfalia and Hildesheim in Southern Lower Saxony. Hofmann and Schneider's congress transactions (2001) truss short studies on Lüneburg, Lübeck, Stralsund and the Baltic Sea area, Kristiansen's publications are an important contribution on the Danish material (2008 with further references).

The basic lines of development are very similar (Figure 6). In Switzerland, the typology starts with beaker types of the late 11th century until the 13th century (Figure 6: 1-3), over dish-shaped vessel tiles of the 13th-14th century (Figure 6: 4). A very important, innovative step is visible in the appearance of the 'mushroom' tile in the 14th century (Figure 6: 5). It represents the fundamental turning inside-out of the vessel base towards the face of the tile stove. This change enables to apply moulds on the base and transforms a bare heating system into a decorative room feature. It is only a short step from moulded mushroom tiles to panel tiles (Figure 6: 6), which was achieved in the 14th century. The composite niche-tiles as last step and most complex product in this development appear by the 14th century (Figure 6: 7) in Switzerland (Tauber 1980: 341f).

In the Lower Mountain Range area, conical vessel tiles mark the beginning of the development in the late 12th century; the western region close to the Rhineland seems to prefer niche tiles, whereas the eastern area uses dish-shaped vessel tiles in the 14th century before both regions adopted panel tiles (Hallenkamp-Lumpe 2006).

In Lübeck, a flourishing city with widespread trade contacts, tile stoves evidently came into use in the 12th century (Figure 6: 8). Here, the Swiss pattern of evolution is repeated in an abbreviated development which omits the 'mushroom tile' from beaker tiles (Figure 6: 8-11) over dish-shaped vessel tiles (Figure 6: 12, 14). The first panel tiles appear in the 15th century (Figure 6: 13). Finally, niche tiles (Figure 6: 15) are known in the 16th century (Falk 2001). Denmark followed a hundred years later, starting with Kugeltopf-shaped beaker tiles in the 13th century until the 14th century. Dish-shaped vessel tiles have been known since the 15th century, which is the moment when Danish developments appear to parallel those in Lübeck (Kristiansen 2008).

Consequently, the tile stove as a comfortable and economic heating system spread within a hundred years in the zone between Alps and Baltic Sea. Not surprisingly, this innovation was first apparently used by the upper classes in monasteries and on castles, trickling down by the late Middle Ages to urban and rural houses. The interesting aspect is, in how far the connected ninefold ground plan was also diffused. This house structure started in the 12th or 13th century in the Upper German speaking region and it reached the urban buildings in the Lower Mountain Range zone between the 13th and 16th century. The Northern Region soon was adopting the heating system, but it took until the end of the Middle Ages to start the adaptation of the ninefold ground plan ('midtforstueplan'). So, evidently, the system of heating is one, but not the only key to the explanation of a social system of a house.

Conclusion

This paper has suggested that the layout of a house and its ground plan not only reflects practical needs, such as the creation of a heated comfort zone for daily work and life, close to the kitchen providing warm food. Symbolic and traditional values determine the sequence of rooms and access routes within

and between them. Hierarchical divisions could be created in traditional forms of common living rooms used for cooking, preparing meal and daily living. However, the position of the stube and its separation by a corridor that enabled access to the majority of rooms without crossing or entering the living room could facilitate the creation of more formalised degrees of privacy and expressions of hierarchy. The tile stove heating was more appropriate to such a subdivided use of a house than the older subfloor heating, which was quite efficient, but rather inflexible. The use of a more differentiated ground plan afforded inhabitants the opportunity of controlling who could, and who could not, enter this smoke-free heated, comfortable room. Future research will seek to examine how this new heating system was technically implemented and transformed, why it fell out of use in the early modern period, where and why the ninefold ground plan was overtaken. Last but not least, it will seek to explore who was responsible for this process of innovation and its wider meanings.

Acknowledgements

I would like to express my thanks to Roman Grabolle M.A., who has permitted me to use his unpublished paper on heating systems at castles held on the congress "Die Burg" on the Wartburg castle in 2010. Moreover I would like to thank Elizabeth Jill Archer who revised my English text.

References

Altwasser, E. et. al (1997) *Die Limburger Fachwerkbauten des 13. Jahrhunderts.* Limburg: Der Magistrat.

Barz, D. (2008) Schlössel bei Klingenmünster. Befunde und Funde einer salierzeitlichen Burg, *Mitteilungen der Deutschen Gesellschaft für Archäologie des Mittelalters und der Neuzeit* 20, 189-196.

Bedal, K. (2002) Bohlenstuben in Süddeutschland. Bemerkungen zum Forschungsstand, *Hausbau im Alpenraum = Jahrbuch für Hausforschung* 51, 12-27.

Bedal, K. et al. (1987) *Ein Bauernhaus aus dem Mittelalter.* Schriften des Fränkischen Freilandmuseums Bad Windsheim 9. Bad Windsheim: Fränkisches Freilandmuseum.

Biller, Th. (2001) *Burgen geistlicher Bauherren.* München: Deutscher Kunstverlag.

Binding, G. & M. Untermann (1985) *Kleine Kunstgeschich-*

te der mittelalterlichen Ordensbaukunst in Deutschland. Darmstadt: Wissenschaftliche Buchgesellschaft.

Bingenheimer, K. (1998) *Die Luftheizungen des Mittelalters. Zur Typologie und Entwicklung eines technikgeschichtlichen Phänomens.* Hamburg: Kovac.

Brather, S. (2001) *Archäologie der westlichen Slawen. Siedlung, Wirtschaft und Gesellschaft im früh- und hochmittelalterlichen Ostmitteleuropa.* Ergänzungsband zum Reallexikon der Germanischen Altertumskunde 30. Berlin/New York: Walter de Gruyter.

Cramer, J. (1988) Ein mittelalterliches Gerberhaus in Geislingen. In: *Hausbau im Mittelalter III.. Jahrbuch für Hausforschung Sonderband*, ed. K. Bedal, 347-362. Bad Sobernheim: Arbeitskreis für Hausforschung.

Dapper, M. (2007) Die Neuinterpretation der Grabungsergebnisse auf der Pfalz Tilleda. In: *Zentren herrschaftlicher Repräsentation im Hochmittelalter*, ed. C. Ehlers, 151-169. Deutsche Königspfalzen 7. Göttingen: Vandenhoeck und Ruprecht.

Dohrn-Ihmig, M. (1996) *Die früh- bis spätmittelalterliche Siedlung und Kirchenwüstung „Krutzen" im Kalbacher Feld, Stadt Frankfurt am Main.* Materialien zur Vor- und Frühgeschichte von Hessen 16. Wiesbaden: Landesamt für Denkmalpflege Hessen.

Engqvist, H.H. (1976) Über die Gestaltung und Disposition des Bürgerhauses in Dänemark um 1500. In: *Häuser und Höfe der handeltreibenden Bevölkerung im Ostseegebiet und im Norden vor 1500*, ed. G. Svahnström, 173-190. Visby: Museum Gotlands Fornsal.

Feld, I. (2006) Zur Frage der Beheizung auf mittelalterlichen Burgen. In: *Alltag auf Burgen im Mittelalter*, ed. J. Zeune, 100-107. Veröffentlichungen der Deutschen Burgenvereinigung B 10. Braubach: Deutsche Burgenvereinigung.

Falk, A. (2001) Hoch- und spätmittelalterliche Ofenkeramik in Lübeck. In: *Von der Feuerstelle zum Kachelofen; Heizanlagen und Ofenkeramik vom Mittelalter bis zur Neuzeit*, eds. C. Hofmann & M. Schneider, 64-78. Stralsunder Beiträge zur Archäologie, Geschichte, Kunst und Volkskunde in Vorpommern 3. Stralsund: Kulturhistorisches Museum.

Frischer, B. & P. Geary (2012) *The Plan of St. Gall, Carolingian Culture at Reichenau & St. Gall.* Los Angeles: University of California Los Angeles: http://www.stgallplan.org/en/index_plan.html (visited 2.1.2013).

Franz, R. (1969) *Der Kachelofen. Entstehung und kunstgeschichtliche Entwicklung vom Mittelalter bis zum Ausgang des Klassizismus.* Forschungen und Berichte Kunsthistorisches Institut Universität Graz 1. Graz: Akademische Druck- und Verlagsanstalt.

Furrer, B. (2002) Bohlen- und Bohlen-Balken-Decken in Bauernhäusern der Voralpen und Alpen, *Hausbau im Alpenraum = Jahrbuch für Hausforschung* 51, 29-38.

Großmann, G.U. (2010) Wohnräume im Burgenbau des 12. und 13. Jahrhunderts. In: *Die Burg*, eds. G.U. Großmann & H. Ottomeyer, 176-187. Dresden: Sandstein.

Hähnel, J. (1975) *Stube. Wort- und sachgeschichtliche Beiträge zur historischen Hausforschung.* Schriften der Volkskundlichen Kommission des Landschaftsverbandes Westfalen-Lippe 21. Münster: Aschendorff.

Hallenkamp-Lumpe, J. (2006) *Studien zur Ofenkeramik des 12. bis 17. Jahrhunderts anhand von Bodenfunden aus Westfalen-Lippe.* Denkmalpflege und Forschung in Westfalen 42. Mainz: von Zabern.

Hecht, K. (1983) *Der St. Galler Klosterplan.* Sigmaringen: Thorbecke.

Henkel, M. (1999) *Der Kachelofen. Ein Gegenstand der Wohnkultur im Wandel. Eine volkskundlich-archäologische Studie auf der Basis der Hildesheimer Quellen.* Göttingen: Niedersächsische Staats- und Universitätsbibliothek online-publication. http://webdoc.sub.gwdg.de/diss/1999/henkel/ (visited 2.1.2013).

Hofmann, C. & M. Schneider (2001) *Von der Feuerstelle zum Kachelofen; Heizanlagen und Ofenkeramik vom Mittelalter bis zur Neuzeit.* Stralsunder Beiträge zur Archäologie, Geschichte, Kunst und Volkskunde in Vorpommern 3. Stralsund: Kulturhistorisches Museum.

Jacobi, L. & A. von Cohausen (1897) *Das Römerkastell Saalburg bei Homburg vor der Höhe.* Homburg v.d.H.: Staudt & Supp.

Jacobsen, W. (2002) Der St. Galler Klosterplan. 300 Jahre Forschung. In: *Studien zum St. Galler Klosterplan II.*, eds. P. Ochsenbein & K. Schmuki, 13-56. St. Gallen: Historischer Verein des Kantons St. Gallen.

Jankuhn, H. (1986) *Haithabu. Ein Handelsplatz der Wikingerzeit.* Neumünster: Wachholtz.

Keim, H. (2002) Mittertennbauten des 16. Jahrhunderts aus dem östlichen Oberbayern, *Hausbau im Alpenraum = Jahrbuch für Hausforschung* 51, 64-72.

Kirchner, W. & W. Kirchner (1988) Zum spätmittelalterlichen Holzbau in Regensburg. In: *Hausbau im Mittelalter III. Jahrbuch für Hausforschung Sonderband*, ed. K. Bedal, 475-558. Bad Sobernheim: Arbeitskreis für Hausforschung.

Kluge-Pinsker, A. (1992) Kachelöfen. In: *Das Reich der Salier 1024-1125.* Katalog zur Ausstellung des Landes Rheinland-Pfalz, ed. Römisch-Germanisches Zentralmuseum & Bischöfliches Dom- und Diözesemuseum Mainz, 215-219. Sigmaringen: Thorbecke.

Kohnert, T. (2008) *Die Forchheimer Burg genannt „Pfalz". Geschichte und Baugeschichte einer fürstbischöflich-bambergischen Stadtburg.* Schriften des Deutschen Burgenmuseums Veste Heldburg 4. Petersberg: Imhof.

Kristiansen, O. (2008) Kakkelproduktion i Danmarks middelalder og renæssance, *KUML. Aarbog for Jysk Arkæologisk Selskab*, 245-285.

Krongaard Kristensen, H. (2004) Land, by og bygninger. In: *Dagligliv i Danmarks middelalder*, ed. E. Roesdahl, 55-81. København: Gyldendal.

Liebgott, N.-K. (1972) Kakler. Hovedtræk af kakkelovnens historie ca. 1350-1650. København: Nationalmuseum.

Mahler, F. (2001) Heißluftheizungen in Uelzen. In: *Von der Feuerstelle zum Kachelofen ; Heizanlagen und Ofenkeramik vom Mittelalter bis zur Neuzeit*, Stralsunder Beiträge zur Archäologie, Geschichte, Kunst und Volkskunde in Vorpommern 3, eds. C. Hofmann & M. Schneider, 22-27. Stralsund: Kulturhistorisches Museum.

Matter, A. & W. Wild (1997) Neue Erkenntnisse zum Aussehen von Kachelöfen des 13. und frühen 14. Jahrhunderts. Befunde und Funde aus dem Kanton Zürich, *Mittelalter. Zeitschrift des Schweizerischen Burgenvereins* 1997/4, 77-94.

Meyer, D. (1989), Warmluftheizungen des Mittelalters. Befunde aus Lübeck im europäischen Vergleich, *Lübecker Schriften zur Archäologie und Kulturgeschichte* 16, 209-232.

MGH LL (1868) *Monumenta Germaniae Historica Leges IV*, ed. G.H. Pertz. Hannover: Hahn.

Peine, H.W. (2001) Von qualmenden Herdfeuern und Wandkaminen zu rauchfreien Räumlichkeinten mittels Warmluftheizungen und Kachelöfen. In: *Von der Feuerstelle zum Kachelofen; Heizanlagen und Ofenkeramik vom Mittelalter bis zur Neuzeit*, eds. C. Hofmann & M. Schneider, 43-63. Stralsunder Beiträge zur Archäologie, Geschichte, Kunst und Volkskunde in Vorpommern 3. Stralsund: Kulturhistorisches Museum.

Reichmann, Ch. (1991) Der ländliche Hausbau in Niederdeutschland zur Zeit der salischen Kaiser. In: *Siedlungen und Landesausbau zur Salierzeit.* Teil 1, ed. H.W. Böhme, 277-98. Sigmaringen: Thorbecke.

Renfer, Ch. (1988) Zur Regionalisierung der Hauslandschaft im Kanton Zürich. In: *Hausbau im Mittelalter III. Jahrbuch für Hausforschung Sonderband*, ed. K. Bedal, 419-474. Sobernheim/Bad Windsheim: Arbeitskreis für Hausforschung.

Reuther, St. (2003) Der Um- und Neubau des Schlosses Rochlitz von 1375 bis 1400, *Jahrbuch Staatliche Schlösser, Burgen und Gärten Sachsen* 11, 112-119.

Reuther, St. (2009) Schloss Rochlitz in der Zeit von Markgraf Wilhelm I. Ein Überblick zum Baubestand. In: *Wilhelm der Einäugige, Markgraf von Meissen (1346-1407)*, ed. I. Gräßler , 173-184. Dresden: Sandstein.

Ring, E. (2001) Herdstelle, Heißluftheizung, Kachelofen, Kamin. Wärmequellen in Lüneburger Häusern. In: *Von der Feuerstelle zum Kachelofen; Heizanlagen und Ofenkeramik vom Mittelalter bis zur Neuzeit*, eds. C. Hofmann & M. Schneider, 28-42. Stralsunder Beiträge zur Archäologie, Geschichte, Kunst und Volkskunde in Vorpommern 3. Stralsund: Kulturhistorisches Museum.

Roesdahl, E. (2004) Boligernes indretning og udstyr. In: *Dagligliv i Danmarks middelalder*, ed. E. Roesdahl, 82-109. København: Gyldendal.

Roesdahl, E. (2009) Housing culture: Scandinavian perspectives. In: *Reflections: 50 years of Medieval Archaeology, 1957-2007*, eds. R. Gilchrist & A. Reynolds, 271-288. Leeds: Maney Publishing.

Roth Heege, E., A. Heege, & C. Meiborg (2004) Ofenlehm und Napfkacheln. Ein ungewöhnlicher Kachelofen des 15. Jahrhunderts aus dem Marburger Schloß, *Zeitschrift für Archäologie des Mittelalters* 31, 95-114.

Roth Kaufmann, E. (1997) Ofen und Wohnkultur. In: *Material Culture in Medieval Europe*, eds. G. de Boe & F. Verhaege, 471-483. Medieval Europe Brugge 1997, I.A.P. Rapporten 7. Zellik: Vlaams Instituut Voor het Onroerend Ergfoed.

Ryhl-Svendsen, M., G. Clausen, Z. Chowdhury & K.R. Smith (2010) Fine particles and carbon monoxide from wood burning in 17th-19th century Danish kitchens. Measurements at two reconstructed farm houses at the Lejre Historical-Archaeological Experimental Center, *Atmospheric environment* 44, 735-44.

Schmitt, R. (2007) Schloß Neuenburg bei Freyburg (Unstrut). Zur Baugeschichte vom späten 11. bis zum mittleren 13. Jahrhundert nach den Untersuchungen der Jahre 1986 bis 2007, *Burgen und Schlösser in Sachsen-Anhalt* 16, 6-138.

Schmitt, R. (2012) Die romanische Neuenburg und ihre Stellung im hochmittelalterlichen Burgenbau. In: *Schloss Neuenburg*, eds. B.E.H. Schmuhl & K. Breitenborn, 67-136. Wettin-Löbejün OT Dössel: Stekovics.

Sennhauser, H.R. (1996) *Wohn- und Wirtschaftsbauten frühmittelalterlicher Klöster.* Zürich: Hochschulverlag an der Eidgenössisch-Technischen Hochschule.

Skov, H. & J. Fenger (2008) Air pollution from fireplaces. From the Iron Age to Modern Times, *Probleme der Küstenforschung im südlichen Nordseegebiet* 32, 27-32.

Skov, H., C. Stenholt Christensen, J. Fenger, M. Essenbaek & L. D. Sorensen (2000) Exposure to indoor air pollution in a reconstructed house from the Danish Iron Age, *Atmospheric Environment* 24, 3801-3804.

Stelze-Hüglin, S. (1999) *Von Kacheln und Öfen. Untersuchungen zum Ursprung des Kachelofens und zu seiner Entwicklung vom 11.-19. Jahrhundert anhand archäologischer Funde aus Freiburg im Breisgau.* Freiburg i. Br.: Freiburger Dissertationen Microfiche.

Stelze-Hüglin, S. (2004) Von Kacheln und Öfen im Mittelalter, *Historische Ausstattung = Jahrbuch für Hausforschung* 50, 319-339.

Stiewe, H. (2007) *Fachwerkhäuser in Deutschland.* Darmstadt: Wissenschaftliche Buchgesellschaft.

Svart Kristiansen, M. (2008) Der dänische Bauernhof im Mittelalter. Daten und Deutung. In: *Haus und Hof in Schleswig und Nordeuropa*, ed. P. Dragsbo, 108-126. Heide: Boyens Verlag.

Tafur, P. (1926) *Travels and Adventures (1435-1439).* The Broadway Travellers series, eds. Sir E. Denison Ross & E. Power. New York & London: Harper & Brothers.

Tauber, J. (1980) *Herd und Ofen im Mittelalter.* Schweizer Beiträge zur Archäologie und Kulturgeschichte 7. Olten & Freiburg i. Br.: Walter.

Trochet, J.-R. (2006) *Les maisons paysannes en France et leur environnement (XVe – XXe siècles).* Paris: Editions Créaphis.

Tuchen, B. (2001) Heizeinrichtungen im öffentlichen Badehaus des 14.-18. Jahrhunderts. In: *Von der Feuerstelle zum Kachelofen. Heizanlagen und Ofenkeramik vom Mittelalter bis zur Neuzeit*, eds. C. Hofmann & M. Schneider, 194-200. Stralsunder Beiträge zur Archäologie, Geschichte,

Kunst und Volkskunde in Vorpommern 3. Stralsund: Kulturhistorisches Museum.

Twain, M. (1923) *Europe and Elsewhere*. New York: Harper & Brothers.

Voß, L. von & L. von Gersdorff (1830) Über die Luftheizungseinrichtung im Schloß Marienburg in Preußen, *Verhandlungen des Vereins zur Beförderung des Gewerbefleißes in Preußen* 9, 41-57.

Wackerm, J. (2012) Cottbus im Mittelalter – Cottbus in the Middle Ages. In: *Archäologie in der Niederlausitz – Archaeology in Lower Lusatia*, eds. F. Schopper & D. Dähnert, 318-327. Zossen bei Berlin: Brandenburgisches Landesamt für Denkmalpflege.

Wand, N. (2002) Die Ausgrabungen in der Dorfwüstung Holzheim. In: *Holzheim bei Fritzlar. Archäologie eines mittelalterlichen Dorfes, Kasseler Beiträge zur Vor- und Frühgeschichte 6*, ed. N. Wand, 49-156. Rahden/Westfalen: Leidorf.

Zettler, A. (1988) *Die frühen Klosterbauten der Reichenau: Ausgrabungen – Schriftquellen – St. Galler Klosterplan.* Sigmaringen: Thorbecke.

Zimmermann, H. (2002) Kontinuität und Wandel im Hausbau südlich und östlich der Nordsee vom Neolithikum bis zum Mittelalter. In: *The rural house from the migration period to the oldest still standing buildings*, Ruralia IV, Pamatky Archéologické Suppl. 15, 164-168, ed. J. Klápstĕ. Prague: Academy of Sciences.

Medieval Houses in Aalborg, Denmark – a Study of Excavated Timber Houses

Christian G. Klinge

Abstract

Based on a study of house plans and interior in excavated timber houses in Aalborg, it has been possible to shed new light on urban housing culture in Denmark in the period 1050-1600 AD. In this period houses comprised only two or three rooms. Hearths usually occur in one of the rooms only. From the early Middle Ages until the 14th century, cooking facilities were situated in the room facing the street. The adjacent room was comfortable, with the possibility of a stove fed from the cooking room. After the 14th century the cooking area appears to have been moved towards the back of the house. As the kitchen was moved away from the front room, it became possible to arrange this room even more comfortably. This type of house plan is commonly known from half-timbered houses in Jutland from the 16th century. It is likely that relocation of the kitchen fire from the front to the back of the house was caused by the changes in family structure that occurred in the 14th century.

Introduction

Among many other things, luck plays an important role in the success of urban archaeological excavations. Often, only a small part of a house, a single well or a few paving stones are uncovered. At other times, fortune smiles, and it is possible to excavate complete, well-preserved houses. Over the past 10 years, Aalborg Historical Museum has been fortunate in this respect, and Aalborg is one of the towns in Denmark where it has been possible to excavate numerous well-preserved timber houses from the Middle Ages. This article presents a synthetic analysis of the evidence of house plans and interiors of excavated timber houses in Aalborg dating from the 11th to 16th century.

Material

This study is based on 42 excavations carried out from 1911 to 2008 in Aalborg, where it was possible to document the existence of timber houses. However, not all of the excavations provided suitable material. It is a prerequisite for such a study that most of the area of the original house is exposed. In addition, it is important that the houses studied are exposed in the horizontal plane. This was the case for 39 of the timber houses excavated in Aalborg as documented in 12 separate excavations[1] (Figure 1).

In this study, timber houses are defined as houses in which all the important load-bearing structures are made of timber. Thus, half-timbered houses are also included in this definition. In Aalborg there is good evidence of half-timbered houses that date from before the 17th century. 23 half-timbered 16th-century houses were, therefore, included in the study. Of these houses seven are still standing at their original locations. 16 half-timbered houses were demolished, but eight of these were later rebuilt.

The houses date from 1064 until the mid-16th century, and although most can be dated to the late

Figure 1. Distribution of the material in Aalborg. The green triangles denote excavations where the timber houses were exposed in the horizontal plane, the big green triangles represent where the houses have a well-defined description of both the plan and the interior. The red triangles represent other timber house finds. The purple rhombic denote recorded half-timbered houses from prior to 1600 AD. The background map is a digital copy of a cadastral map from 1872.

Middle Ages, they can be allocated to all the centuries of this period:

11th century: 2 excavated houses
12th century: 8 excavated houses
13th century: 8 excavated houses
14th century: 5 excavated houses
15th century: 14 excavated houses
16th century: 2 excavated houses and the 23 half-timbered houses

The distribution is somewhat different if only houses for which there is a well-defined description of the house plan and the interior of the rooms is included.

These comprise 23 houses, recorded in seven separate excavations and two half-timbered houses, which give a more even distribution throughout the Middle Ages, although the 14th century is represented by only two houses.

11th century: 2 excavated house
12th century: 7 excavated houses
13th century: 5 excavated houses
14th century: 2 excavated house
15th century: 6 excavated houses
16th century: 1 excavated house and 2 half-timbered houses

Methodology

It is important to set the study of house plans and layouts of rooms in Aalborg in the regional context of the area of Denmark known as North Jutland. It is important to remember that housing traditions varied in different parts of Denmark (Stoklund 1969: 66-76), particularly with regard to the location and design of fires used in cooking, as is illustrated by the following example of an ethnological study of a farmhouse examined in the 18th century. In Jutland and on the island of Funen, cooking was carried out in the main room of the dwelling, and this type of house is therefore often referred to as a 'chimney house' (Danish: 'kaminhus'). A similar arrangement of rooms was common throughout most of Western Europe. On the Danish island of Zealand, in some parts of Scania, and in North Jutland, however, the cooking fire was traditionally placed in a kind of entrance-hall kitchen. A stove in the main room could be fed from the cooking hearth, and such a house was known as a 'stove house' (Danish: 'ovnhus'). This organisation of rooms bears witness to communication to the south across the Baltic Sea to Central and Eastern Europe where this type of dwelling was also common. In Scania generally, a type of house known as the 'stue-herberghus' dominated. The source of heat in this house was a so-called 'smoke oven' (Danish: 'røgovn') located in the main room – there was no chimney or flue, and the smoke remained inside the house. Cooking was done on an open hearth in front of the oven. This ancient type of dwelling is considered to have its origin in Scandinavia (Krongaard Kristensen 2003: 169f; Stoklund 1969: 66-76).

Ethnological studies that describe these three types of house show that the differences in housing culture from one of the three areas of Denmark to another (Zealand, Jutland and Scania), did not necessarily follow strict geographical boundaries (Figure 2). Certain characteristics of the ovnhus and the kaminhus could be seen on either side of the body of water known as The Great Belt, and the housing culture of North Jutland was sometimes seen to be identical to that of Zealand. This crossing of geo-

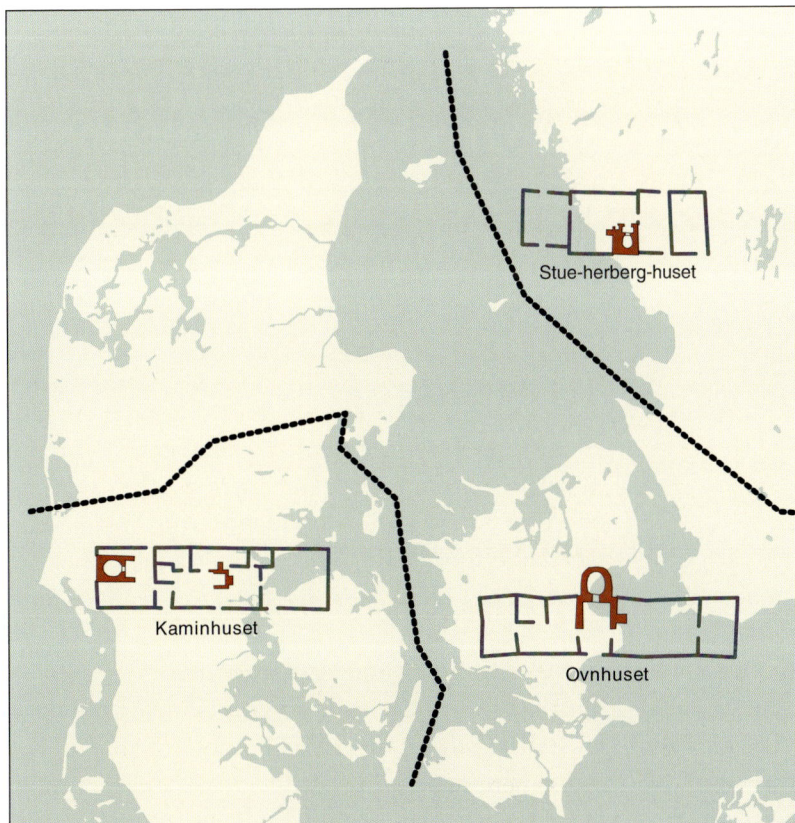

Figure 2. Cultural boundaries of farmhouses in 18th century Denmark and southern Sweden. Note that the boundaries between the various types of houses are not identical with the traditional regional boundaries. Data from Stoklund 1969: 69, 74; 2003: 26, figure compiled by author.

graphical boundaries should therefore be considered when studying the arrangement of rooms in urban, as well as rural houses.

Social differences must also be considered. It is likely that the arrangement of rooms in houses constructed at the same time varied to accommodate occupants from different levels of society. It can, therefore, be difficult to compare houses in the same area if their occupants had different positions in society (Krongaard Kristensen 2003: 171).

Taking the above into consideration, three things are apparent from the material in this study. First, with a single exception, the gables of all the houses faced the street. In Aalborg, excavations that revealed all of the structures on a plot were carried out only at Bredgade 7 and Algade 9. In this study, therefore, only dwelling houses nearest the street at the front of the plot are described. Excavations at the back of the plot at Bredegade 7 revealed traces of workshops, latrines and a few buildings, as well as houses with fireplaces. Although remains of the houses with fireplaces were poorly preserved, they were interpreted as dwelling houses. The back part of the plot at Algade 9 was also excavated, and no dwelling houses were seen here. This is a familiar pattern of building in other places in Denmark. Second, with a single exception, all the houses in this material followed the course of the streets Algade, Bredegade and Nørregade, Aalborg's main thoroughfare throughout the Middle Ages and today. It must, therefore, be assumed that it was not the poorest people who occupied these houses. Finally, all the houses stand in close proximity to a densely-populated area. Although the material is limited, the similarities between the houses suggest that they are part of a homogeneous group.

The size of the houses

Determining the size of the houses presented a problem, as none of the 39 houses excavated were preserved in their entirety, nor could they be completely excavated. Although there was no definite evidence as to the overall size of the houses, for some, sufficient material was preserved to enable a reasonable estimate of their size. Taking the above

into consideration, a comparison of the archaeological evidence from all of the houses enabled an estimation of the size of the houses in Aalborg throughout the Middle Ages.

Apparently, the width of the houses remained unchanged throughout the entire period. The actual width of 19 houses could be measured. All the houses, with two exceptions, were between 4 and 6m wide; only one house was seen to be only 4m wide. Thus, it appears that a width of c 5-6m was common throughout the Middle Ages. A comparison of the width of the excavated houses with the width of the 23 half-timbered houses in Aalborg changes this picture very little. With one exception, all of the Renaissance houses were between 6 and 7m wide, *ie* just 1m wider than the medieval houses.

This similarity in width can almost certainly be attributed to construction requirements. Wider houses would have called for longer tie beams, resulting in a weaker construction. The construction of a wider house would have necessitated the addition of aisles, calling for two rows of parallel, load-bearing posts, or, construction would have had to have been different from that of a half-timbered house.

It is more difficult to establish the length of the houses, and evidence of their length is available for only 12 of the houses. The length varied from 9 to 20m and appears to have followed no set pattern. This may well be because these houses were constructed of modules. The length could be extended simply by adding a module and had no direct influence on the strength of the construction.

The house plan

23 of the houses excavated provided good evidence of the overall house plan and interior of the rooms. In addition, archaeological evidence from two demolished half-timbered houses is also available, making it possible to identify partial or complete plans for a total of 25 houses (Figure 3). Only these 25 houses are included in the following discussion.

Common to all of the houses is evidence only of a crosswise (axial) internal wall, showing that all the rooms spanned the full width of the house. In three of the houses there was good evidence of the arrange-

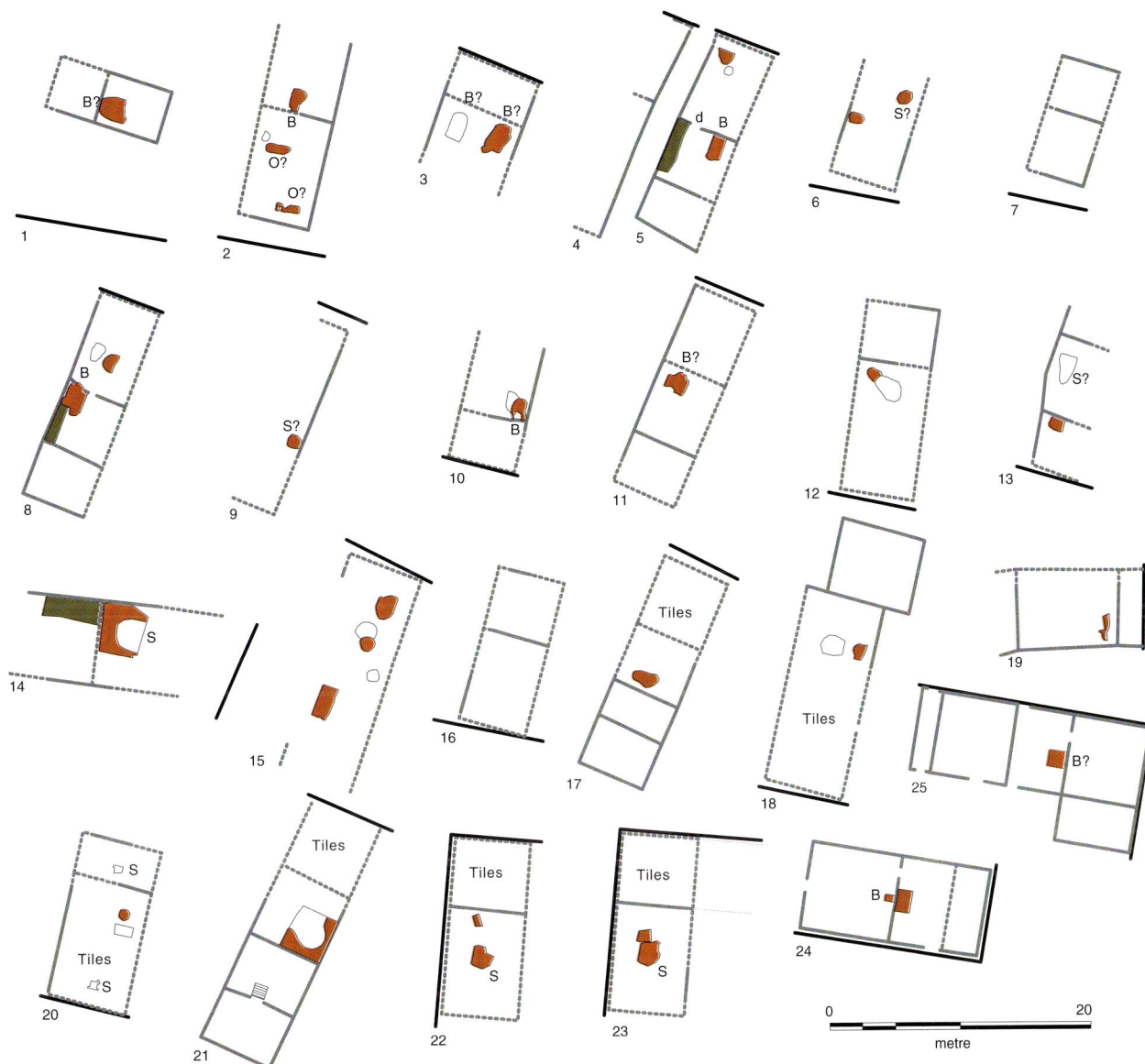

Figure 3. A schematic illustration of the 25 houses discussed in the article. Note developments in the placement of the hearths. The red broken line denotes weak evidence of the wall. Orange signature: Hearth, the empty signatures indicate that it is assigned to a later phase of the house; S: Stove, B: Stove fed from an adjacent room; Tiles: Finds of tile fragments indicate the possible presence of a tiled-stove; The black line denotes the course of the street in 1872. 1. End of 11th to mid 12th century (4158A570); 2. End of 11th to mid 12th century (4158A795); 3. First half of the 12th century (2481A-AUM); 4. First half of the 12th century (5698A503); 5. 1120s to 1160s (5698A504); 6. Second half of the 12th century (4158A420); 7. Second half of the 12th to mid 13th century (4158A535); 8. 1160s to mid 13th century (5698A452); 9. 1160s to mid 13th century (5698A427); 10. First half of the 13th century (1239A-P/Q); 11. Second half of the 13th century (5698A428); 12. Second half of the 13th to mid 14th century (4158A540); 13. Mid 13th century to 1390s, rebuilt in 1320s (4158A244); 14. 1280s to 1330s, rebuilt around 1300 AD (4439A271); 15 Around 1300 AD to 1320s (5698A376); 16. 1390s to mid 15th century (4158A152); 17. 15th century (5698A221); 18. Beginning of the 15th century to c 1557 (4158A466); 19. c 1432 to the end of the 15th century (3536A197); 20. Middle of the 15th century to c 1557 (4158A093); 21. Second half of the 15th to c 1574 (5698A055); 22. Second half of the 15th around 1500 AD (5695A177); 23. Around 1500 AD to the 19th century (5695A080); 24. Povl Pop's House, 1571 AD to 1909; 25. Vesterågade 9, 1580s to 1962 AD.

ment of rooms (Figure 3: 3, 10, 14) but no physical evidence of interior walls. Although the walls are not described in the excavation report, they are clearly shown in the excavation plans and in the description of the cultural layers. In house 3 the charred remains of clay, interpreted as part of a wall construction, were seen at the site of a possible interior wall. The archaeologist who excavated the house suggested the existence of an interior wall (Møller 2000: 23-27). In house 10 there was evidence of vertical wooden planks at the site of the interior wall, and the floors on either side of the wall were different. In house 14 an interior wall is indicated by the fact that two parts of the house were paved with different materials. This is no direct evidence, but the existence of partitioning here seems likely.

From the year 1050 to 1600 AD houses comprised two or three rooms. A closer look at small differences between the oldest and the newest houses, however, shows a less homogeneous picture. There are well-documented plans for seven houses from the period from the year 1050 to 1300, and in houses from this period, one large room facing the street appears to have been common. This room occupied the first 4 to 7 m of the house, and all seven of the houses were heated. The room behind this front room was generally a little smaller or the same size as the front room. Although two houses (Figure 3: 5, 8) had a third room, this was not interpreted as living quarters. In general, the 14th century is under-represented as regards excavated houses in Aalborg, in particular when it comes to well-documented house plans. Only one house is represented throughout all its three phases of construction. This house has alternately two and three rooms.

The 15th century is without question the best archaeologically-documented century in Aalborg. This is also true as regards house plans, as there are well-documented plans for six houses from this period. Although none of the houses has been excavated in its entirety, it has been possible to identify parts of the plans. All of the houses had large rooms facing the street. It was not always possible to find traces of a source of heat in the front rooms, but this was to be expected. The digging of cellars in more recent times has disturbed the most recent cultural layers nearest the street, and the front parts of the houses were rarely preserved. In every house from the late Middle Ages, there were traces of a fireplace in the room or rooms toward the back of the house.

The house plans from the 16th century were identical to those of the 15th century. In the study of hous-
es from the 16th century it was, however, possible to draw on plans from the half-timbered houses known in Aalborg. Thorough studies have been made of the plans of two of the Renaissance houses. Both houses had a large room facing the street. There was no open fire in this room, and it had been heated by a stove fuelled from an adjacent room. Behind the room facing the street was a smaller room, heated by an open fireplace. In both houses, both rooms had outside entrances.

One of the advantages of the half-timbered houses is that they were either preserved or had been documented prior to their demolition. In contrast to the excavated medieval houses, it is also possible to study the second storey of these houses. Two of the half-timbered houses in Aalborg (Figure 3: 23-24) were recorded before being demolished (Engqvist 1968: 30-40; 1975: 33-66; 1986: 47-51). The second storeys of the houses were remarkably similar; both had one large room and one smaller room at the gabled end of the house, facing the street. The large room had been a storeroom, while the smaller one was probably a dwelling.

In general, one can say that the plans of the houses in Aalborg from the Middle Ages and the early Renaissance were not very complicated. Without exception, the houses were divided crosswise with interior walls, and there were very few rooms. The houses from the early and the late Middle Ages are well documented, while only sporadic information is available for the period in between. Two half-timbered houses from the 16th century have been studied before demolition, and the house plans from the 16th century are very similar to those from the Middle Ages.

Heating methods

The fireplace, either in the form of an open hearth or a stove, was a central element in the design of a house in the Middle Ages and in the Renaissance. The fire was necessary both for cooking and as a source of heat. In the following, various types of fireplace from the Middle Ages and the Renaissance will be described, both as regards the fireplaces themselves and their location in the houses included in this material. Different terms can be used to describe sources of heat used for warmth and for baking and cooking. The term 'stove' is often used to describe an enclosed hearth used purely for generating warmth and that of 'oven' for sources of heat also used for baking and cooking as well as heating. However, it is not always possible to distinguish between ovens and stoves in the early Middle Ages, because both the construction and the excavated evidence of these are identical, until the tile-stove becomes common in the 15th century.

In archaeology, it is relatively easy to find evidence of a permanent hearth. Both charcoal and burnt clay are stable materials and are, therefore, easily identified archaeologically (Foged Klemensen 2003: 142f). In the 39 houses in this material, there were only 12 in which it was not possible to identify a hearth. The majority of the houses with no identifiable hearths were only partially excavated. The lack of a hearth is an interesting issue. A house without a hearth would typically not be thought of as a dwelling. However, this interpretation raises some questions. A house may well have been heated without leaving archaeological traces. The use of a warming-pan (Danish: 'ildbækken') would not, for example, have left distinctive remains. In the course of the Middle Ages, the fire was situated on a raised bench (Danish: 'ildstedsbænk'), and neither would this necessarily have left archaeological traces. It cannot, therefore, be categorically concluded that a house had no form of heating simply because this left no archaeological remains (Foged Klemensen 2003: 143f).

One important consideration in the interpretation of sources of heating is the visible differences between an open hearth and a stove. Often only the bottom of the hearth was preserved. There is little difference between the bottom of a stove built of stones and clay and the bottom of a hearth built of the same materials, but where there was an open fire. It is, however, possible to demonstrate differences if traces of the construction of the stove's hood are found. There may, for example, be remains of the wicker frame over which the hood was built, or traces of an opening through which the fire was fed. In some cases, it is also possible to demonstrate that the hearth had no hood. This may be the case if the hearth had obvious boundaries, or if traces of the construction indicate that there simply was no room for a hood.

It is often necessary to take the word of the excavator at face value. In the discussion of stoves and hearths, one should, therefore, keep in mind that an initial interpretation may have been incorrect (Foged Klemensen 2003:142f). In the houses under consideration here, there are several instances in which documentation of whether the traces found were of an open hearth or the bottom of a stove is inconclusive. In these and in several other cases, it is not possible to positively identify the traces found. The same reservations should be kept in mind in the following discussion.

A hearth in a house can have had several functions, the most obvious of which was as a source of heat and a place for cooking food. In pre-historic times, one fireplace probably served both functions. This became more difficult with the advent of the smoke stove. It was, however, possible to cook food right in front of the stove's opening (Stoklund 1969: 66). It was, therefore, not necessary to have an open hearth if the house had a stove (Roesdahl 1999: 87). The hearths and chimneys of the late Middle Ages were well suited for cooking, and a number of pictures from this period show food preparation taking place at the fire over an open hearth (Roesdahl 2003: 239-241).

There are indications that in Aalborg, stoves were common throughout the Middle Ages and the early Renaissance. 47 hearths were registered in the houses in the current material, and of them, 23 were shown to be stoves, while the remaining 24 were open hearths. There was an even distribution throughout the period, and there does not seem to have been more open hearths in the early Middle Ages. This is in opposition to the generally accepted view that hearths were replaced by stoves in the course of the Middle Ages (Foged Klemensen 2003: 146f). In 2003, Foged Klemensen (2003: 155-167) published the following overview of the distribution of open hearths and stoves:

12th century: 9 open hearths and 2 stoves
13th century: 7 open hearths and 4 stoves
14th century: 7 open hearths and 9 stoves
15th century: 4 open hearths and 9 stoves
16th century: 2 open hearths and 3 stoves
(The numbers are taken from the catalogue, uncertain descriptions are not included)

The numbers are not in any way statistically rigorous. The information on which the catalogue is based is, for the most part, taken from short abstracts from excavation reports (Foged Klemensen 2003: 155). The catalogue is based on the excavators' own interpretations, and varying definitions can, therefore, confuse the picture. The absence of hearths can either indicate a genuine absence or that the source of heating was on a raised bench and could not, therefore, be recorded.

However, bearing in mind these reservations, it still appears likely that open hearths were replaced by stoves in the mid-Middle Ages. The evidence and analysis presented above suggest that conditions in Aalborg differed from those of Denmark in general.

The oldest stoves in Denmark were smoke stoves, in which there was only one opening, which allowed smoke to escape through the same opening as that used to fuel the stove, hence the name (Roesdahl 1999: 87). The smoke stove dates from pre-historic times. The hoods of the oldest stoves were constructed over a wicker frame, which was then covered with a thick layer of clay. This method of construction was common throughout the Middle Ages. The smoke stove was probably originally designed for baking and other food preparation, but because the thick clay hood became very warm, it also became very useful as a source of ambient heat. It was, therefore, not necessary to have a fire in the stove at all times.

If the smoke stove was placed so that the opening was in one room, and the main body of the stove was placed in an adjacent room, it was possible to heat a room without the nuisance of the smoke. In Danish, this type of stove was called a 'bilæggerovn'. It would also have been possible to put all of the dwelling's sources of heating in one or a few rooms. That would also have reduced the danger of fire. In order to optimise the heating value of a stove, it became common in the Middle Ages to attach tiles to the outside of the stove. With its outer surface thus enlarged, the tiled stove (Danish: 'kakkelovn') could heat a room more efficiently.

Some of the oldest examples in Denmark of a stove fed from an adjacent room have been found in Aalborg. Thus, this stove is of particular interest when studying the timber houses in Aalborg. The two best examples of such a stove were excavated at Algade 9. Dendrochronology was used to date both houses: one to 1115-30 (Figure 3: 5), the other to 1157-70 (Figure 3: 8), the earlier being replaced by the later (Figure 4, Figure 5). In both houses, the stove heated the second room from the street, probably making this a comfortably warm room without the unpleasantness of smoke.

Two other houses in Aalborg from the early Middle Ages probably also had stoves fed from adjacent rooms. One of the houses was excavated at Algade 19 (Figure 3: 3) and can still be seen today at the underground Franciscan Friars' Museum in Algade. It is dated to the first half of the 12th century. An almost identical stove to the one described above was excavated in this house. The stoves are so similar that it is likely that their placement and function were the same, *ie* that they were used to heat a smoke-free room. It has not been possible to identify any partitioning of the rooms in the house at Algade 19. Considering the construction of the house and its poor degree of preservation, however, an interior wall would not necessarily have left archaeological traces. A line of charred wall material in front of the stove's opening has been cautiously interpreted as an interior wall.

Another house that may have had a stove fed from an adjacent room is dated roughly to the 13th century, and was excavated at Strandstien in 1981 (Figure 3: 10). The interpretation of this house is somewhat problematic, as the extent of the excavation was only 18 m² and, therefore, very little of the house has been excavated. The descriptions in the documentation are brief. For example, only the stoves and not the house itself are mentioned in the excavation report. The house is, however, described and given prominence in literature about buildings in Aalborg in the early Middle Ages (Knudsen & Kock 1992: 23-26). Two stoves were found in the house (Figure 6). The later of the two was located adjacent to a row of planks hammered into the ground that may have formed a wall. The floor is different on either side of the planks, thus strengthening the interpretation that they constituted a wall. The stove can, therefore, cautiously be interpreted as a stove fed from an adjacent room. Thus, it seems likely that by reviewing earlier

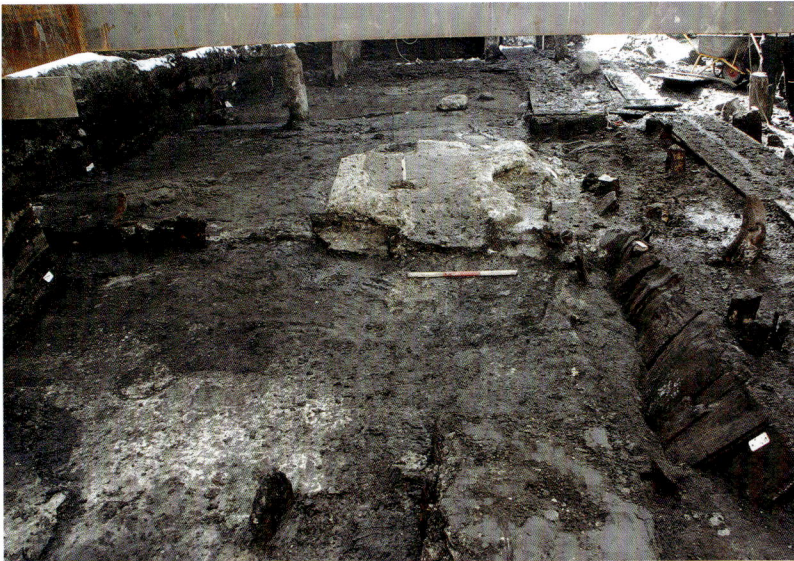

Figure 4. A look inside the later house at the excavation at Algade 9. The stove can be seen at the right. The opening is denoted by an arrow. The interior wall can be clearly seen to the left of the stove. Photo Aalborg Historiske Museum.

Figure 5. A stove fuelled from an adjacent room in the earlier house at the excavation at Algade 9, dating from the 1120s. The opening is outside the field, while the interior wall can be seen at the bottom to the left of the stove. Photo Aalborg Historiske Museum.

excavations it would be possible to find additional examples of stoves fed from an adjacent room from the period before the 14th century. It is, however, also problematic to reinterpret or expand the interpretation of older, already thoroughly-investigated excavation material.

The only other examples of town houses from the early Middle Ages with stoves fed from an adjacent room have been found in Store Sct. Pedersstræde in the town of Viborg. The houses have been dated to around the 12th and 13th centuries. Each has at least two rooms, one of which was heated with a stove fed from the adjacent room in the same manner as in the houses in Aalborg (Krongaard Kristensen 1987: 79f). The gables of the houses from Viborg do not face the street, indicating that this type of stoves was used in different urban environments. The houses in Viborg and Aalborg are from the same period, also suggesting that stoves fed from an adjacent room were not uncommon in the early Middle Ages.

In the stoves fed from the adjacent room described so far there is no evidence of the use of tiles in the stove shell. There are only a few evidences of tile fragments in Aalborg before the 15th century. Thus, the absence of tiles should not be taken as evidence that stoves fed from the adjacent room were not pre-

Figure 6. A stove fuelled from an adjacent room in the house at Strandstien. The stove in front, also the newest stove, is situated like a stove fed from an adjacent room, while the house plan around the earlier stove is not quite as distinct. Photo Aalborg Historiske Museum.

sent before the 15th century. The introduction of the stove fed from the adjacent room appears in Aalborg four hundred years before the introduction of tiles.

In the material available currently, information about the heating methods in more recent houses is often more difficult to establish than in earlier houses. This may reflect the destruction of upper levels of stratigraphy in these contexts but also the fact that it became common to situate the hearth or stove above floor level during the later periods. Archaeological traces are more difficult to interpret if a hearth bench or stove is completely removed when a house is torn down. Likewise, traces of hearths in the area near the street also disappear. In addition, in some houses there are very distinctive traces of hearths in the middle and back parts of the house where previously no traces of sources of heating were seen (Figure 3: 17-18, 20-23).

Tiled stoves clearly became more common in Danish towns after the 14th century. Fragments of tiles can therefore be taken as indirect proof that houses in the late Middle Ages had stoves as a source of heat, regardless of the fact that there are few traces of

hearths preserved. In Aalborg fragments of tiles are very common onwards the 15th century, but uncommon before 1300 AD.

There is surviving information about the location and type of heating method used in two of the Renaissance houses in the material. One is a house known as 'Povl Pop's house' and the other a house at Vesterågade 9 (Figure 3: 24-25). The heating methods in both houses were almost identical. Both were described as having open chimneys in the second room from the street. The chimney was built next to the wall of the room facing the street. The front room could be heated by a stove fed from the open chimney in the adjacent room and was, therefore, a heated but smoke-free room (Engqvist 1986: 47-51).

The home in Aalborg throughout the Middle Ages

The current material provides a clear indication that the interior arrangement of dwellings in Aalborg changed throughout the Middle Ages. Almost all of the houses in this study were gabled houses in which the gable end faced the main street of Aalborg. From the houses in this material it can be seen that the main tendency was for the cooking fire to be moved from the front room, facing the street, further back in the house. In Aalborg, in the first centuries of the Middle Ages, the arrangement of rooms in dwelling houses followed a relatively similar pattern. In the front of the house, facing the street, there was a smoke-filled room. A stove fuelled from this front room heated the room behind it. Food preparation and other work that called for fire must have taken place in the entrance room. From our perspective, the room behind this front room must have been by far the most comfortable. In some of the houses, built-in benches indicate that this was the living and sleeping room.

When it comes to archaeological documentation in general, there is less information in Aalborg about the 14th century than about the other centuries of the Middle Ages. This is also true of the material in the current study. House plans from the period after the 14th century is very similar to the plans in Aalborg's older timber houses; there were few large rooms and a crosswise division of the house. The differences lie in the location of the hearth. After the 14th century, the hearth was no longer placed in the entrance room of the house, indicating a major shift in planning. From the 15th century onwards in Aalborg, hearths were situated in the back of the house in six out of eight houses (figure 3: 17-18, 20-23). In one of the half-timbered houses (Figure 3: 24) the front room was heated by a tile-stove. In all the six houses mentioned above tile-fragments were found in the primary layers of the house, indicating that these houses contained a tile-stove, possibly in the front room. With the main source of heating moved toward the back of the house, it was possible to arrange the front room more comfortably. This is in contrast to the early Middle Ages, when the more comfortable room was toward the front or in the middle of the house.

It is not clear just when this change in interior arrangement took place, but it appears to have been in the course of the 14th century. If this is the case, the change corresponds to other profound chang-es in this century, among others those caused by decline in population due to the Black Death and the subsequent reorganisation of the rural economy and production and changes in family structure (Poulsen 2003: 33-35). It is likely that changes in living habits have their background in such significant changes.

Changes in the arrangement of rooms meant that the front room now had a new function. In Aalborg's preserved half-timbered houses from the 16th century, the front room was often arranged like a kind of entrance hall (Danish: 'forstue'), that is, a room where out-going activities such as the making of crafts and commerce were carried out (Engqvist 1986: 47-51). It may be just such an entrance hall that is shown in the excavated timber houses from the late Middle Ages. As noted above, the hearths are placed toward the back of these houses, just as they were in the houses of the Renaissance. It is, therefore, natural to assume that the front rooms of these houses are identical with the entrance halls in the Renaissance houses.

It appears that this interior arrangement of houses in the late Middle Ages was maintained until the end of the 16th century, after which changes took place again. House plan development is documented in the half-timbered house situated at Vesterågade 9 in Aalborg. The house dates from about 1580 and was measured and documented when it was taken down in 1968 (Engqvist 1968: 34-40; 1986: 48-51). The oldest plan followed a pattern that was similar to that seen in the late Middle Ages. The house was rebuilt around 1620; when a small porch was added to the front room at the door facing the street, making this front room a living room. At the same time, the walls and ceiling were covered with inlaid panels. The room with the kitchen hearth was divided into two rooms, a separate kitchen and a smaller room. Both these rooms were heated by a stove fuelled from the kitchen. In general, the houses had more rooms than had previously been the case. The new housing customs that can be seen in the house at Vesterågade 9 became popular in Jutland in the beginning of the 17th century. The housing culture of the Middle Ages in the timber houses in Aalborg ended in the years around 1600.

Notes

1. The following 12 excavations carried out by Aalborg Historiske Museum, comprised well preserved remains of timber houses that are exposed in the horizontal plane: ÅHM707 Vesteraagade 9, ÅHM711 Strandstien I, ÅHM1239 Strandstien II, ÅHM2481 Algade 19, ÅHM3536 Møllegade 8-10, ÅHM4158 Bredegade 7, ÅHM4439 Boulevarden, fase 2, ÅHM4914 Bredegade 9, ÅHM5475 Boulevarden, fase 3, ÅHM5621 Algade 5, ÅHM5695 Bredegade 18, and ÅHM5698 Algade 9.

References

Engqvist, H.H. (1968) *Aalborg bindingsværk*. Aalborg: Historisk samfund for Aalborg Amt.

Engqvist, H.H. (1975) Povl Pops Trefoldighedshus, *Købstadsmuseet "Den gamle By"*1975, 33-66.

Engqvist, H.H. (1986) Jyske gavlhuse. In: *Grønnegade 12 i Ribe*, eds. S.M. Søndergaard et al, 37-56. Ribe: Den antikvariske Samling.

Foged Klemensen, M. (2003) Udgravede træhuse i danske byer ca. 800-1600. In: *Bolig og familie i Danmarks middelalder*, ed. E. Roesdahl, 129-167. Højbjerg: Jysk Arkæologisk Selskab.

Knudsen, B.M. & J. Kock (1992) Anden del. Fra 975-1536. In: *Fra Aalborgs fødsel til Grevens Fejde 1536. Aalborgs Historie 1*, eds. E. Johansen et al, 108-45. Aalborg: Aalborg Kommune.

Krongaard Kristensen, H. (1987) *Middelalderbyen Viborg*. Århus: Centrum.

Krongaard Kristensen, H. (2003) Planløsninger i byernes stenhuse. In: *Bolig og familie i Danmarks middelalder*, ed. E. Roesdahl, 169-192. Højbjerg: Jysk Arkæologisk Selskab.

Møller, S.B. (2000) *Aalborg Gråbrødrekloster*. Aalborg: Selskabet for Aalborgs Historie.

Poulsen, B. (2003) Privatliv i middelalderens huse. In: *Bolig og familie i Danmarks middelalder*, ed. E. Roesdahl, 31-45. Højbjerg: Jysk Arkæologisk Selskab.

Roesdahl, E. (1999) Boligens indretning og udstyr. In: *Dagligliv i Danmarks middelalder*, ed. E. Roesdahl, 82-109. København: Gyldendal.

Roesdahl, E. (2003) Møbler og Indretning. In: *Bolig og familie i Danmarks middelalder*, ed. E. Roesdahl, 223-246. Højbjerg: Jysk Arkæologisk Selskab.

Stoklund, B. (1969) *Bondegård og byggeskik før 1850*. København: Dansk Historisk Fællesforening.

Stoklund, B. (2003) Andre veje til middelalderhuset. In: *Bolig og familie i Danmarks middelalder*, ed. E. Roesdahl, 15-29. Højbjerg: Jysk Arkæologisk Selskab.

Burned-down Timber-framed Houses in Medieval Odense, Denmark

Anne Katrine Thaastrup-Leth

Abstract

Four burned-down timber-framed houses from the 14th to the 16th century were excavated in Odense, in 2010. The houses were smaller buildings close to the ancient main street across Funen, Overgade, south of the excavation. One of the houses was the workshop and dwelling of a coppersmith and later on another craftsman. This house was particularly well preserved and showed several details of the construction and interior. The function of the other houses was unknown.

Introduction

Prior to the construction of a new exhibition hall at Odense City Museum, 1200 m² cultural layers were excavated in the centre of Odense from May to November 2010. This is the biggest excavation in Odense so far. The excavation was located in the parish of the church of Vor Frue (English: Our Lady) with the Blackfriars to the northwest and the medieval main street Overgade to the south (Figure 1). The results of some scientific analyses are still pending and final conclusions about these excavations have yet to be published. This paper therefore presents the preliminary interpretations of the site. During the excavation the remains of buildings from the Iron Age to the 20th century were identified. The focus of this paper will be the analysis of the remains of a burned-down row of timber-framed houses consisting of three contemporary buildings (K1, K9, K8) dating from the 14th to the 16th century. It also aims to compare the results of these exceptionally-preserved houses with other excavation data from Odense and other parts of Denmark. The paper raises a number of questions about the archaeological interpretation of the excavated remains of timber-framed houses more generally.

A main street, a narrow street and an alley

Overgade, south of the excavation, was part of the main medieval street crossing Funen from east to west. It dates back to the 11th century at least. The remains of several medieval cellars can be identified in the much-altered houses along Overgade itself (see further Christensen 1988: 81-84). The area of Overgade was outside the excavated area (Figure 2). The plots to the north of Overgade were long and narrow and faced the churchyard of the Blackfriars and further to the north, meadows and gardens.

The excavation did not yield evidence of a street to the north, but this must have existed, as the excavated remains of the row of three houses were found parallel to, and in line with, the existing Sortebrødre Stræde (English: Blackfriars' Street). As the site is located on the outskirts of the medieval city, it is likely that the predecessor of Sortebrødre Stræde was a reasonably narrow street. East of the houses were the remains of an alley, Møntestræde, which existed contemporaneously with the houses (Figure 2). The alley dated back to the 12th century and linked the main street Overgade and the predecessor to Sortebrødre Stræde.

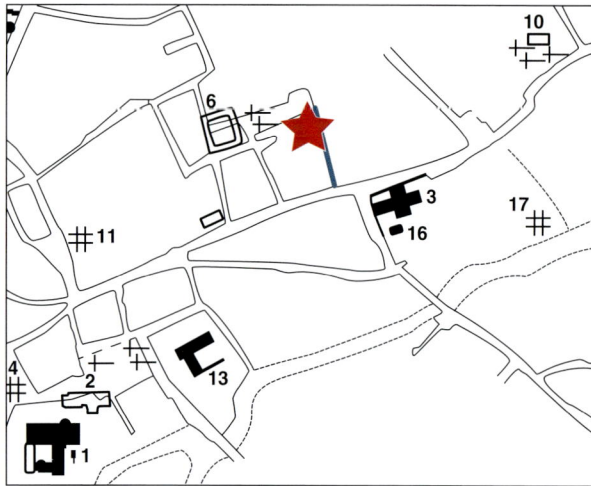

Figure 1. The excavation is marked by a red star, the Blackfriars convent is no. 6, the church of Vor Frue (Our Lady) no. 3, the cathedral Skt. Knud at the centre of the city is no. 1, the leper hospital just outside the medieval city is no. 10. Møntestræde is marked by a blue line. Preserved buildings are shown in black, destroyed buildings are outlined in black. After Christensen 1988: fig. 67.

In 1420, a mint was situated near Møntestræde (Christensen 1988: 121). This accounts for the name, as 'mønt' in Danish means coin. During excavation no clear evidence of the mint was discovered. Three possible circular blanks were found, but no dies were recovered (indeed, it is only in special circumstances that these are preserved (Vellev 2002: 213)), nor were raw or forged bars or strips. The excavators concluded that the mint was therefore located outside the main excavated area – or had disappeared due to the subsequent disturbance of the stratigraphy.

The excavated houses were smaller to the north by Sortebrødre Stræde. One of the houses, K8, could have faced the alley of Møntestræde (See discussion below). East of Møntestræde, another burned-down house, K16, was discovered (Figure 2). The remains were quite disturbed, but the stratigraphy showed that the house burned down in the same fire as the row of houses west of the alley. A large amount of burned clay, probably from plastering, and the remains of wattle-and-daub recovered from the area in and around the house indicate that this house was also timber-framed.

In 1528 a special license issued by the King banned all thatched roofs to prevent fire (Thrane 1982: 420).

This was clearly a response to an ongoing problem and is a common feature of attempts by civic and royal authorities across the towns and cities of Northern Europe. However, the following year the northern part of Odense burned down (Thrane 1982: 420f). Almost a third of the city was destroyed including, it seems likely, the timber-framed houses in the excavated area. The fire could have reached as far as the leper hospital just outside the city to the east (Arentoft 1999: 98).

Parts of the areas surrounding the burned-down houses on both sides of Møntestræde were unfortunately quite disturbed. This means that it is difficult to trace the degree of re-organisation of the plots through time. The area just outside K1, K9 and K8 to the south was undisturbed. No yards, paving, pits, wells or latrines were located here – the area appears to have been a garden. The timber-framed row of houses, Pernille Lykkes Boder, date to 1617 and are now the oldest buildings in the Møntergården complex still situated on their original site (Figure 2). The buildings were without paving and seem to have had a garden at the back – just like the excavated houses, suggesting some evidence of continuity in form and layout.

The artefacts found in the houses

In order to try to interpret the function of some of the rooms in the houses, the floor layers and the deposits above them were divided into square metres, and artefacts carefully plotted in relation to the square metre in which they were found. This methodology is a well-established means of interpreting activity areas and not only reveals the distribution of each type of artefact but also offers some clues about the possible functions of rooms and houses.

Generally, the excavations yielded relatively few artefacts, and at first glance their potential seemed rather limited. One explanation for the general paucity of artefacts was the fact that inhabitants would have sought to remove as many possessions as possible before the fire reached them. This might be particularly likely in the case of craftsman's tools or treasured domestic possessions. Another explanation is that people in the Middle Ages simply did

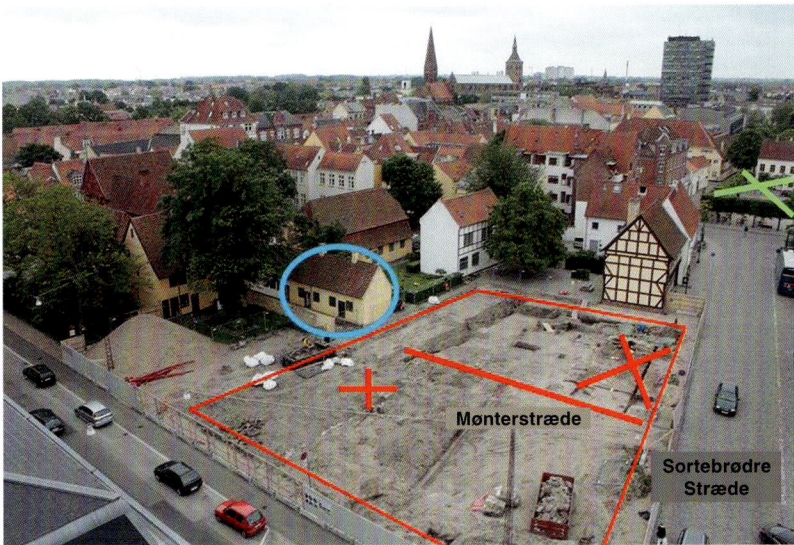

Figure 2. The main street Overgade, to the south of the excavation by the red gable (left), Sortebrødre Stræde to the north and Møntestræde crossing the excavation, seen from the north-east. The excavation is marked by a thin red line. The large red cross marks the houses K1, K9 and K8, the smaller red cross marks house K16. The green cross (back to the right) marks the now destroyed Blackfriars convent, the blue line Pernille Lykkes Boder.

not possess as many personal belongings or domestic furnishings as we might imagine. Of course, some artefacts may also have been recovered from the burned remains after the fire. It should also be remembered that despite wet-sieving of the residues from the site, at this scale it is often difficult to differentiate between fragments of timber which once comprised structural building materials and those of wood originally associated with fittings, fixtures or artefacts.

House K8

However, despite the general paucity of household artefacts recovered from the excavations, one of the houses west of Møntestræde, K8 at the corner of the row, turned out to be rather well-preserved, showing several details concerning construction as well as details of the interior (Figure 3). The preliminary dating of the house is from the end of the 14th century to the beginning of the 16th century. The house was 10 x 5 m and consisted of 7 bays. It had two rooms connected with a door; the room at the east end consisted of 3 bays, the room to the west of 4. The layout shows two phases.

The southern wall and western gable were recognized as a sill of stones. The northern wall was probably just outside the excavated area in line with the street but later truncated by the construction of

a pavement. The eastern gable was not identified and was also probably destroyed in recent development activity. The burned-down remains revealed a collapsed wall, lying outside the house to the south (Figure 4). The wall was timber-framed with posts indicating a bay width of about 1.25-1.30 m. The stones in the sill were the same width as the bays, with flatter and bigger stones fitting together with remains of burned posts. The remains of a diagonal brace (Danish: 'ranke'), were also recognized. In the later part of the Middle Ages it was common to have diagonal braces on a stone in the sill at the corner of the house (Graabach-Klinge 2009: 38-44). If this was actually the case in House K8, the position of the remains of the diagonal brace indicates that only one post in each wall was missing, the corner posts. The 5 m width of the bays and the house was common for a medieval timber-framed urban house. Its length of about 10 m (assuming only a few stones and corner posts are missing) is a little bit below average, but not unusual (Graabach-Klinge 2009: 54-104).

The remains of wattle-and-daub as well as the remains of collapsed planks, probably originating from an inner coating of the wall, lying on top of the wattle-and-daub were found in the wall itself. There was no evidence of a continuous sill-beam, and the sill of stones was probably too uneven to carry such a feature anyway. However, the remains originating from shorter stretcher-beams between

Figure 3. House K8, from the north, dated from the end of the 14th century to the beginning of the 16th century. The sill of stones is at the top of the picture. The interior wall with a doorway is marked by a red line.

Figure 4. Part of the collapsed wall in K8 lying outside the house, from the north. Posts are marked by a red line. The diagonal brace, marked by a red dotted line, indicates only one stone missing in the sill, marked by a blue line.

the posts were discovered. A large amount of burned clay was recognized among the remains of all three houses in the row and in the surrounding areas. (For a discussion of the interpretation of clay in connection with houses see Foged Klemensen 2003: 138f). The remains of the ceiling and tie beams were also recognized among other burned material which had collapsed down into the house.

A large amount of burned straw found among the remains of the burned wall indicates that the roof was probably thatched. An alternative explanation is that the straw was being stored in the loft of the house. Future analysis of this material may resolve the issue.

There was no clear evidence for the original entrance to the house. It is therefore impossible to say whether the hearth was located at the back of the house, as it generally was in the later Middle Ages, or at the front (Graabach-Klinge 2009: 90-104). It seems most likely, however, that the original entrance to the building was located in either the northern wall or eastern gable facing one of the two streets, which were either located outside the excavated area or destroyed. During excavation the fairly large stones in the sill, which measured 50 x 50 cm were interpreted as evidence that the house might originally have supported two storeys. When the diagonal extent of the corner braces were plotted, they met at a height at about 5 m, which suggests that a first floor could have been accommodated. However, no evidence of building elements from a second storey or a staircase to the second storey was recovered from the site. Taken together, these conditions point towards the house having only one, probably reasonably high storey. The large stones in the sill might easily have been re-used from an older building nearby.

The house plan

The house had two phases. In both it consisted of two rooms – the dividing wall with a door, crossing the house (Figure 3). The oldest phase had a hearth in the middle of the western room. As the remains of this were fragmentary, it is difficult to say anything specific about its form or the technology with which it was associated, and thus it seems unlikely that it was smoke-free. The room certainly housed craft activity; lots of cut-offs of copper alloy and rivets were recognized on top of the oldest floor. These rivets suggest that the room (and the house) was the workshop of a coppersmith.

Traditionally, the hearth is taken as an indication of a dwelling house. But it is notoriously difficult to discern whether a hearth was used for cooking, for heating and lighting a room or in performing a craft. Indeed, a formal distinction between domestic, craft and trade-related functions might not be relevant in

such an urban context. Instead, the hearth probably served more than one purpose (Foged Klemensen 2003: 148). It is hoped that the analysis of soil samples taken from House K8 might give further clues about the function of the room and the purpose of the hearth within it. For now, it is suggested that the house accommodated both domestic and craft activities.

In Phase 2, a hearth and a new floor were added to the house. The remains of an open hearth (Danish: 'skorstenskøkken'), were recognized by the western gable (Figure 5). From this phase no traces of craft-working were identified. A new clay floor was laid down and the hearth had both a brick foundation in clay and was made from bricks. Lots of fragmented bricks were recovered from around the hearth, but no glazed or unglazed tiles indicative of an oven. The hearth was 2 x 2 m, the width of the brick wall corresponding with the length of a medieval brick. The northern and eastern walls were laid in stretchers, the western and southern walls were irregular with both stretchers and headers. Only one course was visible. The hearth was not an original part of the house but rather a later addition built on top of the clay floor from the earlier phase. North of the hearth a considerable quantity of charcoal and ash indicated that it was open to one side. The open side provided space for someone to step into the hearth area and cook under a hood, or heat whatever was

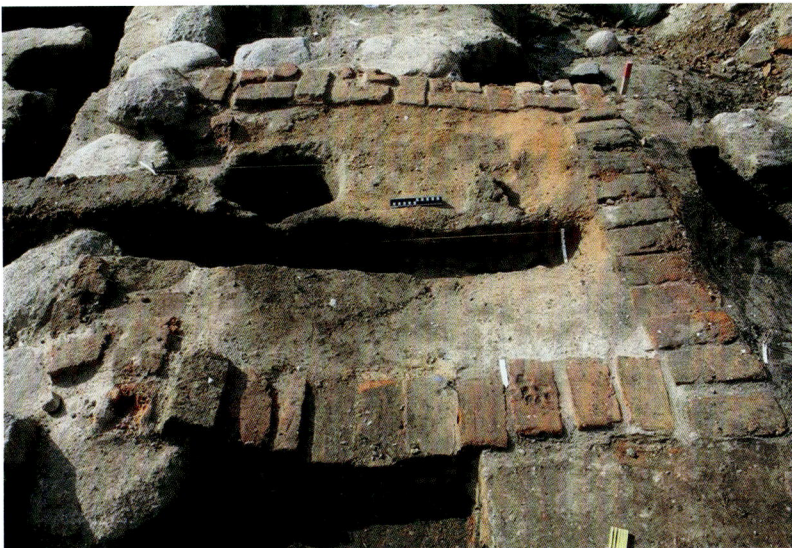

Figure 5. The hearth by the western gable in K8, from the east. Notice the charcoal to the north of the feature. This is where you stepped into the hearth to work – and cleaned out the charcoal.

Figure 6. House K8, phase 2, from the north. The hearth is marked by a red line, the area lacking the younger floor by a red dotted line.

needed in the performance of a craft. The debris from these processes was then cleaned out from the hearth. Traces of a chimney were not identified, but the size and strength of the foundation certainly indicate that one must have existed. It is striking that no traces of stoves fed from the neighbouring room were recognized, as this type of heated living rooms is known in Denmark from the 12th century in several Danish cities (Graabach-Klinge 2009: 77-79; Krongaard Kristensen 1999: 74).

In this western room a rectangular spot lacking any trace of the later floor indicates the presence of a large piece of furniture by the south wall. This may have been an original built-in feature such as a bench or maybe an alcove, where you could keep warm at night close to the hearth (Figure 6). The area measured 0,8 x 3 m. Built-in benches are known from medieval Denmark but seem to disappear around 1200 (Foged Klemensen 2003: 148). Thus, if this was a bench it may have been considered a rather old-fashioned feature by the 14th – and certainly by the 16th century. On the other hand, alcoves are not commonly known before around 1500. If this was the case, it would therefore be an early example of the type. Alternatively, the evidence might suggest the presence of a heavy piece of furniture that the residents could not or would not move, when the new floor of clay was laid down – such as a large chest? Another possible explanation for the absence of a

floor layer in this area was that the heat from the hearth was being used in this area to dry out malt or cereal. Indeed, in one part of the eastern room some burned grains, probably wheat, were recognized. This indicates that the room was used for storage, and further analysis of these cereals may shed further light on this function of the room. Whatever the outcome, it therefore seems likely that this room was more than a private living room; a multiple-functioning space which probably accommodated craft or processing activities as well as domestic use and storage – according to the situation in Phase 1.

The houses next door to the west

The west-gable of K8 was shared with the neighbouring house to the west, K9. This house turned out to be less well-preserved, but its burned-down remains still yielded clues about the house. The gables were facing north and south, the house also had a sill of stones and it had probably been timber-framed. The width of the house was about 6 metres, but the length is unknown.

This house also consisted of two rooms. In the northern room remains of a stove were identified. The stove was quite big, and was probably used for baking. No trace of the entrance to the house was recognized, and although it is once again uncertain whether the stove was located in the back or front room, the presence of the street to the north and a garden to the south suggests that the latter was more likely. Due to the location of the hearth in K8 to the east, however, it is possible that the chimney was shared between the two houses.

West of this second house a third house, K1, was found. Due to recent demolition K1 was only recognized as a clay floor in the profile. The house burned down in the same fire as the previously mentioned houses and no further conclusions can be drawn from the few remains recovered.

The function of the houses

Due to the nature of the surviving evidence it is not possible to say that the houses were connected with each other by doors. K8 and K9 do not appear to have been connected to each other, and the evidence for connections between but K9 and the third house, K1, is also unclear. The location of doors and access routes between these houses would facilitate their interpretation, either as three independent small back houses on three different plots, each with a main house at the front of the plot in line with Overgade; or as houses by Sortebrødre Stræde accommodating a mix of craft and domestic activities. The latter seems most likely; the houses are in line with Sortebrødre Stræde or Møntestræde, and entrances were probably facing one of these streets. This might suggest a reorganization of the plot in the 14th century, with Sortebrødre Stræde or Møntestræde becoming more important than it had once been.

Timber-framed houses in Odense

After about 1400, few medieval Danish urban buildings are of post-hole construction (Foged Klemensen 2003: 133). In 1473, due to a shortage of wood, the Funen nobility ordained that wooden houses (that is houses consisting only of wood) should no longer be built and posts must not be set in the earth but rather on stones (Foged Klemensen 2003:132; Knudsen & Myrtue 2000: 11). The answer to this was an increase in the number of timber-framed buildings, as a timber-framed house used a minimum of wood compared with houses built entirely of wood. The

excavated houses from Odense correspond closely to these changing construction traditions.

Two houses, K8 and K9, had few rooms, and interior walls crossing the house itself. This plan is known from the northern part of Jutland (Krongaard Kristensen 1999: 77-79), and was common until just after 1600 – at this time it becomes common to have more rooms in a house, and for rooms to have more specialized functions. This development was probably influenced by countries south of Denmark (Foged Klemensen 2003: 142; Graabach-Klinge 2009:110).

Conclusion

In Odense only a few timber-framed houses from the Middle Ages have been excavated and there are not many undisturbed existing buildings to con-

Figure 7. Ejler Rønnows Gård from 1547, the oldest surviving timber-framed building in Odense. To the left a crane at the construction site of the new exhibition hall of Odense City Museums.

sider, but the few results we do have seem to be reminiscent of the plans from the well preserved House K8 excavated by the museum (for a description of excavated houses in Odense see Arentoft 1999: 76-105 and Christensen 2003: 111-117). The Møntergården museum complex consists of houses from different ages, constructions and functions, many of which have been moved to their present site. One of the houses, Ejler Rønnows Gård, from 1547 is the oldest surviving timber-framed house in Odense (Christensen 1988: 74). The house was moved to the museum complex in 1939 from the medieval main street Nørregade at the centre of Odense. The house shows the standard of dwelling houses between the Middle Ages and the Renaissance (Figure 7). The three excavated houses K8, K9 and K1 were probably more modest than this example. As mentioned above, the form of the houses might be a result of a reorganization of plots in the 14th century. The excavation raises a number of other questions concerning the relationship of urban buildings to streets and the meaning of different forms of heating for the interpretation of domestic and craft activities. Future archaeological work therefore needs to move beyond small-scale, developer-led excavation to explore larger areas of the urban fabric with these questions in mind.

References

Arentoft, E. (1999) *De spedalskes hospital. Udgravning af Sankt Jørgensgården i Odense*. Odense: Odense Universitetsforlag.

Christensen, A.S. (1988) *Middelalderbyen Odense*. Århus: Centrum.

Christensen, J.T. (2003) En 1300-tals hustomt på voldstedet Gåseholmen i Odense. In: *Bolig og familie i Danmarks middelalder*, ed. E. Roesdahl, 111-117. Højbjerg: Jysk Arkæologisk Selskab.

Foged Klemensen, M. (2003) Udgravede træhuse i danske byer ca. 800-1300 – konstruktion og indretning. In: *Bolig og familie i Danmarks middelalder*, ed. E. Roesdahl, 129-167. Højbjerg: Jysk Arkæologisk Selskab.

Graabach-Klinge, C. (2009) *Træhuse i Aalborg 1050-1600. Bygningskonstruktioner, planløsninger og Rumindretning* (Wood houses in Aalborg 1050-1600. Building constructions, house plans, and interior). MA thesis, Aarhus University.

Knudsen, L.G. & A.S. Myrtue (2000) Funen building traditions. In: *Guide to The Funen Village*, eds. L.G. Knudsen, A.S. Myrtue & M. Schultz, 11-13 [also available in Danish]. Odense: Odense City Museums Press.

Krongaard Kristensen, H. (1999) Land, by og bygninger. In: *Dagligliv i Danmarks middelalder – en arkæologisk kulturhistorie*, ed. E. Roesdahl, 55-81. København: Gyldendal.

Thrane, H., T. Nyberg, F. Grandt-Nielsen & M. Venge (1982) *Fra boplads til bispeby. Odense til 1559*. Odense: Odense Universitetsforlag.

Vellev, J. (2002) Udmøntningen på Hjelm. In: *Marsk Stig og de fredløse på Hjelm*, eds. P. Asingh & N. Engberg, 203-219. Højberg: Jysk Arkæologisk Selskab.

The House as a Social Project in Northern-Central Italy, *c* 700-1000

Paola Galetti

Abstract

Initially, this paper compares Italian and European historiography on the subject of houses as social projects and presents the evidence from different kinds of written, archaeological, artistic, and ethnographic sources for the study of medieval Italian houses. It proposes an outline of the evolution and development of both rural and urban houses, explaining their material culture (typologies, imported and local models, materials, technologies, spatial organization, furnishings) and connections between houses and their inhabitants (families and/or social groups).

Introduction

The house must be seen as a complex social product. Two observations, the first by an historian of architecture and the second from a sociologist, help to illustrate the idea of a building as a social product and as both a mirror and a projection of its inhabitants.

> "The architecture is a complex phenomenon, which doesn't involve only the building art ... The work is not a closed system, independent, but the result of the relationship between political order, environment, practical demands and the local taste of community"(Tosco 2003).

> "The house reveals the position of man in the social and symbolic space, intifying the factors which form his economic, cultural, social and symbolic capital" (Bourdieu 2005).

Habitations are complex organisms which combine many remarkable features. The house is a constructive entity, the shelter of a family or of an enlarged group, the reference point of family traditions. Moreover, the rural house is often a landmark within a wider estate, the synthesis (in terms of settlement) of what takes place inside its bounds; the urban house can represent the place where trades and hand-crafted activities take place.

Therefore, the habitation can be seen as a marker of its inhabitants' quality of life, insofar as it is a social status symbol of a mononuclear or enlarged family group, depending on different time-space contexts. In this case, the house should not only be considered as a container for its content, like the household effects, the furnishings and the fittings. The building's history reflects a number of interactive phenomena: being the center of anthropic activity, it is the result of geographic and cultural influences, technologic skills, power relations between different social classes, individual choices and collective behaviors (Deffontaines 1972; Galetti 1998; 2008; Roux 1982). Consequently, nowadays our perception of a building emerges from a multiplicity of messages generated by multiple sources that we have to decode. First of all, it is necessary to rely upon typologies derived from written sources but also upon material sources (archeological, architectural, artistic), as well as ethnographic ones.

Ethnographic research can in fact yield significant evidence of different ways of living, in particular about functional typologies of houses, about their persistence in time, about their spread and about building techniques (not only about the building's materials but also their implementation). These facilitate the analysis of the structures built in perishable materials which are typical of the early medieval (7th-11th centuries) residential housing. This sort of buildings is less perceptible in its components and internal articulation through the traditional sources, because of its characteristics and troubles with their conservation. The newest methodology is connected with reciprocal exegetic work. This is not easy to apply particularly because of the specific characteristics of each source (Augenti 2003; Brogiolo 1988; Chapelot-Fossier 1980; Eiroa Rodriguez 2004; Furet & Le Goff 1973; Galetti 2006; 2010; Higham 2001; Samson 1990; Wickham 1998).

Different approaches define European historiography. Elsewhere I have given a brief assessment of the tendencies of the English, French, Spanish, German, Eastern and Northern European historiography (and of course Italian as well) (Galetti 2009; 2010). I would like to emphasize that the issue of housing in the European framework (analyzed through written and material sources) found its favorite field of observation in the transformations of the rural settlement organization: many works of synthesis emerged from the study of rural settlements, however they are absent from studies about urban residential settlements. The latter had been considered according to the theme of urban persistence or the discontinuity between the classic and the early medieval world and focused on the private and public buildings' characteristics, according to the topographic and urban transformations of cities between the 4th and the 7th centuries (Augenti 2006; Brogiolo & Ward-Perkins 1999; Brogiolo, Gauthier & Christie 2000; Christie-Loseby 1996; Lepelley 1996). Less attention was paid to the results of this process, namely the Carolingian and the post-Carolingian age (8th-11th centuries) (Galetti 2010; Hodges 2000).

In Italy in the 1960s and 1970s the remarkable development of agrarian history triggered more interest in environmental and human relationships. At the same time, urban settlement studies, especially early medieval ones (7th-11th centuries), became more important, centered on urban and topographical shape and facilities. During the last twenty years we have witnessed the flourishing of medieval archaeology in the study of settlement patterns, which yielded important results about rural and urban residential housing, about perishable materials structures (firstly wooden structures), about building materials in general, about the architecture of castles, about different building typologies of regional areas and their transformation and about cultural features of ways of living. A deeper understanding has emerged from the use of different historical sources to explore the processes of change in Carolingian and post-Carolingian settlement systems (from Late Antiquity onwards) in Italy than perhaps in many other European countries. Research on Italian medieval residential housing is far from approaching a complete synthesis, based on a reciprocal exegetic work between different historical sources. Within the study of buildings, rural examples have received more attention from archaeologists than urban examples; moreover currently, archeologists appear more interested in housing than their historical colleagues (Brogiolo 1994; Francovich & Noyé 1994; Galetti 2009: 12-16).

This paper follows two trajectories. It starts by outlining the material structures of settlements between the 7th and 11th centuries in Northern and Central Italy, through the evidence of written sources and artifacts; it then takes into account different types of building and their distinctive features on a social level, in addition to exploring techniques of construction, furniture and the daily equipment of houses.

Previous steps: 5th-7th centuries

These centuries witnessed profound changes in the Roman institutional, economic and social system: the rule of Roman-Barbarian regimes; the emergence of an occasional taxation system; the development of a local economy; transformations in the social and cultural composition of *élites* and population; prevailing social relationships based on personal links rather than institutional ones; and changes in the system of values which dominated contemporary society.

This resulted in profound changes in the relationship between countryside and town. The rural popu-

Figure 1. Siena, Grubenhaus, 7th century. After Francovich, Valenti & Cantini 2006: 286.

lation increased, towns experienced crisis, the traditional link between the country and the town was broken; the town witnessed the progressive decay of the classical city (including public spaces, facilities, private and public housing) and the emergence of new urban hierarchies; whilst the countryside experienced the end of the *villae* system (the ancient great farms), the expansion of *castra* (the castles), the persistence of villages and dispersed settlements (Brogiolo 1996; Brogiolo & Chavarria Arnau 2005; Brogiolo & Chavarria Arnau 2007; Christie 2004; De Lachenal 1995; Durliat 1990; Francovich & Hodges 2003; Liebeschuetz 2001; Pohl 1998; Ward-Perkins 2005; Wickham 2005).

In these contexts, domestic architecture modified itself through an extreme diversity in building tech-

niques and types; the achievement of a new simple building 'culture', linked to the transformation of handcrafted work and the revival of local (but marginal) construction techniques (Figure 1) (Brogiolo 1996; Galetti 2004; 2009: 17-25; Laval, Ozgenel & Saranis 2007).

8th-11th centuries

With regard to the domestic architecture, the previous transformation processes were simplified. Residential housing was characterized by new construction techniques based on simplified production cycles; the increasing importance of a basic building culture which used perishable materials (timber, earth), which were easy to detect *in situ* and less expensive, to create simple types and plans. Building activity slowed and became simpler; specialized skilled labour was reduced and the use of complex construction technologies lessened. Urban and rural private housing shows a widespread uniformity until the 10th century, when it began to change. The signs of such change (which were certainly not linear) can be observed particularly in urban areas (Cagnana 2000; Galetti 1998; 2004; 2006; 2008; 2009: 25-35; Mannoni 1989).

Town

During this period there was a shift in the culture of the town: a reduction in its civil function; the emergence of a predominantly agrarian economy (which characterized urban territories too); the achievement of a new life-style in which social prestige expressed itself in forms other than private architecture. This is apparent, for example, in the provision of rich grave goods, in the location and form of burial-places, in religious "euergetism" and in the possibility to reuse building materials robbed from ruins (by means of public authorization). Consequently, the *élites* adopted building types and techniques widespread in the rural world, which even unskilled labourers could master in a relatively short time.

The townhouses in this period exhibited a less articulated sense of domestic space; a non-compact dislocation of functions in which the dwelling place and the outbuildings were separated, facing open spaces, the so-called *struttura a corte (courtyard house)*; the use and reuse of perishable building materials (timber, earth, straw). The larger size and greater articulation of the household could be used to reflect social ranking, especially when combined with good-quality furnishings and fittings (Brogiolo & Gelichi 1998: 9-43; Brogiolo, Chavarria Arnau & Valenti 2005; Brogiolo & Chavarria Arnau 2007; Ermini Pani 2009; Francovich, Valenti & Cantini 2006; Galetti 1998; 2004; 2006; 2008: 33-57; 2009: 26-30; Gelichi & La Rocca 2004; Jarnut 2005; La Rocca 2002; 2006).

At the turn of the 10th century domestic urban architecture began to be transformed, as is well documented in towns like Ravenna, Rome and Lucca. A new building type called *casa solariata* emerged between the 10th and 11th century. This was a one block dwelling, with a compact plan, quite different from the *domus* with scattered buildings which characterized the Roman imperial age. This building had two floors, the first one used for a residential functions and the lower one as a service area; sometimes these habitations had a porch and an often also a fenced courtyard. The *opus mixtum* building technique spread.

In the written documentation of the Archbishop of Ravenna we can find rich evidence of these different examples. This is supported by evidence from archeological excavations in Ravenna and in Rome, for example inside the Nerva *forum* (Figure 2). This new building typology meets the demands of new functional, military, ecclesiastical, administrative *élites*, which were different from the late-Roman senatorial aristocracy (which was certainly poorer) (Augenti 2006; 2007; 2010; Belli Barsali 1974; Cirelli 2008; Coates-Stephens 1996; Galetti 2005; 2009: 29-31, 34-36; 2010; Gelichi 2000; Meneghini & Santangeli Valenzani 2004; 2008; Santangeli Valenzani 2004; Zanini 2007).

The Countryside

In the countryside there were different types of settlements, which were characterized by ephemeral and temporary structures. Rural settlements were dispersed around nearby successful urban centers; but smaller centralized settlements could also gradually evolve in *castra* (Galetti 2009: 31-33).

Types, Materials, Size

It is possible to identify two different *structural types* of rural houses in written sources: the so-called *'courtyard house'* and the *'unitary cell house'* (or *'elementary house'*).

The first type consists of a building unit (called the *sedimen/casalivo/casalino*) which is complex and sometimes enclosed with natural or artificial boundaries and enclosures; it consists of different structures, each of which had a specific function. The house *strictu sensu* is surrounded by service structures and cottages, distinct buildings which work as oven,

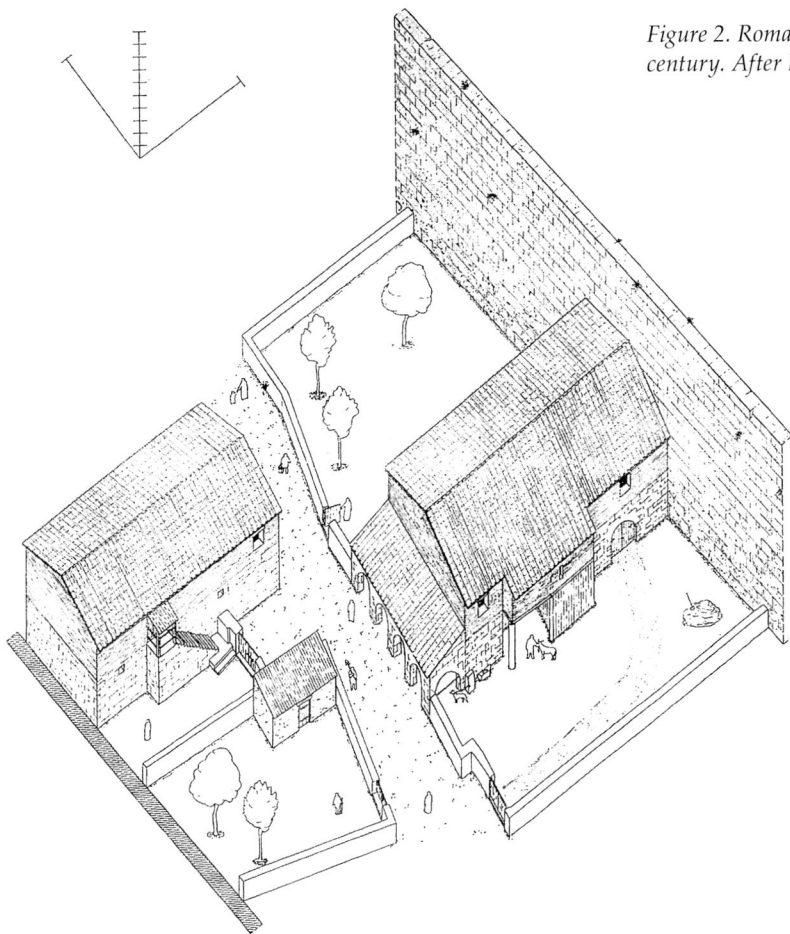

Figure 2. Roma, Nerva forum. Buildings reconstruction, 9th century. After Brogiolo & Gelichi 1998: 146.

kitchen, cellar, wine-making room, warehouse, stable, granary, barn, canopy, all connected around a central court, in which there is the farm-yard with the well and the vegetable garden. This unitary housing scheme contrasts with the 'elementary house', which consists of a single building with a single multipurpose room or split inside.

Written sources inform us about the expansion of these houses horizontally; their different functions; their wooden and other perishable wall materials; their roofing (which are mainly vegetal, straw, *scandolae*/wooden clapboards). Archaeological research gives us some more information about their architectural structure. The buildings (either inside the courtyard structure or the 'elementary houses') were partially excavated (the 'grubenhauser' are the earliest huts) or built directly on the ground. The latter can have different shapes (circular, rectangular, squared, elliptical), either with poles set in the ground, with a masonry wainscot and wooden walls

or with stone foundations and the walls built up using the *opus mixtum* technique. Service buildings and cottages can have the same features. Significant examples were found in early medieval (7th-11th centuries) settlements in Central-Northern Italy (Figure 3) (Fronza & Valenti 1996; 2005; Galetti 1998: 59-92; 2004; 2008: 31-101; 2010; Valenti 2004; 2008).

Written sources do not give us accurate information about the size of rural habitations, since they focus their attention more on the land under the structures than on the dwellings themselves. Nevertheless, it is clear that the size of the 'courtyard houses' (*sedimina*) changed in response to the needs of the estate, rather than the size of the family per se. The more the estate was developed and extended, the more it needs a functional, articulated and broad residential complex. During the 9th-10th centuries we have a few cases in which written documentation gives us some information about the 'sedimina' size, together with the whole surface of the estate's prop-

Figure 3. Reconstruction of different type buildings in Poggio Imperiale- Poggibonsi (SI) Village. After Francovich & Valenti 2005: 249.

erty: their size can be very variable and, in most cases, varies from 2000 m² to 4000 m² (Galetti 1992; 1998: 70-73). The archeological evidence enables the following tabulation of the sizes of rural houses to be made:

– in Poggio Imperiale of Poggibonsi a partally-excavated circular hut (dating to the 6th-8th centuries) has a diameter of *c* 8 m; in Donoratico the same structure (8th century), has a diameter of 3.5 m approximately.

– in Poggio Imperiale of Poggibonsi a rectangular hut (of the 9th-10th centuries) *with poles set in the ground extends c* 33sq and measures 6.9 x 4.8 m; in Scarlino, rectangular huts (dating to the 10th century) measure from 5 x 3.5 m and 10 x 4-4.5 m; in Montarrenti, rectangular huts (dating to the 7th-8th centuries) measure 4.5 x 2.5 m and *extend by c* 11 m².

– in Poggio Imperiale of Poggibonsi circular huts built *directly* on the ground (8th-10th centuries)

have a diameter of *c* 8 m; in the same period we have the same in the sites of Miranduolo (SI) e Rocchette Pannochieschi (GR).

– in Poggio Imperiale of Poggibonsi some elliptic huts built *directly* on the ground (of the 8th-10th centuries) are small and medium in size and *extend by c* 20 m² and *c* 52-53 m² .

– in Piadena (CR) (9th-10th century) a wooden house measures 7 x 4.5 m; two other structures have 4.5 x 7 m and 6.5 x 7 m size (Brogiolo-Mancassola 2005: 121-141; Valenti 1996; 2004: 21-24; 2008).

Construction

Most of the peasants generally built their own dwellings. This is indicated by public regulations, agrarian contracts, the data related to the rural farm's equipment or to the dominical center of the *curtes*, the spread of technical skills related to the wood carving and implementation, and the relatively small number of craftsmen specialized in buildings. Medieval contracts preserve the requirement for peasants to maintain and repair the buildings in which they lived, which ensured access to land and houses but which must have resulted in the construction of ephemeral structures (*Capitularia Regum Francorum: Admonitio generalis*, a.789: 61; *Capitulare Papiense*, a.850 exeunte: 87f; *Edictum Pistense*, a.864: 322; Galetti 1998: 93-106; Pasquali 2002).

Marks of social distinction

The 'courtyard house' is a feature either of the main building of a noticeable size estate, for the farm of an employed peasant or for a minor landowner. The differences between these social groups were reflected in the overall size of the 'sedimen', in its complexity, and furthermore on the larger and better-equipped space which was available as private space. The housing centre of a *domocoltile* could also include buildings for hand-crafting activities in which domestic servants and dependent peasants were often engaged.

These social-economic differences can be highlighted in the terminology of the written sources, through the opposition between the 'courtyard'/*mansio dominicale*, which belonged to the managing houses of the estates, and the 'courtyard'/*casae massariciae*, which instead belonged to the settlers. The pattern is the same but what generally changed was the overall disposition of the buildings and the quality of their architectural structure. Other different aspects which could be used to signal status included the use of different building materials (stone/brick for genteel dwelling, timber and other more perishable materials for settlers' houses) and the choice of distinctive typologies. Some examples are the 9th-century longhouse found in Poggio Imperiale of Poggibonsi and the big houses in Scarlino and Miranduolo (9th-10th century), which were connected to cottages and service buildings separate from the smaller dwelling (Figure 4, Figure 5).

Another distinctive feature can be represented by the raising of houses, such as the 'solarium' structure (with a top floor): this is quite uncommon in the early

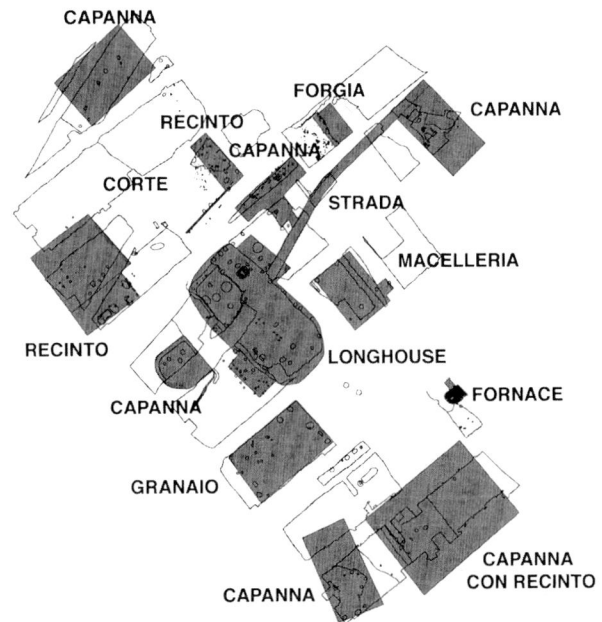

Figure 4. Excavation plan of Poggio Imperiale-Poggibonsi (SI) Village. 9th-10th centuries. (Translation: corte = court; forgia = forge; recinto = fence; granaio = barn; fornace = kiln; macelleria = butcher's; strada = street; capanna = type buildings. After Valenti 2004: 124.

medieval documentation, at least until the 10th century in the countryside. The *casa solariata* required a greater construction complexity and higher economic cost: it represented the privileged social status of a person/family within a community. Initially, the vertical raising of houses developed in urban areas because of the lack of space; it then spread more slowly to the countryside, following the 11th-12th century urban revival as a model of urban organization of the housing space (Galetti 2008: 31-57, 74-80; 2009: 31-33; Gloria 1877, n.42:62; *Inventari altomedievali* 1979: 66, 84, 90, 127; Valenti 2004: 26-31; 2010).

The value of houses

It is extremely difficult to assess the value of houses according to the documentary evidence. Surviving documents often refer to different areas and settlement systems and, above all, to both rural and urban areas. The documented price may well have been fictitious, subject to fluctuations and may tell us little about the form of the houses themselves. However, it seems reasonable to suggest that there

Figure 5. Reconstruction of excavation plan of Poggio Imperiale-Poggibonsi (SI) Village. 9th-10th centuries. After Valenti 2004: 109.

was an increase in urban house prices during the 10th century and that in general the 'casae solariatae' cost much more (Galetti 1998: 62-64).

The inner space of the house/ household belongings and domestic furnishings and fittings

The 'elementary house' and the dwelling place inside the 'courtyard house' could be constituted either by only one room or by more than one. The room can be multifunctional: inside it different activities and objects are often mixed together. The multi-functionality of the domestic space shows the tight connection between house life and the working activity. This contrasts with the 'casae solariatae' which was often more articulated, with a functional division of the inner space. A common feature of all these houses must, however, have been the smoke

from open fireplaces, which have been revealed by archaeological research.

Most of the farm implements (also present inside the house), household belongings, domestic furnishings and fittings are made of wood, although there were also ceramic and more perishable food containers. The metal artifacts and instruments (other more or less precious materials) do not survive in great numbers, which suggests their high cost and value. Their presence is a marker of a socially-distinctive material culture which was often connected to a hand-crafting work, while wooden instruments could be manufactured by the peasants themselves.

Information regarding the furnishings and fittings of these houses reveals some common patterns in the relationship of furniture to the social class of its owners, although there could be distinctions based on quantity, level preservation, quality and refinement (Fois Ennas 1981: 107, 140; Galetti 1998: 107-115; 2008: 57-63, 74-80).

Conclusion

The domestic life inside these fragile and temporary buildings must have been uncomfortable, influenced by the turning of the seasons and by the requirement to meet the most basic of needs. Most of these observations can be extended also to situations which characterized broad areas of Northern and Central Italy during the central and the final phase of the Middle Ages (Galetti 2008: 80-96,114-128).

References

Augenti, A. (2003) Archeologia medievale in Italia. Tendenze attuali e prospettive future, *Archeologia Medievale* XXX, 511-518.

Augenti, A. (ed.) (2006) *Le città italiane tra la tarda Antichità e l'alto Medioevo*. Firenze: All'Insegna del Giglio.

Augenti, A. (2006) I ceti dirigenti romani nelle fonti archeologiche (secoli VIII-XII). In: *La nobiltà romana nel Medioevo*, ed. S. Carocci, 71-96. Roma: École française de Rome.

Augenti, A. (2007) Immaginare una comunità, costruire una tradizione. Aristocrazie e paesaggio sociale a Ravenna tra V e X secolo. In: *Archeologia e società tra tardo antico e alto medioevo*, eds. G.P. Brogiolo & A. Chavarria Arnau, 193-204. Mantova: S.A.P.

Augenti, A. (2010) Tutti a casa. Edilizia residenziale in Italia centrale tra IX e X secolo. In: *Edilizia residenziale tra IX-X secolo. Storia e archeologia*, ed. P.Galetti, 127-151. Firenze: All'Insegna del Giglio.

Belli Barsali, I. (1974) La topografia di Lucca nei secoli VIII-XI. In: *Atti del V Congresso Internazionale di Studi sull'alto Medioevo*, 461-554. Spoleto: Fondazione Centro italiano di studi sull'alto Medioevo.

Bourdieu, P. (2005) *Le strutture sociali dell'economia*. Trieste: Asterios.

Brogiolo, G.P. (1988) *Archeologia dell'edilizia storica*, Como: New Press.

Brogiolo, G.P. (ed.) (1994) *Edilizia residenziale tra V e VIII secolo*. Mantova: S.A.P.

Brogiolo, G.P. (ed.) (1996) *La fine delle ville romane: trasformazioni nelle campagne tra tarda antichità e altomedioevo*. Mantova: S.A.P.

Brogiolo, G.P. & S. Gelichi (1998) *La città nell'alto medioevo italiano. Archeologia e storia*. Firenze: All'Insegna del Giglio.

Brogiolo G.P. & B. Ward-Perkins (eds.) (1999) *Idea and Ideal of the Town between Late Antiquity and the Middle Ages*. Leiden-Boston-Köln: Brill.

Brogiolo G.P., N. Gauthier & N. Christie (eds.) (2000) *Towns and their Territories between Late Antiquity and the Early Middle Ages*. Leiden- Boston- Köln: Brill.

Brogiolo, G.P., A. Chavarria Arnau & M. Valenti (2005) *Dopo la fine delle ville. Le campagne tra VI e IX secolo*. Mantova: S.A.P.

Brogiolo, G.P. & A. Chavarria Arnau (2005) *Aristocrazie e campagne nell'Occidente da Costantino a Carlo Magno*. Firenze: All'Insegna del Giglio.

Brogiolo, G.P. & A. Chavarria Arnau (eds.) (2007) *Archeologia e società tra tardo antico e alto medioevo*. Mantova: S.A.P.

Brogiolo, G.P. & N. Mancassola (2005) Scavi al Castello di Piadena (CR). In: *Campagne medievali. Strutture materiali,economia e società nell'insediamento rurale dell'Italia settentrionale (VIII-X secolo)*, ed. S. Gelichi, 121-220. Mantova: S.A.P.

Cagnana, A. (2000) *Archeologia dei materiali da costruzione*. Mantova: S.A.P.

Capitularia Regum Francorum, I (1883), Monumenta Germaniae Historica, ed. A.Boretius, Hannover: Impensis Bibliopolii Hahniani.

Capitularia Regum Francorum, II (1897), Monumenta Germaniae Historica, eds. A. Boretius & V. Krause, Hannover: Impensis Bibliopolii Hahniani.

Chapelot, J. & R. Fossier (1980) *Le village et la maison au Moyen Age*. Paris: Hachette.

Christie, N. (ed.) (2004) *Landscape of Change. Rural Evolutions in Late Antiquity and the Early Middle Ages*. Aldershot: Ashgate Publishing.

Christie, N. & S.T. Loseby (eds.) (1996) *Towns in Transition. Urban Evolution in Late Antiquity and the Early Middle Ages*. Aldershot: Scholar Press.

Cirelli, E. (2008) *Ravenna: archeologia di una città*. Firenze: All'Insegna del Giglio.

Coates-Stephens, R. (1996) Housing in Early Medieval Rome. A.D. 500-1000, *Papers of the British School at Rome* 51, 239-260.

Deffontaines, P. (1972) *L'homme et sa maison*. Paris: Gallimard.

De Lachenal, L. (1995) *Spolia. Uso e reimpiego dell'antico dal III al XIV secolo*. Milano: Longanesi.

Durliat, J. (1990) *Les finances publiques de Dioclétien aux Carolingiens (284-889)*. Sigmaringen: Jan Thorbecke Verlag.

Eiroa Rodriguez, J.A. (2004) La relacion entre documentos ecritos y Arquelogia in el estudio de la Edad Media in Europa: reflexiones para un debate teorico y metodologico, *Agora* 10(1/2), 113-127.

Ermini Pani, L. (2009) Evoluzione urbana e forme di ruralizzazione. In: *Città e campagna nei secoli altomedievali (LVI Settimana di studio)*, 659-696. Spoleto: Fondazione Centro Studi italiano di studi sull'Alto Medioevo.

Fois Ennas, B. (1981) *Il "Capitulare de villis"*. Milano: Giuffré.

Francovich, R. & G. Noyé (eds.) (1994) *La storia dell'alto medioevo italiano (VI-X secolo) alla luce dell'archeologia*. Firenze: All'Insegna del Giglio.

Francovich, R. & R. Hodges (2003) *Villa to Village. The Transformation of the Roman Countryside in Italy, c. 400-1000*. London: Duckworth Publishing.

Francovich, R. & M. Valenti (2005) Forme del popolamento altomedievale nella campagna toscana (VII-X secolo). In: *Campagne medievali. Strutture materiali, economia e* società nell'insediamento rurale dell'Italia settentrionale (VIII-X secolo), ed. S. Gelichi, 245-258. Mantova: S.A.P.

Francovich, R., M. Valenti & F. Cantini (2006) Scavi nella città di Siena. In : *Le città italiane tra la tarda Antichità e l'alto Medioevo*, ed. A. Augenti, 273-298. Firenze: All'Insegna del Giglio.

Fronza, V. & M. Valenti (1996) Un archivio per l'edilizia in materiale deperibile nell'altomedioevo. In: *Poggio Imperiale a Poggibonsi: dal villaggio di capanne al castello di pietra. I. Diagnostica archeologica e campagne di scavo 1991-1994*, ed. M. Valenti, 159-218. Firenze: All'Insegna del Giglio.

Furet, F. & J. Le Goff (1973) Histoire et ethnologie. In: *Mélanges en l'honneur de Fernand Braudel. Méthodologie de l'histoire et des sciences humaines* II, 227-243, Toulouse: Privat.

Galetti, P. (1992) Per una storia dell'abitazione rurale nell'alto medioevo: le dimensioni della casa nell'Italia padana in base alle fonti documentarie, *Bullettino dell'Istituto Storico Italiano per il Medio Evo e Archivio Muratoriano* 90, 147-176.

Galetti, P. (1998) *Abitare nel medioevo. Forme e vicende dell'insediamento rurale nell'Italia altomedievale*. Firenze: Le Lettere.

Galetti, P. (ed.) (2004) *Civiltà del legno. Per una storia del legno come materiale per costruire dall'antichità ad oggi*. Bologna: Clueb.

Galetti, P. (2005) Caratteri dell'edilizia privata in una città capitale. In: *Ravenna da capitale imperiale a capitale esarcale*, 887-914. Spoleto: Fondazione Centro studi italiano sull'alto medioevo.

Galetti, P. (ed.) (2006) *Forme del popolamento rurale nell'Europa medievale: l'apporto dell'archeologia*. Bologna: Clueb.

Galetti, P. (2006) Tecniche e materiali da costruzione dell'edilizia residenziale. In: *Le città italiane tra la tarda Antichità e l'alto Medioevo*, ed. A. Augenti, 67-79. Firenze: All'Insegna del Giglio.

Galetti, P. (2008) *Uomini e case nel medioevo tra Occidente e Oriente*. Roma-Bari: Laterza.

Galetti, P. (2009) Edilizia residenziale privata rurale e urbana: modelli reciproci? In: *Città e campagna nei secoli altomedievali (LVI Settimana di studio)*, 697-731. Spoleto: Fondazione Centro italiano di studi sull'Alto Medioevo.

Galetti, P. (ed.) (2010) *Edilizia residenziale tra IX-X secolo. Storia e archeologia*. Firenze: All'Insegna del Giglio.

Galetti, P. (2010) Edilizia residenziale tra IX-X secolo: storia e archeologia. Un'introduzione. In: *Edilizia residenziale tra IX-X secolo. Storia e archeologia*, ed. P. Galetti, 7-13. Firenze: All'Insegna del Giglio.

Galetti, P. (2010) Edilizia residenziale privata tra IX-X secolo: fonti a confronto. In: *Edilizia residenziale tra IX-X secolo. Storia e archeologia*, ed. P. Galetti, 59-74. Firenze: All'Insegna del Giglio.

Gelichi, S. (2000) Ravenna, ascesa e declino di una capitale. In: *Sedes regiae (ann. 400-800)*, eds. G. Ripoll & J.M. Gurt, 109-134. Barcelona: Reial Academia de Bones Lletres de Barcelona.

Gelichi, S. & C. La Rocca (eds.) (2004) *Tesori. Forme di accumulazione della ricchezza nell'alto medioevo (secoli V-XI)*. Roma: Viella.

Gloria, A. (1877) *Codice Diplomatico Padovano. Dal secolo sesto a tutto l'undecimo*. Venezia: Deputazione veneta di storia patria.

Higham, N.J. (2001) Archaeology and History. In: *Medieval Archaeology. An Encyclopedia*, ed. J.P. Crabtree, 5-8. New York: Garland Publishing.

Hodges, R. (2000) *Towns and Trade in the Age of Charlemagne*. London: Duckworth Publishing.

Inventari altomedievali di terre, coloni e redditi (1979). Roma: Istituto Storico Italiano per il Medio Evo.

Jarnut, J. (2005) Dove abitavano le aristocrazie longobarde? In: *Dopo la fine delle ville. Le campagne tra VI e IX secolo*, eds. G.P. Brogiolo, A. Chavarria Arnau & M. Valenti, 343-347. Mantova: S.A.P.

La Rocca, C. (2002) Lo spazio urbano tra VI e VIII secolo. In: *Uomo e spazio nell'alto medioevo (L Settimana di studio)*, 398-436. Spoleto: Fondazione Centro italiano di studi sull'alto Medioevo.

La Rocca , C. (2006) Residenze urbane ed élites urbane tra VIII-X secolo in Italia settentrionale. In: *Le città italiane tra la tarda Antichità e l'alto Medioevo*, ed. A. Augenti, 55-65. Firenze: All'Insegna del Giglio.

Laval, L., L. Ozgenel & A. Saranis (eds.) (2007) *Housing in Late Antiquity. From Palaces to Shops*. Leiden: Brill.

Lepelley, C. (ed.) (1996) *La fin de la cité antique et le début de la cité médiévale. De la fin du IIIe siècle à l'avènement de Charlemagne*. Bari: Edipuglia.

Liebeschuetz, J.H.W.G. (2001) *Decline and Fall of the Roman City*. Oxford: Oxford University Press.

Mannoni, T. (1989) General remarks on the changes in techniques observable in the material culture of the first Millennium A.D. in North-West Italy. In: *The birth of Europe. Archaeological and social development in the first Millennium A.D.*, ed. K. Randsborg, 152-155. Roma: L'Erma di Bretschneider.

Meneghini, R. & R. Santangeli Valenzani (2004) *Roma nell'altomedioevo. Topografia e urbanistica della città dal V al X secolo*. Roma: Istituto Poligrafico dello Stato.

Meneghini, R. & R. Santangeli Valenzani (2008) *I Fori Imperiali. Gli scavi del Comune di Roma (1991-2007)*. Roma: Viviani.

Pasquali, G. (2002) La condizione degli uomini. In: *Uomini e campagne nell'Italia medievale*, eds. A. Cortonesi, G. Pasquali & G. Piccinni, 73-122. Roma-Bari: Laterza.

Pohl, W. (ed.) (1998) *Kingdoms of the Empire. The Integration of Barbarians in Late Antiquity*. Leiden-Boston-Köln: Brill.

Roux, S. (1982) *La casa nella storia*. Roma: Editori Riuniti.

Samson, R. (ed.) (1990) *The Social Archaeology of Houses*. Edinburgh: Edinburgh University Press.

Santangeli Valenzani, R. (2004) Abitare a Roma nell'alto

medioevo. In: *Roma dall'antichità al medioevo. II. Contesti tardo antichi e altomedievali,* eds. L. Paroli & L. Venditelli, 41-59. Milano: Electa Mondadori.

Tosco, C. (2003) *Il castello, la casa, la chiesa. Architettura e società nel medioevo.* Torino: Einaudi.

Valenti, M. (ed.) (1996) *Poggio Imperiale a Poggibonsi: dal villaggio di capanne al castello di pietra. I. Diagnostica archeologica e campagne di scavo 1991-1994.* Firenze: All'Insegna del Giglio.

Valenti, M. (2004) *L'insediamento altomedievale nelle campagne toscane. Paesaggi, popolamento e villaggi tra VI e X secolo.* Firenze: All'Insegna del Giglio.

Valenti, M. (ed.) (2008) *Miranduolo in Alta Val di Merse (Chiusdino-Siena).* Firenze: All'Insegna del Giglio.

Valenti, M. (2010) Villaggi, strutture abitative e di servizio nella Toscana di IX e X secolo. I casi di Poggibonsi e Miranduolo. In: *Edilizia residenziale tra IX-X secolo. Storia e archeologia,* ed. P. Galetti, 91-125. Firenze: All'Insegna del Giglio.

Ward-Perkins, B. (2005) *The Fall of Rome and the End of Civilisation.* Oxford: Oxford University Press.

Wickham, C. (1998) Early medieval archaeology in Italy: the last twenty years, *Archeologia Medievale* XXVI, 7-19.

Wickham, C. (2005) *Framing the Early Medieval Ages. Europe and the Mediterranean 400-800.* Oxford: Oxford University Press.

Zanini, E. (2007) Archeologia dello status sociale nell'Italia bizantina: tracce, segni e modelli interpretativi. In: *Archeologia e società tra tardo antico e alto medioevo,* eds. G.P. Brogiolo & A. Chavarria Arnau, 23-46. Mantova: S.A.P.

The Development of Dutch Townhouses 700-1300

Jeroen Bouwmeester

Abstract

The origins of the Dutch Townhouse lie in early trade-settlements such as Dorestad in the 8th and 9th centuries. The earliest houses were closely related to Carolingian farm buildings and were used for storage and craft functions. During the 10th century the house-building tradition developed along its own path which was determined by the development of the earliest towns. The rapid growth of these settlements had a great impact on townhouse development. The growth of technological skills of the High Middle Ages made it possible to adapt local circumstances and to make the construction of heavy stone buildings possible on unstable substrates. House building then became the symbol of a new social group of traders and craftsmen: the bourgeoisie (Figure 1).

Introduction

This paper ties in with a project being run currently by the Netherlands' Cultural Heritage Agency (RCE), to compile a Dutch Reference Collection of house plans.[1] The aim of the project is to set up an online database of house plans excavated in the Netherlands, arranged by period and region.[2] A subject review article is also to be published for each period and region.[3] The project initially focused largely on farmhouses. However, in a country which, along with Northern Italy, was one of the most urbanised regions in Medieval Europe, wooden townhouses must not be omitted from any such review. It is for this reason that my research has been included in this project.

No review of this kind has ever been produced for the archaeology of houses in the Netherlands, merely for certain towns or parts of towns like Deventer (Mittendorff 2007) and 's-Hertogenbosch (Cleijne 2011). This is no coincidence. Dense and continuous building in Dutch towns and cities has caused considerable damage to the subsurface archaeology. Old wooden buildings have been demolished, and new stone foundations and cellars have destroyed what was left of many of these houses. Complete ground plans of wooden townhouses like those found occasionally in Lübeck (for example: Gläser 2001) are encountered only sporadically in the Netherlands. We have to make do with fragments of buildings, which cannot always be identified as houses or type of houses. Despite the damage to the remains, and thus to the ground plans, many remains have been excavated. Unfortunately there is a serious backlog in the analysis and publication of these excavations. At most, they are mentioned in the 'grey' literature.[4] Finally, while traces of wooden buildings will certainly still be buried under a number of towns and cities, we simply cannot access them because of the more recent buildings that still stand above them. In new projects developers try preserve the archaeological remains in situ to avoid the high costs of an archaeological excavation. This means that the remains of ancient buildings will still be safe underground, but unexamined. This paper examines the emergence and early development of the wooden townhouse until the start of stone building (which occurred in the 14th century). It relates this process both to that of urban development and to contemporary developments in rural farmhouses.

Figure 1. The Netherlands with 1. Alkmaar; 2. Amsterdam; 3. Deventer; 4. Dordrecht; 5. Dorestad; 6. 's-Hertogenbosch; 7. Leiden; 8. Medemblik; 9. Nijmegen; 10. Rotterdam; 11. Tiel; 12. Utrecht; 13. Voorburg. J. Bouwmeester – Cultural Heritage Agency.

Phase 1. The pre-urban settlement (750-850)

Unlike in many neighbouring countries, the two Roman cities in the Netherlands – Forum Hadriani (Voorburg) and Ulpia Noviomagus (Nijmegen) – disappeared towards the end of the Roman period. In the subsequent period there appear to have been settlements, with no vestiges of urban features, either morphological or functional. After the Roman period, trading centres where goods were brought from great distances to be bought and sold grew up alongside the existing agricultural settlements. One of the most famous of these was Dorestad. This settlement had a clear agricultural component in its hinterland, and a trade and craftsmen's quarter on the river side.

The 8th- and 9th-century farms in Dorestad were rectangular or slightly boat-shaped (type Odoorn C and Odoorn C') (Bouwmeester in prep; Waterbolk 2009: 90, 94) (Figure 2). The buildings were single-aisled with external posts that shored up the roof supports. They were, on average, 10 m wide and 26-28 m long. In Dorestad, they not only had an agricultural function; traces of handicrafts and cottage industry have been found around the farmhouses, including smithing, bronze casting, spinning, weaving and the working of wood and bone (Botman 1995: 10f). However, most of these activities took place in other buildings on, or close to, the river bank. These buildings bear a strong resemblance to the farmhouses described above (Figure 3). One rectangular building that has been investigated and published was 6 m wide and 12 m long (Van Es & Verwers 2000: 36, fig. 11,6). On the outside of the house there were posts that would have shored up the roof supports, as in the farmhouses. Dorestad is suspected as playing a key role in the spread of the farmhouses described above (Waterbolk 1999), and this smaller type of building does indeed also occur in other countries, including in Scandinavia and Germany, *eg* at Haithabu (Elsner 1989: 26). It has been determined on the basis of waste pits that this type of building had a workshop on the river side with waste pits outside of the building for production waste, and living quarters at the back with a well and waste pits for household waste. Paths ran between the houses (Botman 1995; Bouwmeester in prep; Van Es, van Doesburg, Botman & Greving 1996).

Dorestad is without doubt the best-known settlement of this period in the present-day Netherlands, but there were more trading settlements of this type, including Tiel and Deventer. Evidence of a house similar to those in Dorestad has been found in Deventer (Bouwmeester in prep). The nature of the buildings in these settlements reflects the limited space available and the limited space required by craftsmen. As noted above, these were houses with living quarters combined with storage and/or craft activities. When Dorestad ceased to exist – which was probably more as a result of the silting up of the Lek river rather than the infamous Viking invasions (Sarfatij 1990a: 183) – the forerunners of these two towns largely took over its role. From the 10th to the 12th century the character of the original trading settlement changed dramatically, to what would eventually become a medieval town. Such settlements are therefore referred to as proto-cities. They had

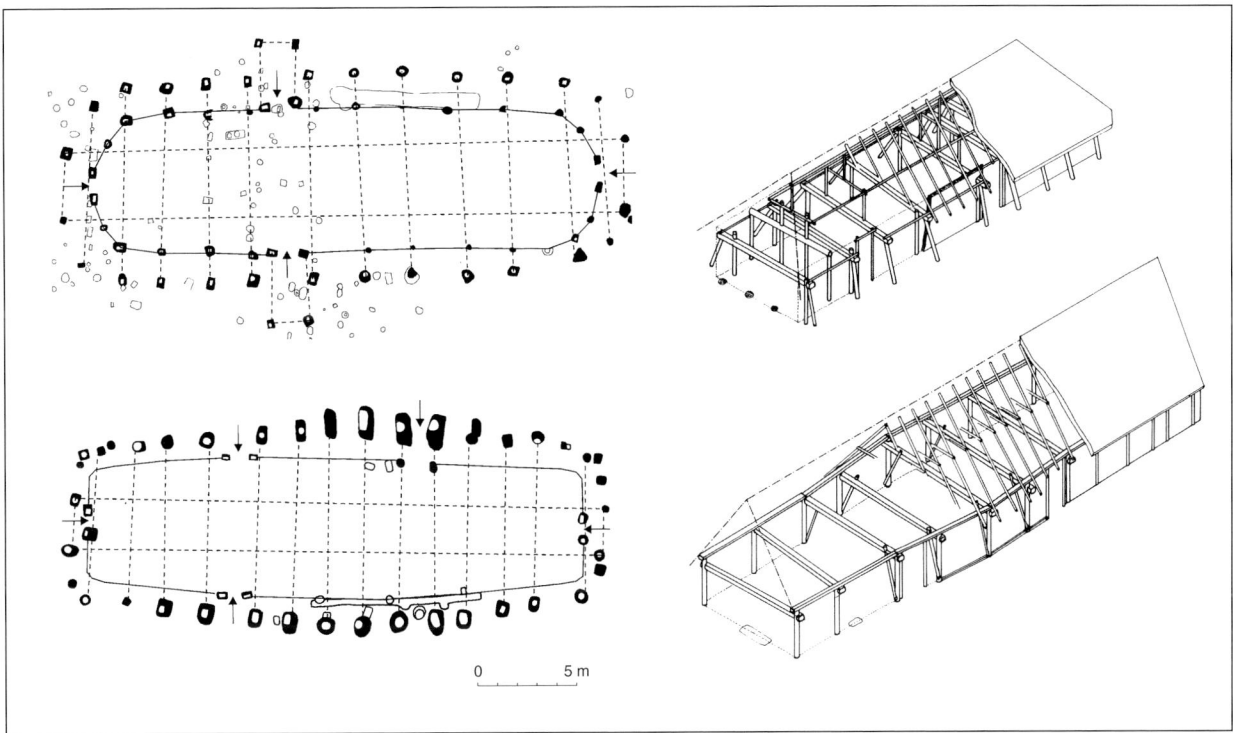

Figure 2. Farmhouses from Dorestad (type Odoorn C followed by type Gasselte A) with a reconstruction. After (clockwise) Waterbolk 1999: 111; Huijts 1992:156; Huijts 1992: 170; Waterbolk 1999: 111.

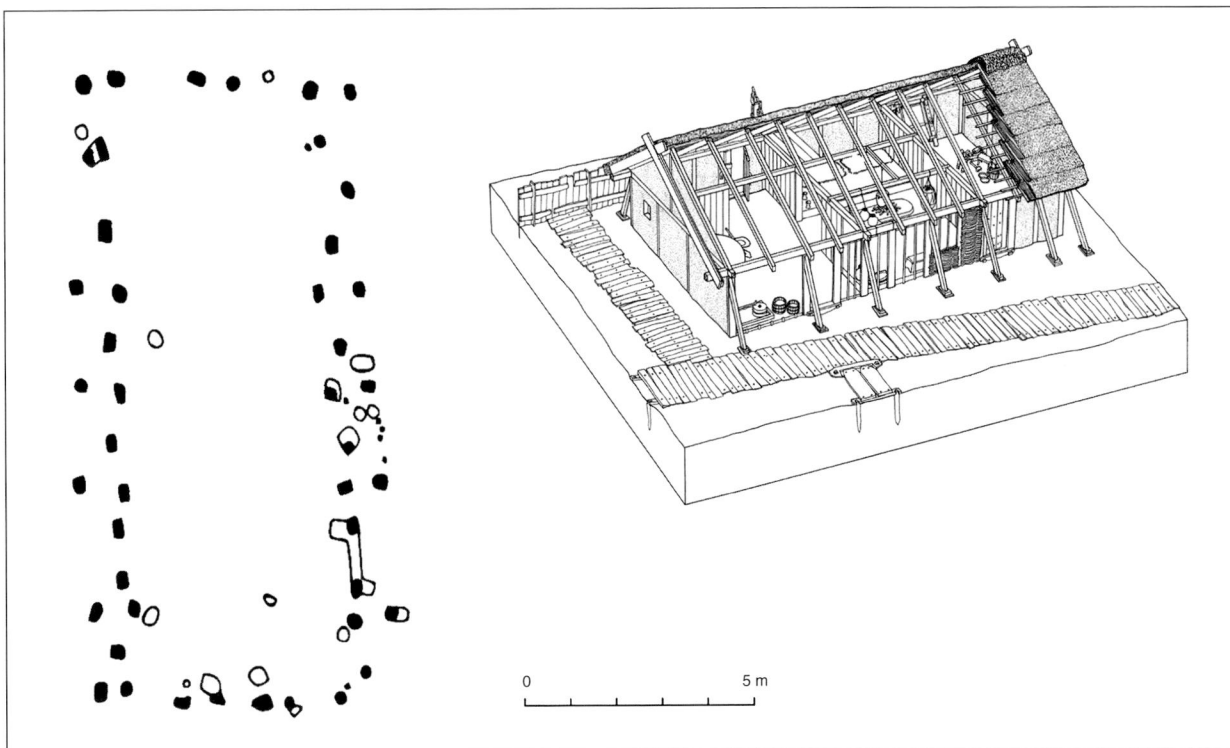

Figure 3. Craftshouse from Dorestad with a reconstruction from Haithabu. After Van Es & Verwers 2000: 36; Elsner 1989: 26.

functions that transcended those of a local agricultural settlement. As a result, they grew rapidly, as did the pressure on space, particularly in the commercial zones along the river. However, like the later medieval towns, the proto-cities always retained an important agricultural element.

Phase 2. The development of timber framed houses (850-1250)

In the subsequent period the boat-shaped farmhouses with external posts of types Odoorn C and C' described above developed into the large single-aisled boat-shaped structures of the Gasselte type, whose external posts had entirely disappeared (Waterbolk 2009: 109). This was initially achieved by shoring up the roof supports on the inside, rather than on the outside. But in the same period the structure of the roof supports themselves underwent a new development. With the beam – known as the anchor beam[5] – penetrating through the posts and secured with pegs, this structure was so strong that it no longer needed to be supported. A curved brace on the inside of the roof supports was sufficient. This allowed the internal space to be used more effectively. It also made timber-framed houses possible, so the posts eventually no longer had to be dug into the ground, but could stand on a padstone. These farmhouses are known as the Pesse type (11th – 13th century) in the farmhouse typology of the Netherlands (Waterbolk 2009: 101, 109).

External posts disappeared fairly quickly from the houses being built in the emerging proto-cities, from the mid-9th century AD onwards. That is about half a century earlier than the farmhouses (Gasselte type). This may have been because the houses with external posts took up precious space in the settlements. Another, more likely, explanation is that these posts, which played a vital role in the structure, were exposed to the elements and to damp, and therefore had to be replaced regularly. Whatever the truth of the matter, the disappearance of external posts meant that the weight of the roof had to be supported in some other way. The solution was to shore up the roof supports on the inside, to prevent them

from being pushed outwards by the weight of the roof. Houses of this type have been found in Tiel-Koornmarkt phase 1 (Dijkstra 1998: 23f), Deventer (Mittendorff 2007: 253) and other places. They are single-aisled houses 4-5 m wide and 9-13 m long. They had relatively light foundations consisting of posts approximately 25 cm in diameter (for example Dijkstra 1998: 23f).

Sometime later, in the 10th century, the structure of houses in these settlements changed dramatically. Instead of the relatively light structures found in the houses described above, the new buildings were heavy, with deep foundations. A fine example has been excavated in Tiel-Koornmarkt phase 2. The load-bearing posts – heavy oak posts with a diameter of 36-40 cm – were buried deep in the ground, and stood in the long wall at remarkably regular two-metre intervals. The walls consisted of horizontal planks with tongue-and-groove joints that connected them to each other and to the rest of the structure (Dijkstra 1998: 24-27). Wattling anchored by pickets in a horizontal joist along the ground, known as a sillbeam or foot-plate, and a horizontal joist at the height of the roof support, known as a wall-plate, was also used.

What prompted these radical changes in the construction of houses? They might have represented an attempt to increase the usable space inside the building. The struts inside a building of an average width of 6 m would have caused an obstruction. The idea might have been that, by using heavier load-bearing posts and burying them deep in the ground, it would be possible to absorb the outward pressure of the roof. It is difficult to say whether fully-fledged anchor beam frames were used in the 10th century, or whether this was merely a stage in their development. It is, however, clear that with these technological innovations house building was undergoing dramatic change at this time.

Eventually, this type of structure paved the way for timber-framed houses. However, the construction tradition of using heavy posts buried deep in the ground (which was not structurally necessary for fully timber-framed structures), did not disappear entirely. Buildings with deep wall posts continued to be built into the 13th century, for example

Figure 4. Remains of the basement of a timber framed house from Deventer – Muggeplein. After Mittendorff 2007: 260.

in 's-Hertogenbosch-Postelstraat (Janssen & Treling 1990: 93; Janssen & Zoetbrood 1983: 78). This method was particularly common in areas where the subsurface was wet, so a building required sturdy foundations, and it was decided not to use a 'separate' foundation beneath the structure. It is highly likely that fully-fledged timber framed houses were also being built by that time. This technique was already widely known, and it made the structure considerably stronger, thanks to the anchoring of the roof support and the use of curved braces to absorb the outward pressures and loadings of the roof and walls.

The earliest proven timber-framed structures without buried posts occurred from the second half of the 10th century. Early examples have been found in Deventer and other places (Mittendorff 2007: 255-260). They can be divided into types of buildings with a partial cellar and buildings with no cellar. This latter category is also the most problematic from an archaeological point of view. Since the structure stood on the clay floor, when a replacement structure was built the entirety of the old timber frame was often removed, leaving barely a trace in the archaeological record. Only in the event of destruction by fire, for example, have traces of the structure been found (Figure 4). Fortunately, more

traces of houses with cellars can be found, and they provide a great deal of information about the nature of their construction.

In this form of timber-framed structure the load-bearing posts are no longer buried deep in the ground, but rest on horizontal joists on the ground (foot-plates). These lay on a clay floor, and in wetter regions sometimes on a foundation of broken iron ore or padstones, fascines or separate underground piles. The wall was built between these load-bearing posts. It might have consisted of wattle and daub, or of horizontal or vertical planks attached to the structure by tongue and groove joints. In the cellars, the planks were generally placed on the outside of the load-bearing posts rather than between them. They did not need to be anchored in the structure because they were held in place by the pressure of the earth outside (Gläser 2001: 285).

The load-bearing posts and the anchor beam formed the roof support. As in farmhouses, they were attached to the studs on the outside using pins, and on the inside using a curved brace. At first, these houses had only one storey. There is later evidence that they had more storeys, including the fact that the hearth was no longer situated in the centre of the space, but rather on the edge of it. The timber-framed houses in Deventer have been dated to 1200 (Mittendorff 2007: 255-260). But their continued existence in the town after 1200 cannot be ruled out. The buildings were 4-5 m wide and between 10.25 and 14.5 m long (Mittendorff 2007: 255-260).

Evidence of timber-framed houses has been found in many places in the Netherlands, albeit in most cases in the form of floors, rather than remains of the structure itself. In towns where the subsurface is wet – consisting of clay or peat, for example – the remains of the foundations of timber-framed structures have been found. The first stone buildings began to appear in the 11th century. This does not mean that timber-framed construction ceased altogether, however. Only a relatively small proportion of urban buildings were made of stone, and timber-framed structures remained the norm in large parts of every town. These may have been complete timber-framed houses, but often they were replaced by structures in which only the side walls and/or the bottom of the facade were built of brick, with a timbered structure above. It took Utrecht city council a great deal of effort, lasting into the 18th century, to ensure that wooden facades disappeared entirely from the city's streets (Kolman 1990). The earliest roof structures, even in stone houses, were basically still those of timber-framed buildings, with studs incorporated into the wall (wallpost) and a console often made of natural stone.

Phase 3. Stone buildings (from 1250)

The introduction of building in stone commenced in the second half of the 11th century in places like Deventer. The houses were not built of brick, however, but of tuff. Tuff is a volcanic rock of which a plentiful supply was available in Deventer. The town was in the hands of the bishop, and was situated at a major transit point for tuff from the Eifel region en route to the north (Mittendorff 2007: 280). Many churches were built of tuff in this period, but the local elite – who were probably closely associated with the church – were also able to use this material for their own houses (Mittendorff 2007: 280). Clearly, these tuffstone buildings must have stood out among the timber houses around them, which were generally lower. Interestingly, in Deventer timber houses with cellars, presumably the former houses of the elite, were no longer built once the larger tuffstone houses began to appear (Mittendorff 2007: 280). After 1200, no new houses were built of tuff in Deventer, probably as a result of the fact that brick became a widely-used building material around that time (Mittendorff 2007: 68).[6] The first brick houses were also built in other towns in the Ijssel region, such as Zutphen, in the mid-13th century, and widespread replacement of timber with brick began in the first half of the 14th century (Fermin & Groothedde 2006: 28, 99) (Figure 5).

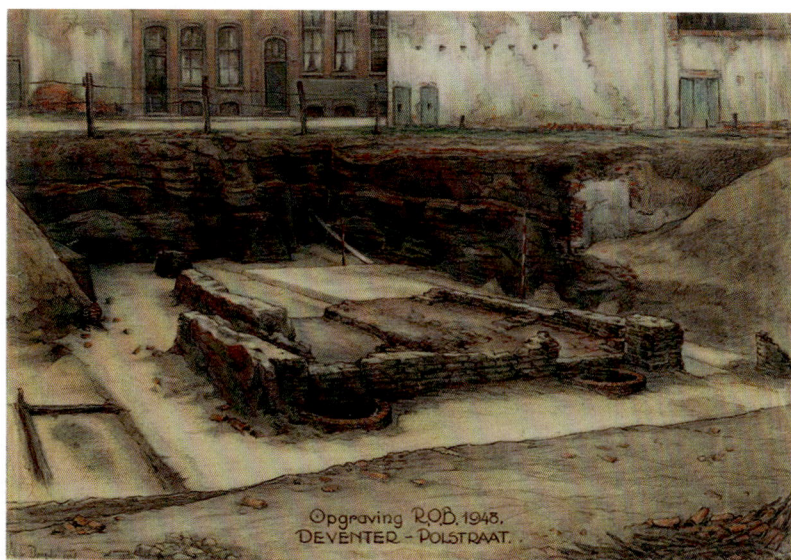

Figer 5. Remains of a tuffstone building from Deventer – Polstraat, excavated in 1948 by A.E. van Giffen. Drawing by A. Dorgelo, Collection Historisch Museum – Deventer.

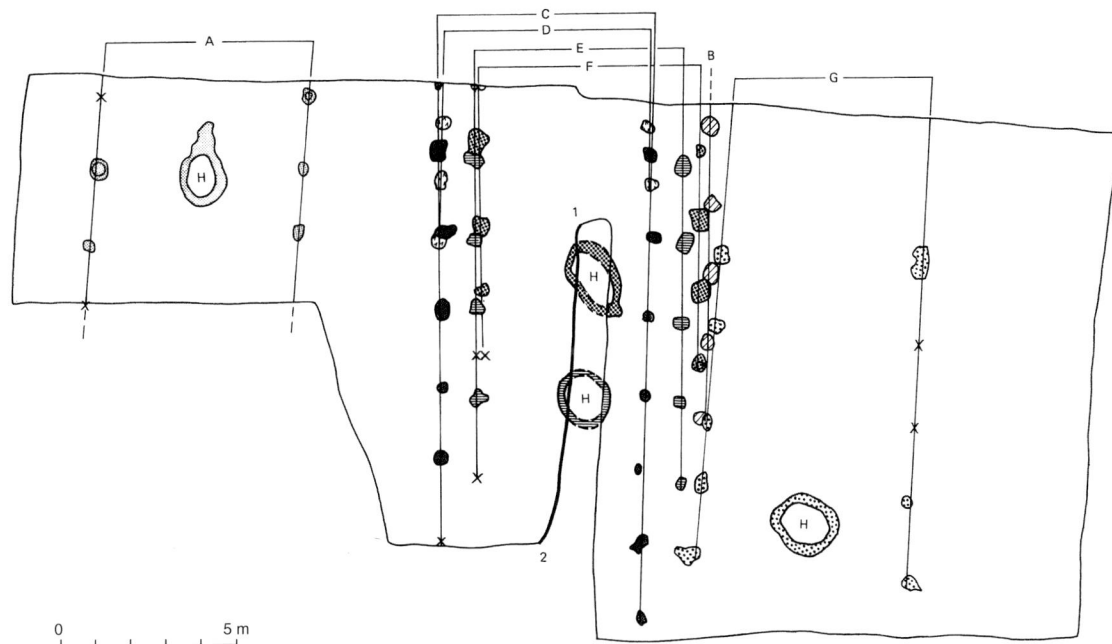

Figure 6. Houseplans from the 9th-11th century from Medemblik – Torenstraat/Muntstraat. After Besteman 1989: 15.

The first brick building in the Netherlands was Klaarkamp monastery near Rinsumageest in Friesland province, which dates from the second half of the 12th century. Brick buildings occurred in other places in the northern Netherlands in this period, particularly churches and monasteries. 12th-century brick has been found in secular buildings in the rest of the Netherlands, too, including in parts of the Leiden fortress and some houses in Utrecht (Berends 1990: 71f). All in all, the introduction of brick differed from one town and region to another. As with natural stone buildings, the first brick buildings were church buildings and a few houses belonging to the elite. When brick became more common, particularly from the 14th century onwards, houses were not always built entirely of this material. At first, it was often just the foundations and the side walls that were made of brick, for fire safety reasons (Kolman 1990: 283).

The development of town houses in the western Netherlands

When settlements like Deventer and Tiel, and also Zutphen, Utrecht, Nijmegen, Maastricht and Zaltbommel, for example, began to develop into proto-urban settlements from the 10th century onwards, the western Netherlands consisted largely of primarily agricultural settlements. One exception was Medemblik, where house plans of timber-framed buildings with buried posts similar to those in Deventer and Tiel have been found. The positions of the posts, spaced at regular 2 m intervals, and the dimensions of the buildings – 5.5 m wide and at least 8 m long – are clearly similar. One interesting feature of the house plans in Medemblik is the fact that the walls consisted of wattle and daub, with turf on the outside. In this respect, they resemble the local building traditions seen in rural farmhouses. Despite the strong resemblance to the houses in the two towns in the central and eastern Netherlands, there is clear evidence that the settlement of Medemblik was highly agricultural at the time (Besteman 1989: 16)[7] (Figure 6).

At this time, the farmhouses in the western Netherlands were usually light, three-aisled structures. This may have been the case because of the generally weaker clay or peat subsurface and the limited supply of oak. The load-bearing posts made of lighter species of wood such as alder were generally flattened at the bottom, and often stood on wooden planks to prevent them from sinking into the soft

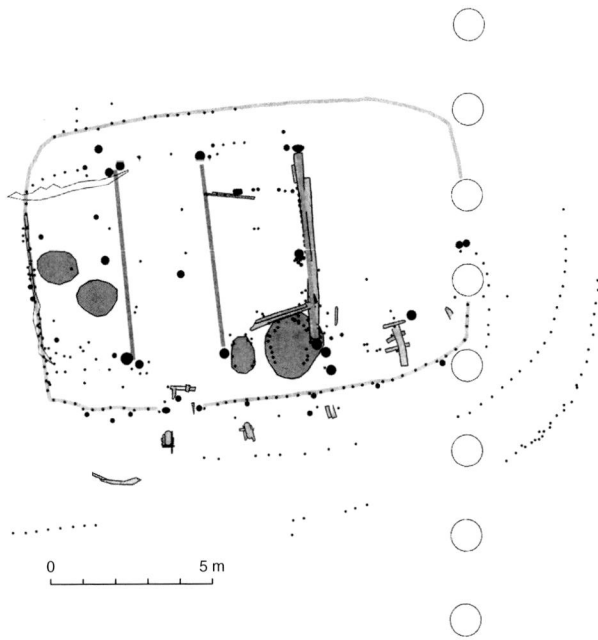

Figure 7. Plan of a farmhouse from the 10-11th century from Rotterdam-Markthal. At the south- and west side are ovens. The horizontal beam divides the building into two compartments. After Guiran & van Trierum 2010: 33.

subsurface. The walls consisted mainly of wattle-and-daub, sometimes with turf on the outside.

The earliest pre- and proto-urban settlements in the western Netherlands were markedly agricultural. Nevertheless, that does not mean that no other activities took place there. Excavations at Rotterdam-Markthal found a three-aisled farmhouse ground plan of the pre-urban settlement known as Rotta dating from the 11th – possibly the 10th – century. One interesting feature is the presence of a number of hearths or ovens in the western part of the building that suggest it had both a domestic and a craft function. A piece of horizontal timber was found between two posts in the east of the building. This may have divided the western living quarters from the animal stalls (Guiran & Van Trierum 2010: 32-34). Other research in Rotterdam has shown that the old settlement of Rotta certainly had another function besides farming, with residents engaging in trade and crafts. The excavation at the Hofdame site, for example, revealed remains that may be associated with agricultural and fishing settlements, as well as drops of metal and a bronze bar that suggest "a traditional form of cottage industry" (Guiran & Van Trierum 2010: 19). Also a struck

penny from Tiel and other 11th- and 12th-century coins provide evidence that the settlement was part of or had access to a large trading network (Guiran & Van Trierum 2010: 40) (Figure 7).

A 12th-century expansion of proto-urban Alkmaar consisted of a very regular pattern of adjacent farmhouses (Cordfunke 1992: 359-363). More than 20 buildings were built at regular intervals, with narrow paths between them (Bitter 2002: 92). This suggests a planned expansion that must have begun around 1120. C14 analysis has established that the houses were built at roughly the same time, further substantiating the planned expansion theory (Cordfunke 1992: 362f). As in Rotta, it is important to bear in mind that various handicrafts were practised around these buildings (Bitter 2002: 92). Townhouses like those in Deventer and Tiel would appear to have been rare at that time.

One town in the western Netherlands that developed fairly early is Dordrecht. The earliest settlement there dates form the second half of the 12th century, and consisted of two rows of dwelling mounds divided by ditches. The first expansions took place here before 1200, and the settlement developed rapidly. Dordrecht was granted a charter as early as 1220, and the first brick building – the Lakenhal (Huis Scharlaken) – was built in 1235. Dordrecht underwent several large-scale expansions from 1250 to 1400, during which large parts of the town were raised and infilled (Sarfatij 1995: 17f). One of these was the harbour area. Here, the subsurface was strengthened down to a depth of 5-6 m using piles with large wooden boards between them to keep the soil in place. This formwork was filled with clay and household waste (Sarfatij 1990a: 105f). This made the subsurface so strong that new houses could be built on it without any extra foundations (Sarfatij 1990a: 106). These houses were not built completely of timber, virtually all of them having at least a stone base from the 13th century onwards (Sarfatij 2007: 213f). In the 14th and 15th centuries, Dordrecht's heyday, closed brick facades appeared along the main streets (Sarfatij 1990b: 151). This was a sign of the great wealth the town had amassed in just a short time. Just how early Dordrecht became predominantly brick-built becomes clear if we compare it

Figure 8. The massive formworks of the land extensions at the harbour side of Dordrecht. After Sarfatij 2007: 63.

with other towns in the western Netherlands. In Amsterdam, for example, bricks became common around 1325 (Sarfatij 1995: 13). In Rotterdam, too, the first brick buildings date from the 14th century (Sarfatij 1995: 17) (Figure 8).

Conclusions

As we consider the development of townhouses in relation to urban development and the development of farmhouses, two issues are evident. The earliest houses with storage space and craft functions like those in Dorestad were still closely related to the farmhouses of the period. However, houses soon began to undergo a separate development. Under pressure from the lack of space, in particular, solutions were sought that would make houses more functional by freeing the interior space of braces, including a cellar and later also adding more floors. This was ultimately possible thanks to the development and introduction of timber-framed construction in the course of the 10th century. This seemed

to mark a shift in the initiation of architectural developments from farm buildings to residential building. From then on, new developments first occurred in the dynamic environment of the pre-urban and urban settlements, and were later adopted in the building of farmhouses.

But there was more to it than this. The ancient tradition in farmhouses was for construction methods to adapt to local circumstances. In the relatively wet areas of the west farmhouses were considerably lighter structures because of the risk of subsidence and the scarcity of oak. Further to the east, farmhouses were heavier, sturdier structures. The higher-lying sandy soils provided a firm base for the houses and building materials were in plentiful supply. In the first proto-urban settlements, the shortage of space soon became an important issue. Houses therefore had to extend upwards and downwards. New houses also had to be built on poorer ground within the city walls. For this purpose, the ground in wetter zones was strengthened, as seen in Dordrecht. Timber buildings were also given special foundations, in the form of wooden piles, planks, fascines and brick dies. The city-dweller's relationship with his environment was not the same as that of the farmer, as he adapted nature or circumstances to suit his own needs. This transformation is particularly evident in the development of urban housing. But that is not the only change. Urban building clearly shows that houses were not merely functional spaces where people lived and worked, they also had a representative function that reflected power and status. The same applied to many other buildings in towns and cities, such as the clothmakers' hall (Dutch: 'lakenhal'). It is no coincidence that this was the first stone building in Dordrecht. This was a statement by a new class, the bourgeoisie, with its own ideals of freedom, independence and, above all, entrepreneurship.

Notes

1. Website Dutch Reference Collection: www.referentiecollectie.nl
2. Covering the whole of the Netherlands, from prehistory to the Middle Ages (until stone building commenced).
3. This article explores various aspects examined in the present paper in greater depth (Bouwmeester in prep.). The research also ties in with my PhD research on the archaeology of urban development in the Netherlands.
4. Most of these publications are in the archives of the archaeological services of the various towns. Several annual reports are also present in the library of the Cultural Heritage Agency. But then still it's very complicated to find the right articles.
5. "Anchor beam: a horizontal timber, the head of which portrudes beyond the wall post or staves with which it articulates" (Brigham, Goodburn, Milne & Tyers 1992: 14).
6. The earliest use of brick in Deventer has been dated to shortly after 1235 (Mittendorff 2007: 287).
7. It should however be noted that a large proportion of the archaeological investigation of this settlement has not yet been analysed.

References

Berends, G. (1990) Backstein in den Niederlanden des Mittelalters. In: *Hausbau in den Niederlanden. Bouwstenen voor oude woonhuizen in Nederland,* ed. G.U. Grossmann, 71-77. Jahrbuch für Hausforschung 39. Marburg: Jonas Verlag.

Besteman, J.C. (1989) The pre-urban development of Me-

demblik. In: *Medemblik and Monnickendam. Aspects of medieval urbanization in northern Holland. Cingula* 11, eds. H.A. Heidinga & H.H. van Regteren Altena, 1-30. Amsterdam: Universiteit van Amsterdam.

Bitter, P. (2002) *Graven en begraven. Archeologie en geschiedenis van de Grote Kerk van Alkmaar.* Hilversum: Uitgeverij Verloren.

Botman, A.E. (1995) *Van Dorestad naar Wijk bij Duurstede. Sporen uit de 8ste-12de eeuw op het terrein aan de J. van Ruysdaelstraat te Wijk bij Duurstede, Intern Rapport ROB.* Amersfoort: Rijksdienst voor het Oudheidkundig Bodemonderzoek.

Bouwmeester (in prep.) *Het ontstaan en de vroegste ontwikkeling van het Nederlandse stadshuis.*

Brigham, T., D. Goodburn, G. Milne & I. Tyers (1992) Terminology and dating. In: *Timber Building Techniques in London c.900-1400. An Archaeological Study of Waterfront Installations and Related Material,* ed. G. Milne, 14-22.

Cleijne, I.J. (2011) *Late medieval house construction and parcel history in 's-Hertogenbosch, compared to Helmond and Dordrecht.* MA thesis, University of Leiden.

Cordfunke, E. (1992) Thirty Years of Archaeological Investigations in Alkmaar's Town Centre, *Berichten van de Rijksdienst voor het Oudheidkundig Bodemonderzoek (BROB)* 40, 333-387.

Dijkstra, J. (1998) *Archeologisch Onderzoek in de binnenstad van Tiel. Juni t/m september 1996. Lokaties Koornmarkt en Tol-Zuid.* Rapportages Archeologische Monumentenzorg 57. Amersfoort: Rijksdienst voor het Oudheidkundig Bodemonderzoek.

Elsner, H. (1989) *Wikinger Museum Haithabu: Schaufenster einer frühen Stadt.* Neumünster: Wachholtz Verlag.

Van Es, W.A., J. van Doesburg, A. Botman & K. Greving (1996) REMU-terrein (putten 880-882), *Jaarverslag ROB 1995,* eds. M. Alkemade, G.H. Scheepstra & A. Steendijk 192-194. Amersfoort: Rijksdienst voor het Oudheidkundig Bodemonderzoek.

Van Es, W.A. & W.J.H. Verwers (2000) De voorgeschiedenis van Wijk bij Duurstede. In: *Wijk bij Duurstede 700 jaar stad. Ruimtelijke structuur en bouwgeschiedenis,* eds. M.A. van der Eerden-Vonk, J. Hauer & G.W.J. van Omme, 25-40. Hilversum: Uitgeverij Verloren.

Fermin, H.A.C. & M. Groothedde (2006) *De Zutphense ringwalburg van de 9e tot de 14e eeuw. Nieuwe gegevens en inzichten uit archeologisch onderzoek en boringen op de Zutphense markten – deel 1 and 2.* Zutphense Archeologische Publicaties 22. Zutphen: Gemeente Zutphen, Sector Ruimte, afdeling BMA/Archeologie.

Gläser, M. (2001) Archäologisch erfaßte mittelalterliche Hausbauten in Lübeck. In: *Lübecker Kolloquium zur Stadtarchäologie im Hanseraum III: Der Hausbau,* eds. B. Dahmen, M. Gläser, U. Oltmans & S. Schindel, 277-305. Lübeck: Verlag Schmidt-Römhild.

Guiran, A.J. & M.C. van Trierum (2010) Op zoek naar de nederzetting Rotte uit de 8e-12e eeuw; nieuwe vondsten en inzichten, *Boorbalans* 6, 13-50.